THE YEAR'S BEST SPORTS WRITING 2023

ROBERTO JOSÉ ANDRADE FRANCO

BRUCE ARTHUR

JERRY BREWER

JORGE CASTILLO

ALEX COFFEY

BENNETT DURANDO

ASHLEY FETTERS MALOY

DERRICK GOOLD

SARAH HEPOLA

RYAN HOCKENSMITH

CHANTEL JENNINGS

JULIET MACUR

JANA MEISENHOLDER

IAN MENDES

HAMILTON NOLAN

LEX PRYOR

CASSIDY RANDALL

DAVID REMNICK

DAN ROBSON

MICHAEL ROSENBERG

KATIE STRANG

KURT STREETER

WRIGHT THOMPSON

JONATHAN TJARKS

JENNY VRENTAS

GRANT WAHL

SEAN WILLIAMS

THIS YEAR'S FEATURED WRITERS

T0037597

The Year's Best Sports Writing 2023

Edited and with an
introduction by
Richard Deitsch

TRIUMPH
B O O K S

Library of Congress Cataloging-in-Publication Data available upon request

This book is available in quantity at special discounts for your group or organization. For further information, contact:

Triumph Books LLC
814 North Franklin Street
Chicago, Illinois 60610
(312) 337-0747
www.triumphbooks.com

Printed in U.S.A.

ISBN: 978-1-63727-445-3

Design by Sue Knopf
Page production by Patricia Frey

Contents

Introduction

As he often recalled with robust humor, professional calamity beckoned for Grant Wahl on the night of July 12, 1998. Hired by *Sports Illustrated* as a fact-checker just 20 months earlier, Wahl was covering his first World Cup, in a role best described as a utility player. As eight national teams turned into four and four into a final pair, the two more senior writers *SI* had assigned for the quadrennial soccer tournament had gone home—one for a wedding, one after the departure of the U.S. national team. So the magazine's editors gambled: They assigned a rookie to write a 2,500-word story on the World Cup final.

But the problem Wahl faced on the night France famously beat Brazil was not inexperience; it was that he had failed to bring his laptop to Stade de France, the massive stadium located in the Paris suburb of Saint-Denis. He left the device at the apartment he was staying at near the Bastille, assuming, quite incorrectly, that favored Brazil would win easily and the streets of Paris would be relatively clear for him to return to his temporary home, write the story from his notebook, and file to his bosses in New York City with plenty of time to spare.

Of course France, led by the transcendent Zinedine Zidane, crushed the Brazilians, 3–0. While the masses swamped *les rues* of Paris in ecstasy, Wahl experienced a different sensation from inside a media shuttle bus stuck in the gridlock, envisioning his professional career slowly going up in flames. So at around 2 a.m. Paris time, the writer hopped off the bus and spent hours walking through the streets of the city. He darted down the

Champs-Élysées and zigzagged through besotted French fans, stopping every so often to scribble down ideas in his notebook. He finally arrived at his rented apartment (and his laptop) at 5 a.m., and with his adrenaline flowing at full blast, he beat his 3 p.m. ET deadline by a few minutes.

Here's how Wahl led the piece, which was published in the July 20, 1998, issue of *Sports Illustrated*:

> In Saint-Denis, the Paris suburb where the French once buried their kings, a new one ascended last week. Zinedine Zidane certainly doesn't look the part. He's quiet, usually gazing down at the ground. He's going prematurely bald. He can appear slow and sometimes clumsy. At one point on his way through the interview room at the Stade de France after the World Cup final on Sunday, he stumbled on the carpet like a young girl wearing her first high heels. Give Zidane a ball and put him on a soccer field, though, and he becomes the Baryshnikov of the midfield, deftly toe-poking a pass in one direction, gamely looping a long ball in the other, holding his head regally erect all the while. It should be noted that Zizou, as he is known, never trips on grass.
>
> He also scores, but not very often and almost never with his noggin. Which made the two goals he netted with his ever-expanding forehead against Brazil on Sunday nearly as shocking as the game's outcome: a 3–0 victory that gave France its first world championship after 68 years of futility. Not since the 1978 World Cup in Argentina had the host country won the 11-pound gold trophy. Never had mighty Brazil, the defending and four-time champion, suffered a more lopsided defeat in 80 World Cup games dating to 1930.
>
> That Zidane is the son of Algerian immigrants was appropriate. The increasing number of immigrants in France is a hot political topic there, and the team that dethroned Brazil included players who were born or had roots in lands ranging from Armenia to Ghana, Guadeloupe to New Caledonia. Two years ago the leader of France's right-wing National Front

party, Jean-Marie Le Pen, had complained that it was "artificial to bring players from abroad and call it the French team," even though every member of the World Cup squad has been a French citizen for years. As Les Bleus marched to the final, however, the racial and cultural diversity of the team became a point of Gallic pride. Wrote a columnist for the news magazine *Le Nouvel Observateur*, "They can be blacks, whites and all shades of beige, but that doesn't prevent them from singing their national anthem with conviction, even if that irritates Mr. Le Pen."

Grant Wahl was 24 years old when he wrote those paragraphs. The story was a massive hit among *SI*'s editors—and a journalism comet was launched. Wahl quickly joined the ranks of the magazine's most well-known voices, writing memorable college basketball profiles and a February 18, 2002, cover story about a 16-year-old basketball prodigy from Akron, Ohio, named LeBron James. Wahl would become *SI*'s lead soccer writer and ultimately the most famous American chronicler of the world's most popular sport. He profiled a litany of soccer greats, from Ronaldinho to Leo Messi and Carli Lloyd to Abby Wambach. It is not hyperbole to credit Wahl's coverage of the sport with helping soccer grow in the United States.

Along with millions of soccer fans, I had anticipated two more decades of thrilling work from Wahl, who left *Sports Illustrated* in 2020 and had branched out as an independent multimedia journalist, with his own Substack, podcast, and producing career. But last December 9, while covering the Argentina-Netherlands World Cup quarterfinal in Qatar, Wahl collapsed while working in the press section of Lusail Iconic Stadium. An autopsy revealed that he had experienced a catastrophic rupture in the ascending aorta, which carries oxygenated blood from the heart. He was 49 years old when he died, covering his 14th World Cup between the men and women.

Wahl's last editor, Mark Mravic—who, like Grant, was a longtime colleague of mine at *Sports Illustrated*—told me that the story Grant was most proud of in 2022 was his reporting from inside Qatar months before the start of the World Cup. Wahl traveled to the authoritarian Persian Gulf nation to report on what life was like on the ground for the migrant workers who had come to Qatar as part of the development boom around the World Cup. His findings from that reporting, "The Qatar Chronicles," are included in this anthology.

Along with Wahl, this collection features another gifted writer who was cruelly taken away from us in 2022. Jonathan Tjarks of The Ringer wrote about his cancer diagnosis, his family, and an uncertain future in a poignant piece titled "Does My Son Know You?" The odds of Tjarks's being diagnosed with Ewing's Sarcoma, a rare bone cancer, were about 25 million to 1. Last September, the writer passed away at the age of 34. His work lives on here, as well as with the basketball fans who enjoyed his writing and podcasting for years.

The essay before you, which introduces this collection from the curator, has a charge to inform how this anthology was put together. The challenge was multifold: There is a surplus of great work every year, and this book can only house a finite number of stories. There was also self-doubt from this year's guest editor. Previous iterations of this collection have featured writers of thunderous prose and relentless reporting drive. I had reservations to accept this assignment given the names that had come before me.

But the responsibility also provided the opportunity to assemble an advisory panel with a passion for sports writing. That excited me. I wanted a group of contributors who looked different from me, thought differently than I did, and could fill in my blind spots. Each of their lists of story picks was distinctive, which was immensely helpful. The group, with more than a century of sports journalism experience among them, consisted of J.A. Adande, the director of sports journalism at Northwestern University's Medill School of Journalism (and the editor of last year's edition); Paola Boivin, director of the Cronkite News Phoenix Sports Bureau at

Arizona State University; Gregory Lee Jr., an editor and writer at Front Office Sports; Jane McManus, executive director of Seton Hall's Center for Sports Media; Iliana Limón Romero, deputy sports editor of the *Los Angeles Times*; and Shalise Manza Young, a columnist for Yahoo Sports. They were a tremendous sounding board, and all would be tremendous guest editors for future books. Glenn Stout, the longtime steward of this project, was an invaluable resource in answering the many questions I had as my deadline neared midnight. His love for this project is real.

The nightmare is the actual selection process: There was extraordinary work done in 2022, and culling it into a final group proved excruciating. The entries in the Honorable Mention section could easily form multiple main collections.

I read the essays of previous guest editors and found their rationales for selecting entries to be remarkable and thorough. Mine was more elementary: Which pieces stayed with me days after I let them go? Which pieces reflected who we were in sports in 2022? Which pieces demanded I read them again and again?

The gift of this book, as an editor, is the opportunity to marinate inside so many brilliant minds. It was thrilling to discover the prose of Cassidy Randall, whose harrowing tale of British sailor Susie Goodall for The Atavist Magazine is written with such force and detail that you feel lashed by the ocean, rain, and wind on the Southern Ocean alongside Goodall. Sean Williams of *Outside* had me deeply invested in Kurt Steiner, who has dedicated his entire adult life to the lost art of stone skipping. Sarah Hepola brilliantly explored the cultural impact of the Dallas Cowboys cheerleaders for *Texas Monthly* and gave voice to those who were commercialized for the profit of others. Defector's Hamilton Nolan described what it was like to punch, and be punched, as good as any writer I have read on it. ESPN's Ryan Hockensmith wrote the best story I've ever read about shit—a deep history of the nexus between sports and the port-a-potty. I wanted to include a memorable Serena Williams piece, and Lex Pryor of The Ringer made that decision easy.

The profession is fortunate to have such investigative sports reporters as Katie Strang, Dan Robson, and Ian Mendes of *The Athletic*, and Jenny Vrentas of *The New York Times*. I included their pieces given the impact of their reporting. The other authors included in this collection—Roberto José Andrade Franco, Bruce Arthur, Jerry Brewer, Jorge Castillo, Alex Coffey, Bennett Durando, Derrick Goold, Chantel Jennings, Juliet Macur, Ashley Fetters Maloy, Jana Meisenholder, David Remnick, Michael Rosenberg, Kurt Streeter, and Wright Thompson—are equally brilliant, diligent, and thoughtful.

The small but hearty group at Triumph Books with whom I worked care deeply about this project. My eternal thanks to Adam Motin and Clarissa Young for many reasons, including a first phone call about this project from Clarissa in August 2022 in which she convinced me that I could do this.

My wife and children moved with me to another country when I was presented with a lottery ticket of a job opportunity in Canada. I love how passionate they are about what they love, and I love them.

When I was a teenager, I had a goal of finding a job that would pay me to travel. Working for nearly two decades at *Sports Illustrated* opened up a larger world for me, including the opportunity to cover seven Olympic Games around the globe. My current employer, The Athletic, offered the rare prospect of helping to build something new. Each provided me with unmatched creative freedom. Professionally, I drew a straight flush.

The year 2022 concluded with Lionel Messi finally claiming the crown he had desired most. Argentina defeated France in the World Cup final on December 18, ending a title drought of 36 years for the soccer power, with Messi scoring twice (and France's Kylian Mbappé scoring a hat trick) in the most exciting World Cup final in history.

It was also a somber occasion for many of us. Grant Wahl first fell in love with global soccer in 1994 when he was awarded funding to travel to Argentina following his sophomore year of college. He returned to Buenos Aires less than two years later for his senior thesis, an exploration of how soccer and civic institutions intersected. He would have been overjoyed to chronicle the triumph of his adopted country. This book concludes with his words—those of a friend who left the pitch far too soon.

Richard Deitsch
Toronto, Ontario, Canada
Summer 2023

The Year's Best Sports Writing 2023

Stone Skipping Is a Lost Art. Kurt Steiner Wants the World to Find It.

SEAN WILLIAMS

FROM *Outside* • SEPTEMBER 20, 2022

On a clear-skied morning in March, Kurt "Mountain Man" Steiner stood at a lonely bend of Sinnemahoning Creek, deep inside Pennsylvania's Elk State Forest. He was dressed in a black hoodie and Dollar General jeans that hid his athletic 56-year-old frame, and wore a brown beanie that pressed his long gray hair and Rasputinesque beard into a single wild mane.

Steiner stared across the creek and raised his right arm into an L, clasping a coaster-size sliver of shale the way a guitarist might hold a plectrum during a showstopping solo. But rather than fold his torso horizontally, as you might expect somebody skipping a rock to do, he stretched his five-foot-nine-inch body vertically, and then squeezed down like an accordion and planted his left leg to crack his throwing arm, placing the rock under so much gyroscopic force that it sputtered loudly as it left his hand, like a playing card in a bicycle wheel.

The rock appeared for a brief moment to fly. Then it dipped and plunged, kicked up a wave, rode it like a surfboard, and became airborne again. Standing behind Steiner, I counted at least 20 skips before the rock slowed, scrolled gently right, and sank in the calm water some 50 yards away.

This would have been the greatest throw of my life. To Steiner it was a bullpen toss, and an average one at that. He grunted disapprovingly, then stooped to grab another stone from the small pile he'd gathered from a 25-gallon tub sitting in the bed of his 1989 Toyota truck—one of the quarter-million rocks he estimates he's thrown in his lifetime. One hour and dozens of stones later, we headed back to Steiner's tiny, *Walden*-like home, 30 minutes down back roads and dirt tracks into the bowels of the forest. His shoulder was stiff, and the biggest throwing season of his life loomed. "This could be bad news," he told me.

Kurt Steiner is the world's greatest stone skipper. Over the past 22 years, he has won 17 tournaments in the United States and Europe, generating ESPN coverage and a documentary film. In September 2013, he threw a rock that skipped so many times it defied science. This year he hopes to smash records on both sides of the Atlantic, giving him a platform for sermonizing about a sport he believes is nothing short of a means for the redemption of mankind—"a legitimate path to an essential inner balance," he says.

Skipping has brought Steiner respite from a life of depression and other forms of mental illness. It has also, in part, left him broke, divorced, and, since the death of his greatest rival, adrift from his stone-skipping peers. Now, in middle age, with a growing list of aches and pains, he must contemplate the reality that, in his most truthful moments, he throws rocks not simply because he wants to, but because he has no choice.

Is THERE A more universal littoral pursuit than skipping rocks? Russians call it baking pancakes. Czechs throw froggies, while Swedes say they're tossing sandwiches. Competitors of Japanese *mizu kiri*, which translates as "cutting water," are judged not just by a throw's distance or the number of skips but by its aesthetic beauty.

Ancient Greeks held stone-skipping contests, and Tudor Britons later took it up, calling the pastime "ducks and drakes." Eighteenth-century priest and scientist Lazzaro Spallanzini determined how stones can push down on the surface of water to generate lift, knowledge humans later employed to kill each other more effectively—first with skipping cannonballs, then with the bouncing bombs invented by British engineer Barnes Wallis to bombard Nazi dams.

Today's professional stone-throwing world is divided into two disciplines on either side of the Atlantic. British tournaments measure distance, not skip count. This is called skimming, and the World Stone Skimming Championships take place every fall at an abandoned slate quarry on the Hebridean island of Easdale. Perhaps the greatest stone skimmer is Scotland's own Dougie Isaacs, who has won eight world titles and holds the Guinness World Record for the longest skim: 399 feet.

American skippers have no such global title to compete for, but the most prestigious event has, since 1969, taken place every July 4 on Mackinac Island, Michigan, a wooded, high-end tourist destination wedged between the state's Upper and Lower Peninsulas. Competitors have six chances to impress a handful of judges—some on the shore, some positioned knee-deep in the water. The thrower with the highest average score wins, with a contestant's second-highest-scoring throw used to break ties. The victor receives a trophy—and a pound of the island's renowned fudge.

Anybody can show up and pay $5 to enter Mackinac's amateur event. But to throw for the fudge at its pro tournament, you must win one of a small number of regional events, by far the most popular of which is the Rock in River Festival in Franklin, Pennsylvania, which, since its inception, has become Mackinac's principle feeder. The rules at Franklin are identical—only, to compete among its pros, you must skip a rock at least 30 times at its amateur event, held an hour before. Miss that milestone and it's back to the showers for another 365 days.

In recent years, smaller competitions have cropped up in Vermont and Arkansas. But Mackinac and Franklin are skipping's major championships, and each has its peculiarities. Franklin, which considers itself blue-collar, is held at a pan-flat confluence of French Creek and the Allegheny River that fans out like an easy fairway and rewards strength and raw technique. Mackinac's festivities happen in and around the Grand Hotel—a vast, colonnaded national historic landmark that has welcomed Mark Twain, Thomas Edison, and at least five U.S. presidents. The event's competitors face a stretch of Lake Michigan crammed with tourists, piers, and ferries that churn the surface. Typical winning throws at Mackinac may total half as many skips as you'd see at Franklin, because even the best pros throwing their best rocks can lob skipless duds into the surf. "You can't use all your power," Kurt told me. "It'll ruin your shot. You have to finesse."

My time with stone-skipping's greatest living legend began late one evening in February, when Kurt picked me up from the Greyhound station in Erie, Pennsylvania, and drove us to his sister's Victorian home, in the city where he spent almost all of his youth. The next morning we drove half an hour along the shore of Lake Erie to a secluded bight where, under frigid gray skies, we gathered rocks and aimed them down a thin, unfrozen vein of water. Throwing the stones felt meditative and timeless, transporting me back to childhood weekends on the pebble beaches of southern England.

Back then I imagined myself to have a pretty good arm. Kurt quickly put that idea to rest, fizzing stones down narrow lanes and bending them around promontories and broken masonry while I janked mine into the shore. His throws were trick shots he'd developed as a kid, when he wandered the edge of the lake between fishing trips and family camping holidays. These were happy times in an otherwise difficult childhood. Kurt's mother, Nancy, a retired flower-shop owner in Erie, and his machinist father, Karl, were teenage trailer dwellers when they had their first and only son in 1965. Nancy gave birth to a daughter, Erika, two years later. But the couple split in 1973, when Kurt was eight, and the kids lived with Nancy in an old cottage house in Erie.

Kurt never quite felt like he fit in the world. He struggled to eat, hobbled by a compulsion never to mix the items on his plate. While other kids burst with energy, he often felt exhausted. He craved sleep so much that he winnowed his morning routine—waking, showering, scarfing some breakfast, and running to the bus stop—down to 11 minutes. Doctors suspected he was fatigued or hypoglycemic, but tests for those conditions came back negative. Physically he was healthy. He excelled at science and loved to write, but he struggled with social interaction.

Literature offered an escape; so did his high school's Apple computers, on which he coded rudimentary mazes. But for him, nothing could match the vast, glorious silence of nature, and Kurt would disappear for hours into the forests surrounding Erie. At the lake, he was perfectly happy to skip rocks, alone, for hours.

Over time he developed a sixth sense for the adjustments required for a mean toss. The first morning he and I skipped stones together, it took him mere minutes to suggest changes in wrist rotation and foot placement that I could use to "attack the water" better. Within an hour, I could skip a rock a dozen or so times. When he told me that one of my throws was good enough for tournament competition, the endorphin rush almost completely masked the painful throbbing of my blown-out elbow.

If Kurt teaches stone skipping like a Zen master, he talks like he's on his seventh cup of coffee, at a breathless pace, switching between topics rapidly. As we stood on that shoreline, we touched on Socrates, George Carlin, Albert Einstein, Paulo Coelho, quantum physics, Taoism, the Sanskrit *Mahabharata*, and how the dogma of Christ's divinity was, according to Kurt, "where the Western mind went off the rails." He has theories on the true purpose of the Antikythera mechanism, an ancient Greek device used to track astronomical positioning. "Ask him, 'How do you tie your shoes?'" Paul Fero, a close friend, told me, "and you could be there for half an hour."

I FIRST ENCOUNTERED Kurt online in 2018, in a video posted on Wired's website. It asked whether it was physically possible to beat his 2013 world record, and I quickly plunged down a hole of YouTube videos, podcasts, and subreddits detailing his achievements and his shamanic views on the sport and life. It took me another year to reach him via email; Kurt often goes weeks without cell coverage or access to the internet. We exchanged dozens of messages before he agreed to spend a week with me— first for a few days in Erie, then at the far-flung Pennsylvania cabin he's been building for several decades. But then the pandemic hit, and pro sports at all levels wound down. Mackinac and an unsanctioned Franklin tournament went ahead, but they were pared back, and only professional throwers were able to attend.

In 2020, Kurt placed first in Michigan and second in Pennsylvania, and then, competing under the same restrictions in 2021, he scored a win at Mackinac and third place at Franklin— so it seemed, on paper at least, that he was as strong as ever. By October of last year, restrictions had lifted and I was planning my trip. Then I received a text file labeled "appologies" [sic].

"October through March is pretty much my psychic recovery phase," Kurt wrote. "I will spend most of the next six months in super-isolation—no power, no heat, no water, no phone … getting high, maybe drunk … watching video, reading, writing, taking hikes … and crapping everyday in a bucket in the basement. All just trying to get myself centered for the next year.

"I need this time for mental health," he added, "and that has to be me alone."

Finally, in February, after pursuing Kurt for more than two years, I flew from Europe to Detroit, where border guards had a hard time believing I was entering the U.S. to interview a stone skipper. Then I showed them a video of Kurt's magical record throw, and before long a group was gathered around a computer screen, counting the skips and hollering "*No fucking way!*" before letting me through. From the moment I met Kurt in Erie a day later, it was clear that his hibernation had ended. By 10 p.m. on our second evening, when he fashioned a can of Monster energy drink into a makeshift bong, we'd spoken for 12 hours straight.

KURT TOILED WITH the duality of his mental life throughout his teenage years, lurching from hyperfocus to apathy. Classmates would crowd around to watch him at a pinball machine, where he could go hours without losing a ball. He excelled at chess, could pick apart a radio and put it back together, and racked up an *Asteroids* score so crazy he assumes it broke any known record. "He was seeing the back end of the coding rather than the graphics on the screen," Victor "Chip" Susol, one of Kurt's oldest friends, told me.

But the thought of dating filled him with dread, so instead he indulged in wild sexual fantasies and wrote poetry encrypted in a shorthand only he could read. He was a skilled linebacker in football but wouldn't learn the plays. He enjoyed the "pure contest" of wrestling, but during one bout, an opponent dumped him on his collarbone, and Kurt took a year off from the sport. By 1985, when he enrolled as an English major at Penn State Behrend, in Erie, he says he was more interested in "me-against-myself stuff": cycling, weight training, canoeing. Hiking became an obsession.

At first Kurt hit established trails near home. Then he linked up sections of abandoned railroad, ATV trails, and footpaths, sleeping wherever it worked out. Before long he was bushwhacking for weeks across mid-Pennsylvania with a compass and a 75-pound pack, fasting for days and testing the limits of his body's endurance. Fellow travelers were good for a quick chat here and there; then they were gone, just the way Kurt liked it. Walking gave him the time and distance to restock his mental stores before returning to the city.

Whenever he discovered a body of water on these sojourns, he skipped rocks. It felt natural, as if by clasping a stone he was anchored to the planet, able to "hold infinity in the palm of your hand," in the words of William Blake. Skipping was "safe from development and capitalism, and in control," he told me, at odds with a society that seemed "hell-bent on detaching itself from the natural world."

He was great at it, too, able to exert enough spin on the stone that it would stabilize after each skip, maintaining the same gyroscopic effect that holds a spinning top in place. When Kurt returned to Erie, skipping became something of a circus act. His friends would hand him a random lump of something and he'd skip it. "He threw a cinder block," said Susol, "and it actually skipped."

After Kurt graduated from Behrend, he earned money delivering flowers for his mom and laying bitumen roofs. But he couldn't face regular work, and eventually he registered for unemployment. Doctors refused to prescribe talk therapy, and for the general sense of depression that would later be refined to diagnoses of schizoaffective disorder and obsessive-compulsive disorder, he was given only Zoloft, an antidepressant, which he sometimes supplemented with recreational psychoactive drugs. During one week in 1994, he couldn't get his prescription filled and got into a store argument that involved the police.

Shaken, Kurt left Erie and headed out on a 300-mile trek from Mount Greylock, in northwestern Massachusetts, to the Canada-Vermont border, searching for Thoreau's "tonic of wilderness." When he returned, he moved to a motel in Reynoldsville, two hours southeast of Erie, and enrolled in a welding program at a local vocational college. In December 1995, he bumped into a woman named Paula, who was clearing out her locker following a course. After almost a year of exchanging letters, they got together again in person. A year after that they got married, moving into the home of Paula's elderly mom in Kane, an hour north of Reynoldsville.

The couple enjoyed hiking together—Paula nicknamed them Pair o' Pathetics, a pun on "peripatetic"—and hoped to honeymoon somewhere far from Pennsylvania. But Paula's mom was housebound, and neither of them were fit to work. They lived on welfare and rarely hung out with friends.

"There were always three people in our marriage," Kurt told me on day four of my trip, as we passed Kane on the three-hour drive from Erie to his cabin. "We really had the cards stacked against us."

Twenty-five years later, Kurt still doesn't jibe with Kane or other parts of "Pennsyltucky," Pennsylvania's Appalachian interior. Partly this is because of his half-redneck, half-Talmudic-prophet appearance: he looks like a figure who stepped off the stained glass of a local prayerhouse to score Big Gulps and jerky. It's also an outgrowth of his politics: in a region dominated by Let's Go Brandon flags, he donates to Bernie Sanders, fears climate change, and despises evangelists. He worries that cashiers judge him when he uses food stamps, and he shrank with embarrassment as we loaded up on supplies at Costco.

In 1997, feeling trapped in Kane, Kurt searched for somewhere that he and Paula could escape to. He unfurled a map of Pennsylvania and focused on the green areas. Then he triangulated a spot as far from crowded areas as possible, landing on a corner of Elk State Forest, around 15 miles from the lightbulb-manufacturing town of Emporium.

There he found a 16-acre plot that backed onto a creek and faced south. The moment he saw it, he felt time stand still. It was a "heaviness," he told me. "The weight of the silence, like a deep cave."

With help from Kurt's dad, the couple bought the plot, and they spent the next two years driving between there and Kane, occasionally camping under star-filled skies. Kurt leveled the land and dug the foundation using nothing more than a shovel and a wheelbarrow. He scavenged timber wherever he saw it and scored remnants from local construction sites, but by 2000, he still hadn't completed the core of what became a two-story home, so he and Paula camped in sleeping bags.

In the fall of 2000, Kurt was reading local classifieds when he came across an advertisement for an amateur stone-skipping contest being held 100 miles west in Franklin. It would be the city's first, and a feeder for the July 4 tournament on Mackinac Island. Kurt still had a pretty mean throw, and Paula encouraged him to sign up. "My marriage played into my skipping," he told me. "Ironically."

That September, Kurt lined up on the bank of Franklin's Riverfront Park, ready to put his years of throwing to the test. Beside him was a local guy named Russ Byars, who had a towering physique and a shock of blond hair. The two were neck and neck going into the final throw, but Kurt nailed it and won the event, qualifying for the following year's Mackinac pro tournament.

Byars won at Franklin the following year, earning his golden ticket to Mackinac. Kurt struggled during his debut on the island's choppy water. This meant that, in 2001, both men would meet in Michigan. It was the beginning of an era-defining rivalry.

"YOU CAN FALL in love with a rock," Dave "Spiderman" Ohmer, a five-time Franklin winner, told me. "It's that rare—it's just got everything." It was my third day with Kurt, and the three of us were sitting in the corner of an Erie bar, several IPAs deep and discussing the topic of searching for competition-worthy skipping stones.

"You can search for years and say, 'OK, this is the best stone I have found,'" said Kurt. "And then you'll find another one. And if you take the time to look at the differences between the two, they have unique characteristics. And it's not just size, it's not weight, it's not thickness. It's every little feature. You start to pick up on things over time."

Becoming a world-class stone skipper is as much an asymptotic quest for the perfect rock as it is about honing technique. Some skippers, and most skimmers, use slate, specifically the kind of slate most commonly found in Britain and the northeastern United States. Japanese throwers mostly skip sparkling, metamorphic schist.

Kurt has only sourced rocks from Lake Erie, whose 13,000-year-old basin is crammed full of the kinds of wafer-thin, Devonian-shale chunks that cause skippers to swoon.

To find rocks, Kurt combs the lake for about an hour, appraising the stones like a diamond merchant. One in three he picks up makes it into his five-gallon bucket. Ideally, it weighs between four and seven ounces, has a smooth, flat bottom, and measures between a quarter-inch and five-sixteenths of an inch thick. Once he's gathered 60 pounds' worth—around 200 rocks—he sits on a crate and sorts the rocks into four rows of descending weight, arranged left to right.

He also sorts them for quality, placing better ones—those with tapered edges or easy-to-grip lobes—at the top of each row. "If I can find one stone in a hundred that I really like," he told me, "that's about right." Then he puts them back in the bucket in four layers: decent midsize stones; large, heavy, poor-quality stones he calls "chunky junkies"; high-quality midsize stones; and lighter ones he can skip at the end of practice without throwing his arm out. On rock-searching days, he goes through this process twice, which takes around five hours. Then he drives home. By his own calculations, Kurt has taken enough rocks from Lake Erie to load up almost 16 big-rig trucks.

I should note that the most important rocks he finds never make it into the bucket. These are "pocket rockets" that he keeps in his jeans. They're all of average weight, and he'll separate them into the rockets he'll use as tournament warm-ups—as practice rocks for certain techniques—or, in the case of a few dozen each year, for contest throws. These chosen few are the rocks he thinks have a shot at a trophy or a world record.

A top thrower will tell you that to skip a superior rock is Promethean, like unleashing some wild energy that has lain dormant for millions of years. It is also—like a sunset or a birth or a shooting star—a lesson in the impermanence of nature's beauty. The rock may skip for what feels like forever, but its ripples will fade, and it will sink into the fluvial void, likely never to be skipped again.

"There is so much poetry," Ohmer said as the three of us sat the bar. "Because you find that stone, then you've thrown it in the river and it's gone. You've pursued this endeavor until you have it all figured out. And then you hand it over to the world and see what comes of it."

KURT'S FIRST APPEARANCE at Franklin changed his life. Skipping rocks competitively felt as profound as anything he had experienced before. It was primal and pure, he said, "a little slice of utopia." Everything else, including his marriage, could feel like a distraction. He dived into physics, writing stone-skip theories on a scroll, Jack Kerouac–style, sketching models of gyroscopic inertia, vibratory components of rocks, or ripple patterns—"z waves," as he called them, that could propel them farther along on the water.

His hypotheses only got him so far, however, and Kurt placed second at Mackinac in 2001 behind Dave "Lefty" Kolar. He's the younger brother of John "The Sheriff" Kolar, a long-time skipper who I met during my U.S. trip. Kolar and his clique treated Mackinac as a lark, but Kurt was deadly serious, and he won the following year with a 21-hopper, beating the elder Kolar by a single skip. Organizers offered Kurt the nickname Slap-Happy, but he insisted on Mountain Man, owing to his love of the Appalachian wilderness. Every hotel on the island was packed with throwers, attendees, and organizers.

That same year, Kurt faced a Franklin showdown against Russ Byars, the blond-haired local he'd squeezed past a couple of years before. At 39, Russ was the anti-Kurt, a six-foot-one, 250-pound Marine Corps vet with a beer belly and a saucy grin. He was a gambler, with the languid posture of a guy on a Vegas weekend. To him, each throw was like an arm-pull on a slot machine: you never quite knew what you'd get.

Russ often had a drink in his hand, and he competed in Hawaiian shirts and tees emblazoned with phrases like I Beat Anorexia. Fellow skippers nicknamed him Rock Bottom. He claimed he'd never skipped a rock before moving to Franklin in 1999—and he didn't share Kurt's love of scientific inquiry. "There has been a lot of physics on this, and I don't understand any of it," he once told an ESPN reporter. "Grip it and rip it, that's my motto."

But boy could he throw. Russ cranked out 20 skips like Babe Ruth belted homers: effortlessly and often, with a knack for throwing final-round humdingers. He called them "Jesus fishes," because they hopped along the surface as if carried by divine hands. In 2001, Russ qualified for the pro event at Franklin, and he placed second among the pros, while Kurt took his second title in a row. In 2002, Kurt was looking for his hat trick. But after five of six throws, both men were dead even. Kurt, taking a page from his opponent's book, decided to go all in. His stone had an "aggressive" shape, he told me—so he switched styles, gripping it with his middle rather than his index finger and squeezing it a little tighter. Then he planted his foot and launched a throw that traveled what looked like a mile down a pinched seam of calm water.

For ten years, Jerdone "Jerry" McGhee's 38 skips along Texas's Blanco River had stood as the Guinness World Record for "most consecutive skips of a stone on water." Judges that day in Franklin decided that Kurt's clutch throw had skipped 40 times. "To land that stone was like threading a needle," he told me. "It was a sweet shot."

From then on, *Kurt and Russ* were stone skipping's Federer and Nadal. Between 2001 and 2007, one of them won every Franklin—Russ's four to Kurt's three. But Russ dominated Mackinac, taking home the fudge in '04, '05, and '07, besting Kurt's solitary victory in 2002. "I was the guy when I first started," Kurt told me. "Then Russ figured me out."

On July 19, 2007, Russ skipped a stone 51 times at Franklin, destroying Kurt's world record. TV crews invited him to Paris and China, and he competed against a robot on Discovery's slo-mo science show *Time Warp*. He launched a website and marketed a line of merchandise that included Russ Byars–branded writing pens. Kurt was furious. Self-promotion was a rejection of stone skipping's spiritual purpose. Besides, he was the science whiz: *he* should have faced that robot.

When the director of an indie movie invited Russ to consult on its stone-skipping scenes, Kurt felt left out. He convinced the director to let him on set, but argued in front of the crew. The director didn't want a stone-skipping consultant after that.

At loose ends, Kurt and Russ headed to a nearby river and threw rocks. They swapped stories, of Kurt's reclusive lifestyle and Russ's military service. "I was like, you know what? Russ is basically like me. He's a big kid," Kurt recalls. "He's also somebody who really has had a rough go of it in his own way. And he's just finding the thing that he is kind of proud of.

"I went into that movie kind of hot under the collar," Kurt added. "I came out with real respect."

RUSS'S 15 MINUTES of fame presented Kurt with an inconvenient truth: The general public didn't care who won which tournament or where. It was all about the *record*. He had never been more convinced that stone skipping offered "undeveloped natural purity, a refuge against the consumerist, plutocratic, kleptocratic, fucking destroy-and-build-up-everything mentality." To earn a platform to say so, he'd have to get the record back.

First he got ripped, speed-hiking uphill every day, then going hard on a single strength exercise—either push-ups elevated on soup cans or pull-ups using a bicycle handlebar drilled into a ceiling beam. He also calculated that, contrary to the 20-degree attack angle that physicists deemed optimal for skipping, he could hold a rock high and spear it into the water at 50 miles per hour at an angle closer to 30 degrees and still rip it hard enough to beat gyroscopic inertia.

Russ continued to run away with contests, winning Mackinac in '08, '09, '10, and '12, and Franklin in '08 and '10. But by 2013, Kurt had dialed his body-fat percentage way down and was ready for a comeback. "I felt like I could punch a hole through a brick wall," he told me.

On September 6, 2013, while Paula filmed from a bridge overhead, Kurt flung a stone from a bank of the Allegheny Reservoir, near Kane, that hit the water, took off, and didn't sink below the surface for seven seconds. It certainly *looked* like a record. Kurt sent Paula's footage to physicists in Pennsylvania and Australia and an aeronautics expert in Dubai. Responses were slow.

The following August, Russ was setting up his own camera to film a demonstration with Max Steiner—no relation to Kurt— and Max's father, Eric, a Mackinac stalwart. The 22-year-old was good. And when Russ checked his footage, he discovered that Max had skipped one of his rocks 65 times. They called Guinness, which approved the record.

"I was furious about this upstart who won one tournament a month ago and thinks he can come into my backyard and step on a record I spent six months beating myself to death to get," Kurt told me. "I wasn't going to have it."

A fortnight later, the result of Kurt's September 2013 throw came back. It was a new record, and it wasn't even close. According to the scientists, Kurt had skipped his rock at least 88 times. "Everybody's trying to break the two-hour mark in the marathon," Chip Susol told me. "What Kurt did was basically show up and run it in an hour and a half." People around the world marveled. It was an "unbreakable" achievement, Japanese *mizu kiri* champion Keisuke Hashimoto told me, "a product of miracles." Author Tom Whipple called it Kurt's Sistine Chapel: "He's given this gift to the world, this stone that floats along the lake."

Suddenly, folks wanted to hear what Mountain Man had to say. But the record had drained him, physically and economically:

each contest-quality stone had cost around $10 to find, he reckoned, and he'd won less than a thousand dollars of prize money in over a decade.

Paula hoped the record might quell an obsession that was contributing to the destruction of their marriage. But when she asked Kurt to cut back, she sounded to him like the pharmacist in Erie years before—only this time the medication was actually helping him.

At the same time, his great rivalry faded. Russ suffered nerve flare-ups and polymyalgia rheumatica, an inflammatory condition that causes pain and stiffness. In 2014, Russ's mother died. Then he got cancer, and by 2017, his T-shirts hung off him like bedsheets. That year Russ won his final Mackinac with a 31-skip Jesus fish. Soon after, Kurt visited him in Franklin. "We finally had that grand realization. It was a real kinship," Kurt told me.

"This wasn't about us," he continued. "This was bigger shit. We fought hard enough, we beat each other up enough, that we didn't have anything to prove to each other anymore. And now we were just friends."

A few weeks later, Russ died. It "hurt Kurt a lot," Paul Fero, Kurt's friend, told me. "Kurt has told me flat out that he would have never done what he did, throwing the 88, without Russell. Russell was a counterbalance, something to shoot for. They kept each other going. They both kept each other striving for more."

Kurt and Paula split in 2017. As Kurt and I drove to the cabin, he wiped away tears when he described that period. "I like to solve puzzles," he said. "My marriage was the biggest puzzle of all."

"Everything good was there, for a couple of fucked-up people," he said. "But she ultimately couldn't cope with my particularities of being fucked up—and it was mutual." Then he added, "I couldn't be that somebody who was deserving of some kind of normalcy and love, I couldn't be that. I tried. But I couldn't get it the way she needed without damaging myself further."

We turned off the highway at Sinnemahoning Creek and onto a snow-covered dirt path that led into forest. Thirty minutes later, we arrived.

KURT STEINER'S CABIN is his masterpiece. Since 1997, he's been adding to it, fixing it up, using other folks' junk or whatever he can buy with the few bucks he has left at the end of the month. There is no central heating or shower, and he still craps in a bucket under the basement floorboards. But he loves it to death, he said, and enjoys it "as much, perhaps, as I enjoy stone skipping. There's a very strong pull in me to want to work on this place."

We spent four days there. The cabin is surrounded by mechanical flotsam—skeins of chicken wire, engines, old tools. Nothing is decorated, and some of the walls have yet to be insulated. The ground floor is divided into two halves, marked by a blanket draped across a doorway. On one side are the 250 or so square feet where Kurt lives. The space holds a bed, a kitchenette, a couple of chairs, a desk and a dresser for his computers, a couple of bookshelves (full), and plastic tubs of papers and writing (overflowing). The other half is filled with five-gallon water jugs, workout gear, tools, food supplies, building materials, and everything in between.

Sleeping on a roll with my head beside a gas heater, I began to decrypt the cabin's contents. Each aspect embodies precision in chaos, "a recognition that when things are arranged a certain way, with a certain use of angles and curves, it echoes something of my soul," Kurt told me. "Even here there's a fairly conscious, loose interpretation of feng shui—a structure that, if you spend time in it, imprints itself on you."

We spoke most intimately at the cabin: this is where Kurt is most himself, rather than Mountain Man. He writes poetry and works on the Toyota. He eats very little and relies on seasonal fruits and vegetables. He can squat 100 times in six minutes and knock out 55 sixty-pound curls in the same amount of time. He can run up the valley with surprising speed.

Kurt won Mackinac tournaments in 2020 and 2021, but the sport is changing. In 2018, ESPN approached Eric and Max Steiner about televising a contest. Last year a camera crew came to Franklin, later airing Dave Ohmer's victory on ESPN 8, between other sports marginalia like Putt-Putt and marble runs. Eric Steiner is keen to expand skipping, perhaps even monetize it. "I think it's just a fun sport," he told me. "With ESPN picking it up, it's really brought it to a bigger audience."

Kurt would like skipping to be less commercial, of course— he still believes it can save the world. "This culture is pushing people to be all the same, and incurious," he said. "To me, all that's against humanity. I really believe I'm in a fight for the soul of humanity. And you can call me crazy, but you need crazy people."

To stay the course, Kurt has one more wild ambition: to become the world record holder in both skimming *and* skipping. That would mean beating Dougie Isaacs, which is possible: Kurt has already thrown a rock to within 26 feet of Isaacs's record. One thing holding him back is his financial situation and the cost of gas. Another is his body. Soon after I left Pennsylvania, Kurt had surgery on his busted shoulder, and he fears his 2022 season may already be over.

It's not his only challenge, though. One day Kurt would love to coach a female skipper and make his sport more inclusive. Fast-pitch softball techniques could easily be adapted to skipping, he told me—especially at Mackinac, where raw power counts for way less.

But finding somebody with whom he could skip into his twilight years is a tougher test. "I've had to accept that there are things about myself I'm never gonna get right," he said. Sometimes he dreams he's dating a woman with brittle, walnut-like teeth that crumble when he tries to kiss her. "Maybe the most responsible thing for me to do…," he said, tailing off. "I have to accept that I'm gonna be alone."

"I don't want to say I am never happy, or that I don't know what that is," he told me. "Stone skipping does reward me, in the way it makes me forget, in the way it gives me hope, in the way it brings me to people I like. The mystery never gets tired, never gets solved. Skipping stones makes me happy, because there are hints of happiness writ large. That happiness is not dead."

On our final day at the cabin, Kurt was fumbling with a dog-eared box of special rocks. Some were signed by fellow skippers. Others were handmade or fixed with tiny motion sensors, the products of decades-old experiments. "Should I go for a record in skimming?" he asked me. "Should I make another insane stone-skip video? Or should I take care of my house, which is crumbling down around me?"

Outside, the winter snow melted in a bright blue sky. We grabbed our jackets, hopped in the Toyota, and headed for the creek. It was time to throw.

SEAN WILLIAMS is a British reporter and photographer based in Wellington, Aotearoa New Zealand. His subjects range from human rights and conflict to sport, culture, and tech.

A Half Century of High Kicks and Hot Pants

SARAH HEPOLA

FROM *Texas Monthly* • SEPTEMBER 2022

On a sweltering Saturday in August, seven cheerleaders stood in the tunnel of the new Texas Stadium, just beyond the city limits of Dallas, wearing a uniform unlike anything that had ever been seen in professional sports: White go-go boots that zipped up the front. Teensy white hot pants. A plunging royal blue crop top knotted at the rib cage, just one suggestive tug from coming untied.

This was 1972, and Vonciel Baker was nervous about the crowd. The twenty-year-old was short and skinny, and she used to shimmy to James Brown in her living room as a kid. She was one of five raised by a single mom in South Dallas, on the wrong side of the tracks in a status-obsessed city, but Baker had a quality you might call sparkle. Earlier that spring, she'd heard a radio spot on the local station KVIL announcing that the Dallas Cowboys were looking for a new kind of cheerleader—dancers, that was the idea. More than a hundred showed up for tryouts; only seven made the cut. (Actually, eight did, but an aspiring model dropped out before the season began.) They would become known as the Original Seven: Baker, Anna Carpenter, Rosemary Hall, Dolores McAda, Carrie O'Brien, Deanovoy Nichols, and Dixie Smith.

Each of them stood in that tunnel, staring at the artificial turf and the stands of a new football stadium named for the state whose glory it hoped to capture.

The Dallas Cowboys had had cheerleaders before, including a group of high schoolers in bobby socks and pleated skirts who yelled "Charge!" They didn't dance, and they didn't wear *that*. It's tough to remember in our skin-saturated age, but cleavage and bare midriffs weren't just unusual back then—they were scandalous. This moment in 1972 marked the debut of a bold experiment, a very Texas hybrid of pageant beauty, good-girl etiquette, and come-hither slink.

Baker looked up at the sky whenever she got anxious, and she could see the sunlight fading and the stadium lights blazing from where she stood in the mouth of the tunnel. Texas Stadium had a hole in the roof, a design quirk (plans for a retractable roof were squelched because of the price tag) spun into an asset. "So God could watch his favorite team," one player famously put it.

As the drums of the live band started to pound, the seven cheerleaders burst from that tunnel. "And all of a sudden, we heard noise from the fans, and we're going, like, 'What's going on?'" Baker told me in her honeyed twang. Texas Stadium erupted in a joyful noise she can still hear, fifty years later. "And they're pointing at us. We didn't know that we had introduced something new to football."

What they introduced was sex and glamour into the gladiator arena of modern sports. They launched a wave of imitations across the NFL, creating a blueprint for beauty that's practically branded on the cultural imagination.

It was a watershed year for women, a time when the forces of freedom were starting to be unleashed but also clash. *Roe v. Wade* was making its way from a Dallas courthouse through the Supreme Court, where it would ignite a battle that's still raging. It was the year *Deep Throat* hit American theaters, launching a vogue for "porno chic." And it was the year Title IX passed, opening the door for women in athletics.

The Dallas Cowboys Cheerleaders were a watershed too, combining the precision of the East Texas drill team the Kilgore Rangerettes with the class of the Radio City Rockettes and adding a dose of old-fashioned Texas razzle-dazzle. "We're looking for an all-American, sexy girl," choreographer Texie Waterman once told a local news station, taking a bite out of that word, "sexy." And this internal contradiction—of being good but also a bit bad, of being innocent but also a bit dangerous—became an essential part of their brand, and their explosion.

To follow the Dallas Cowboys Cheerleaders over the next half century is to watch the pop sexualization of women: on television, on billboards and magazine covers, in swimsuit calendars that became making-of DVDs that became a reality TV show. Though their spot in culture is singular, their struggles and triumphs speak to women's rising place in the world: how we look, how we behave, who and what determines our value.

These days, they're seen as a legacy, a throwback to another era. Their instantly recognizable uniform was donated to the Smithsonian in 2018, a piece of American lore alongside Dorothy's slippers and Abraham Lincoln's top hat. But the squad has also slipped from its pedestal. Across the NFL, the past decade has brought fair-wage lawsuits, sexual harassment claims, and bad press. Professional cheerleaders for other teams are moving away from sexy sideline dancing, adopting more-modest uniforms, and adding men to their squads. The Carolina Panthers recently brought on the first openly trans cheerleader. (Whether fans want these changes is another matter.)

In February, scandal hit the Dallas Cowboys when ESPN broke the story that the team's number one PR guy, Richard Dalrymple, had been accused of using his phone to film four cheerleaders in their dressing room back in 2015, resulting in a $2.4 million settlement. The company line had always been that the cheerleaders were protected. The extensive rules that had been put in place decades earlier—dictating everything from how the cheerleaders dressed to the way they conducted themselves off the field—were supposedly for their own good, meant to guard their safety as well as their image. Yet here was the team's own PR guy being accused of creating a PR disaster. For a squad that prided themselves on "wholesome sexiness," this was seedy indeed.

The Cowboys and Dalrymple denied any wrongdoing. But my phone blew up with cheerleaders I'd gotten to know during the year I spent interviewing them for the *Texas Monthly* podcast *America's Girls*. How had this happened? Had it happened other times? On sports radio and Twitter and in casual conversation, I heard questions that had dogged me since I'd started this project: Did the world still need professional cheerleaders? Did we ever?

Cowboys' history books won't tell you the true origin story of the cheerleaders. "The Dallas Cowboys Cheerleaders began as the creation of one man: Texas E. Schramm," reads a 1984 tome on the Cowboys. Nope, try again. General manager Tex Schramm, who helped launch the franchise, in 1960, was a visionary, a former CBS executive who saw that the future of professional sports was television. And it's true he kept the squad alive during the years when born-again coach Tom Landry wanted them gone. But the Dallas Cowboys Cheerleaders are actually the creation of a few women, whose innovative ideas and contributions have mostly been forgotten.

Dee Brock was a woman of the world when the world could be quite small for women. She got her PhD in literature at the University of North Texas after marrying longtime *Dallas Times Herald* columnist Bob Brock, with whom she had three sons. She taught high school English, though she'd later become a founding faculty member at the city's first community college, El Centro. She was uncommonly beautiful—blond and five feet seven—and she modeled on the side. She also had a sense of humor. "I don't really like girls that have that much breast," Brock remembered legendary clothier Stanley Marcus once telling her as she prepped for a Neiman Marcus fashion show. "Well, I'm sorry," she replied. "But there they are."

Sometime before the Cowboys' second season, in 1961, Schramm tapped her for a Big Idea: beautiful models on the sidelines. Respectfully, Brock told him this dog wouldn't hunt. Models didn't move much, and they required money, something Schramm didn't like to spend. She hatched a different plan. Recruit local high school girls. Pay them with a couple of tickets to the game, give them some kerchiefs and pom-poms. It's free! Schramm placed her in charge, and she spent the next decade trying to make this formula work, though it ultimately did not. She recruited teenage boys for an experiment in coed cheerleading remembered mostly for its dumb name: the Cowbelles and Beaux.

"That is one of my embarrassing moments," Brock, now in her early nineties, told me at her home in Tyler. The name was a PR guy's stunt, and, sadly, it stuck. "My teams were strong. They were not Belles and Beaux." She practically spat that last part.

Brock had long been a woman ahead of her time. She integrated the squad in 1965, with the help of a local Black teacher named Frances Roberson. The Cowboys had several Black players by then, but much of Dallas was still segregated. In 1971, half of the Dallas Cowboys Cheerleaders were Black.

The following year, a skimpier uniform, an age bump, and an open audition marked the start of a brave new era. "I think we need an older group of girls," Brock remembers telling Schramm.

"Old?" He was not convinced.

Older, she explained. Eighteen and above. "And I wanted them to have a sexier costume," she said.

She didn't use that word with Schramm, but it was on her mind. Back in the fifties, Brock had landed a spot as a "bathing beauty" in a Dallas summer musical, where she turned heads as one of only two women audacious enough to wear a bikini. That revealing number made her a celebrity in local modeling circles. She wanted her cheerleaders to get that same kind of attention. She also wanted the cheerleaders to be dancers. To put on a show.

And she knew exactly who to hire in order to do that: the other woman bold enough to wear a bikini in that summer musical.

TEXIE WATERMAN WAS a petite pistol of a redhead who kept a cigarette forever smoldering between her fingers. She was also the go-to dance instructor in Dallas. "When they told me they wanted dancing cheerleaders, I told them they were crazy," Waterman said, according to the 1982 book *A Decade of Dreams*, still the only history of the Dallas Cowboys Cheerleaders ever published, though it's long been out of print.

Waterman grew up in Dallas and was a Highland Park High School grad who began teaching dance at seventeen. In her twenties, she had a run in New York City, where she performed in lavish supper clubs like the Copacabana. By the time Brock approached her, she was managing a studio along with her mother. (A very Texas detail: Her mom was also named Texie.) She wasn't sold on the idea at first. "There's no stage, no light, no illusion," she said in *A Decade of Dreams*. But she went for it anyway, introducing a sexy and playful style of dance that would go on to shape stadium entertainment.

Her initial annual salary was $300. Actually, Schramm didn't want to pay her at all, but Brock wasn't about to ask the choreographer to work for free, so she split her own salary, which was $600 at the time. So there you go: $300 a year to build a legendary squad.

The appalling compensation for the women behind the Dallas Cowboys Cheerleaders is a reflection of both the times and a team known for being cheap. The Cowboys didn't become all-powerful by giving anything away. That new squad of cheerleaders that burst out of the tunnel in 1972? They got $15 a game, $14.12 after taxes.

"It was enough to fill up my gas tank and buy me a Slurpee," Baker said. The money was a joke, but it made sense at the start. The cheerleading gig was only a side hustle, but it brought status, sisterhood, the chance to be part of something bigger.

The Original Seven quickly became local sweethearts. Fans started lining up after games to get their autographs. Little girls, little boys, adult men who had never before shown much interest in the action on the sidelines. More cheerleaders were soon added, because 7 wasn't nearly enough to meet crowd demand. First 15, then 21. They appeared at car dealerships and got their picture in the paper, like hometown pageant queens. It was, in those initial years, a low-key kind of celebrity.

But the cheerleaders were about to go global.

IT WAS NOVEMBER 10, 1975, and the Cowboys were squaring off against the Kansas City Chiefs on Monday Night Football. At the time, the weekly ABC broadcast was a blockbuster, with tens of millions training their eyes on the same game. Three years had passed since the cheerleaders' debut, and still no other team in professional sports had a squad like Dallas's. And on this night, the cameras didn't let you forget. They kept cutting away to those lovely lasses, sipping a cup of water, smiling and laughing on the sidelines.

Then came the moment: A cheerleader named Gwenda Swearengin is shaking her pom-poms overhead as she faces the field between plays. She's a former Miss Corsicana first runner-up, her long brown hair cascading across both shoulders, and the camera zooms in so tight on her that the white swish of her poms is barely visible at the top of the screen. As the shot lingers, she does something no cheerleader has ever done. She looks straight into the camera—and winks.

"I think she was doing that for you, Frank," host Howard Cosell cracks to his cohost, Frank Gifford.

"She was very effective," Gifford responds.

Coy but flirtatious. The perfect tease. One beautiful woman shining her light on every viewer in their living room recliner.

"The wink" became a part of Cowboys mythology, a way to explain the squad's rocket ride over the next years, and like many myths, it's about half-true. The moment was a bold breaking of the fourth wall—the cheerleaders had mostly ignored the cameras before then. And that game ramped up their profile, as did their appearance two months later on the sidelines of the 1976 Super Bowl. But even before the wink, the cheerleaders were already a fixture of an enterprise that was casually turning everyday sports fans into armchair voyeurs—not in a single moment, but over a season of televised games.

Football's exploding popularity through the seventies had a lot to do with TV sets moving to the center of American households. The cheerleaders went along for the ride. Waterman had designed the squad to play to enormous stadiums, where their exaggerated movements could be seen high in the bleachers, but television collapsed the distance, with close-ups that were startling in their intimacy, almost as if the cheerleaders were performing in your living room too.

"Honey shots" was the industry term for these cutaways, the invention of a former Dallas TV guy turned ABC sports director, Andy Sidaris. "I got the idea for honey shots," he said in the 1976 documentary *Seconds to Play*, "because I am a dirty old man."

That same year, Dee Brock left the cheerleaders. She eventually landed a gig as a senior vice president at the Public Broadcasting Service, where she developed educational programming. Waterman stayed on, but the demand created by the massive TV exposure was proving too much for one person. And so Schramm asked his secretary, Suzanne Mitchell, to run the cheerleaders "in your spare time," a diversion that would soon take over her life.

As the story goes, when Schramm first interviewed her for the job of secretary, Mitchell was back in Dallas after a stint in New York City, where she'd worked in publishing. He asked where she saw herself in five years. "Your chair looks pretty comfortable," she told him. He hired her on the spot. She would soon transform an upstart group of pretty sideline dancers into a sleek media machine.

She ruled by fear and never pretended otherwise. Full hair and makeup had to be done for rehearsal. No appearing in uniform around alcohol. No chewing gum. The cheerleaders had always had rules. "No fraternizing with players" was gospel from day one, an attempt to keep players from distraction (and the wives from mutiny). But Mitchell was the daughter of a military man, and she introduced a boot-camp mentality, making the rules a way of life. Scales showed up in the studio. Cheerleaders were rebuilt in a new image, like soldiers enlisted in the army of glam. She expanded the squad, ultimately settling on 36, and fashioned a sort of seventies Spice Girls: there was the sporty one, the sweetheart, the beauty queen. The idea was that every little girl would see herself—and every man would see his fantasy.

In 1977 the cheerleaders landed on the cover of *Esquire*, one of the most sophisticated and influential titles in the heyday of magazines. "The Best Thing About the Dallas Cowboys," it read. A cheerleader named Debbie Wagener, a dead ringer for Blondie's Debbie Harry, stands with her hands on her hips. The Cowboys merchandising arm got cranking soon after that: there were cheerleaders calendars, playing cards, Frisbees, even a toy van.

Annual auditions ballooned to more than a thousand hopefuls by 1978, with swarms of gorgeous, talented women all competing for the same 36 spots. "You can be replaced in a second," Mitchell used to tell anyone who stepped out of line, though most didn't. These women weren't going to jeopardize their first taste of fame.

"We were put on a pedestal," said Shannon Baker Werthmann, who joined the squad in 1976. "You did have to pinch yourself." Through the late seventies, her Farrah Fawcett hair and killer high kicks made her a poster girl and the cheerleader who always seemed to get the most fan mail. It's easy to forget how young these women were as they blasted into the zeitgeist. Werthmann was seventeen when she first tried out for the cheerleaders. The rule was you had to be eighteen, but she didn't want to wait, so she lied on her application.

In 1978 the squad was flown to Utah for its first big TV spot, a special hosted by the Osmond Brothers. "We were treated like princesses," Werthmann told me. "We rode in limos. There was a large spread of food waiting for us." This was the dream. They even toured Donny and Marie's home. Marie, a teenager at the time, had a pink bedspread and a collection of dolls, a detail that stuck with Werthmann. "She was a girl, just like us."

Tami Barber was there too. The only child of a Cowboys diehard, Barber came from a small Nebraska town and had made the squad in 1977, at nineteen. Suddenly, she became known as "the one with the pigtails" and found herself signing autographs. She recalled appearing on Jerry Lewis telethons in Las Vegas. "I got to see Johnny Carson and Frank Sinatra and Dionne Warwick," she said. "I mean, I was the fan at that point."

But these events stood in stark contrast to the reality for many at home. The cheerleaders never got a slice of the merchandising profit, and the $15-a-game pay wouldn't budge until the nineties. Rehearsals could be as frequent as five nights a week, sometimes lasting till midnight, in an un-air-conditioned studio meant to prep them for the Texas heat. Many of them were broke, hustling to make rent, falling asleep at their desks during work or school. Wagener was a checker at Tom Thumb when she appeared on that *Esquire* cover—ringing up the glossy magazine she graced and quietly putting it in someone's bag.

IN 1977 THE cheerleaders released their own poster: five glamazons lit by neon, with smoke billowing around their ankles. At the center was a brunette named Suzie Holub, her eyes smoldering as she looked directly into the lens. "Damn if that ain't a come-hither look," Tex Schramm told photographer Bob Shaw when he saw the image, a shot that would sell around a million copies and turn the cheerleaders into the country's hottest pinups. But this popularity came with a dark side.

That year, after a performance in Wichita, Kansas, the cheerleaders were walking back to their bus when fans descended on them in a way they never had before. "A couple of girls started running, then we started running, and then the crowd was running," Tami Barber remembered. "It was our Beatles moment. We were running for our lives because these people were grabbing at us." Barber sat inside the bus as strangers pounded the sides. "My heart was beating so fast, and it was the first time I thought, 'Why are people crazy? We're just us.'"

The visibility brought threats even Suzanne Mitchell couldn't manage. One night, Barber picked up the phone in the apartment where she lived alone. "Good-night, Tami," said an unfamiliar man's voice. She hung up, but he called back another night, and she was so scared she moved. She wasn't the only one. "You'll have to have an unlisted number," Mitchell instructed the cheerleaders, but often that wasn't enough. A cheerleader named Billie Mitchell once opened her eyes in the middle of the night to find a strange man standing beside her bed. She chased him out, and then she moved too.

The Dallas Cowboys Cheerleaders had become a bona fide global sensation. They starred in a hit 1979 made-for-TV movie; they became part of the story arc in a two-part episode of *The Love Boat*; they faced off against some Cowboys football players on *Family Feud*. And along the way, Mitchell had the impossible task of managing these internal contradictions: she had to keep the cheerleaders safe while presenting them as endlessly available; she touted their singularity in public while quashing their egos in private. She had to control this wildfire at the same time she fanned the flames.

Cheerleaders across the NFL started copying the Cowboys, with more than twenty squads transforming seemingly overnight into sexpot dancers. *Sports Illustrated* called it "the Great Cheerleading War of 1978." The Cowboys had become the most visible and most valuable franchise in the NFL, and a huge part of the brand was these fetching women. It was a match made in marketing heaven: in the center of the field, Captain America

Roger Staubach, and on the sidelines, 36 Miss Americas in a famously tarty uniform.

The year 1978 was also when an adult film actress by the name of Bambi Woods donned that glorious uniform (or at least an imitation of it) in a less-than-glorious scene. *Debbie Does Dallas* was a shoestring porno film whose plot, so to speak, followed a young woman with the dream of cheering for a certain legendary Dallas football team. The marquee outside the New York City theater where it debuted falsely claimed that Woods was an "ex–Dallas Cowgirl cheerleader," and the Cowboys—presumably incensed that the "wholesome sexiness" they'd pioneered had gone full frontal—sued for trademark infringement, resulting in the deliciously named lawsuit *Dallas Cowboys Cheerleaders v. Pussycat Cinema*. Newspapers and TV stations devoured this saga. The Cowboys eventually won the case. But the media frenzy turned a fly-by-night skin flick into a blockbuster.

In turn, the cheerleaders doubled down on their wholesome image. They launched a line of children's clothing that included a little satin jacket and developed a new logo of a doe-eyed cartoon girl dressed as a cheerleader and looking all of seven. Young girls had by then become a major fan base for the cheerleaders. But the sexual tease the squad had introduced was tricky to put back in the bottle.

That same fall of 1978, five women dressed as cheerleaders posed for a feature in *Playboy*. The group was a rogue outfit called the Texas Cowgirls, a rival Dallas-based agency formed by women who had quit the Cheerleaders (fed up with the rules, worn down by the demanding schedule and low pay) or been nixed from the squad as auditions became cutthroat. The Cowgirls made appearances at places where the cheerleaders wouldn't dare to go, often events where alcohol was served. And their fees were shared evenly among the members, unlike the cheerleaders, whose occasional appearance fees went to a select group of favorite members of the squad, and who did not see a dime from the squad's numerous merchandising deals.

The Texas Cowgirls' splashy debut in *Playboy* was a riff on the Cheerleaders' top-selling 1977 poster, five glamazons in triangle formation, except for one detail. This time, their tops were untied.

DESPITE THE CONTROVERSIES of the late seventies, the cheerleaders rarely encountered any sort of public backlash. But in 1982, they arrived at Fresno State University, in California, to rehearse for a halftime performance, and as they entered the campus they were greeted by a big white bedsheet hanging out the window of a building, spray-painted with the words "Hearts and Minds, Not Bumps and Grinds."

The cheerleaders had transformed culture in the previous decade, but so had second-wave feminism. *Ms.* magazine debuted the same year, 1972, as that iconic uniform did, and the consciousness-raising publication cofounded by Gloria Steinem had helped popularize ideas about sexual objectification and the male gaze during a decade when legal victories like *Roe v. Wade* and the 1974 Equal Credit Opportunity Act were changing women's lives. By 1982, a feminist vernacular had seeped into the American vocabulary in the same way hot pants and jiggle had seeped into network programming, and on the sidelines of Fresno State, those two forces were about to collide.

The drumbeat of protest had been building all week. A professor in the physical education department named Rhita Flake started a petition, swiftly picked up by the news media, calling the cheerleaders "demeaning to women" because their primary function was "to provide sexually suggestive entertainment for male sports fans."

"Sex objects"—that was the slur that followed the squad, even if the cheerleaders, and many fans, saw themselves as more: role models, goodwill ambassadors, talented performers. In 1979 they'd even begun doing USO tours to visit soldiers in Korea and elsewhere overseas. So when director Suzanne Mitchell heard about Flake's comment, she shot back in the press, "The first thing

I'd like to ask her is, what has she ever done for her country? We helicopter into the DMZ."

Things got ugly at the performance later that day, when protesters gathered outside the stadium. Dana Presley Killmer, who joined the squad in 1981, remembers the ominous vibe. "It was so nasty that the faculty at the university had to form a human fence on either side of us so we could get out of the bus and get onto the field without [protesters] throwing rocks." The confusing part for the cheerleaders was that the appearance was a charity event to raise money for the college's athletics department. But in the heated battle of the sexes, the cheerleaders were now deemed to be on the wrong side.

The cheerleaders may have been thought of as eye candy for men, but they had become a lightning rod for many women, and still are to this day. Their popularity raised complicated questions about women's beauty and sexuality—how do you extol those qualities without being defined by them? "Exploitation" is a word that often gets thrown around by critics of the cheerleaders. But who decides that these women are being exploited if they say they're not?

"We really were doing what we wanted to do," Killmer told me from her home in East Texas. "No one forced me to be a Dallas Cowboy cheerleader." Quite the opposite—she beat out more than two thousand women for her spot.

By the end of the decade, the cheerleaders' tightly calibrated mixture of sweetness and licentiousness was about to face an entirely different challenge—the team's new owner.

ONE SATURDAY IN early 1989, Mitchell's assistant, Debbie Bond Hansen, arrived at the office to discover all sorts of unfamiliar men wandering the halls, shuffling through papers. "There were all these suits," remembered Hansen. She called Mitchell, who was at home. What was happening? The evening news would tell them soon enough. An Arkansas oilman named Jerry Jones had bought the Dallas Cowboys. A new sheriff was in town.

Hansen had been with the cheerleaders since 1979. Through much of the following decade, she'd proven a trusty second lieutenant to Mitchell. Once, after hearing a rumor that one hopeful was moonlighting as a stripper, Mitchell dispatched her to visit every strip club in Dallas. "I had never been to a strip club, okay?" said Hansen. "I was hiding in the corner because I didn't want anybody to recognize me." She slunk around in oversized sunglasses and a fur coat. Since her last name at the time was Bond, this detective work earned her the nickname "Double-Oh-Seven."

Mitchell and Hansen had steered the cheerleaders out of the scandalous late seventies and the feminist pushback of the early eighties by leaning on the rules. The rules were used to keep things steady and predictable, but they also offered instruction in a certain kind of Southern womanhood. "A lot of people don't know this—we were a grooming school too," Hansen told me. The matter of when to wear heels and what fork to use with the salad might seem like trivial concerns, but those questions could be overwhelming to small-town women hoping to be something more. The ultimate goal of each cheerleader was made clear in Mitchell's photocopied handouts, which were given to rookies: "A girl becomes a LADY."

Jerry Jones didn't seem to be a fan of rules—not theirs, anyway. He fired Coach Landry. He shunted Tex Schramm to the side till the legendary manager walked off the field he'd built, and the ever-loyal Mitchell quit soon after. "They were America's Team," she told a reporter after she resigned. "[Now] they're Jerry Jones's team."

Mitchell installed Hansen as her successor, but the scene had changed in distressing ways. "I'd be having a rehearsal in the dance studio, and Jerry Jones would come down with his friends and his cocktails," Hansen said. Prior to this, the cheerleaders had always been strictly siloed. They entered and exited through different doors than the players did and often only saw them on the field. Under Jones, the girls' school vibe had turned strip club. There was the owner, "clinking the ice, watching the girls rehearse," Hansen remembered. "I was just like, 'Gosh, this is not like the old days.'"

According to Hansen, Jones brought her into his office and explained he was relaxing the rules. Let the cheerleaders date players, let them appear around alcohol. Who cares? He also wanted to change the uniform. At least that's what Hansen told reporters who ambushed her at the office a few days later. On the news clip, she speaks in a solemn voice as microphones cluster near her chin. "I have received pressure from within the front office to add to the cheerleaders' uniform during the summer months biking pants and halter tops." She tells reporters how this Jones character responded to her objection that cheerleaders should not be seen in untoward scenarios. He told her, "Debbie, alcohol is here to stay."

Hansen resigned, and she wasn't the only one. Fourteen cheerleaders quit, although Jones sweet-talked them back, saying it was all a misunderstanding. He brought in his Stanford-educated daughter, Charlotte, to help straighten out his PR mess, and in time she'd become president of the cheerleaders and a major power player in the Jones family business.

This particular standoff evokes a tension that has existed in women's lives for generations. The old regime wanted to protect the women, but the strict rules also constrained their behavior—and placed all responsibility exclusively on the women's shoulders. Cheerleaders were kicked off for dating players, who never suffered a thing. Cheerleaders were kicked off for much less, in fact—drinking in uniform, wearing a salty Halloween costume, any behavior deemed unladylike. Suddenly, a new regime wanted to loosen the corset, granting the women more leeway—but to do what? One cheerleader, a two-year veteran named Cindy Villarreal, said she quit after getting an unusual request to appear with another cheerleader on Jerry Jones's private jet. (The Cowboys organization declined several interview requests. A spokesperson for the team disputed Hansen's and Villarreal's accounts but offered no details.)

It was, indeed, Jones's team now. And over the next decades that team would nab three Super Bowl championships, garner a heap of tabloid scandal, and become the most lucrative brand name in sports, valued at more than $6 billion.

"WE REALLY WANTED this year's calendar to be special," cheerleaders director Kelli Finglass tells an ESPN film crew on a windswept Caribbean beach in 1999. "We wanted it to be classy and elegant and to expose the cheerleaders as the premier group of women in all sports."

"Expose the cheerleaders"—was that a cheeky joke or a slip of the tongue? The swimsuit calendars, first released in the early nineties, certainly did expose those cheerleaders: over time, the bikinis got smaller, the poses more risqué. The women were busy keeping pace with a culture gone wild. The nineties saw the rise of Victoria's Secret Angels and MTV Spring Break, all of which amounted to a lot of soft-core porn on cable channels just as real porn started running rampant on the internet. It was now mundane to see a nearly naked woman rolling in sand in a commercial for watches, for cologne—for anything, really.

Finglass had been a Dallas Cowboys cheerleader from 1984 to 1988, when her last name was McGonagill. Raised in the small East Texas town of Lindale, she was known for her outgoing personality and radiant smile. She'd studied marketing in college, and Jones eventually hired Finglass as the new director in 1991. She turned out to share her boss's marketing prowess and knack for corporate partnerships. Every last detail on those cheerleaders got a sponsor, from their Lucchese boots to their visits to Planet Tan.

The swimsuit calendars became a fixture of display tables at Barnes & Noble, next to *Sports Illustrated* pinups and *Far Side* desk calendars. Their reach was extended even further when ESPN decided to film those making-of-the-swimsuit-calendar specials, hoping to fill up programming on an expanding cable network. It was one long hour of behind-the-scenes moments:

cheerleaders getting their makeup done, cheerleaders posing beside rocks as waves crash against them, all set to tropical club music. A few years later, the Cowboys produced their own swimsuit special, which they sold on DVD.

But in 2006, the cheerleaders' exposure hit a new level: they got their own reality show. *Making the Team* was the brainchild of writer-producer Eugene Pack, whose many credits included the Miss USA Pageant. This was high tide for reality TV, a genre that exploded around the turn of the century with *Survivor, Dancing With the Stars,* and *American Idol,* shows that allowed viewers to pass judgment from the comfort of their couches. Like those hits, *Making the Team* followed the audition process each year, as the judges—led by the ever-poised Finglass—whittled down hundreds of hopefuls. The show had built-in dramatic tension: only 36 women would (metaphorically) survive. Thrilling competition, tearful eliminations, and plot twists drawn from real life (injuries, heartbreaks, personal tragedies) became a part of the narrative.

Unlike shows such as *The Real Housewives, Making the Team* did not traffic in catfights, and it felt earnest in a way that swept you up into these women's hopes and dreams. Whether or not the producers were scheming behind the scenes to drum up ratings (I was told by several crew members they weren't), the women who made the cut seemed chosen because they were the best candidates, not because they would instigate drama. Although early seasons included a certain mean-girl snideness and casual body-shaming endemic to the era, the show started to move away from that. Perhaps the most surprising thing about *Making the Team*—given all the cleavage, hip thrusting, and hair flicking— was how endearing it could be.

"I used to watch that when I was stoned in college with my friend Suzy," *New Yorker* writer Jia Tolentino, who grew up in Houston, told me. "It was the kind of thing where we thought we might be watching it in a snarky, we-will-laugh-at-these-people way, and then we were like, 'I would f—ing die for these women.'"

Tucked away on a cable channel called CMT (Country Music Television), it was ignored by most media even as it caught on with a hard-core fan base of women, many of whom might never set foot inside a football stadium. If honey shots had reduced the cheerleaders to cutaway sex objects, the reality show expanded them into bona fide talents. Dance became the central theme, from the opening cattle call, when groups performed a number in front of a panel of judges, to the long studio practices, as newbies struggled to perfect their high kicks and jump splits. The most entertaining segments were the solo performances, when the women revealed a finesse for pirouettes and grand jetés that seemed to surprise even them. Early seasons had an *American Idol*–style tendency to mock less talented performers, and the threat of reality show cameras may have tanked the audition numbers, leading fewer hopefuls to try out, but the women who did show up were top-notch. *Making the Team* became one of the longest-running and most popular reality series in CMT's history, and it turned women who'd long been anonymous into characters whose journey viewers could follow through the seasons.

But another reality was emerging alongside the show, and this one didn't get airtime. In 2014 two Oakland Raiders cheerleaders filed a class-action suit against their squad, claiming wage violations. The lawsuit ended in a $1.25 million settlement for the cheerleaders and launched a wave of litigation across the NFL. For decades, low pay had been industry standard, and some even argued that this was a good thing. "You get a better quality of girls who aren't doing it for the money but for the love of dance," Dallas Cowboys Cheerleaders choreographer Judy Trammell told a reporter from E! News back in 1996, when the pay rate was still $15 a game.

A new generation of young women, steeped in social media activism, were revealing this tradition to be something else entirely: against the law. Similar suits followed with the Cincinnati Bengals, New York Jets, and Buffalo Bills, while ones that cited body-shaming and discrimination hit the Houston Texans and the New Orleans Saints, respectively. A chill shot through the NFL.

So much of what had made it possible for the Cowboys cheerleaders to become a global phenomenon—the armchair voyeurism, the throwaway pay, the strict weight requirements ensuring a supposedly ideal body, one that could be dissected by cameras—began crashing into conflict with the #MeToo era, as treatment of women took center stage. Squads started wearing more-modest costumes, adding men, trading hip thrusts for the kinds of stunting seen on Netflix's *Cheer*, moves that were less "all-American, sexy girls" and more Cirque du Soleil.

In 2018 the Cowboys were hit with a lawsuit too. Erica Wilkins had been a star on the squad who appeared on the cover of a Cowboys *Star* magazine swimsuit issue in 2016. It was her most lucrative year, and, according to her complaint, she raked in a total of about $16,500, including game day and appearance fees. The most damning detail found in the complaint was that Rowdy, the team's mascot, made about $65,000 per year during that same period.

Though Wilkins filed the suit as a collective action, no other cheerleaders joined her. High-profile veterans, including *Real Housewives of Dallas* star Brandi Redmond, instead circled the wagons on social media. "I would do it all over again for free," she wrote, a common sentiment among cheerleaders but one that isn't actually relevant to the legality of a contract. According to Wilkins's suit, the Cowboys classified their cheerleaders as employees, but they weren't making minimum wage. They received $200 for game day and $8 an hour for rehearsals. The seventies girls may have died for that kind of scratch. But even with the pay bump, Wilkins said, her pay often fell far below minimum wage once she logged all the hours. She settled her suit out of court, and while no cheerleaders ever joined her, it benefited them anyway. Game day pay reportedly doubled to $400.

Meanwhile, much of the media, which had once treated cheerleading as the ultimate fantasy, started to treat it more like a waking nightmare. "A Ponzi scheme in hot pants," read a piece on Deadspin. "So, Uh, Why Does the NFL Have Cheerleaders Again?" asked the Ringer. What was once new and sexy now looked outdated and sexist. And yet, each May, hundreds still vied for the honor.

LAST NOVEMBER, THE cheerleaders performed a sixtieth anniversary halftime show at AT&T Stadium, a.k.a. Jerry World (it replaced Texas Stadium in 2009), where the Miller Lite and Pepsi logos were displayed right below the American flag. The number sixty actually came as a bit of a surprise. For a long time, the cheerleaders dated their inception to 1972, when the uniform debuted. But now they were dating it back to the very beginning, 1961, the year Dee Brock started the squad.

I bought a cheap standing-room-only seat in the rafters and jockeyed for a better view as cheerleaders from each decade— white-haired ladies from the seventies, followed by long-haired ladies from the eighties, followed by even more long-haired women from the nineties—took the field for a choreographed routine, one danceable hit after another. And then all of them took the field together for the finale, "We Are Family," by Sister Sledge.

The Dallas Cowboys Cheerleaders have always been a family. At least, that's what people I interview tell me. And so the scandal that erupted in February was more than just an alleged transgression. Because the offense was coming from inside the house.

PR maven Rich Dalrymple had unexpectedly retired earlier that month. He was greeted with hosannas from local sports journalists, who didn't seem to notice that for the organization to quietly disappear one of Jerry Jones's top advisers without so much as an announcement on their website was very weird. Weeks later, veteran investigative reporter Don Van Natta Jr. broke the story on ESPN. Dalrymple had been accused of secretly filming as four cheerleaders changed in their dressing room.

It was shocking, but not surprising. During a 2001 postgame show for a playoff matchup hosted by the Philadelphia Eagles, a sportscaster revealed that visiting players, whose locker room was adjacent to that of the Eagles cheerleaders', were caught peeping at the women as they undressed and showered. A lawsuit followed, with claims that such behavior had been going on for nearly twenty years, that the peepholes were "common knowledge among virtually the entire National Football League," and that they were "considered one of the special 'perks' of being a visiting team of the Eagles." More recently, the Washington Football Team (now the Commanders) had their own voyeurism scandal after a former executive was accused of having staff create a lewd video that pieced together nip slips and other risqué B-roll footage from their cheerleaders' swimsuit shoot.

Representatives from the Cowboys claimed that an investigation into the Dalrymple incident, which took place in 2015, revealed no wrongdoing. Yet the team still paid that confidential settlement of $2.4 million. At the time, my podcast on the cheerleaders had just wrapped, and I went on the Dallas sports station the Ticket. One of the questions I'd been pondering was how to protect against toxic voyeurism, when, as I explained on-air, "low-key voyeurism is part of their brand." I noted that in 2013 fans were invited to pay $6,999 to travel to Mexico and watch the swimsuit calendar shoot in person. Among the listeners that day was Kelli Finglass, who later messaged me on Instagram, where we had occasionally traded direct messages. Kelli had complimented my work on the podcast (though she'd declined to participate), but she wasn't thrilled with me that afternoon.

"Your comment that the DCC were designed for low key voyeurism made me gasp," she wrote. I had a momentary stab of guilt, wondering if I'd gotten the story wrong. But I'd often suspected that many of the cheerleaders didn't fully know their own story, and that modern audiences hadn't fully absorbed the extent to which we've all become voyeurs—watching the grand spectacle through the screens in our living rooms, which became our bedrooms, which became our laptops, which became the phones in our palms.

Cheerleaders began texting me, eager to talk but wary of going on the record. The team instills fierce loyalty (some might say quaking fear), and it's unusual to hear cheerleaders openly questioning the organization's integrity or griping about current leadership, but several were cutting loose that day. "Don't Tarnish the Star" was a mantra those women had taken to heart. They followed the rules, they toiled for next to nothing—and the people tarnishing the star turned out to be the ones in control all along. "Every decision I've made in my life, I thought about that team," Tami Barber, now 64 and staring down a cancer diagnosis, told me. She was one of the rare few who didn't mind being quoted. Her heart would always be with the cheerleaders, she said, but the Cowboys? "If I were in AT&T Stadium today, I would puke on the star."

It became a long, dark off-season for the Cowboys. In March, news broke that Jones had been slapped with a paternity suit by a 25-year-old woman alleging he was her father. (She later dropped the suit.) Later that month, *Making the Team* was quietly canceled. No reason was given, but it was hard not to speculate either that the scandals had given CMT cold feet or that the cheerleaders, scrambling to control the narrative, felt that reality cameras came with too much risk. The Cowboys kept on as if there were nothing to see here. There was a big NFL draft party outside the team's Frisco practice facility later that month, with cheerleaders high-kicking and shaking their silver-and-blue pom-poms.

Of course, the franchise has been nothing if not bulletproof. By summer, talking heads were debating when (if?) they'd win the Super Bowl again, and Jones was awarded a bid to host the 2026 FIFA World Cup in his behemoth stadium. The future of the cheerleaders, on the other hand, was less clear.

The cheerleaders changed the world. And the world changes. They burst out of that tunnel and shifted the way we saw sex and beauty, commerce and culture. But as our perspectives shift, so do our heroes. Women don't want to be on the sidelines anymore. Sexiness in service of men's sports strikes many as painfully outdated. The erotic contagion the cheerleaders sent through the NFL is heading in the other direction now, with many squads reinventing themselves as coed, more athletic, family-friendly. Can the all-American sexy girls stick around in a landscape that seems to be crumbling? A landscape they helped build? I wouldn't bet against them.

Still, fifty years is a long time to hold on to tradition. Several of the women who shaped this phenomenon have passed on. Texie Waterman died in 1996, Suzanne Mitchell in 2016. But the original architect is still around.

On a sunny afternoon in early June, a Cowboys bus pulled up alongside a curb in Tyler. Eight current cheerleaders stepped out in summer dresses, followed by a few former cheerleaders in jeans and sparkly Cowboys jerseys. All of them made their way up the sidewalk and into a home whose entryway led to a cozy book-lined room. Sitting in an armchair was Dee Brock, 92 years old but with the same fine bone structure, her long white hair swept to the side in a ponytail. Brock hadn't been able to attend the sixtieth alumni reunion, so the cheerleaders brought the celebration to her.

"Dee knew how to get people's attention back in the day," Finglass said once everyone had gathered inside. And so her gift, she explained, should be similarly eye-catching. She pulled out a lifetime achievement award, a white leather football studded with rhinestones that caught the light when Brock turned the ball in her hands, before gamely tucking it under her left arm, as if she were about to run for a touchdown. Her central role had long been forgotten, so it felt like a sign of institutional health that she was being honored, as if the present could shake hands with the past.

The young cheerleaders lingered by Brock's side all afternoon like long-lost granddaughters, leaning their heads on the chair where she sat, soaking up her wisdom, holding her hand, almost as if they never wanted to let it go. The squad began as only an experiment—but what an experiment it turned out to be.

———

SARAH HEPOLA is the host/creator of the *Texas Monthly* podcast *America's Girls*, about the cultural impact and lost history of the Dallas Cowboys Cheerleaders. Her memoir, *Blackout: Remembering the Things I Drank to Forget*, became a *New York Times* bestseller in 2015, and she's currently working on her second memoir, *Unattached*. She's a writer-at-large for *Texas Monthly* and the co-conspirator, with Nancy Rommelmann, of *Smoke 'Em if You Got 'Em*, a culture podcast on Substack. She lives in Dallas with a ridiculously handsome cat named Wallace.

The World's Cornhole Elite, Chasing That One Perfect Toss

ASHLEY FETTERS MALOY

FROM *The Washington Post* • AUGUST 11, 2022

ROCK HILL, S.C.—The surface of a professional-grade corn-hole board—two feet wide and four feet long, give or take a quarter-inch, and made of birch or oak with a polyurethane finish—can change texture with the temperature. On a hot day, even indoors, the clear varnish can get tacky, slowing bean-bags down as they slide toward the 6-inch scoring hole. Near an air-conditioning vent, boards "play faster." Farther away they get stickier.

Which is why, here at last week's American Cornhole League world championships, held in a massive indoor sports facility in humid South Carolina, Corey Gilbert, 33, has opted for the "Sniper" set from his sponsor, Lucky Bags. It's a middle-of-the-spectrum, Goldilocks option—not the firmest or the floppiest, neither the silkiest nor the craggiest, but it will slide comfort-ably on the boards, which have been playing on the slow side. It also suits both his own rocket-like throws and his doubles partner's loftier, softer tosses. "You can just chuck it and it'll be like *skrr-rr-rt* but it'll still stop," he says. The two often fine-tune midgame by changing which side of the bag—the smoother or the rougher—will hit the board.

It wasn't a slam-dunk strategy, though it also wasn't disastrous. When he arrived in Rock Hill, Gilbert was officially the 43rd best cornhole player on planet Earth; when we speak on Sunday, as the tournament winds down, he thinks his ranking may have slipped, but only a little. As Gilbert explains all this to me animatedly, his parents, 63-year-old Anita and 66-year-old Jerry, glance over, anxious to get him to the airport on time to fly back to Sacramento.

A barber in his weekday life and a former softball pitcher, Gilbert plays cornhole almost every night of the week, sometimes on boards he built himself. Among the accoutrements that have to make it onto the plane home with him: Gilbert's rolling cornhole bag, which contains six sets of beanbags and weighs 28 pounds.

Tailgates, barbecues and frat quads have all done their part to raise awareness of cornhole, known in some regions as "bags," and played in its modern form since the 1970s. On lawns and decks all over America, the game offers a way to pass the time while the burgers get grilled; a way to benignly bond with a father-in-law; a way to assert momentary, marginal athletic dominance over one's buddies while holding a Bud Light in one hand. Cornhole is shorthand for relaxed summertime fun, an easygoing enough pastime that pharmaceutical commercials sometimes include it in their soft-focus "after" montages.

In recent years, though, many have gotten acquainted with the elite levels of the game by flipping past ESPN coverage of major cornhole tournament finals. For five years running, cornhole has been part of Ocho Day—ESPN's annual celebration of niche and novelty sports, a whole genre of haha-no-way-OK-but-wait-what-a-*shot* TV spectacles. For the 1,800 players competing at "worlds" in the Rock Hill Sports & Event Center, a 170,000-square foot athletic complex built in 2019, 'hole is life. And almost everyone here shares the earnest belief that the game is poised for global domination.

Behind Gilbert, stretching out across a prairie of hardwood floor under fluorescent lights, are 132 cornhole courts, every one occupied by either two or four players. A gigantic American flag looms over the expanse. The air smells like sweat, $2 pizza slices and the occasional discreet puff of vape smoke, despite PSAs ringing out now and again to remind attendees that vaping is off-limits. Sideline chatter accompanies the thwacking sound of competitors' beanbags landing plumply on the boards (or, God forbid, the floor). There's no official uniform of cornhole, but you could be forgiven for thinking it consists of a jersey, baseball cap and cargo shorts. Amateur players wear jerseys with the names of their local leagues: North Country Cornhole, Montana Vigilante Cornhole, A-Town Baggerz. Pros wear jerseys proudly advertising Bush's baked beans. Beards are optional but popular. Women, who make up about a quarter of competitors at worlds, often pair their jerseys with leggings.

Every one of them has come here, some from hundreds or even thousands of miles away, with a goal: Some want to win their amateur division, others want to win their way to a pro card, still others want to win a pro singles or doubles title. Gilbert, who earned his pro ranking last year, wants to someday win a championship on ESPN.

Though the tournament's main court is just two boards set up on half of a dramatically lit basketball gymnasium, under ESPN's red-tinted TV lights it looks and feels like the Arthur Ashe Stadium of cornhole; its Colosseum, even, maybe. Competitors enter, prizefighter-like, through an inflatable tunnel sponsored by Johnsonville Sausage.

It was there, on Saturday afternoon, that Mark Richards, a 25-year-old first-year pro from Valparaiso, Ind., who came in tied for No. 1, claimed the pro singles championship title. Some spectators wore white foam wedge hats in the shape of cornhole boards; others held up yellow signs reading "4 BAGGER" when a player or team managed to sink all four bags. At tense moments—like when Richards reached 18 points against 51-year-old janitorial supply salesman Matt Guy of Alexandria, Ky., and found himself one clean shot from victory—the arena went spooky-silent, other than the frequent *pop-chhh* of aluminum cans emanating from the beer garden. When Richards's last bag instead went skipping off the back of the board, the roar of anguish from the crowd rattled the bleachers.

Richards, a gym teacher, doesn't have as much time to devote to the game as his contemporaries who play cornhole full-time. Nineteen-year-old Alex Rawls, Richards's co-No. 1, graduated high school this year. He practices for up to three hours each weekday at an LA Fitness near his home in Jacksonville, Fla., that lets him set up boards in its dance studio. Jamie Graham, 24, ranked No. 3 behind Richards and Rawls, throws hundreds of bags every day. His girlfriend, 20-year-old Kaylee Hunter, a rising cornhole star herself, throws with him at their home in Hamlet, N.C.

Still, Richards plays about eight to 10 hours a week. He works on his wrist flick, his backswing, making shots from different angles, whenever he can make time.

Up 20-7 with one bag left, Richards needed only to land it on the board to claim the championship. When he instead fired it cleanly into the hole, his girlfriend, sitting courtside, brought her hands to her face and burst into tears.

Indeed, Rock Hill Sports & Event Center is an insular social ecosystem unto itself, with its own gossip networks and cliques and scandals and royalty. Amateur players speak in hushed tones about how No. 7-ranked pro Matthew Creekkiller throws bags for, *like, eight hours a day.* (Creekkiller, a 20-year-old from Cloud Creek, Okla., tells me it's actually more like four.) A score-entry error in an early-round women's singles game sent cornhole podcasters into a tailspin; Trey Ryder, the chief marketing officer of American Cornhole League, whose additional work as an analyst has earned him the nickname "the Tony Romo of cornhole," says he got death threats over it. And 2020 and 2022 women's singles champion Cheyenne Renner, 22, is getting married this

November to—who else?—an amateur cornhole player. Sarah Cassidy, who teamed with Renner to win this week's women's doubles championship, will be a bridesmaid.

In the championships' vendor hall, one can purchase a generic fan replica of this year's Bush's Beans-emblazoned pro jersey. Nearby, sets of League-regulation cornhole bags—with names like "Karnage," "Assault," "Sniper" and "Juggernaut"—are sold for upward of $50 each. Some have skulls; some have camouflage. It's a curiously violent, militaristic aesthetic choice for a sport that, rather than requiring its athletes to maintain any sort of fighting shape, is instead rather forgiving. What it takes to be a good cornhole player is mastery of a variety of shots and the wisdom to know when to deploy them—not any impressive degree of strength, or agility, or reflex quickness, or stamina.

Or even sobriety, really. True to cornhole's origins as a bar or yard game, players at almost every level are known to drink before, during and after. Not everyone partakes. But Shannon Thompson, a contractor with the ACL, opens the beer garden at 8 a.m. every day of the tournament to a morning rush hour: "There's guys who can't throw their first bag until they've had their first beer." Domestics are most popular, she adds ("obviously"), though Samantha Finley, a top women's player, tells me with a laugh that she prefers to warm up with Fireball. Matt Guy has been playing cornhole competitively for 22 years and is widely understood to be the greatest to ever do it; he says his sweet spot is somewhere around six beers in. (Those are, he clarifies—after ACL media chief Marlon LeWinter shoots him a look—consumed over the course of several hours before a big game.)

Stacey Moore, the former tennis player who founded the ACL in 2015 and now acts as its commissioner, welcomes the obvious question with a laugh when we speak on Saturday evening, the ESPN crew packing up their gear behind us. No, he doesn't have any plans in the immediate future to institute an alcohol policy, though "we definitely talk about it every season," he says. On the one hand, rarely do cornhole players cause problems with their drinking; some players find it calms their nerves. "I want players to feel like they have the right to do what they feel like is going to put them in the best position to win," Moore says. Beers, he adds, sometimes used to be affectionately called "PEBs" (a riff on PEDs, or performance-enhancing drugs). Eventually, though, he expects cornhole to go the way golf did—years ago, some players were notorious for how much they could knock back on the course. But eventually, Moore says, competition reached a level so fierce it paid to stay sober.

Already, the rate at which the game of cornhole has crystallized into a thousand tiny trackable, analyzable strategies and statistics has astonished even Moore. When he founded the league, "I felt like, 'Okay. There's basically two or three basic shots,'" he says. Now, there are seven or eight, and Moore is still learning the new ones. He laughs as he ticks them off: Cut shot. Rollback. Bar of soap. Penguin.

Moore's eventual dream for the American Cornhole League is for more tournaments with bigger cash prizes so that more participants can do it full time. (Richards, for example, won a $10,000 cash prize for winning the singles final, and split an additional $7,500 with his partner when they finished second in pro doubles.) He'll need continued support from sponsors and an ever-expanding base of players who'll pay entry fees for tournaments (yes, like this one), but he's not worried. He's courting new fans, players and sponsors with events like this week's SuperHole series, which pairs up celebrities with pro cornhole players for doubles. In Friday's final, Matt Guy and NFL great Doug Flutie bested Richards and basketball Hall-of-Famer Dawn Staley. Though the buzziest contestant on-site was "Jersey Shore" star Mike "The Situation" Sorrentino.

And after the tournament, Moore was scheduled to travel to the Netherlands for the first official ACL international tournament.

International interest, he emphasizes, is key to getting cornhole recognized as an Olympic sport. Initially, he set his sights on 2028. He doubts that will happen, "even though when L.A. 2028 rolls around, we'll be in over 50 countries, easily," he says. So he's aiming for 2032.

The next day, the ESPN set gets swiftly dismantled after the network's last broadcast is over, and the tournament's main stage begins to look once again like a gymnasium. The day after that, an Uber driver who lives 30 minutes away in Charlotte laughs when I tell him what I've been doing in town.

"Cornhole," he repeats, and shakes his head. "I did not know about that."

ASHLEY FETTERS MALOY is a feature reporter at *The Washington Post*. She is a graduate of Northwestern University, and her work has also appeared in *The New York Times*, *The Atlantic*, *GQ*, and elsewhere. She lives in Brooklyn with her husband.

Alone at the Edge of the World

CASSIDY RANDALL

FROM The Atavist Magazine • OCTOBER 2022

In the heaving seas of the Southern Ocean, a small, red-hulled sailboat tossed and rolled, at the mercy of the tail end of a tempest. The boat's mast was sheared away, its yellow sails sunk deep in the sea. Amid the wreckage of the cabin, Susie Goodall sloshed through water seeping in from the deck, which had cracked when a great wave somersaulted the boat end over end. She was freezing, having been lashed by ocean, rain, and wind. Her hands were raw and bloody. Except for the boat, her companion and home for the 15,000 miles she'd sailed over the past five months, Goodall was alone.

The 29-year-old British woman had spent three years readying for this voyage. It demanded more from her than she could have imagined. She loved the planning of it, rigging her boat for a journey that might mean not stepping on land for nearly a year. But she was unprepared for the attention it drew—for the fact that everyone wanted a piece of her story.

The thing was, her story was a fantastic one. Goodall was the youngest of the 18 skippers resurrecting the Golden Globe Race, a so-called "voyage for madmen," and the only woman. Last run 50 years prior, the race entailed sailing solo and nonstop around the world in a small boat without modern technology. The media were hungry for it, and people were drawn to Goodall in particular: Here was a blue-eyed, blond, petite woman among the romantic mariners and weathered adventurers. All of them were chasing the limits of what humans are capable of physically and mentally, but much of the coverage singled out Goodall, who wanted no part of the sensationalism. She had been a painfully shy child and was a private and introverted adult. The fervor surrounding her participation in the Golden Globe made her feel like a caricature, an unwilling icon. All she wanted was to sail, to search out the connection sailors had with the sea before satellite phones and GPS.

When the race began, she was almost able to leave the attention behind. There were quiet days gliding south in the calm Atlantic; ecstatic mornings surfing swell in the Southern Ocean; the sudden appearance of a magnificent sunset through persistent clouds. But the spotlight tailed Goodall like a subsurface current. Now, after two days of brutal storm, she knew the world was watching to see whether she would survive.

I.

In 1966, an English bookstore owner named Francis Chichester riveted the world when he set out alone in a boat to circumnavigate the globe. He wasn't the first to do so; Canadian-American Joshua Slocum completed the first known solo circumnavigation in 1898, and the feat may have been achieved long before but gone unrecorded. Yet the 65-year-old Chichester chose a dangerous route—one that no one, according to sailing lore, had ever attempted alone: From England he would sail south in the Atlantic, along the coast of Africa to the bottom of the world. There he would pass under the Cape of Good Hope, Australia's southern coast, and South America's treacherous Cape Horn before sailing north across the Atlantic again. The remote lower reaches of the Indian, Pacific, and Atlantic where Chichester would spend much of his voyage are known collectively as the Southern Ocean. The region is a vast field of sea unobstructed by land in any direction, with enormous waves, riotous gales, and dramatic skies. Stories abound about ships meeting their end in the Southern Ocean and heroes enduring impossible circumstances.

Chichester stopped only once on his journey, at the halfway mark in Australia, to perform major repairs to his 53-foot boat, which had been battered by three and a half months on the open sea. When he stepped ashore in England nine months after he'd left, he was greeted like a rock star. Queen Elizabeth II knighted him nearly on the spot. Meanwhile, fellow seafarers understood that, after Chichester's feat, one great ocean challenge remained: sailing solo around the world without stopping. No one knew if a boat could stand up to 30,000 uninterrupted miles at sea, or what might happen to a human mind so long without company. Nine different men decided to find out.

They ranged from a former British submarine commander to storied French and Italian sailors to thrill seekers with little seagoing experience. GPS hadn't been invented, satellite communications and solar panels were scarcely commonplace, and computing had yet to transform weather forecasting. So the men would sail with the accessible technology of the era: a radio, a windup chronometer, and a barometer. They would catch rain for fresh water and navigate with a sextant and the stars.

The Sunday Times decided to brand the men's individual attempts a formal race, announcing the Golden Globe in March 1968. The event had virtually no requirements or regulations, as the competitors were already planning their voyages, each with its own launch date. But in offering a trophy for the first man to complete the challenge—to incentivize urgency—and a cash prize for the fastest time—to incentivize competition—*The Times* instantly created one of the greatest adventure stories in history.

Only one man finished the race. Twenty-nine-year-old Brit Robin Knox-Johnston's heavy, 32-foot boat *Suhaili* had been considered a long shot. During the voyage, *Suhaili*'s water tanks polluted, her sails tore, and the self-steering—a primitive autopilot system consisting of a wind vane that attached to the boat's rudder—fell apart. The radio malfunctioned two and a half months in; Knox-Johnston had no way of calling for help should trouble have arisen. He jumped overboard multiple times to perform underwater repairs, once shooting a circling shark before diving in. While rigging near impossible fixes to his equipment, he splashed battery acid in his eye and stitched his mustache to a sail while repairing it. When against all odds he reappeared in the harbor of Falmouth on April 22, 1969, after nearly a year at sea, Knox-Johnston sailed into legend.

The other eight competitors sank, abandoned the journey, or worse. Alex Carozzo bowed out in Portugal, vomiting blood from a peptic ulcer. John Ridgway surrendered to intense loneliness and a poorly constructed boat, exiting the race near Brazil. Nigel Tetley barely survived 80-foot waves in the Southern Ocean, only to have his boat sink a thousand miles from the finish. A storm destroyed Bill King's mast, and he ended his journey in Cape Town. Favored winner Bernard Moitessier, a sea mystic who practiced yoga naked on deck, was well in the lead after passing Cape Horn. But, imagining the glare of the international spotlight that surely awaited him, he used a slingshot to hurl a message onto the deck of a passing ship, informing the world that he was abandoning the race "to save my soul," and continuing on to the tropics.

And then there was Donald Crowhurst. He sailed slow circles around the Atlantic in his rushed build of a leaky boat, transmitting fake radio reports of progress in hopes of fooling the world into believing he was winning. His log told the story of a man slowly going insane under the pressures of deception and monstrous debt to his sponsor, until his transmissions went silent. His trimaran was later found floating on the waves, its skipper having slipped into the ocean in an apparent suicide.

It would be half a century before anyone attempted the Golden Globe again.

SUSIE GOODALL'S FATHER was obsessed with the sea first. Stephen Goodall learned to sail as a teenager and taught his Danish wife, Birgitte Howells, to sail too. "Sailing is one of those things where people either have a yearning to get back on the water, or they have no particular desire to," he told me. Susie and her older brother, Tim, began sailing and racing small boats on a lake near where they grew up outside Birmingham. In 2004, when Goodall was 15, English sailor Ellen MacArthur set out to break the record for fastest nonstop solo circumnavigation; Susie and Tim followed her journey. After that, Susie read countless books about single-handed sailing and the noble explorers, salty adventurers, and sages who entered into a relationship with the sea as if it were a living thing. Maybe one day she, too, would sail around the world.

When Susie was 17, she told her parents she wanted to attend university, and they took her to visit several campuses. One day she announced, "I'm not going to go to university. I'm going to the Isle of Wight to become a sailing instructor." Yes, her father thought. That's what she should be doing.

Susie got her instruction certificates and taught sailing courses. She also worked on superyachts, delivering boats to port for their wealthy owners or crewing them while the owners were on board. She loved long ocean passages and taking night watches to memorize the patterns of the stars. But the yachts were so mechanized that her work felt like operating a computer. She marveled at stories of sailors once keenly in tune with the ocean and the boats they helmed: Ancient Polynesians, for instance, found their way by swell direction and the flight patterns of certain birds. She taught her students celestial navigation, but there was always backup—a GPS or their smartphone could be turned on at any time.

Susie voyaged to Iceland, Greenland, Svalbard, and the Baltic, and rose through the ranks of instructors and crew to become a skipper, the small-boat equivalent of a ship captain, in an over-whelmingly male industry. Still, she doubted her abilities. She rarely felt pressured by her crewmates to prove her worth, but that hardly mattered; with few female role models to look to, her internal critic was more than happy to pick up the slack. Susie found herself wondering: Am I smart enough or strong enough? Am I good enough to do this job?

It didn't help when, in her early twenties, she voiced her dream of sailing around the world to her boyfriend. "Well, that's just ridiculous," he replied. "You can't sail around the world by yourself."

IN JULY 2015, Goodall, then 25, was teaching in Iceland when one of her crewmates mentioned that a rerun of the Golden Globe was in the works. When her boat came ashore, she used a computer in her tiny hotel to look up the details. And there it was: The race was set to launch in 2018, the 50th anniversary of the original voyage. Don McIntyre, a decorated Australian adventurer who'd grown up idolizing Robin Knox-Johnston, was masterminding the event. On the edge of 60, McIntyre knew that if he didn't re-create his hero's journey now, he never would. And if he wanted to do it, he figured a few others might, too.

Boats would be limited to the same class as the intrepid *Suhaili*, between 32 and 36 feet. Sailors would have to navigate with paper charts and sextant, catch rain for water, handwrite their logs, and communicate by radio. No outside assistance would be allowed: no physical contact with anyone else, no help with repairs, no supply deliveries. The specifications couldn't have been more different than those of the only other solo, nonstop, round-the-world race on offer, the Vendée Globe. That event, which took place every four years, was high-tech, high-speed, and high-cost; the boats alone were worth $300,000 to $5 million. But the new Golden Globe seemed more about the journey than the competition. Goodall downloaded the application and sent in the $3,000 entry deposit.

Telling her parents wasn't easy. She called her mother—her parents were by now divorced—first. Howells knew something was up just by the sound of her daughter's breath.

"What's the matter?" Howells asked in her light Danish accent before Goodall could speak.

"Nothing, nothing, all is good," said Goodall.

Howells waited.

"There's this race," Goodall said. "Round the world. Robin Knox-Johnston has done it before. I've applied to join it." She didn't mention that the race would be nonstop, and run solo without modern technology. She hoped to drip-feed the more worrying details to her family. What Goodall didn't know was that Howells, on her first sailing trip with Goodall's father, had read *The Strange Last Voyage of Donald Crowhurst*. The book recounted the original Golden Globe and Crowhurst's haunting end. Goodall's mother knew exactly what her daughter would face. And she also knew from her own experience that the sea offered a connection to something greater and deeper, something perhaps beyond words.

"I've been waiting for you to do something like this," Howells said.

In the ensuing months, Goodall didn't tell many people that she planned to sail the Golden Globe. When it did come up, she dreaded a particular question: What made her think she was capable of sailing around the world alone? She had no response to this. It was true that the farthest she'd sailed single-handed was four miles across the Solent, a strait between the Isle of Wight and mainland Britain. Still, she knew she was a strong sailor and could cope with being alone.

In truth, that she didn't know whether she'd make it was part of the reason she wanted to try. She wasn't content to merely read about the size of the Southern Ocean's waves, the ferocity of its wind. She wanted to feel those forces, face them on her own. Only then would she know what she was capable of.

INTEREST IN THE new Golden Globe came fast and heavy. Dozens of people wanted to run it. McIntyre eventually sacrificed his own entry to devote himself to overseeing such a large event and securing the necessary funding.

The first meeting of participants was held in London in December 2015. There Goodall was introduced to Barry Pickthall, a former yachting correspondent for *The Times* who had written dozens of books on sailing. McIntyre had enlisted Pickthall to publicize the race in hopes of gaining a major sponsor. Pickthall was a teenager when Knox-Johnston went around the world, and remembered following the voyage. Of the rerun, he said, "In the end we had 18 starters, with 18 different reasons for going, and very few had aspirations to win it. That wasn't what they were doing it for at all. They wanted to prove something to themselves, to other people, or just do something they'd always dreamed about."

In Goodall, Pickthall saw a golden opportunity. Indeed, Goodall remembered him telling her as much the first time they met. He said that having a woman in the race made it more glamorous and he wanted to get *The Sunday Times* to feature her. "We're going to dangle you like a puppet for the media so we can attract a sponsor for the race," Goodall recalled him saying. She was immediately put off. During my conversations with him, Pickthall disputed Goodall's characterization of their meeting, but conceded that he knew she had media appeal. "It was the sex side of things! Pretty girl sailing around the world," he said. "And I made the most of it."

In *A Voyage for Madmen*, a book about the 1968 race, author Peter Nichols writes about the "Ulysses factor" in human mythology, "the lone hero figure in society, the rare character who by his or her exploits stimulates powerful mass excitement." The archetype encompasses a set of characteristics—imagination, endurance, selfishness, discipline, courage, and social instability. Francis Chichester was such a figure, Nichols writes, as were many of the other original Golden Globe sailors. Goodall didn't fit the Ulysses mold in many ways. It would be difficult to call her selfish, and although she's an introvert, she's socially adept, with valued connections to friends and family. But she was a woman at an unprecedented time of women's empowerment, when the public was hungry for stories of lone heroines who'd found success in male-dominated arenas.

When Goodall told her mother about what Pickthall had said, Howells was surprised. Back in 1989, when she'd just had her daughter, Howells followed Tracy Edwards's history-making circumnavigation during the Whitbread Round the World Race. Edwards had worked as a cook in the 1985 edition of the race, and she was treated like a servant or worse. One crew member wrote "For sale: one case of beer" on the back of her thermal underwear. After that, Edwards refinanced her house to buy a yacht she named *Maiden*, and she assembled an all-female crew for the 1989 Whitbread. The media skewered her. Journalist Bob Fisher called the crew a "tin full of tarts" in *The Guardian*. While other crews were interviewed about experience and strategy, Edwards was asked about packing waterproof mascara and how such a "gorgeous slip of a young girl" expected to raise the millions of dollars needed to participate in such an extravagant race.

Among the journalists lambasting the *Maiden* crew was Barry Pickthall. In his telling, it was essentially the women's fault for the things that were written about them. "They hadn't done very well in their preparations. We saw all sorts of catfights," Pickthall told me. "We said, 'How are these girls going to get round the world?'"

When the women came in third and then first in the first two legs of the race, Pickthall said, "We were absolutely astounded. Bob had to change his view to a 'tin full of *smart, fast* tarts.'"

Howells saw how the media had treated Edwards, but that was nearly three decades before her own daughter planned to embark on a similar endeavor. This is a whole new century, she thought. Surely we've moved on.

In April 2016, Goodall combined her savings with a bank loan and bought a Rustler 36 sailboat named *Ariadne*. Rustlers are sleek and British-built, which meant she could view them close to home—Goodall didn't have much of a travel budget. Once she'd purchased *Ariadne*, Goodall packed her bags and moved aboard; she had no money left for rent. The media were already watching her. One story written four months prior had pointed out that Goodall faced "minor issues such as not having a boat or much experience of solo sailing." She'd addressed the first concern. A solo Atlantic crossing would address the second.

Ariadne was mostly in good enough condition for the crossing, but to make it around the world, it would need a refit to the tune of $50,000 or more. For that Goodall would require a sponsor. She set a timeline for herself: If by the end of 2016 she hadn't secured financial support, she would go back to working on superyachts to pay back the money she'd borrowed to buy *Ariadne*. She would have to abandon her Golden Globe dream, but she'd at least have a boat. She lived on *Ariadne* on a mooring near Southampton. She woke at 4 a.m. each day to put together packets describing the race and then ship them off to everyone she could think of who might consider supporting her.

In late fall, Goodall got an email from Tim Stevenson, an investment banker who had a Rustler of his own. He popped over for a cup of tea. They chatted about the race, and Goodall told him about her refitting ideas. Not long after that, Stevenson was at a meeting with Ken Allen, an executive at global shipping enterprise DHL. "I've been thinking of sponsoring some women's sports," Allen told Stevenson. "Maybe equestrian." Stevenson replied, "What about sailing?"

Just before Christmas, with mere days remaining before Goodall's self-imposed deadline, she signed a sponsorship contract with Allen's billion-dollar company. She thought she'd be over the moon; she *was* excited. Relieved too. She had what she needed to race. But she felt something else—that it was real now.

A massive company with thousands of employees was supporting her. She couldn't let them down.

IN A SMALL harbor on Antigua, Goodall was facing one of her sailing fears. She dashed from cockpit to bow on *Ariadne*, trying to get into position to drop anchor. Other boats dotted the surface on all sides, like obstacles in a pinball machine, and cliffs loomed ahead. If she ran into them, it could damage or destroy her boat. But dodging them would be difficult—Goodall's engine, which sailors used for precision movement when coming into a harbor and anchoring, had cut out more than a week before in the middle of the Atlantic. Goodall knew how to service it and was annoyed she hadn't been able to fix the problem. Now the wind in the harbor was blowing at nearly 30 knots, pushing *Ariadne* with it. Finally, Goodall got into position and dropped anchor. She stood on the bow watching, waiting. Please hold, she thought, *please hold*.

The anchor stuck. She exhaled.

In that moment, Goodall completed the first half of her Atlantic loop, which she'd planned as a crash course in getting to know how *Ariadne* handled, and how she herself would handle on a long solo sail. When Goodall left the Canary Islands three weeks prior, isolation had weighed heavily. She focused her attention on what she wanted to improve on the boat for the Golden Globe, logging ideas in a notebook: where to stow the life raft, how to arrange her sleeping space, where to solder more steel rings around the deck so she could clip a harness to *Ariadne* in rough seas. She soon got into a rhythm that eased the loneliness, but trade-wind sailing was too straightforward for much excitement. Even with a broken engine, the journey to Antigua was fairly boring.

That's why she'd planned a different return route. One thing that worried her about sailing alone around the world was hitting a big storm. Sailors can practice for most things, but it's not as if a colossal tempest can be conjured up on command to test themselves and their boat. Her return leg, at least, would pit her against prevailing winds and send her into spring squalls.

She spent a month in Antigua fixing the engine, but it broke again on her homeward leg. She sailed through moderate gales and another length of solitude. Having to be alert to changes in the weather meant her mind was far less likely to wander. This was more like what the Golden Globe would be like, Goodall knew. She loved it.

But as she neared the Azores, a chain of islands 1,000 miles west of Portugal, a scattering of anchored boats and a maze of docks lay ahead, an arrangement far more constricted than what she'd encountered in Antigua. The prospect of coming into harbor with no engine, no room for error, and certain consequences if she hit someone's boat had been weighing on her mind for days. Heavy weather was close on her heels. She hoped desperately to outrun it, and that some harbormaster might pick her up on the radio and agree to tow her in.

"Please," she said out loud. She wasn't sure who or what she was talking to. Maybe the ocean itself. "Show me a sign. I just need to know that everything's going to be OK."

Suddenly, *Ariadne* was surrounded by dolphins.

It reminded her of something Moitessier had written in *The Long Way*, about passing Stewart Island off the southern tip of New Zealand on a misty day. He heard whistling and hurried on deck to find nearly a hundred dolphins in the water around him. As he watched, 25 of them swam from stern to bow and then veered off at a right angle. They repeated the move over and over. He looked down at his compass. He was headed straight for the fog-shrouded rocks of Stewart Island. He changed tack to the right, and one of the dolphins celebrated with a somersault.

Goodall had crossed most of the Atlantic without seeing much wildlife at all. Now she'd gone from an empty sea to surrounded by dolphins in minutes. It was as if they were telling her everything would be all right.

Moments later her radio crackled to life. It was the harbormaster. She got a tow before the storm hit.

IN THE TWO weeks leading up to the Golden Globe launch on July
1, 2018, the skippers brought their boats to Les Sables-d'Olonne,
on the Atlantic coast of France. The race contract required that
they reserve two full days for interviews with journalists, but
few outlets wanted to speak with the other participants, who in
turn were freed up to make last-minute preparations. Goodall,
by contrast, was swamped.

Some asked her about the work she'd done on *Ariadne*, and
she was happy to show them around the refitted boat. Since pur-
chasing the vessel, she had transformed it almost from top to
bottom into what was effectively a tiny floating home. She rein-
forced the windows of the cabin to stand up against the Southern
Ocean's powerful waves and installed a submarine-style entrance
to keep out water in case of knockdowns—when a boat is flung
sideways—or capsizes. There were two backup systems at the
ready if her mast broke. She stowed an emergency rudder and
extra sail-repair kits. In addition, she created a two-week menu
of canned and dehydrated food and had enough provisions to
repeat it for ten months. She spent hours staring at the world map
pinned to the cabin wall, breaking her journey into wayposts in
her mind and deciding on dates to celebrate. She laid in cakes and
small bottles of wine for special occasions: crossing the equator,
reaching the Southern Ocean, her birthday, Christmas, and New
Year's. She learned a visualization exercise that involved hovering
above a situation to gain a fuller perspective of it, in case loneliness or tough conditions tempted her to quit.

But other journalists didn't bother to ask Goodall how she'd
prepared her boat, or herself, to cross the world alone. They were
far more interested in asking some version of the same question:
"So, Susie, you're the only woman?"

"Well, that doesn't really matter in rigging my boat—"
Goodall began one of her replies in Les Sables-d'Olonne.

"Please just say it for the camera: 'I'm the only woman.'"

Sitting through interviews, she came to feel like a clumsy ballet dancer trying to pivot away from this one thing that everyone wanted her to say. She usually managed it, however gracelessly. But as the race loomed, all the talking wore her down. "Yes, I'm the only woman," she said.

Goodall had become the unwitting face of the race—singled out, it seemed, because she was the only woman in it. "As the youngest and only female competitor, there is international focus on Goodall's participation and pragmatic zeal," wrote *Forbes*. *Yachting Monthly* framed the story like so: "At face-value Susie Goodall appears to be a 'normal' looking, petite, elegant young lady."

Goodall of course understood the arguments for why women and girls needed to see role models in male-dominated sports, jobs, and so on. But the emphasis on her being the sole female seemed to create a whole separate playing field, and she was alone on it. Whether she wanted to or not—and she did not—Goodall felt like some journalists were holding her up as representative of *all* women in sailing: their navigational skills, endurance, and capacity for handling fear and danger.

The effect was isolating for Goodall, who was already exhausted from preparing for the race. Even McIntyre knew it. "She was just too popular," he said. "It was getting crazy. At the same time, so much is involved with preparing your boat."

Goodall hoped the frenzy would die down once the race began—that, like Knox-Johnston fifty years prior, she would sail off the grid in search of an elemental connection with the ocean. But the race stipulated that participants remain linked to the world during their journey. Golden Globe sailors were required to make weekly satellite phone calls to race headquarters that would be recorded and shared with media, and to send daily texts that would be automatically posted online. Race organizers also asked that they shoot footage of themselves using an old-school film camera, and stop at a series of gates—Lanzarote in the Canaries, Hobart in Tasmania, and the Falkland Islands—to drop it off. The race website would track each boat's progress in real time.

In a mandatory self-recorded prerace clip I watched while reporting this story, Goodall held a set of questions from the race team, speaking each one aloud before answering. "How many cassette tapes do you plan on bringing, and what type of music? What books? And how many toilet paper rolls?" Goodall read. She replied that she was bringing a pile of eighties music cassettes and several sailing books, and that she would be keeping the number of toilet paper rolls aboard to herself, thank you very much.

"What is the most likely thing that would keep you from finishing the race, and how are you trying to solve that?" she read.

Goodall paused. She'd prepared the boat for every eventuality she could think of. If it was as fail-safe as she hoped, then her will to finish was the only question mark. She had no intention of letting that break, either—not with the whole world watching. But she wasn't about to say that into the camera.

"I think from a boat perspective, the most likely thing would be something going wrong, like with the mast or hitting something," she said. "But I've done everything I can to minimize that." Goodall moved on to the next question.

SOON THERE WAS nothing left to do but say goodbye to her family. They'd rented a house by the harbor to help her get ready. Goodall wouldn't be able to speak directly with them for up to nine months—the expected duration of the race, assuming all went well.

Howells had also been busy. She couldn't imagine being alone for nine months, and she aimed to do everything she could to support her daughter in her isolation. Howells had bought a teddy bear dressed in a raincoat and, over an entire year, photographed various friends and family hugging the stuffed animal. She laminated the photos and collected them in an envelope: an imprint of love to carry her daughter through. Howells gave the package—and the bear—to Goodall the night before the race. Goodall's father, Stephen, for his part, had spent three years perfecting a recipe: fruitcake that would keep in baking paper and tinfoil. He made 24 of them and presented them to his daughter.

"So, where should I meet you?" he asked her as they packed the cakes aboard. "At the end of the race, where will you sail to?"

Goodall knew he was joking, as if she'd do like Moitessier and avoid the fuss at the finish line. She played along. "Iceland. I've always like Iceland."

"OK," he said. "I'll see you there."

II.

On July 1, 2018, vessels jockeyed for position in the Les Sables-d'Olonne harbor. Goodall sat in the cockpit of *Ariadne*, which had been rechristened *DHL Starlight* by her sponsor. She was too busy to feel the gravity of actually, finally going. She needed to stay focused on navigating among the boats full of journalists, race crew, and family and friends, and of course the other Golden Globe skippers.

Only some of the race's competitors had any designs on winning it: Jean Luc Van Den Heede, a septuagenarian French sailor who'd circumnavigated many times and podiumed in the Vendée Globe; Norwegian Are Wiig, who'd finished second in class in a single-handed transatlantic race; and Dutchman Mark Slats, another veteran circumnavigator. The other skippers had different motivations. Simply finishing would fulfill Estonian Uku Randmaa's dream. Indian Abhilash Tomy hoped to find a kind of nirvana that wiped the mind clean. Young Irishman Gregor McGuckin had crossed the Atlantic and Indian Oceans and wanted to see if he could make it all the way around the world.

As Goodall left the harbor, the sea calmed. Normally, when sailing alone, Goodall would connect the wind vane for self-steering, but she didn't want to move from the tiller. If she focused on steering, she wouldn't have to think about saying goodbye to her family or the enormity of the distance ahead. It was dark before she finally rose from the helm. And quiet—so quiet.

Down in the cabin that evening, Goodall got a radio call from Ertan Beskardes, another skipper in the race. They chatted about what they had for dinner. They didn't speak about what they were feeling, but there was comfort in knowing someone else was probably dealing with similar emotions.

Five days later, Beskardes retired from the race. He wasn't prepared for the challenge, he said. Not being able to speak to his family had robbed sailing of its joy. Goodall was shocked, but then she wondered if Beskardes's decision wasn't admirable in its own way. In the year leading up to the race, she deliberately ensured there'd be no boyfriend to leave behind. She had no children. Skippers like Beskardes who sailed away from their families, Goodall thought, were far braver than her.

SAILING ACROSS THE Bay of Biscay between France and Spain was the first celestial navigating Goodall had ever done without GPS backup; even on her Atlantic loop, she'd kept a system stowed away just in case. In the bay's busy shipping lanes she slept in short bursts, setting an egg timer to wake her every 15 minutes to check for vessels in her path.

On July 9, during her second weekly check-in by satellite phone, McIntyre asked how her navigation was going. It had been frustratingly cloudy, she told him, and she couldn't get as many sun and star sights as she would have liked. "Hopefully, you'll find the Canaries," he said. "We won't talk about penalties until later, but it's a mandatory mark of the course."

Goodall laughed nervously. If she missed the Canaries, the first compulsory gate—skippers had to remain there for 30 minutes—she'd be the female navigator who couldn't navigate, the woman who was bad with directions. But a week and a half after she started the race, Goodall made it to Lanzarote. Sailing toward the island before the sun rose, she could smell it—the rich dryness, the salty rocks and docks. She was pleased with herself, and surprised to discover that she was near the front of the pack, arriving fifth. To the annoyance of the race organizers, she didn't drop any film.

A few days later, Goodall was cruising at a rapid clip when she saw one of her two spinnaker poles flick off from the mast, where she'd been storing it. She dove from the cockpit to grab it, but it fell over the side of the boat before she could reach it and was gone.

She stared into the ocean. That was a critical piece of backup. If she lost her mast in violent seas, the plan was to use the two spinnaker poles, which support the sails rigged to the front of the boat, to fashion a substitute that would hold sail long enough to get to land. At least she had one remaining, along with a boom, the heavy horizontal pole that attaches to the bottom of the mast and allows the sail to harness wind. If she also lost the boom she'd be in trouble. She didn't want to imagine that scenario.

Two weeks later, July 27, was Goodall's birthday. By then, Australian Kevin Farebrother had dropped out of the race, saying he wasn't fit for solo sailing, the lack of sleep, as had Palestinian-American Nabil Amra, who'd struggled with a faulty self-steering system. "Sailing is better with friends," Amra texted from a satellite device.

Other than losing the spinnaker pole, things were going well for Goodall. She'd been holding down a position in the top five, surprising herself, even with light winds making for slow progress through the sweltering tropics. In her daily texts, which she kept as brief as possible, she described the bright starry skies and the magic of marine life.

For people who haven't experienced blue-water sailing—an ocean crossing with no land in sight—it's easy to imagine endless lovely sunrises and frolicking whales. It is not that. The middle of the ocean can seem a great nothingness, at least to those who don't know to look for the elusive green flash as the sun sets on a clear horizon or the endless shades of blue and silver that flicker across swells. On calmer evenings, Goodall brought up her beanbag chair—one of the few frivolous comforts she'd allowed herself—to recline in the cockpit. She passed hours waiting to take a sun sight, a measurement of the sun's angle to determine the boat's position for navigational purposes. She learned to identify land too distant to see by the way clouds formed over it. She thought often of the Southern Ocean. How different would it look compared with this?

Goodall had never spent her birthday alone. She located the mini bottle of wine packed for the occasion and set it out to have with dinner. Then she pulled out the birthday cards friends and family had sent along with her. She'd prepared to be emotional reading through them, but she was fine—until she got to the one from her mother.

It is Danish custom to raise a flag at birthdays. Howells always did that for her children, no matter where they were. In the hot Atlantic, Goodall read her mother's handwriting: "We'll raise a flag for you. But this year there will be no phone call." There was more, but Goodall couldn't bring herself to read it. She folded the note back up to read tomorrow, or maybe the day after.

She looked forward to her nightly radio check-in, when many of the skippers spoke to one another, provided they were in range. One evening, some of them exchanged inventories of leaks. Her boat, she reported, was bone dry. She was quite proud of that, and told her so—*DHL Starlight*, that is. Even boats with male names like Moitessier's *Joshua* go by "she." It's not clear how the tradition started. In some ancient cultures, ships were named after protective goddesses. Others named boats for mothers. This rarely resulted in confusion, since sailors were almost always men. In Goodall's mind, she and her boat had long ago become "we"— each other's companion in the great expanse. Goodall spoke to *DHL Starlight* often, and the boat spoke to her, telling Goodall what she needed and even waking Goodall from sleep when a familiar motion shifted or ceased entirely.

Goodall also learned to feel when she and the boat weren't alone: a rising of the small hairs on her arms, a prick at the back of her neck. The first time, she looked behind her to see a ship on the horizon. Another time, a whale surfaced next to the boat. Once, she'd been below deck when the feeling hit; she went above to find an enormous freighter headed toward her. Goodall altered course, and the ship chuffed by.

GOODALL WIPED SWEAT from her brow in the late August sun. She'd just spent an hour hand-pumping a liter of ocean water through her desalinator. It turned out that the yellow paint on *DHL Starlight's* sails—essential components of her rainwater catchment system—had contaminated Goodall's fresh water supplies. The paint was DHL yellow. Now it meant she had to spend hours each day at the pump just to get a few liters of potable water from the sea. She only had so much canned food before she'd have to turn to her dehydrated stores, which required water to prepare. She took seawater baths. She thought often about how nice it would be to shower after nine months at sea.

There was no wind to cool her skin; there hadn't been for days. Her progress was slow, and Goodall was more frustrated than she'd ever been. There was a general race route but endless options for changing course to leverage winds or currents. Recently, Goodall had chosen to go east instead of south in hopes of saving some time. She ended up in a long, windless high-pressure system. It cost her a few places in the race lineup, but she cared less about that now than the boredom and feeling of helplessness hounding her.

Two more participants had pulled out of the race. French sailor Antoine Cousot retired after admitting to the pressure of the undertaking. And Philippe Péché, who'd violated the rules by contacting his partner by satellite phone, limped into Cape Town with a broken tiller. Sitting in the still sea, Goodall empathized with their decisions. Finishing the race, she now understood, would require resisting the urge to give up. It would also require wind. Where the hell was the wind?

She took a drink of water and went for a swim; it wasn't as if the boat was going anywhere. She treaded water, amazed at the red reflection the hull cast on the surface of the ocean. What a nice change, she thought. She'd had the same point of view—deck, sails, horizon—for nearly two months. It was enough to drive a person crazy.

After more than a week, a hesitant wind gathered momentum, ending Goodall's purgatory of motionlessness. A text from McIntyre beeped on her sat phone. Fifty-eight-year-old Norwegian sailor Are Wiig had been hit by a storm 400 miles southwest of Cape Town. He was below deck when the boat flipped descending a wave. He hit his head against the hatch and was underwater a few moments, wondering if he might drown. The boat righted, but the capsize broke the mast, smashed a window, and split the cabin roof. Wiig was headed back to Cape Town under jury rig, using backup poles to construct a makeshift mast. The race was over for him.

The news shook Goodall. Wiig, an engineer and yacht surveyor who'd run transatlantic races, had five decades of sailing experience. If it can happen to him, it can happen to anyone, she thought. She recalled Wiig radioing her about sailing down the coast of Norway in 70-knot winds. The most she'd taken *DHL Starlight* through was 45 knots. Seventy knots, she thought. What does that even feel like?

IN MID-OCTOBER IN the Southern Ocean, almost halfway around the world, Goodall received a text from McIntyre: "A storm is forming in your path." She felt a flutter of nerves. Another text beeped; the storm was gaining strength. "Turn around and sail west," McIntyre said.

That's ridiculous, Goodall thought. I just came from there. After weeks of frustrating calm, she wasn't about to give up miles. *DHL Starlight* was gaining on Uku Randmaa, the Estonian, who was in third place and with whom she had a good-natured rivalry. She called McIntyre on the sat phone for clarity.

"It's bad. It's really bad," he said. "You won't be able to get away from it entirely. But you can get away from the worst of it." Goodall changed course. That afternoon, she got on the radio with Randmaa and Mark Slats, the Dutchman, who were well east of any weather. She told them she'd turned around.

"It must be a bad storm," Randmaa replied.

Goodall thought of two other skippers, Tomy and McGuckin, who'd been forced out of the race a month before. As they were racing to catch Slats and Van Den Heede, a vicious cyclone screamed over them in the Indian Ocean, more than a thousand miles from land. Seventy-knot winds and 46-foot waves rolled McGuckin's boat twice, ripping away the short mast at the back of the boat and then destroying the main mast. His boat crippled and the storm still raging, he saw a distress text from Tomy, who'd been rolled and dismasted as well: *Severe back injury. Cannot get up.* There followed hours of silence. McGuckin jury-rigged a mast and headed through violent seas toward his rival. In the ensuing days, both men were rescued by a French vessel, leaving their broken, beloved sailboats adrift.

The storm in Goodall's path seemed just as ferocious. She told Randmaa and Slats that she didn't want to risk destroying her boat and being forced to leave the race. Better to head west for a while and get back on course when the skies cleared. "I want to actually make it round the world," she said.

HUNDREDS OF MILES off the coast of Australia's Cape Leeuwin, *DHL Starlight* bobbed gently in the ocean. The red hull reflected brightly on a narrow strip of water that otherwise appeared dull under a cloudy sky. The wind had disappeared hours before. In the cockpit, Goodall sat in the silence. She wouldn't have to face the storm's full force, but she would have to skirt the edge of it.

What could be tied down or put away was lashed and stowed. Lines were tidied, the yellow sails trimmed and ready for winds that were now predicted to be 60-plus knots. "We're ready, aren't we," she said softly to the boat. "We'll get through this."

Goodall stared out at the horizon. The eerie calm went on and on, inviting her fear to expand. Some of the skippers in the race, when they came on the radio after a fierce storm, would say they hadn't been scared. But Goodall could hear the tremble in their voices. Any sailor feels fear when the water turns on them. But what was in her now was different: the nerves before a storm, when it only exists in the imagination.

Goodall had never seen a sky so dramatic. In the distance was an advancing curtain, dark and heavy as lead. Dusk was falling, but what approached looked like midnight. A low rumble traveled across the sea. Surely I can't *hear* the storm, Goodall thought.

The rumble grew. The darkness hulked forward. In her hair, against her skin, through the rigging of the boat, the wind began to rise.

By morning, 25-foot swells pitched the sailboat. Wind howled at 50 knots. It was nothing Goodall couldn't handle. Below deck, she threw on her lightest rain gear; her intention was to raise a storm jib, a small sail that is the bare minimum needed for maneuverability in heavy weather. She climbed out of the cabin and tethered herself to one of the rings she'd soldered to the deck.

And then she looked up.

A great wave towered, ready to break over *DHL Starlight*. Goodall crouched in the open cockpit as it fell, the force like a sledgehammer on her back. When it passed, she raised her head and found that only the mast jutted from the foam left behind by the wave. As the water slowly drained off—the boat was made for this, after all—Goodall looked to the stern. The self-steering flapped uselessly, broken.

She lunged for the helm and wrestled it under control. As she worked the tiller, she examined the self-steering system. The tube on the wind vane was broken. Without the self-steering, she would have to hand-steer every minute of the storm, eliminating the possibility of eating, resting, or making repairs. But fixing it meant leaning out over the stern to insert a new tube, sliding a bolt through the tube, and threading it into a nut on the other side. Another wave broke on top of the boat; there was no way she could repair the wind vane in this. All she could do was brace herself at the helm. If she didn't keep the stern perpendicular to the swells, the boat would slide sideways down a breaking wave and capsize.

The waves kept coming, growing in size until they were higher than the boat's 45-foot mast. They were steeper and faster than anything Goodall had ever seen. The wind topped 70 knots. With each passing swell, the boat rose and then rocketed downward. At the bottom of a trough, Goodall looked behind her and watched as the next wave pulled the boat up its face, far faster than *DHL Starlight* was designed to travel, the whole boat shuddering, until it was atop a rushing, breaking peak, the bow hanging in thin air. Then the boat slid down the back side as the wave rumbled past. A breath of relief. A glance over her shoulder, and another on its way.

And another. And again. Over and over for 11 hours.

Waves broke against Goodall's back, beating the air from her lungs and swamping the cockpit. They knocked the boat on its side, half-submerging Goodall as she gripped the tiller. She prayed for the boat to right itself. "*You did so well,*" she shouted when it did, the gale ripping her voice away.

If she was exhausted, if she was hungry, if she was soaked through and cold to the bone, there was no time to feel it. The intensity of certain situations, when the world brings nearer the thin line between life and death, demands presence. Goodall knew she was afraid, but she couldn't think of anything but the waves. She couldn't rest. She and the boat were crowding up against the absolute limit.

Finally, the sky darkened again—not with clouds, but with twilight. The wind backed off its mad tear, and Goodall realized she hadn't eaten for 24 hours. She was freezing and so tired. But she had to fix the self-steering; she couldn't hand-steer at night, when she couldn't see what was coming. As the boat continued to be tossed by 30-foot swells, she leaned over the stern with numb hands, replaced the wind vane's tube, inserted the bolt, and screwed on the nut. That she managed to pull off the repair—that the waves didn't swallow the boat and spit it back out in pieces—suggested someone or something was helping them through the storm.

Finally, she went below to warm up and make an enormous pot of rice pudding. She spoke to her boat the entire time: "You are amazing. You handled it so beautifully." And then she fell into her bunk.

She closed her eyes, but the waves barrelled down in her imagination. The only way to make them stop was to open her eyes again, keeping her from sleep. If she'd ever wanted to pick up the phone and speak to her family, it was now—to tell someone who loved her what had happened, what she'd survived.

Two weeks later, Goodall had made it nearly halfway around the world and was approaching the second compulsory gate, in Tasmania. She would stop near Hobart and, without leaving her boat, do whatever interviews had been lined up, including one with McIntyre, from a boat that pulled alongside *DHL Starlight*.

She hadn't seen another soul in four months. She'd been through a calm hell and a tempestuous one, had some of the best sailing days of her life, felt lonely and not alone at all, and seen what the Southern Ocean was capable of. What would it be like now to suddenly find herself with people? To show up for the cameras again? Maybe I can just turn off my tracker and head for Iceland, she thought.

Nearing Tasmania, the scent of land nearly knocked her breathless. Soon the flat horizon broke into a rise of mountains, the blues and grays split by a shock of green and brown. She began to feel some excitement at the thought of seeing faces again.

Goodall arrived at midnight. The following morning, McIntyre stood on a boat alongside *DHL Starlight* to record an interview. He started by asking about the most challenging aspect so far, to which she replied succinctly, "Being becalmed." Then he asked, "What challenges do you face as a female sailor that's different to men?"

Goodall raised her eyebrows and laughed. "Come on," McIntyre prodded, "what's different?"

She tried to laugh it off. "Uh, I don't have a very quick answer for that. Um, I don't know. I guess I'm maybe not as strong as—"

"Oh, yes you are," he interjected. "OK, we'll pass on that one."

Several rapid-fire questions later, each of which Goodall answered gamely, McIntyre circled back. "Does being the sole woman push you or not? You know what I mean—feel as if you've got a drive because you're the sole woman?"

"Um, well. Yes and no. I feel like a woman's got to finish it."

She'd been able to transcend the pressure, escape the "sole woman" box, for the past few months. In Hobart, the weight was back on her shoulders.

The following day, Goodall anchored in the sheltered bay of Port Arthur; a storm roiled the Tasman Sea, and she'd decided to wait it out. She found that she couldn't sleep with the boat moored. The three days she spent in the bay were the worst of the race. Across from where she dropped anchor was a lovely beach. "I just want to give up," she said aloud at one point.

But the simple act of saying it defanged the idea. She could quit right then, but she wouldn't.

III.

"*There's a storm front coming*," Billy Joel wailed over the boat's tinny speakers. It was December 4, Goodall's 157th day at sea, and a good one on the Southern Ocean, in the expanse between New Zealand and South America's Cape Horn. Nearly two-thirds of the way through the Golden Globe, a 15-foot swell and 30-knot winds were at Goodall's back, pushing *DHL Starlight* forward. She was still in fourth place and had nearly caught up with Randmaa.

During her weekly check-in with McIntyre the day before, Goodall reported that she was running low on fresh water. While most of the yellow paint had run off the sails, little rain had fallen lately. "I've got about 20 liters in the tank. I've barely been drinking anything," she said on the call, sounding cheerful nonetheless.

"Well, you've got a bit of rubbish coming in the next couple of days," McIntyre told her. "It's not a big deal, but it's a messy low-pressure system that's a bit all over the place. Not a huge storm, but you could get some big squalls."

"Ah, OK. OK. How big?"

"Could be gusting around 55, 60," McIntyre said—less intense than the Cape Leeuwin storm. "Nothing to worry about, you're more than capable of handling it."

Still, McIntyre updated the race's Facebook page with news of the coming storm—some drama for its 41,000 followers.

Goodall was also getting radio updates from a forecaster in New Zealand. He didn't see what McIntyre was predicting, and thought she'd only get winds around 45 knots. But then, below deck, the barometer dropped significantly, and kept dropping. Fast. Even before the Cape Leeuwin storm, the barometer hadn't been in free fall like this. We're not in for just an average blow, Goodall thought.

She spent the rest of the day preparing the boat. She strapped and stowed. She readied her drogue—a series of funnel-shaped parachutes used to steady a boat when sailing in stormy conditions. She put on her heavy-duty weather gear.

By afternoon the wind had picked up to 30 or 35 knots. The boat sped along. Squalls came and went. The sea was confused and chaotic, with swells in three directions—the largest was around 15 feet, and the other two milled around it messily. The rumbling of the storm shook Goodall; she could hear it coming, going, all around her.

Everything felt wrong.

She made an enormous pot of curry and put some in a thermos for an easy meal. She pulled in the sails. She was becoming chilled. As the dark of the approaching night thickened, a wave hit the boat and snapped the safety tube on the wind vane—again. She couldn't hand-steer through this storm in the dark, not without seeing the waves. She sat in the cockpit and debated putting out the drogue, which drags like a series of parachutes through the water to turn the stern into the wind and waves, the safest positioning. If later she decided it wasn't the right decision for these helter-skelter seas, she wouldn't be able to pull the drogue back in, and she'd lose the ability to steer the boat with any agility, allowing the storm to overtake her. But if there were steep waves like in the Cape Leeuwin storm, the drogue should stop the boat from surfing and pitchpoling—somersaulting end over end—down a breaking wave. She decided to release it. As she watched the drogue pull away from the stern, the boat felt instantly steadier.

It was dark now. She went below and crawled into the bunk to get warm. Every half-hour, she'd pop her head out of the hatch with a headlamp to check the drogue.

Soon a thought nagged. Had she tied down the storm jib tightly enough to protect it from the wind, which had gone from whistling to howling to a high-pitched scream? She worried that the flapping jib would be ripped to pieces.

Goodall debated going up. She was just starting to get warm, and it was so cold out there. Then again, she couldn't sleep—although she desperately wanted to. It was too loud, and she always felt herself holding her breath in high winds and big seas. *DHL Starlight* would roll, and in her bunk she'd lean the opposite way, as if helping to steady the boat.

She poked her head out of the hatch every 15 minutes. The jumbled swells were now more than 30 feet, and she could see the pale foam of the breaking waves. She could no longer make out which direction was dominant. She'd never seen seas like this.

Ten p.m. neared, the time when Slats and Randmaa and the New Zealand forecaster would get on the radio after a day of sailing. Goodall made herself a deal: She'd get up to chat, and after that she'd deal with the jib. She turned on the deck light to get a glimpse of the small sail through the hatch. It was well lashed. It didn't even flutter in the riotous gale. She wondered why it was bothering her so much. Slats came on the radio, talking with the forecaster as Goodall put on her clammy rain gear and fastened a harness over it. She picked up the handset, waiting for a break in the conversation to speak into the radio.

At that moment, the screaming wind ceased. The world went silent.

The storm's stopped, she thought. She chided herself: That's ridiculous, storms don't suddenly stop. Then she realized—this must be a wave.

She felt the stern rise. Sound returned in a deafening roar. Clinging to the post by the radio, she was suddenly looking down at the rest of the cabin. She went airborne as a leviathan of water she couldn't see but only feel somersaulted the boat. Her mind blacked out before her head slammed into something, before the beanbag chair tumbled in front of her body right before she hit the wall, before the boat crashed down on its side in a tremendous violent blow.

When Goodall came to, the boat had rolled upright and she was in a heap. Her head throbbed with a horrible grinding noise. When her mind cleared, the sound was still there. She rushed to the deck to assess the damage and find the source of the noise. Immediately she saw it: The mast had been dashed into three pieces, and they were scraping against the hull. They were still attached to the deck by ropes and steel wires and cables, and the weight was pulling the boat underwater.

Goodall hurried below to retrieve a hacksaw, sloshing through knee-deep water; the mast, she thought, had ruptured the hull and caused a leak. She switched on the emergency bilge pumps to drain the water from the cabin, but then remembered that she'd plugged the outlets. The pumps had two outlets, or holes to the outside. Soon after starting the race, Goodall discovered that a swell following the boat could send water into the bilges—the part of the boat designed to collect excess water at the bottom of the hull—forcing her to run the pumps and drain the battery.

So, after the Canaries, she'd filled the outlets with wooden plugs and used a hand pump when necessary.

She ran back to the deck. The outlets were in the stern, and she'd have to pull the plugs downward to remove them. She leaned over the dark, pitching sea. Every time the stern slammed down, it plunged her head and shoulders into the freezing ocean. But she grasped at each plug until she got them out. She tried to pull herself back up, only to find that she was tangled in the steering lines and her hair had caught on something. She reached for the knife she always kept on her and cut the lines free, along with a chunk of hair.

Back below, she turned on the bilge pumps and let them run while she searched for the hacksaw and bolt cutters—she had to cut loose the broken mast before it sank the boat. The cabin's lockers on the port side had all burst open. Nothing was where it should be.

She found the tools and returned to the seething storm. It was nowhere close to wearing itself out. Goodall reached for the first of the stays—wires that hold the mast in place—barely able to see what she was doing. The bolt cutters didn't even leave a mark. So she started in with the hacksaw. The boat was parallel to the swell, with the mast trailing off the side, which meant that every wave smashed the hull into the ruined pieces of mast, threatening more damage.

After an hour, Goodall had severed only two of the boat's 11 stays. Her arms were jelly. Her hands were bloody from where the hacksaw slipped and hit skin. She left a red trail wherever she moved. Then she had a thought: She could pull out the pins. Yes. She could remove the metal pins that fastened the stays to the deck. She ran below to grab her Leatherman from near the chart table. The water was still above her boots, though the pumps had been running nonstop.

She looked at the emergency beacon, also strapped up by the chart table. When activated, it would send a distress call via satellite to the Falmouth Coastguard in England, which would notify race headquarters. There was so much water in the boat, she thought there must be a hole in the hull. If that was true, the boat could sink then and there. But what if she was wrong? She could always cancel the call when she got the situation under control, released the mast into the ocean and located the leak.

She grabbed the beacon and pressed the emergency button.

ON THE AFTERNOON of December 5, a Wednesday, Birgitte Howells's phone rang as she drove down a motorway. It was McIntyre.

"We've received a call," he told her. Goodall's distress beacon had been activated. He didn't know what had happened, and he couldn't tell Goodall's mother anything else. He'd call back as soon as he knew more.

Howells hung up. She pulled off the road. She knew McIntyre would post about the distress call on social media immediately. And indeed, after calling Howells, McIntyre updated the Golden Globe's Facebook page. Based on Goodall's proximity to South America, he said, Chile's marine search and rescue was now in charge of responding to the call. Race organizers had also sent a text message. "It was received," McIntyre wrote, "but not acknowledged at this time by Susie. No further news is available for now."

Howells didn't want the people who loved her daughter hearing about it online. She needed to get in touch with family before word spread. She called Stephen, Goodall's father, first. They both knew that anything could have happened since Goodall activated the beacon. She could have sunk straightaway. They also knew a global audience would be watching to learn if their daughter lived or died. While Howells continued to make calls, Stephen began the longest wait of his life.

GOODALL'S HANDS WERE numb, making it almost impossible to work the Leatherman's pliers. But she needed to get the pins out of the deck, so she kept at it.

She implored her hands to work. Her head spun. She was about to throw up. She swore at herself for being useless.

Finally, the mast slid away. Then came a tug. She looked down. There were ropes around her legs, ropes attached to the sinking mast. She wasn't wearing her harness; she'd taken it off so she could work faster.

She grabbed a handrail, but the boom was what saved her: Still attached to the mast, it became wedged against the boat's stanchions, the slender metal rods slung with safety cable to keep people on deck from falling into the sea. Ironic. Goodall untangled her legs, then slumped in the cockpit and put her harness back on.

She was so utterly exhausted. Dizzy. Her hands were done. For a moment she just sat there, listening to the hull bash against the mast, which refused to come free in a storm that refused to ebb. Then she pulled herself up.

She needed the boom to help make a substitute mast. But as she tried to cut the heavy pole free from the tangled rigging, it came loose and slid underwater with such force that it snapped the stanchions off the deck. She rushed to cut the remaining mast lines so nothing would get caught, and the boom, mast, and sails fell into the sea.

Something didn't feel right. The cockpit was full of water, and the stern was slowly sinking. Then Goodall realized: She had forgotten to cut the backstay, the wire running from the stern to the top of the mast. The rig was dragging the boat under.

Goodall lunged across the deck and cut the backstay loose. Doing that sent the stern surging upward. That was when she noticed the drogue, or what was left of it: a frayed rope that ended after a few feet.

She sagged down once more and lay in the water filling the cockpit. She'd stopped shivering, which she knew was a bad sign. She needed to warm up. But she just lay there.

Then she remembered the emergency beacon. That got her moving.

The water level had dropped in the cabin. She turned off the pumps to identify the source of the leak, but the storm was too loud for her to hear if water was rushing in through a crack in the hull. She turned the pumps on again and took in the wrecked cabin. Food and broken glass were everywhere. Storage containers were smashed to bits. The toolbox had slammed into the bunk right where her head was moments before the wave hit. The satellite phone, thankfully, was where she kept it near the chart table. She called McIntyre.

When he picked up and she spoke, all that came out was gibberish. Her lips were frozen. McIntyre hit record. "The… the boat is destroyed. The boat inside and out is destroyed. I can't make a jury rig, I can make no form of jury rig. The wind vane is ripped to pieces. The boat is, uh, the only thing that's left is the hull."

Despite how she sounded, Goodall felt in control of the situation. She didn't think that the boat was taking on more water than she could pump out, and she'd dealt with the mast, which had been the immediate crisis. She was hypothermic and exhausted, but she told McIntyre that she didn't need to be rescued—she could save herself, whatever that looked like. She just needed time to figure it out.

McIntyre told her to call every hour to keep him updated. Before he signed off, he told Goodall that he'd called her mother to let her know what was happening.

Goodall's heart sank. She couldn't imagine how worried Howells must be. Race rules prohibited Goodall from contacting anyone, but it hardly seemed to matter at this point—the dismasting meant her race was done. It was about saving herself and the boat now. She picked up the sat phone and called her mother.

HOWELLS WAS BACK on the motorway when she realized she had a voicemail, and that it was from her daughter. Goodall's voice was shaking with cold. "Hey Mom, it's me. Don't worry, everything's OK. I'm just calling to say hello. I'm OK."

Howells pulled over again, sat, and waited. A few minutes later, Goodall called back. It was a short conversation. Goodall said she'd pitchpoled and broken the mast, but that Howells didn't need to worry. Goodall would sort it out.

It was the first time Howells had spoken to her daughter in five months. She'd followed the weekly updates, listening in her daughter's voice for clues to her emotional state. Just now Goodall sounded distraught, but also confident that she was physically sound and had the situation in hand. Now all Howells could do was keep the phone close. She knew Goodall was a good sailor, at home in the sea. She could only hope that it wouldn't swallow her daughter whole.

IT WAS MORNING. Goodall didn't move. Her body was stone. She'd wedged herself into her bunk to weather the swells, which were still more than 25 feet high. She was nauseous and needed fluids, but she couldn't get herself to the sink. She looked up at the curry-splattered ceiling. She finally had a moment to think, despite the unceasing pain in her head, about the almost impossible series of events that had led to her being here, alive.

If she hadn't waited to speak on the radio, if she'd gone above just a few seconds before the wave hit, there would have been a moment when she wasn't tethered to the deck, when she might have been flung into the sea. Or, possibly worse, she'd have been tethered when the boat somersaulted and the mast was smashed to pieces, possibly on top of her. If she hadn't left her bunk to take care of the storm jib, she could have taken a hammer to the head. If the beanbag hadn't landed in just that spot at just that second to break her fall. If the mast had snapped in a way that it ripped up the deck and left her in an open boat, exposed to the storm.

Eventually, she managed to rise and turn off the bilge pumps. The battery was low. She moved to plug in the wire attached to the solar panels meant to charge the battery, but the wire sparked and went dead.

She called McIntyre to check in. He told her that American entrant Istvan Kopar was about six days behind her and had offered to give her a spinnaker pole so she could fashion some sort of mast.

She spent the night planning how to save herself. The realization had sunk in that the Golden Globe was over for her. Without a mast, she couldn't make it back to England. But with a spinnaker pole, she might be able to devise a way to get to Chile. If she could fix the solar-panel wire, the bilge pumps might be enough to keep the boat afloat. With the wind vane on the self-steering totally destroyed, she'd have to hand-steer the whole time, but she thought she could manage it.

The only other option was to let herself be rescued and abandon the boat. She would do whatever she could to avoid that. For nearly three years, the boat had been home. It was Goodall's partner in this journey; they were a team. Besides, Goodall wasn't ready to be back on land. Even jammed into the bunk of the broken vessel, dehydrated, injured, and exhausted, she was prepared to stay at sea.

The following morning, Goodall set the sea anchor, a big parachute with a hundred-meter line, to help stabilize the boat. But without a mast, *DHL Starlight* rolled horribly. Goodall couldn't keep anything down—food, water. Seasickness wasn't to blame. Maybe it was the concussion she knew she probably had. But she didn't think so.

She was ill, Goodall figured, because she knew she would not make it around the world.

"THERE'S ALREADY A rescue underway," McIntyre told Goodall the next time she checked in. A cargo ship bound for South America had changed course to come for her. It was two days away. "If we cancel it, and you get halfway to Chile on your own and your boat sinks, then another one has to be coordinated," McIntyre said.

True, Goodall thought, but at least then I'd know the boat was sinking. If she left the boat now, she'd never know if she could have saved it.

"If I just have a spinnaker pole, I can rig something."

"But where's the water coming from into the boat?"

"I don't know. I can't get in this sea to inspect the hull."

McIntyre asked about food and water. If she were sparing, she might have enough to make it to land. She still had the desalinator, four months' worth of dehydrated food, and half a dozen of her father's fruitcakes. McIntyre pointed out that an hour of hard pumping would yield less than a liter of water. Was that sustainable?

Goodall knew in her heart that she was stretching. If another storm hit in the six days it would take Kopar to reach her—difficult to consider, since the current storm was still tossing the boat as if it were in a washing machine—she wouldn't be able to run from it or maneuver through it. The boat would likely sink.

Leaving *DHL Starlight* would be like leaving a piece of herself at sea. But she knew there was no other choice.

That afternoon, Goodall looked around the ruined cabin, still being pitched by the storm. She had to decide what she could take with her in one load. If she focused on the task, perhaps she could keep her emotions from boiling over. Hands cold and bloody, trying to maintain her footing on the heaving floor, she fished out the bag of dry clothes she'd stowed five months before. She grabbed the letters from her family. Her camera and SD cards. Satellite phone and tracker. Passport. The photos her mother had given her of loved ones hugging the teddy bear. The bear itself was too big. It would have to stay with the boat.

That night she lay in her bunk and stared at the dented ceiling as the boat rolled sickeningly. She went over and over what she could have done differently. She'd put everything into this boat, this voyage. It had become her identity. Soon it would be gone.

ON THE EVENING of December 6, Howells and her husband, Goodall's stepfather, sat down to watch the news. They knew that a cargo ship was coming for Goodall, and in her gut Howells never doubted that Goodall would return alive. But now they, too, were navigating a storm: a salivating media eager to get a peek at a family's emotional crisis.

Outside the gated fence, a journalist and a photographer had been parked all day. Messages from other reporters piled up on her phone. "How does it feel that your daughter is stuck in the middle of the most ferocious ocean on earth?" one asked. Another inquired, "What's the first thing you'll say to her when you see her?" Howells didn't reply. "It felt," she later said, "like the sensationalism of somebody's misfortune just to get more views and followers, without any thought to what it may do to those of us who care about her."

Now, as Howells and her husband were watching BBC News, a segment about Goodall came on, and it included audio from her first call to McIntyre. Howells hit the roof.

Earlier that day, race organizers sent that recording to the family, who had asked that it not be released to the media. They thought it was in poor taste to do so while Goodall was still in danger. (McIntyre noted that Goodall had signed an agreement granting the race organizers permission to release audio from satellite phone calls. McGuckin's call after his dismasting wasn't released until after he was safe, because, reported *The Times*, "he feared it would distress his mother and girlfriend if they knew the danger he was facing.")

Headlines immediately appeared around the globe. When outlets had covered Tomy's and McGuckin's rescues a month and a half before, the coverage tended to focus on their bravery. "Irish Sailor Makes Heroic Efforts to Reach & Help Injured Rival Abhilash Tomy!" read a headline in *The Better India*. Those about Goodall took a different tone, shaped in part by Goodall's fame as the only woman and in part by the fact that the race had released only the portion of the call in which Goodall sounded shaken and distraught. The media never heard Goodall say that she was prepared to save herself. "British yachtswoman 'clinging on' as she waits for rescue," heralded the *Daily Mail*. The BBC quoted McIntyre saying, "She was in shock and during a dramatic phone call didn't want to abandon the boat. But we had to make her realize it was more serious than she thought." Just like that, it seemed like race organizers were trying to shift the narrative around her journey from lone heroine to feckless damsel in distress.

JUST BEFORE DAWN on December 7, three days after she pitchpoled, Goodall came on deck to see the lights of *Tian Fu*, a 620-foot-long cargo ship in the distance, a floating city heading her way.

It was the third day of the storm. Though the swells had fallen to 15 feet, getting aboard the Tian Fu wouldn't be easy. A 42,000-ton ship can't just pull alongside a far smaller one—a damaged one, no less—and toss down a rope ladder. This was the plan: The *Tian Fu* had to maintain a steady two knots to have steering capability, so Goodall would motor alongside to keep pace and avoid being crushed between the ship and the waves. Once both vessels were in position, the *Tian Fu* would deploy a crane to pluck Goodall off her boat.

As first light sparked the horizon and the ship approached, Goodall started her engine, which had worked during a test run the day before. Now, though, it smoked like it might explode, emanated an acrid smell, and went dead. Her stomach dropped. She would have to do without.

She grabbed her bag of belongings and looked around the ruin of her home. Before she left the cabin for the last time, she turned the bilge pumps back on. The boat had done so much for her. Goodall would do everything she could in return, even if it meant *DHL Starlight* would stay afloat only a few more hours.

The bow of the massive freighter loomed, a wall of steel blocking the sky. As it passed, crewmen threw down a line; Goodall had a split second to admire the incredible maneuvering by the ship's captain. She caught the line and attached her bag, which was hauled up first. Goodall winced each time her boat made impact with the ship's massive hull.

Now it was her turn. The *Tian Fu* positioned its crane, which was at the ship's stern, above her. The crew lowered a hook, and she clipped it to her harness. With the boat and the ship both rolling in the waves, she struggled to get it attached properly, nearly falling into the ocean in the process. Then she got it on, and it yanked her into the air.

As the crane swung her skyward, Goodall looked down at the husk of her little sailboat. It didn't feel right, to be lifted from her boat like this, to be leaving it alone. Once Goodall reached the deck and unclipped herself, the cargo ship chugged forward, leaving *DHL Starlight* bobbing in the empty Southern Ocean.

Goodall knew she would never forgive herself.

IV.

Goodall spent a week aboard the *Tian Fu*. She couldn't communicate much with the crew, so she spent most of her time in her cabin. She was thankful to be left alone. She went up to the bridge and used gestures to request a pen and paper from the captain. Then she wrote. She wrote down everything about the past three days, willing herself to remember it. When she'd emptied the pen, she got another from the captain. She emptied that one too.

Goodall spoke with her family occasionally by sat phone. On one of the calls, they told her that McIntyre had played them the recording of the first call she'd made during the storm—she had no idea he'd recorded her. She imagined what her family must have gone through as they waited for her to be rescued. *She'd* known she was OK, and she'd told her mother as much, but still, they'd had to listen to that call and worry.

As the cargo ship neared land and the experience she'd weathered settled into her being, the emotions piled on. She'd prepared for every eventuality except failure, a fact that left her feeling pinned, gasping. The sense that she'd put her family through hell only made it worse.

On December 14, the hump of Chile's Cape Horn appeared on the horizon. Goodall went to the back deck and stood facing away from South America, toward the open sea, trying to relieve some of her dread. She was still processing a near-death experience, and far from ready to be back on land. She hoped it would be just her family there when she stepped ashore. She didn't want to speak to anyone else. But the media had been a presence, hounding her, for so long. There was no reason to think it would treat her arrival any differently. Her dread intensified.

Then, down below, dozens of dolphins surfaced suddenly from the sea.

OK, she thought. I can do this.

When the ship anchored outside Punta Arenas, Goodall glimpsed the small boat that had been sent to fetch her. It was packed with cameras. Her heart dropped into her stomach. She held on to the dolphins in her mind.

Once she boarded the small boat, she was directed to a certain side of the deck so that cameras on shore had a better view of her. "No comment," she said again and again. At the dock, someone told her to stay on the boat while journalists set up photo ops. When she was finally allowed to step off the deck, they directed her further: "There's your mom, go hug your mom."

Of course Goodall wanted to hug her mother. She'd had no human contact for months. But to have this private moment stage-directed felt cheap. "When she got off the boat," Howells told me, "she seemed, apart from being bruised from the pitch-poling and the cuts all over her hands, deflated. Totally deflated. It was like hugging a shell. It was all her dreams, aspirations, years of hard work, at the bottom of the ocean. And here's everyone just wanting a bit of a person grieving."

Goodall didn't speak to any journalists that day. Her mother and brother took her to a hospital to have her wounds checked— nothing major, they would heal on their own—and then back to their hotel. Later that day, Goodall gave a statement. She thanked her family, sponsors, and everyone involved in the rescue. On the question of whether she would undertake such a voyage again, she said, "I would say yes in a heartbeat. You may ask why. Some people just live for adventure. It's human nature. And for me, the sea is where my adventure lies. That fire in my belly is far from out."

She took no questions.

BACK IN THE UK, Goodall spent Christmas at her mother's house. The mini bottle of wine she'd packed for the occasion was deep in the Southern Ocean by now. "So many people said to me, 'Thank God she's home. You can have a good family Christmas,'" Howells said. "I'd reply that I'd rather she weren't here for Christmas. She doesn't want to be here. She wants to be at sea."

Goodall was withdrawn and listless. Even after coming home, she used "we" often, unconsciously, to refer to herself—as if she was still aboard her boat and not adrift on land. She found herself wondering what the point of the past four years had been. So many people had offered support and money, and she had disappointed them. Meanwhile, the media didn't let up. Reporters bothered her family every day. Online, her comment that she would undertake the journey again "in a heartbeat" was seized on. "And capsize again at a cost to life and limb best stay in the kitchen luv," someone wrote on Twitter. Another asked, "What about the poor people who have to rescue the silly mare again?" For her part, Goodall only said on social media that she needed time to process things before she told her story. Then she went quiet.

Perhaps she'd been naïve when she signed up for the Golden Globe, Goodall thought. She assumed that she could be one of the sailors circumnavigating the world. But it would never be that simple, by dint of her being a woman and the world being what it is. Now she wrestled with the creeping realization that the

narrative she despised had gotten to her; one can't be the object
of relentless attention without being shaped by it, one way or
another. Goodall sometimes felt awful that she, the lone woman,
hadn't finished. In other moments she wished she'd never thought
about going around the world.

In January, Goodall received a set of questions from a PR
firm arranging a series of interviews in cooperation with DHL.
She didn't want to do it; she was still trying to process what had
happened to her out there. But she also felt that she'd somehow
wronged her sponsor by not finishing the race, and by losing the
boat they'd paid to refit, and owed it to them to participate. So
she steeled herself and agreed. Then she got the questions: What
happened when the wave hit? What do you think went wrong?
How did you feel about leaving your boat?

She choked on a sob. Everyone wanted the story of how her
journey ended, but Goodall had spent 160 days alone with her
boat and the ocean. She'd navigated not one monstrous storm
but two, and at just 29 years old had held her own amid a fleet
of experienced circumnavigators. She couldn't do this to herself.
She couldn't relive her failure, let alone put it up for exhibit. She
couldn't be the rescued damsel.

Two days before the interviews were set to begin, Goodall
backed out. She felt guilty; she knew DHL would be disappointed,
maybe even angry. She knew that all the people who'd followed
her journey expected to hear her speak. She suspected the race
organizers might portray her as uncooperative. But she canceled
anyway.

Over the next few months, she turned down thousands of
dollars for an exclusive first interview. She rejected book deals
and documentary offers. Saying no became her way of protecting
herself and her story. She would speak if and when she wanted to.

THREE AND A half years after returning home from the Southern
Ocean, Goodall spoke to me from the flat where she lives now
in Edinburgh with her fiancé, a professional ship's pilot. A

bright painting of a boat with sails full of wind hung on one wall; shelves loaded with books lined another. After the Golden Globe, Goodall worked in a boatyard to avoid thinking too much and then returned to sea as an instructor. When we spoke, her hands were full with something else: Her newborn was asleep in her arms.

A cup of tea went cold as she talked. This was the first time she'd told the whole story: the preparation, the voyage, the wave, the aftermath.

She agreed to speak with me on the condition that I wouldn't try to paint her as a hero or a feminist icon. Those portrayals still bother her, as does the black cloud the media pressure cast over her. It's only recently that she's been able to grasp the value of the journey she undertook.

Goodall wasn't able to remember much about the wave and the hours after it hit, not until she reread what she'd written on the *Tian Fu*. The rest of the race, though, she remembered like yesterday. As she recounted falling in love with *Ariadne*, Goodall was animated, lighting up like the sun burning through marine fog.

These days she still wants to circumnavigate the globe, but she has no desire to make the voyage alone, without stopping. She wants to show the world to her son, to sail with her fiancé on their own time and whim. Sometimes though, she told me, she dreams that she made it to the finish. Or that she sailed *DHL Starlight* to Chile. That she never left her alone out there.

It was her brother, months after she got home, who urged her to check her social media account; there were some incredible messages on there, he said. She also went through the piles of unopened letters she'd received. Many were from young girls who'd followed the Golden Globe. "A lot of the time," she said, "it was their dads who would follow it, and because there was a woman in it, they would introduce their young daughters to the race."

She went to the bookshelf and pulled down a box. A piece of pink construction paper fell out; it featured a crayon drawing of a boat on a blue ripple of water, and a stick-figure woman with yellow hair waving from it. Goodall read the card that arrived with the drawing aloud:

> *Dear Susie, please find enclosed the picture of you drawn by my two daughters, Lily three, and Penny eighteen months. I wanted you to see this so that in your disappointment about the GGR, you remember what you have achieved. While not tangible like a medal, inspiring young girls to be great is, at least in my mind, a far greater feat.*

It wasn't that Goodall never wanted girls to look up to her. She wanted the fact that a woman tried to circle the world to be an admirable thing, but also a normal one. Now she takes heart in the fact that so many messages sent to her don't mention how the race ended for her. All that mattered was that she'd set off in the first place, that she'd risen to a great challenge.

Goodall told me that her father recently said it was her destiny to survive. She'd never thought of it that way. But the thing about destiny, he suggested, is that you can't see it until it's unfolded.

When I first spoke to Stephen Goodall about his daughter's experience, he told me a story. There's an uninhabited rock, barely an island, off the coast of Scotland, he said, with a cave full of hexagonal basalt formations that served some ancient, mysterious purpose. A ritual was performed there in which an individual was set adrift to face a storm in a coracle, a round boat of animal hide and wood the size of a bathtub. When the storm passed, the others waited to learn whether the seeker had survived, and in doing so touched the thin place between earthly life and the spirit realm.

I scoured the internet for details of this ritual; I reached out to scholars and museums. But I came up short of any reference to coracle boats and spirit-testing ocean journeys. I asked Stephen how he'd encountered the story in the first place. He said that someone had told it to him. Perhaps it was just a myth.

We tell and share stories to explain things. Myths are no different. But when we feel the urge to birth new myths for new eras, it can be difficult to deviate from the paths our heroes were sent down before, to move beyond archetypes. We go with what is already known, what is easy.

Before Stephen told me about the cave, I'd been wrestling with the arc of Goodall's story. What I came to understand is that it isn't about the trappings of adventure or the silver linings of failure; it certainly isn't about anything measurable, like Goodall's impact on sailing or young women. It was about how a journey shaped a person, in ways knowable and not.

Some stories are ours to consume. But some, perhaps, are best left to the seeker and the thin place where they touched grace.

CASSIDY RANDALL is a freelance writer telling stories on environment, adventure, and people expanding human potential. Her work has appeared in *Time*, *The New York Times*, *National Geographic*, *Rolling Stone*, and elsewhere, and she's an adventure travel columnist on Forbes.com. Her first book, *The Hard Parts*, with Oksana Masters, came out in February 2023.

Serena Williams Refused to Bend. She Bent Tennis Instead.

LEX PRYOR

FROM The Ringer • SEPTEMBER 8, 2022

I.

Moonlight has long since graced the floor of Arthur Ashe Stadium, but Serena Williams pays the glare little mind. She will not be pushed off stage. On Friday, a night that began firmly balanced on the tightrope of victory has tumbled to within an eyelash of fate's unforgiving mat. Williams let the first set slip on her racket. With the right dose of offensive steel, her challenger, the 46th-ranked Australian Ajla Tomljanović, should've been overwhelmed. But the American swung and grazed her opponent's temple; four unforced errors, only one ace. She tried to recover. Out of something sweeter than spite, Williams managed to grab hold of the second set. It took 85 minutes. Then she went up a break in the third, and gave it right back. The bill was due, Serena had three dollars. She lost five games in a row.

This is how it ought to have ended, at the foot of the athletic afterlife, heels barbed, tendons tattered. But Serena, war-worn, 23-time champion, mother of one, does not bend. She digs her feet in. Once, then twice, then three times. And her people—sitting courtside, in the second deck, flowing over the top of the bowl that is this monstrous stadium—wail, and they gasp,

and they love it. "*Serena*," they chant in three separate parts—
"*Se-re-na*"—they shake the floor, again, again, and again. She
withstands four match points. She screams. She claws. The game
stretches 14 minutes and 19 seconds. She loses on point 22, with
a forehand return into the net. Even in the end, even as it dims,
her light continues to shine.

The 2022 U.S. Open didn't wrap on Friday, but its memory
is sealed. No matter who wins, no matter how awesomely they
might go about doing so, the moment Serena Williams (possibly?)
announced her impending retirement—or *evolution* away from
the sport—the tournament morphed into something greater. It
belonged to her. You could feel it on the ground, in the form of
attendance surges and ticket-price hikes, hashtag tributes and fare-
well videos, but especially in the general and pervading vibe that
all this hubbub was not really up for discussion. That the present
moment was as much in honor of Serena, as it was, justifiably,
pulled into her orbit.

There is a kind of poetry in this: The most dominant athlete
of our time exiting as she operated. Serena, just by existing, just by
doing what she does, turns everything upside down once more.
She is herself upheaval, even at the end, even as she floats off
into the realm of sports eternity. It's the inconvenient truth of
her reign. She didn't set out to inspire anyone or piss anyone off,
to embody the fissures that line America's social and political
battlefields. She didn't grow up wanting to be a role model, a
martyr, or anything in between: She wanted only to never once
yield a single point of tennis to anyone else on this earth. This
was her edict. This was her beauty. To see her topple all those
records, those moments, those walls—whatever it is, if it's in her
way, she will bend anything.

II.

The godfather of Black tennis was first a football player who
refused to use a helmet and became a doctor who refused to learn
his place. His name was Robert Walter Johnson. His hair was long

and then he went bald. Folks called him "Whirlwind" back when he was a halfback. It's tricky trying to fit the whole of a history, or at least responsibility for a series of advancements, into one figure. Like golf, baseball, or any other game that white America tried to segregate, efforts to integrate U.S. tennis were multigenerational, diffuse, and collaborative. But there's one person with ties to the biggest success stories before the Williams family, and that's Dr. Johnson, the man who forged jewels on a clay court in Lynchburg, Virginia.

Starting in the mid-'40s, Johnson put together a team of pupils, whose living expenses, equipment, and travel costs he covered out of pocket. He had two cars and he'd use them to drive the groups to Black-run tournaments in D.C., North Carolina, New Jersey, and Michigan. He had a set of standards for what he'd eventually call his development teams. Players had to do yard work, weed his garden, maintain the bushes out front, prune his apple trees. And they had to follow his instructions on the court, both in form and behavior.

Before newbies were allowed to use racquets, they were resigned to broomsticks. They were taught to return all shots within two inches of the boundaries. There was to be "no racquet throwing, no hollering, no indication of discontent with officials' calls." It is through this regimen that Althea Gibson transformed herself from Harlem street fighter to leading lady of American tennis, that Arthur Ashe grew from exuberant Southern cub to internationally cool and affectless beau. The most vital of Johnson's precepts shadowed all of his lessons. "I want you to be accepted without being a center of attraction," Johnson told his pupils. "I want you to be able to take care of yourself in any situation where habits or manners are important, so that you don't stand out."

Thing is, Serena's whole vibe been centripetal. After Johnson's students, there were a handful of Black U.S. players. By the time the Williams sisters burst onto the scene there were just a few Black women ranked in the top 100 worldwide. Venus and

Serena were ink in a pail of whiteout. They came in with their hair beaded and braided, and they didn't move an inch when the sport tried to censure them for it.

Serena got older and her body filled out. Which ain't a thing, until it is, and at the country club it often was. Various episodes included: the backlash to her catsuit at the 2002 U.S. Open; repeated implications by players and coaches that she and Venus were "masculine"; the time a white player walked out onto the court and *impersonated* Serena by stuffing towels beneath her shirt and skirt; a final catsuit kerfuffle in 2018, this time in the form of an outfit ban and a scolding from the French Tennis Federation president that she ought to "respect the game and the place." For as long as Williams has existed within tennis she has been branded—by the media, by supposed friends and peers, by the controlling institutions of the sport itself—as aggressive, masculine, unattractive, and hyper-sexual, even as these tropes trip over one another in multiple angles.

And all that's without even saying anything. Even as a teen, her confidence brimmed. Folks were always trying to chip away at it, a fact that her mother, Oracene, was keenly aware of. ("It's like, 'Squish them down, they can't have that confidence,'" she said of the reaction to both Venus and Serena.) In 1999, a 17-year-old Serena famously said of then-all-time singles leader Steffi Graff, "No, I'm not intimidated by Steffi, I've never been intimidated by anyone." Avoid the center of attention? She Crip walked on the lawn of the All England Club. Dr. Johnson's racquet rule? Laughable. She went through them like Tic Tacs. Any representative-of-the-race-style complaint ban? Out of the question. At the 2004 U.S. Open, she was robbed repeatedly in the course of a heated loss, so she called a spade a spade, and got a belated apology and eventually the modern replay system to boot.

And yes, it might've gone overboard sometimes (an "I swear to god I'll fucking take the ball and shove it down your fucking throat" here, a "You're just unattractive inside" there). That's the kind of behavior that's lined the underbelly of many a great in and outside tennis. Connors called an umpire "an abortion." McEnroe told a supervisor to "go fuck your mother" at the Australian Open. Is there anything more alpha, more Tiger, more Michael, more wonderfully and ridiculously competitive, than Williams, in the midst of yet another Grand Slam victory, reacting to a bad shot by throwing her arms back, arching her spine, and screaming "Fuck are you doing" into the sky?

Part of Serena's genius—competitively, personally—is that she never can quite be anything but herself when she's desperate. And she's desperate every time she steps foot on a court. But another more conscious part of her genius is that she showed no shame in this, or any other segment of her being that she could not control. She sidestepped the trap, the one that predates her, Dr. Johnson, tennis itself. The American dilemma. Serena's refusal to couch herself, to fit what the game was in order to be what the game is, recalls all the ancestors—breathing and not— who eyed down worlds meant to twist them and derived freedom from the revelation that there were places they could not be bent.

III.

Althea Gibson is standing next to Arthur Ashe. Not his body but his stadium. And Althea's in stone. Her likeness is carved onto a gray granite cube with sharp beige lettering at the base. This statue of Gibson receives little attention as wandering currents of patrons exit Billie Jean King National Tennis Center following (possibly) the last doubles match played together by Venus and Serena Williams. Even with a stretch of lighting at its feet, by the middle of the evening session the monument blends into the foreground.

In Flushing, Ashe may cast a larger shadow, but on the court, Gibson reached just as high. She grew up in Harlem, 10 miles from the headquarters of the U.S. Lawn Tennis Association. She spent most of her Depression-era childhood on the streets, playing basketball. Gibson didn't pick up tennis until her mid-teens. She built herself up, from local tournaments among the Harlem elite, to Robert Walter Johnson's fledgling academy, to what few white-run events would have her. It took her white peers advocating publicly for Wimbledon and the U.S. championships to open their doors. She won five Grand Slam titles from 1956 to 1958, but still she was never fully embraced on tour. Fans sometimes hurled slurs at her from the safety of the stands. Gibson's longtime doubles partner, a Jewish Liverpool native named Angela Buxton, initially teamed up with her because no one else wanted either of them as partners. Years later, at the unveiling of Gibson's statue, Buxton was proud and appreciative that her friend was finally getting her due. There was just one problem. "You want an honest opinion?" Buxton said at the time. "Well, it doesn't resemble her at all. Sorry to say that. I would have passed her any day and not known who it was."

The monument is still a bit incongruous in person. Seeing her there, carved (however roughly) in granite, you can't help but wonder what remembrance means to the person being remembered. How exactly they'd want to be etched in stone. Serena's legacy might be as a trailblazer: the woman whose response to racist harassment at Indian Wells was to refuse the tournament her entry for 14 consecutive years. The activist who wouldn't play in South Carolina while the Confederate flag flew. The champion of equal pay. The voice for the voiceless, particularly post-Ferguson.

There is value and honor in this. But where it resides—like the mark of her playing career—is in how she touched her people. In this way, Serena's reign endures in Naomi Osaka's serve *and* her strength outside the sport, through Coco's on-court resolve *and* her off-court scruples. "Maybe it didn't work out for me," Williams phrased it after another perceived slight at the Open in 2018, "but it's going to work out for the next person." Even then she was a step ahead of everybody, even then she was calling her shots: It's not how the patrollers of the game remember you that matters, it's how your folks do. How you live on through them.

IV.

This is the part where we talk about the fact that Compton was a sundown town before it was a ghetto. That the Compton you know (of John Singleton wide angles and swap-meet slo-mos) and the Compton you don't know (the one that's too sharp, beautiful, infuriating to wrap the mind around) are both the product of white Californians thumbing the scales of fate. And by thumbing fate, we're talking cross burnings and bombings and death threats and mobs scattered by shotgun shells (and absolutely no public "negro housing"). And then, when that fails, we're talking blockbusting, property devaluation, labor shortages, tax-base erosion. In 1950 Compton is less than 5 percent Black; in 1960 it's over 40 percent; in 1970, nearly three-quarters of the population is Black. They've got a word for that and it's called sabotage. But sometimes things left to rot manage to sprout all the same.

This is the part where we discuss that without Compton there is no Serena as you know her. That she is an impossibility. That because the scales of fate were tipped, in April 1980, a Black congresswoman representing a virtually all-Black district secured $582,000 in funding to build a 3.3-acre park on the corners of Atlantic Avenue and Compton Boulevard—a park where a Louisiana exile named Richard Williams would teach his two daughters how to play tennis a decade later.

That all the roadblocks made a path but that only those two girls could walk it. America built a gate around Serena Williams and Serena Williams fitted herself through. The question we ought to ask is less what the hole in the gate means for others, and more whether it means that the gate is still a gate at all. And there she is again, just by her will, just by her presence, warping everything around her.

The slippery truth—the one that if you know, you know, and if you don't, you don't—is she made it out but never all the way. It's how she loses a sister to a mistaken bullet and is called a "lost cause" and has an embolism and wins, and wins, and wins, 23 times over. How she finds out her sister's killer was paroled minutes before playing a match. The trick of a place like Compton is that it sticks. Can't get it off you. Then again, you might not want to.

And Serena will do what she wants.

V.

It's Y2K season and those beads from '97 are back on your nearest plasma screens. Different girl this time, same family. Sixteen years old and out for title no. 1. Arthur Ashe Stadium opened two summers ago but this might as well be its christening. The teen's up against the 1-seed and running her ragged. She's louder visually and sonically. Range of movement quicker than something reptilian. She takes the first set in a breeze. Her power's untapped; the aim is precise. Backhand winners at every angle, a forehand capable of reaching Row 305. She's up 5-3 in Set 2 but blows match point twice. Others would fall apart. She digs in mid-tumble. Forces a tiebreaker, then like nothing, holds steady while her opponent starts to slide. She will not bend. Third time's the charm. "Oh my god, I won," she says, "oh my god." This is an upset, a coronation, a new order in the making. Serena, shaper of worlds, has suddenly arrived.

LEX PRYOR is a staff writer at The Ringer. He covers race, pop culture, and sports. He lives and loves in Harlem.

A New Bat, Old Friends, and Timeless Magic as Cardinals' Albert Pujols Soars to 700

DERRICK GOOLD

FROM THE *St. Louis Post-Dispatch* • SEPTEMBER 24, 2022

LOS ANGELES—In his first season as batboy for the visitors' dugout at Dodger Stadium, Oscar Ramirez studies the arrangement of bats in the bat rack, so when one splinters at the plate he can swiftly greet the batter with two new ones. He wants to offer the hitter a choice.

In the third inning Friday night as Pujols walked back toward the dugout holding a bat fractured at the handle by a slider he smashed for a foul ball, Ramirez hustled onto the field with only one Marucci model AP5 he picked out for Pujols.

"It was in the heat of the moment," Ramirez said. "It was crazy. I looked for the engraved '5'. There were two. Something told me go right. I went with the right bat."

He handed the magician his wand.

With that familiar flair for timing and talent for giving the biggest stage his best show, Pujols' next two swings—his first two swings of the evening with that bat—launched himself into the most exclusive club of hitters in Major League Baseball history. The pitch after breaking his bat, Pujols rocketed the 699th home run of his career. An inning later he lofted No. 700 into the bleachers at Dodger Stadium. Albert joins Babe, Hank, and Barry as the only members of the 700-homer club. He is the first Latin player to reach 700 and one of only two players ever with 700 homers, 3,000 hits, and 2,000 RBIs. Hank Aaron is the other.

As he started his 700th lap around the bases, Pujols looked elated, his arms outstretched toward his teammates and the "600" medallion he's been wearing bobby against his chest. His latest and greatest gust of history came in the first game this season with all five of his children present to see.

"Because of this—my beautiful family," Pujols said, gesturing to his sons and daughters gathered around him. "After the Lord, that's who I play for. They've been walking through this journey, through the ups and downs, through the cries and the hurts and the injuries. Knowing they have my back, and having them in the stands, at this game, like this, become part of this history, means a lot to mean. Everything, pretty much, to me."

Pujols' milestone home runs produced the first five runs of the Cardinals' 11-0 rout of the Dodgers. The homers were Nos. 20 and 21 of the season. Fifteen have come since the All-Star break. With the bat handed to him by Ramirez, Pujols mashed No. 699 off a 94-mph fastball from Dodgers starter Andrew Heaney, a lefty. The ball traveled 434 feet—one of the Cardinals' longest homers of the season. An inning later, in the fourth, LA brought in right-handed reliever Phil Bickford. Jose Quintana nudged teammate Jordan Montgomery, a fellow lefty, in the Cardinals' dugout and mentioned how cool it would be if No. 700 came against a right-hander.

Cool it was, Quintana later confirmed.

Before going to the plate, Pujols told Ramirez and MLB's authenticator that he was going to use the same bat as No. 699 one more time. He took a strike and a ball from Bickford and then jumped a hanging slider, sending it 389 feet into the stands and forever into the highlights.

"As soon as he looked into the dugout with his arms up, it was like, 'I did it,'" manager Oliver Marmol said.

"A lot of sensations. I almost cried," said Quintana, who pitched 6⅔ scoreless innings for the win. "That happened on my day. I'm never going to forget this night."

The baseball from No. 699 was confirmed by MLB and returned to the Cardinals for Pujols. The three-time MVP met with the fan who caught it late Friday night. The fans who snagged No. 700 had the ball authenticated by a Major League Baseball representative and then, one official said, "walked."

Pujols stressed that "souvenirs are for fans."

Ramirez, the first-year batboy, is a 20-year-old college student from nearby El Monte, California. He takes a full course load and works a full-time job at the ballpark. Already this year he's manned the bats for an All-Star Game, witnessed Clayton Kershaw make Dodger history, and prepped for his first post-season. He was setting up the dugout and checking through his pre-game chores as Pujols circulated on the field during batting practice.

Pujols hugged his former teammates with the Dodgers. He lifted up the LA batting coach who helped him modify his leg kick to generate better timing and more power. He laughed with Dodgers execs, including CEO Stan Kasten, and they chided him about the size of his bejeweled 600 necklace, asking how big is the 725 pendant? Pujols repeated to them what he's repeated to everyone—he's not coming back to chase numbers or changing his mind about retiring. These are his final swings. He told them privately what he would later say to the entire crowd, explaining how being a Dodger last season "brought back the joy" he felt playing the game as a boy.

Without that spark, he was going to retire.

Without that time as a Dodger, he would never have returned as a Cardinal.

Without ending his career as a Cardinal, he never would have hit 700.

"If they weren't going to give me the opportunity, I don't think I would be sitting here today," Pujols said of the Dodgers signing him a year ago. "You guys wouldn't see the history tonight. ... It's great when you have great people around you who believe in you."

During BP, Pujols chatted with Hall of Fame-bound third baseman and fellow Dominican Adrian Beltre, the All-Star whose record Pujols' surpassed to become the all-time leader for hits by a player born outside the United States. Beltre came to witness history, and Pujols told him, "Man, I want to do this for our country." He could not have picked a more fitting day.

On Sept. 23, 1956, Ozzie Virgil Sr. started at third base for the New York Giants and became the first Dominican Republic-born player to debut in the majors.

Sixty-six years, to the date, Pujols became the first Dominican with 700 homers.

"God works his thing in amazing ways sometimes we don't understand," Pujols said when told of the anniversary by the *Post-Dispatch*. "I'm just glad I was able to do it tonight."

"It means a lot for us," said Quintana, who grew up in Colombia and counts Edgar Renteria as a mentor. "He tried to say something with that, 'Hey, guys, you can do that, too.' No matter where you're coming from, we can do good things in baseball, at this level. I think he delivered that message for Latin guys."

After the win, after they trimmed that magic number for the division title to four, the Cardinals gathered in the clubhouse for their second champagne toast of history this month. They previously gathered to honor Adam Wainwright and Yadier Molina for setting the major-league record for starts by a battery, at 325. Special labels featuring Pujols, his signature, and a neon-glow "700," were prepared and packed for the possibility of Friday's feats.

Pujols was also showered in water and beer by his teammates after Wainwright and Molina stuffed him and spun him in a laundry cart.

"Imagine me jumping in there," said Pujols, 42. "I struggled getting out."

His children laughed at that line.

Marmol had a sense coming to the ballpark Friday that the confluence of events—a return to Dodger Stadium, a playoff chase, Hollywood, and his family at the ballpark—primed the weekend for something special, just not so soon, or so rapidly in back-to-back at-bats. During his post-game toast of the newest 700 man, Marmol touched on that and Pujols' promise in spring.

"That's what he's known for—doing big things in the big moments," Marmol said. "That's what I told the club. This is just helping us win. His whole thing coming back and signing was, 'I can help you win a championship and in the midst of doing that he's hitting homers.'"

Not too far from the bat rack from which Ramirez pulled the AP5 that had one remarkable game before retirement, and not quite out of sight from the dugout, Pujols found a spot to be alone after No. 700.

His manager saw him crouch down, put his face in his hands, and remain still.

"Coolest part for me," Marmol said. "Him by himself, no cameras, no nothing, just him taking in the moment."

A few hours later, still sticky from some beer spritz, Pujols mentioned the people who came to mind in the calm that came after 700. He mentioned his grandmother, his father, his family in the Dominican Republic, and the others who could be watching. He talked about the scout who befriended him and quit when Tampa Bay didn't draft him. Fernando Arango, who was later hired by the Cardinals, "was somebody who believed in me in 1999. Someone I almost considered my dad." Arango died several years ago of cancer, Pujols said, and he paused in the dugout to think how Arango's would have been the first text he received about No. 700.

Pujols was soon back with teammates, grinning with Molina, and watching home runs from several of the youngest hitters on the roster light up the scoreboard. The scoring that began with Pujols' Nos. 699 and 700 home runs ended for the Cardinals when rookie Alec Burleson pinch-hit for Pujols and homered for his No. 1.

Pujols said the location of his homer meant the world.

So did the laundry.

"To do it with this uniform is even better," he said.

The jersey and the batting helmet he wore for the two homers received an authentication from Major League Baseball. They are his to keep or donate to a Hall of Fame. The bat he used also finally got that authentication, too. That happened a few steps away from where Ramirez rushed to get it and then deliver it.

As Pujols left the Cardinals' clubhouse late Friday night—one of the last players to do so—Ramirez was still tidying up with his boss and fellow clubbies.

"Picked the right bat," he said. "Part of history now."

DERRICK GOOLD is the lead baseball writer at the *St. Louis Post-Dispatch*, where he's won numerous national awards for beat writing. A University of Missouri School of Journalism graduate, he previously worked at the late, great *Rocky Mountain News* and *The Times-Picayune*. He lives with his wife, Erika, and their son, Ian, in St. Louis.

Does My Son Know You?

JONATHAN TJARKS

FROM The Ringer • MARCH 3, 2022

Waiting for a PET scan is pretty boring. The nurse brings you down a long hallway with a bunch of rooms on each side. Each is just big enough to fit a chair and a sink. They all look the same except for the picture on the wall. I've seen a pond, a lake, and some mountains.

You walk into the room, sit down, and get injected with dye. Then you have to wait an hour for it to go through your bloodstream. There is absolutely *nothing* to do. The doctors want as little brain activity as possible in order to get a better scan. You put your phone in a locker and there's no TV. You can't even bring anything to read. If you are lucky, you get some sleep. Otherwise you are left alone with your thoughts.

I got scanned for the first time last April. That's when I found out I had cancer. I had been in and out of the hospital for two months. The doctors couldn't figure out what was wrong because what I had (a Ewing's-like sarcoma with a BCOR-CCNB3 rearrangement) is so rare. Sarcomas are small tumors found in the bones and connective tissues of the body. They represent about 1 percent of new cancer cases in the United States each year among adults, and BCOR is an even tinier part of that 1 percent. The odds of me getting it were about 25 million to 1. My wife and I ran into a doctor who is friends with her parents. He asked how it felt to get hit by lightning.

Sarcomas are one of the deadliest kinds of cancers. The five-year survival rates for adults with metastatic Ewing's sarcomas are between 15 percent and 30 percent. Metastatic means the tumors have already spread through the body by the time they are diagnosed. There were too many for the doctors to count on my first scan.

Cancer is much easier to treat when it hasn't spread beyond the primary tumor. You can get chemotherapy and radiation and remove whatever is left with surgery. That's not an option for me. The doctors don't even know which tumor was my primary. They will never be able to say that I'm "cancer free," because there could always be tiny sarcomas lurking somewhere in my body that the scans miss.

That's what happened after my first chemo regimen, which lasted about six months. All the tumors were gone at the end. There were only a few potential spots they would check on my next scan. But when I came back in two months, a series of new ones had popped up.

There are two main problems. The first is that the chemo has to kill every single cancer cell in my body. Leave even one behind and that one can turn into a million. The second is that the cells that survive become more resistant to the chemo. You can't use the same type of treatment again and expect the same results. So you have to try a different kind each time they return. One of my doctors compared it to trench warfare in World War I: You build multiple lines of defense so you can keep falling back when the first gets overrun. You just eventually run out of lines.

Being diagnosed with terminal cancer doesn't happen like it does in the movies. The doctors don't actually tell you how long you have to live. They can't predict the future. What they say is: What you have will kill you at some point. We just don't know when. It could be months. It could be years. It could be longer.

The only real hope they can offer is that someone might find a cure before it's too late. All they can do for now is keep me alive as long as they can.

That means a lot of chemo and a lot of scans. My current schedule is chemo every three weeks and scans every nine. The whole process of getting scanned takes about an hour and a half. One hour to sit in the tiny waiting room and another half-hour for the actual scan.

Like I said before, it leaves you with a lot of time to think. I usually end up thinking about my son.

HIS NAME IS Jackson. He was born in late March 2020, the week after Rudy Gobert tested positive for COVID-19. He's now almost 2, which is a really fun age. We can communicate with him. He learns a new word almost every day.

He's obsessed with cars. He stomps around the house with a toy car in each hand and rolls them on any surface he can find. He cries when we drive off a busy street and he can no longer see cars driving past. Sometimes he will be in his high chair and just start saying "ooh da cays."

It makes sense when you think about it. Humans are hard-wired to fear snakes, spiders, and heights. Those things have been killing people since the beginning of time. Cars are still brand-new by comparison. Things that big and that fast *shouldn't* exist. We are just so used to them that we don't think about it anymore.

Jackson isn't used to anything. He sees a car and thinks it's the coolest thing he has ever seen in his life. One of his favorite phrases is "you see it?" He might say it 10 times a day. You never know what exactly you are supposed to be seeing. But apparently it's *something*.

Being a dad has been the greatest joy of my life. I was never someone who debated about whether or not to have a family. It's something that I had wanted ever since I was a kid. I wanted what I didn't have.

My dad was diagnosed with Parkinson's disease when I was 6. Most people know Parkinson's from Muhammad Ali or Michael

J. Fox and the shaking they see. But that's only the beginning.
Parkinson's gradually robs you of your ability to control your body.
My dad went from needing a cane to walk to a back brace and then
a walker and finally a wheelchair. Things really went south after
he had open heart surgery. His body never recovered. He had to
take so much medicine that it became hard to talk. He was there
but he was no longer *there*.

I was 12. That's the age when your parents go from authority
figures to actual people. That never happened for me and my dad.
We never got to know each other. What did he like doing? What
were his experiences growing up? What were his goals in life?

And there's the simpler stuff too. How do you tie a tie? Or
grill a burger? Or fix a car?

I had to figure it all out on my own. Now it looks like my
son might have to do the same. It was the one thing that I never
wanted for him.

I REMEMBER MY dad had a lot of tennis trophies in his office. I
never saw him play, but I was told he was good. He was 6-foot-4
and had a big serve. But the trophy he was most proud of was the
Courage Award that he got from his fitness club. It was for the
toughness he showed in fighting Parkinson's.

He went to the club all the time before he got sick. It had
tennis and racquetball courts, a swimming pool, and an outdoor
track. It's where he made most of his friends.

Everyone was supportive at first. They brought us food, drove
him places, and got him in and out of the car. But those visits
slowly dried up over time. My dad kept getting sicker and could
no longer do the things that had made them friends in the first
place. People moved, or had kids, or got busy at work. Even the
Christmas cards stopped coming. By the end, the only people
who stopped by the house were nurses and health care workers.

My dad died when I was 21. There were a bunch of people
at his funeral whom I hadn't seen in years. They all told me how
sorry they were and asked whether there was anything they could

do. All I could think was I don't know any of you. I know *of* you. I've heard your names. But I don't *know* you.

The lie that society tells us is that our friends can be our family. That's the premise of TV shows like *Friends*, *Seinfeld*, and *How I Met Your Mother*. We can all leave our hometowns behind and have exciting adventures in the big city with people that we meet. And those people will love us and take care of us and be there for us.

But life is more like what happened to the actual actors on *Friends*. Their TV reunion was the first time all six had been together in years. They still cared about each other to a degree, but they had grown apart. They were living in different cities and working different jobs and had a million different things happen to them that they didn't share as a group. It couldn't be the same as it was when they were all single and working on the same TV set.

Americans tend to put our careers first and move around the country. That's what my parents did. My dad was from Nebraska. My mom is from the Philippines. I grew up in Dallas. That's a long way from their families (although one of my mom's sisters ended up moving here). My parents tried to form a community where they lived, but they didn't really have one. Not one that lasted.

I WAS NERVOUS the first time I went to a life group. I'd joined a church the week before and one of the pastors, a guy a few years older than me, invited me. It was a smaller group of people who met at his house every week.

I remember walking up to the door and not knowing what to expect on the other side. There were about a dozen people in the living room talking to each other. I didn't know any of them besides the pastor—and I barely knew him. I didn't know what to do, so I did what most people would do: I headed over to the table with snacks.

Eventually the chatter died down and everyone sat in a circle in the living room. They all introduced themselves with an ice-breaker. Something about their favorite TV show or their favorite snack. I was thinking, either I'm supposed to say I'm an alcoholic or this is a cult.

But nothing that exciting happened. They sang a few songs and then talked about the Bible for a while. At the end of the meeting, everyone paired off to pray for each other and the pastor asked me what I thought of the group. Then he asked if I would come back. I said I guess, but I wasn't sure.

That was seven years ago. Some of those strangers from the house that first night are now some of my closest friends. It didn't happen overnight. It took me a long time to feel comfortable. I usually came after the life group had already started and left as soon as it was over.

But I was seeing the same people every week and I was telling them about my problems and they were telling me about theirs. Do that for long enough and you become friends. You get to know enough people that way and life group goes from being an obligation to something you look forward to.

Making the commitment to come every week is still hard. There are always other things to do. Sometimes you are tired or you had a long day or you just don't feel like it. It gets even harder once you get married and have kids.

Nor are the people always easy to deal with. You may not have a lot in common. You have to search for things to talk about. You can be vulnerable with people and they don't always respond how you would expect. And you certainly won't always agree with them on how they see the world.

The past two years haven't been easy. Our life group met over Zoom for a while. People ask me whether I have to be more careful because of my condition and the pandemic. But it's really the opposite. I don't have the luxury of waiting for life to get back to normal. This might be the only time that I have.

I can't imagine not being in a life group at this point. Human beings aren't supposed to go through life as faces in a crowd. It's like the song from *Cheers*. Sometimes you want to go where everybody knows your name.

Life group is a different kind of insurance. People talk a lot about medical insurance and life insurance when you get sick. But relational insurance is far more important. I didn't need my dad's money, but I could have used some of his friends.

I WISH I could say that getting diagnosed with cancer has brought me closer to God. That my faith is stronger than ever before and that it has comforted me through these tough times. I have read plenty of stories like that. But that's not really how it has worked for me.

I want to believe in a miracle. There have been people with stage IV sarcomas whose tumors never came back. No one knows why. Some things are still beyond the knowledge of medical science. I asked my doctor if I could be one of those people. He replied, "I am not the one who decides those things."

I believe in a God who does. But I also know that He has chosen not to heal me. At least not yet. And that hurts.

The only thing I can say is that there was never a promise that it would be any other way. I think about Terrence Clarke sometimes when I start to feel sorry for myself. He was a Kentucky basketball player who died in a car accident the same week I was diagnosed with cancer. He was coming from a workout. He would have been drafted in a few months.

There's a Bible passage from Jesus's brother that comes to mind: "Now listen, you who say, 'Today or tomorrow we will go to this or that city, spend a year there, carry on business and make money.' Why, you do not even know what will happen tomorrow. What is your life? You are a mist that appears for a little while and then vanishes." (James 4:13-16)

So where does that leave us, the little mists?

There are some things from the Bible that I have been leaning on over the past year:
- "Religion that God our Father accepts as pure and fault-less is this. To look after orphans and widows in their distress."—James 1:27

- "Learn to do right; seek justice. Defend the oppressed. Take up the cause of the fatherless; plead the case of the widow."—Isaiah 1:17
- "You shall not mistreat any widow or fatherless child."—Exodus 22:22

There are hundreds of verses like that. I have already told some of my friends: When I see you in heaven, there's only one thing I'm going to ask—Were you good to my son and my wife? Were you there for them? Does my son *know* you?

I don't want Jackson to have the same childhood that I did. I want him to wonder why his dad's friends always come over and shoot hoops with him. Why they always invite him to their houses. Why there are so many of them at his games. I hope that he gets sick of them.

One thing I have learned from this experience is that you can't worry about things that you can't control. I can't control what will happen to me. I don't know how long I will be there for my son. All I can do is make the most of the time that I have left. That means investing in other people so they can be there for him.

Editor's note: On September 10, 2022, Ringer senior staff writer Jonathan Tjarks passed away. You can find information about how to support Jonathan's family at theringer.com.

JONATHAN TJARKS was a senior staff writer at The Ringer, brilliantly covering the NBA and hosting *The Ringer NBA Show*. He was a devoted husband to Melissa, and his son, Jackson, was his pride and joy. He loved Jesus and Dallas, in that order. Jon passed away on September 10, 2022, after a courageous battle with bone cancer.

The Team History Must Not Forget: Ukrainian Soccer's Fight to Carry On

WRIGHT THOMPSON

FROM ESPN • DECEMBER 11, 2022

Oleksandr Petrakov looked around the airplane at his boys with both love and disgust. He sat in 1A, front left, his usual head-coach seat, as he and the Ukrainian national soccer team flew from Glasgow to Yerevan, Armenia, for their next match. They'd lost 3-0 to Scotland a few hours before, just his second loss as the national team manager, but whatever hurt inside him did not pass his lips. That was normal. He's the son of a hard-drinking Soviet factory worker and came up in the USSR athletics machine. Once he dispatched an eight-question news conference in 37 words.

"I'm a simple man," he said.

The plane's pilots, both Ukrainian, took a looping route through Eastern Europe to skirt the dangers of Ukrainian airspace. It was late September. Eleven times since the war began Petrakov's team had taken the field, every one of them in a foreign country. Nobody on the plane played cards or sang. The players sat in silence. They'd failed tonight but at least they'd done it together.

After seven hours, the team landed and took a bus to a Radisson hotel in Yerevan. The players went to bed and the staff went to work. Their head security guy, an unsmiling brick of a man named Andriy, took down a Russian flag flying on a pole in front of the hotel, ripping it off the rope. Someone called the cops and after a showdown, the flag was returned to the pole alongside all the other national flags on display.

A few hours later players filtered down through the hotel, which the support guys had turned into yet another base camp while they slept. They checked their phones to find that Russian president Vladimir Putin had instituted a draft and fighting-age Russian men were fleeing their country. Reports said flights were completely booked for days to every country that didn't require a visa and there were miles-long lines of cars at the Russian borders. Some deserters were sleeping in tents in forests. Reports from the front showed Ukrainian troops advancing towards the Oskil River while repelling Russian attacks. The players smiled.

Laminated signs directed them to the kit room (Hayq the Small), or to the meeting room (Hayq the Great), or to the place where they shared meals, always the same: pasta, chicken, fruit. Taras Stepanenko, the oldest player on the team, stopped and looked from the first floor lobby down into the hotel bar a level below and watched a replay of the previous night's loss.

The team's communication chief, Alex, leaned up against the railing, too. Some Ukrainian journalists were fiercely criticizing Petrakov for the Scotland loss, he said.

"If the team wins next two games, he'll stay," he said. "If not..."

A bright red bus waited outside to take the team to practice at a nearby stadium. The blue sky of morning had turned bruised and swollen. Snowcapped Mount Ararat vanished in the thunderheads. Trees swayed. Black clouds moved across the valley. Just before 6 p.m., as the players took the field, the sky opened. The temperature dropped and the horizon looked like an illustration in a children's Bible. Swirling winds spun raindrops into strange balls of water that glittered beneath stadium light stanchions. Petrakov stood on the pitch and screamed at his team about their lazy play the day before. They ran laps in the rain.

They kept their heads down, their shoulders folded forward. He began to run with them and looked up at the sky. A wide smile crossed his face—the first real smile from him all day. An idea formed as water ran down his nose. He seemed happy. Order and purpose emerged from their disappointment. He wagged a finger at his boys.

"There is no punishment without guilt!" he bellowed.

IT WAS MY last chance to see this Ukrainian team. Every national squad has a life cycle, depending on scheduling and tournaments, and these players were at the end of theirs. Perhaps no team in history had been asked to do so much, banding together while their lives were under siege, trying to win the biggest matches of their lives while missiles fell from the sky back home. They've all been forever changed by the experience. They've learned things about humanity and their truest selves.

That was clear from my first meeting with Petrakov back in May, when he had hope he could lead Ukraine to the 2022 World Cup in Qatar. Everyone focused on the results then, including me, but Petrakov seemed to see something deeper about a nation at war, something primal, tuned to the ways the fight creates in you the person you'll have to live with for the rest of your life. He already knew then that every wartime decision revealed either strength or weakness. He told a story about the morning of Feb. 24, the day Russia invaded Ukraine. He and his wife slept in their apartment when it began. They switched on the lights. Explosions rocked their city. His daughter came to the door with her husband. The telephone rang. It was his son.

"Dad, we have to get out of Kyiv," his son told him.

"No," Petrakov said. "I won't go anywhere."

Russian cruise missiles detonated close enough that his windows rattled. His wife went to a bunker. Petrakov stayed in their apartment. One day, early in the invasion, he went outside to buy bread. As he walked near his usual subway station he heard a whoosh above his head. He looked up. Seconds later, he felt the jolt of an explosion. The blast killed a girl and a boy, a father and a mother. Petrakov was 64 years old. He wanted to join the fight. As a young man, he'd served in the Soviet Army. Now he went to a local Territorial Defense Forces recruiting office to volunteer. The soldiers told him that he could serve the nation best by coaching his team.

"Just win," they said.

At sandbag and concrete checkpoints near his apartment, Petrakov brought food and cigarettes to soldiers standing watch. He asked about them, about their homes. Petrakov loves Kyiv. Sometimes he has let himself imagine what it will be like after the fighting stops. His eyes and smile seem lit from within when he narrates the future. One day many years from now, if he's lucky, he will walk down the sidewalk on one of Kyiv's wide avenues and he'll pass a café and see some of his former players sharing a toast. They will crowd around a small table and remember bygone days of football and war.

The national team coaches and players first came together seven weeks after the invasion began, playing matches in Scotland, Wales, Ireland, Poland and Armenia. They've become brothers. They've fought together to win and leaned on each other when they lost. They've taken the field long after the world's attention moved on to other things. They've played in games without visible stakes. They've trained miles from home and hungered for updates from family and friends.

Now in Armenia, they were aware their efforts might soon slip into the realm of memory. And so each game, each moment, meant all the more to them. "At first, the Ukrainian anthem before the game did not cause me any feelings," Petrakov said one afternoon as he wiped tears from his eyes. "But now when the anthem plays at the beginning of the game, I feel like a real Ukrainian. This has never happened to me before. Then I'm ready to tear everybody apart on the field."

It was Thursday. Two more games remained, one Saturday in Armenia and another Tuesday night in Krakow, Poland. Then the players would scatter to their clubs around Europe and the coaches and staff would return to Ukraine. They wouldn't gather again until March 2023—at the end of what they knew would surely be the worst winter in their nation's history.

PETRAKOV WORKED OUT alone in the stark hotel gym and then moved through the halls in a practiced orbit, emotional quantum mechanics, checking on players and coaches. The best coaching he's done with this team has had little to do with football strategy. When he looks down his roster, he sees a map of scattered families. He knows who has a brother in the army or parents trapped in occupied basements. The whole world has seen his boys stand at attention for the national anthem, but Petrakov alone has looked into their eyes just before they take the field and as they return to the privacy of their changing room. He knows their birthdays. Only two of his players—his captain Andriy Yarmolenko and Stepanenko—were born before the collapse of the Berlin Wall. Most of his team have only lived in a free Ukraine and don't remember the past. Petrakov tells them of the world before independence. He has seen a country simply cease to exist.

They pledged to reject all Western values in the Soviet days, but his cool older brother knew the local speculator who could score black market Beatles albums and Levi's. Petrakov loved Donna Summer and ABBA. Today his players chuckle when he dribbles a ball around before practice or takes a shot on goal. They wouldn't have laughed when he was a young man, a feared defender who made opponents pay for even approaching the goal.

He was born in 1957, four years after the death of Josef Stalin and four years before Yuri Gagarin completed the first manned orbit of earth. He lived through the peak and the decline of the Soviet empire. His playing career declined with it. In 1990, the last full year of the Soviet Union, he returned to Kyiv after finishing a run with a professional side in Budapest. "When I returned from Hungary, it was a new country, there was nothing in the shops," Petrakov said. "No one knew what to do. Everyone lived for the day. There were no prospects. There were no jobs. The professors were selling cars. PhDs would take any job to support their families."

He found work as a player for a semipro team near Chernobyl—five years after the nuclear meltdown—before injuries pushed him off the field and onto the sideline. In 1991, the year Ukraine declared independence, Oleksandr Petrakov became a football coach. He was 34 years old and remembers struggling to make enough to feed his two children. But he also remembers clearly the day of Ukrainian independence.

"We talked about football," he said.

OVER THE YEARS, Petrakov found his niche with youth teams and his career seemed to peak when his team won the U-20 World Cup in 2019. Ukrainian football was on the rise. The men's national team reached the quarterfinals of the 2020 Euros, coached by the greatest Ukrainian player, Ballon d'Or winner Andriy Shevchenko—whose poster hung on the wall of nearly every child's bedroom in the country.

Shevchenko and federation president Andriy Pavelko got into a public battle and Shevchenko resigned. As fans howled at the loss of such a legend, Pavelko looked desperately for a new coach. He turned to Petrakov, who'd never held a job near the level of the one he was being offered now. Petrakov said yes. Then he went home and looked around his flat in a modest building near the Kyiv Zoo.

"It was night," he said. "I sat down thinking, 'What have I done?'"

He told that story in Ukrainian. The war has made language itself a battlefield. "Since Aug. 17, the day I started, I've spoken Ukrainian," Petrakov said. "I had never spoken it before."

No Ukrainian coach had ever spoken Ukrainian in public.

The Soviet Union waged a cultural war on every part of the nation's identity, so Russian was the native tongue of every member of the Ukrainian national team. When Russia annexed Crimea and invaded portions of Ukrainian territory in 2014, language and culture became increasingly politicized. By trying to destroy a culture, Putin helped create one. Traditional Ukrainian food experienced a renaissance in the bistros of Kyiv. Lifelong Russian speakers searched their grade school memories for fragments of Ukrainian vocabulary.

At practice one afternoon I watched Petrakov yell instructions to the team in Russian. Then a camera crew arrived.

"In Ukrainian, please," he reminded his team.

Now the entire team speaks Ukrainian in public. Many of their fellow citizens do, as well. One morning in a team hotel, the unified heavyweight champion of the world, Oleksandr Usyk, ate breakfast with his young sons. They'd come to town for a game. His boys would ask him questions in Russian but he never failed to reply, even to them, in Ukrainian.

Yarmolenko, Petrakov's captain, looks like a star, with trendy shoes and a carefully managed beard, but he always seems pitched slightly forward, aggressive, ready. Whenever he hears someone speak Russian, in say, London or Dubai, he will start speaking Ukrainian. Loudly. Almost begging them to start a fight.

The war is being contested over territory, yes, but also over identity. In the main squares of Kyiv, sandbags cover statues and monuments to protect them from Russian attack. Putin has written about his theory that there is no such thing as Ukraine, that the nation was created by the West to fracture Russian power and regional control.

"Russians and Ukrainians were one people—a single whole," he wrote last year.

He blames the West for everything wrong with his nation. He criticizes Lenin. He praises Stalin. The fragile web of irrelevant facts and misrepresentations, the basis for every good conspiracy, is laughed at by historians but taken as gospel by many Russian citizens. Putin calls Kyiv the "mother of all Russian cities" and his assault on the capital isn't just about oil or shipping routes, but about grievance and pride. If Ukrainians exist then Russians don't have a divine right to control their corner of the world.

"All evil things in the world come from short people," Petrakov said with a sneer.

We sat in a café on an off day.

"Kyiv has always been called the mother of Rus cities," he said and launched into what was omitted from Putin's essays. More than a thousand years ago, a great civilization rose in Kyiv, the Kyivan Rus', which was rooted in Orthodox Christianity and ruled a huge expanse of territory stretching from the Black Sea to Scandinavia. In the 1200s, the Mongol armies sacked Kyiv and broke apart the Kyivan Rus'. The people scattered and are still dealing with the consequences of that defeat. Some drifted west and became Ukrainians. Some Belarusians. And others moved northeast and turned Moscow from a timber-walled frontier fort into the center of a new empire. For Russia, not having control of Kyiv means it can't rewrite history to put itself at the center of it. Leaders as far back as Catherine the Great tried to erase even the idea of a Ukrainian people and history, and Putin is using artillery barrages and cruise missiles and Iranian drones toward the same end. As the Ukrainian military advances toward the Russian border, the Ukrainian citizens defend the ideas that underpin their old culture and new country alike.

"From here Kyivan Rus' began," Petrakov insisted. "Not the other way around."

THE NEWLY HIRED Petrakov and his Ukrainian-speaking team started winning games in the fall of 2021, beating Finland and then Bosnia in World Cup qualifiers. They earned a spot in a playoff scheduled for March. If they beat Scotland and Wales, two difficult road matches, they'd qualify for just the second World Cup in the history of their country. As January arrived, the Biden administration began warning the Ukrainian government that a Russian invasion looked imminent. Petrakov didn't believe it. He'd played with Russian teammates. "We were like brothers," he said. "I don't know how to explain it. They lost their minds." The war began with Russian tanks rushing across the border and Russian planes flying bombing runs on civilian targets and airborne troopers landing at strategic airports. The global military community wondered if Ukraine might fall in days under this multifront assault, but the citizen-soldiers and the Ukrainian army held firm. A band of outgunned defenders told the captain of a Russian warship to "go f---" himself.

Some national team players hid in freezing bunkers, while others sought refuge in the west part of the country. Some of the major professional teams opened up training facilities and entire families moved in for safety. Later many would describe not thinking about football for the first time in their lives. Even Petrakov found he couldn't watch matches on television. He tried to keep his team together, finding out where everyone was living, calling to check on them.

"Don't worry about football!" man after man told him. "It's a war!"

Petrakov didn't want to leave Kyiv and he didn't want to hide in a bomb shelter. The army didn't want a man of his age. That left football. UEFA floated the idea of petitioning for an automatic spot in the World Cup, but Ukrainian federation president Pavelko and Petrakov said no. They'd earn their way or stay home. Pavelko begged for the qualifying matches to be postponed and FIFA agreed. The games were moved to June. On the day they would have played their first qualifier against Scotland, raid sirens sounded all over east and central Ukraine. Heavy shelling pushed the citizens of Kharkiv further underground. The Ukrainian military destroyed 18 air targets and sank a large warship.

A week later, in early April, Ukrainian forces won the Battle of Kyiv.

In the capital, people began to stand up. Skateboarders did tricks in public squares, the air alive with the scrape of trucks on concrete and metal. Hipsters held court in shabby chic cocktail bars with names like The Cinematographer's Party. Wedding chapels couldn't keep up with the volume. Three brides before lunch on a Wednesday. Huge groups sat around tables in Georgian restaurants with plates of grilled meat and bottles of semisweet wine. Petrakov went to view the horrors in the northern suburbs of Kyiv. He saw where Russian tanks had been stopped within sight of the city. He could picture his boys as part of the resistance, an instrument of a nation standing up and fiercely getting on with life. He picked up his phone and put his team back together.

"He called everyone," goalkeeper Dmytro Riznyk said, "asking how we were doing, how our families were, where we were. He was worried about all of us."

His players arrived in camp in Slovenia out of shape a month after the Battle of Kyiv ended. The staff hooked up monitors to them during those first training sessions and were appalled at their fitness levels. Petrakov looked out from his fancy hotel room window and saw a rolling rural paradise near the training field. He stepped outside and breathed clean, quiet air and thought about those guys manning the bunker on his street in Kyiv. "Even birds are chirping," he said. "In the meantime, our warriors sleep in foxholes and trenches."

The players' minds were in worse shape than their bodies. Everyone worried. One young player said that the hotel's bland elevator music, played as a soundtrack to his thoughts of home, threatened to drive him mad. "Our cause is to play football. It's very hard," Petrakov said. "Everyone has something else in his head. Someone has relatives where the fighting is going on, someone's relatives are dying. I see it all. My guys are always calling. It is very hard. To understand that you have to be in our shoes. God forbid you ever know what war is."

They made the short trip from their hotel to the training pitch and between the lines, surrounded by old forests and towering blue skies, they got a break from the war. These short hours were the only time they didn't carry their phones. The eyes of the world were on them. A documentary crew from Japan followed them. One from America, too. A reporter from an important Spanish newspaper stood on the sidelines of training, as did one from London. Petrakov and his team did every interview. They thanked every interviewer.

The team arrived for the match in Scotland 10 days later to find a gift from President Volodymyr Zelenskyy, who had just visited the front and asked soldiers there to sign a blue and yellow Ukrainian flag for the team. The flag hung in the dressing room before the game and the players quietly read the messages. Many soldiers had written "4.5.0," Ukrainian military code for "everything is fine, everything is calm." *We're good.*

The team defeated Scotland 3-1, and Petrakov ran onto the pitch in the seconds after the whistle, flexing his arms and screaming in the direction of roaring Ukrainian refugees and expats. The victory set up a deciding game. Beat Wales and qualify for Qatar.

They lost.

One to nil in the driving Welsh rain, on an own goal by their captain Yarmolenko.

Petrakov walked into the postgame news conference and took all the blame. He said he'd let down the nation. When he finished, the reporters gave him an ovation. As he left, he turned back towards the room and begged everyone not to forget his nation and the people fighting there. A trip to the World Cup would have brought a lot of attention, needed attention, and he didn't want this failure to hurt the efforts of those in the foxholes and trenches. His face twisted in unnatural snarls, his body trying to expel this feeling while awakening to the knowledge that it would be with him forever.

They went back to their hotel on the south side of Cardiff after losing the biggest match they'd ever play. Yarmolenko locked himself in his room and skipped dinner. Petrakov couldn't sleep. He looked out his window and saw the Ferris wheel that rose up from the Cardiff docks. The lights flashed and changed colors and the wheel went around and around. He lost himself in the repetition. Hours passed. A strange illness swept through the team that night, with most of the starting eleven running fevers as high as 104.

For months they'd all imagined one version of glory. They'd qualify for the World Cup while Russia sat at home, banned by FIFA, and shine light on the Ukrainian cause. They'd even allowed themselves to imagine going down in history. All that was gone in an instant. If they weren't the team that defied all odds and brought honor to their country on a global stage, who were they? Petrakov stared at the Ferris wheel. He could feel the world's attention slipping away. They'd let down their fans. Their country. This moment had been coming since Feb. 24 and he faced a choice now that would define the rest of his life: Hide or fight? *What happens if I, the head coach of the national team, lose heart and give up?*

The team had their next match in Dublin three days later. They were playing in the Nations League, a minor tournament designed to make money for UEFA more than anything else.

Yarmolenko skipped the team lunch. Then he skipped dinner, too.

The next morning, Petrakov knocked on his captain's door.

"It is so hard for me that this happened," Yarmolenko said. "Do you understand me?"

"That day is over. It will never come back," Petrakov said. "We need to get together and start from the beginning."

Part II: Band of Brothers

Taras Stepanenko sat alone at a table in the hotel lobby bar. He smiled at me and gestured to an empty seat.

"Have a coffee," he said.

It was the morning before the Armenia match in September. We'd been in Yerevan for two days. He pulled up the live security feeds from his home in Kyiv. The cameras still work.

"I love my home," he said. "I want to come back."

He showed me the different views with pride. One camera shows the Dnipro River flowing behind his yard. Another shows the trees and flowers. Stepanenko loved the trees most, watching them grow from seeds along with his children. His wife planted berries and vegetables. Gardening is in her blood. Her grandparents left their village when the war began, moving into the Stepanenkos' riverfront home near Kyiv. They lasted about ten days before returning to the active warzone. Her grandmother wouldn't abandon her garden. She had put those seeds in the ground.

Stepanenko feels homesick a lot. So much has been lost already. His home in Donetsk was wrecked by a bomb. His caretaker sent photos that showed how slivers of shrapnel cut through every wall—"like cheese"—and he felt grateful he wasn't there at the time. The village where he grew up has been destroyed. The city where he moved to as a boy looks like something from a black and white newsreel. For now, his wife and children are living in Spain by the beach. His kids go to school with Russian kids. There are fights on the playgrounds. Stepanenko, who once got into the most famous on-field brawl in the Ukrainian league's history, told his children to walk away; they couldn't afford to get expelled, not when they were lucky to have a safe place to live.

Sitting in the lobby, he talked about life after the Wales match. He went home alone to Kyiv. The guards greeted him as he pulled through the gate. He lives in the wealthy suburbs on the same side of the city as Bucha.

Stepanenko's kids went to school with kids from Bucha, which is no longer known for its bucolic surroundings. Now and forever, it will be the place where the Russian army set up an ambush along a supposedly safe civilian evacuation route. As the Russians retreated, they cut people down and left them to rot, leaving behind corpses with ears cut off and teeth removed.

Residents risked their lives to bury strangers and later those shallow holes were uncovered and the bodies removed for proper burial. I went to Bucha while the Ukraine team played Scotland in qualifying this past summer. A hollow-eyed man named Denys showed me the way from his home to one of those graves. The walk took a few minutes. He narrated along the way but there was a delay while his descriptions were translated to me in English. It added menace to his tour. He showed me the chicken coop where he hid from Russians looking to kill him and the long tree-lined country lane where civilians were gunned down. All four of Denys' grandparents are Russian. His family in Russia insists that his neighbors committed suicide to make Russia look bad, he told me.

"I think they're zombies," he said.

We came to a barbed wire fence and slipped beneath a loose strand. Our security contractor, a retired SAS operator, asked about land mines. Denys told him not to worry and then walked us to a shallow hole, maybe 3 or 4 feet deep. He pointed. I leaned in and saw comforters and a woman's dress. The man started talking as I looked into the hole. It took me a moment to realize the splotches on the fabric were bloodstains. My translator began explaining. This was a mass grave. Bodies had been uncovered and returned to their families when Russian troops were pushed back. The shovel used in the work remained standing upright next to the hole.

The bloody dress was robin's egg blue.

THE FIRST THING Stepanenko did in Kyiv after the Wales match was lay down in the soft grass of his backyard. The river ran nearby. Flowers and trees stretched toward the sky above him.

But the kids' toys weren't left at odd angles around the yard. Nobody kicked a ball or climbed a tree or ran. There wasn't a barbecue or a birthday party or even a lazy weekend sunset to look upon. Just silence.

He stayed alone like this for two hours.

He wore sandals because shoes wouldn't fit on the foot he'd injured in the Wales loss. Everything hurt. He thought seriously about quitting international football.

"But if I retire from the national team, I won't be useful for my country," he said.

So he was back on the road playing these final matches that, from afar, seemed rather meaningless and from inside mattered a great deal. They were fighting for their coach. They were playing for their colors. Wearing the Ukrainian jersey gave Stepanenko and his teammates purpose. That purpose was in its final days, too. I'd been surprised at the intensity of practice sessions in Yerevan, but now I understood a little about what was happening around me. They were proving something, to their fans, certainly, but also to themselves. A few days later before their final match in Krakow, Yarmolenko would sit down to tell me that he won't ever be healed after the own goal against Wales, but these "meaningless" games have provided some measure of grace. "A strong athlete is not the one who wins and then rejoices in his victory," he said. "A strong athlete is one who can get back on his feet after a defeat."

When the war began, Stepanenko wanted to join the military and was told by friends and family to keep playing and to use his gifts for the glory of Ukraine. If glory is gone now, fidelity remains. Persistence remains. He thinks about the soldiers. "My emotion is always with them," he said, struggling to find the words in English. "My heart and ... and soul are always with them. Every day I pray about them. I don't know how to explain this. It's very difficult because it's inside your soul."

Watching him run in the rain felt a lot like watching a man search for a home. Home isn't the bombed apartment in Donetsk, and it's no longer an erased village, or a silent mansion along the banks of the Dnipro River. It's not this hotel, or the next hotel, nor is it a rented roof in a Spanish beach resort town. The cocoon of this team brings him comfort but that's not home, either. The closest he feels to home is when he checks his phone for news about the war. Home is a connection, a thread. In the lobby in Armenia, he switched from his security cameras to his Telegram app where he gets the latest dispatches from the front.

"This morning was the news that nine missiles came to Zaporizhzhia and destroyed one important restaurant for my family," he said. "When we had birthdays, our parents celebrated in this restaurant. Six people died."

THAT EVENING STEPANENKO went to practice.

The stadium in Yerevan sat in a bowl and he looked up at the laundry hanging from balconies and an old Soviet building crumbling on top of a nearby hill. Stepanenko ran hard, jockeying close to the team's young star forward Mykhailo Mudryk—the future of Ukrainian football, soon to be 22—and deftly stealing the ball. Stepanenko gave him a little pat afterwards, as if to remind him that experience remained undefeated against youth.

Petrakov stood at midfield and ran his players through drills.

"Faster! Faster!" he yelled.

He grinned at the intensity.

"Very good, boys!" he said. "No mistakes! No mistakes!"

They moved like lions. Later the biometric sensors would reveal this to be the first practice with everyone at pre-invasion levels. It had taken months to repair what the war had damaged and now that they were whole again, their time together was nearly at an end. It seemed unfair. They had needed this kind of fitness on that rain-soaked day in Wales. Perhaps they would be training for Qatar right now. Perhaps there would be folk songs written about them.

Petrakov pushed them harder still.

"Where's your character?" he yelled.

Those were the stakes then. Not wins or losses or advancing in some silly tournament. They were playing to be worthy of their fans.

The team spent the last part of the day defending corner kicks, which cost them their last game. With less than seven minutes left in practice, Stepanenko ran hard into the space in front of the goal and flung himself at the ball. He rammed his head into a teammate and they both hit the ground clutching their skulls.

Stepanenko got the worst of it and the trainers helped him to the bench. He held a blue ice pack on his head. The medical staff crowded around him as he moved the ice pack back and forth between his hands as his arms got tired.

Petrakov came over to check on him.

"How are you?"

Stepanenko leaned back and smiled a little.

"I was hit by a train."

Petrakov said something quietly to his star player and then reached over and gently touched his head, like a father caring for a child with a fever.

OUTSIDE THE STADIUM as the team left, and inside the hotel as they returned, Ukrainian fans waited to thank the players. This happens everywhere they go. There's a rhythm to these encounters. Just after the photograph, the fan whispers something. It never lasts more than a few seconds.

"Not only are the Ukrainian people happy to see us," Yarmolenko said. "We, too, are really happy to see our Ukrainian people."

I saw that proved true over and over again. One memory from the past six months will remain with me forever. I'd traveled to Italy to meet the Ukrainian team for an exhibition match in the hills west of Florence. A crowd of adults and children sat together in a VIP section just off the pitch. The kids cheered while the adults fought back tears. While we waited for kickoff a woman described her escape from Ukraine when the war began. She and her family pulled into some little village early in the morning to find the residents waiting at the main intersection, offering refugees a place to sleep. They followed an old man and woman to their home and walked inside to find the table set for a full dinner. The next day her husband drove her and their children to the border. He stayed behind to fight. Their oldest son joined him.

In Italy one of the adults stood next to me on the side of the pitch. I looked at this huge group of kids and wondered how they came to be at this game. The woman told me calmly that she was an aid worker and many of these children were orphans. The aid worker explained it was vital to get them to safety because among the many atrocities inflicted by the Russians during this war, perhaps the cruelest is a systematic push to place Ukrainian orphans with loyal Russian families. She never cried telling me this story, not even when relating the most violent details, but she sobbed when the national anthem played on the stadium stereo. The players want to play for *her*. "Each one of them understands why he is here," Yarmolenko said. "Each one is aware that all of Ukrainians stand behind him, that the entire country is going to watch him play."

THE NEXT DAY Petrakov gathered the team in the lobby and asked for their attention.

"Let's go for a walk," he said.

Every match day they all walk together through the city where they'll soon play. It's a way to feel connected to the outside world, to see and to allow themselves to be seen. I think they walk together to lessen the load any one individual might be carrying alone. They listen to each other. They listen to fellow refugees. They carry these stories with them.

Stepanenko talked to the team's young goalkeeper Dmytro Riznyk.

The two of them looked like regular football players. They wore tracksuits and sneakers. They walked on the balls of their feet like predators. They looked like any other team.

But Stepanenko has lost a home and his family's village.

Riznyk is a tall, baby-faced new father who sits in the lobby of these endless hotels and FaceTimes with the little boy who was born the night the war began.

"A small child, only ten hours old, and you cannot take him anywhere, because it is a newborn baby," he said. "He has no immunity. It's scary."

The child came home from the hospital to a world of nightly air raid sirens. The family developed a routine. Riznyk would wrap the baby in two jumpsuits, and a cocoon of blankets, and take him down into the cold basement. They kept a diaper bag packed in case they stayed there all night.

Coach led the way on the team walk, moving slowly with his hands behind his back. Every so often he'd stop and stare though the haze at the faint outline of Mount Ararat, where the Bible says Noah's Ark came to rest. Petrakov turned toward the southwest. Two peaks towered over the city skyline, both covered in snow and connected by a long rocky ridgeline. I stopped and looked with him. He seemed deep in thought. Just taking the field tonight would be an achievement, he believed. "The game should be the only thing in their head, but in their head is Mum and Dad in Odesa," Petrakov said, "Grandma and Grandpa somewhere else. Someone died, someone went missing. It's terrible."

The team walked past a World War II memorial and kept going until they could see the whole valley. We stood together and I imagined all this before concrete and rebar and global shipping routes. Once this was just a valley and a river, green fields and wildflowers and people who only went to the jagged higher ground when threatened. All the coaches, players and staff lingered for a moment. They long for their valleys.

Petrakov turned and headed back to the hotel, talking the whole way with his main tactical adviser. They made plans to rest a lot of the stars against a weak Armenian team and to take the field in Krakow with their best players rested and ready. The air smelled like evergreen trees.

The midfielder Oleksandr Karavayev followed his coach back through the park. He's from Kherson, a then-occupied city south of Kyiv. The Russians captured it during the first days of the war. In September Putin had announced a referendum that would make that city part of Russia. Karavayev was always trying to contact his parents. They lived in Kherson. Once they lost the internet and went three days without answering. The scars of those three days won't ever go away.

When he spoke of his father, Karavayev broke down crying. "I saw my father going to work," he said. "There was no money, but he would bring bread and some other food in the evening for us to eat in the morning. And he went to work again at 5:00 a.m. I remember that and it remains in my heart and soul. It will stay there forever."

As he fought the tears something familiar happened: thinking about his family made him think about the situation at home. So many times, a Ukrainian would start talking about something they loved, or hated, or missed, and with no warning they would suddenly be talking about the war. No part of life remained untouched. The idea of a father's sacrifice made him think about the sacrifices everyone is making and then he could barely get out any words at all.

"Because of this war there are always tears in my eyes because..." he said between sobs, "... I don't understand why people ... can't live in peace."

THE GAME AGAINST Armenia passed with no drama, a rare easy win for Ukraine, who scored five goals and allowed none. Petrakov and his team loaded on the bus. A police escort rushed them past all the sidewalk coffee kiosks, the shipping container barbecue stands, the neon dance club signs out on the edge of town. There are few energies in the world as pure and electric as a victorious sports team traveling to the next city after a triumph and for the first time they just felt like a team who'd won a game. They deserved that small mercy. The drive to the airport took maybe 15 minutes. The bus parked at the terminal and everyone rushed through security.

They laughed in the aisles of the duty free.

Stepanenko read the labels of Armenian cognac bottles.

"I asked the barman," he said. "He said the 10-year is very nice."

They filtered out through the shop and then the terminal. Their charter flight waited at Gate 3. Next door was a flight to Moscow. Riznyk cracked open a Sprite. Stepanenko walked around with a Louis Vuitton backpack. Petrakov got some wine to take home. Soon it was time to board. Stepping onto the jet bridge Petrakov reached out and touched the shoulder of the player in front of him. His boys. He took his usual seat, 1A, cracking open a novel with yellowed pages. The plane sat idling on the tarmac, white with a blue tail and nothing written on the side, as the guys found their seats, too.

Players near the back passed around a bottle. Alex, the team public relations man, got on the microphone and started listing off all the statistics from that night's game.

"Yeah, yeah," they jeered in laughter. "Calm down!"

He grinned, too.

"Glory to Ukraine!" he shouted before passing back the mic.

The five flight attendants did the safety presentation. They were all from Ukraine and wanted pictures but felt too nervous to ask. Soon the pilot rolled up the throttles and the plane accelerated down the runway. The flutter of shuffling cards began in the back. Several poker games happened at once. Drum machine trills filtered from a pair of headphones. Twenty-three brothers climbed out over the lights of Yerevan. The plane bucked and shook, rising through the clouds, bouncing side to side a few times as the last of the city lights vanished and everything turned dark.

They were alone.

Mudryk stretched out on a row by himself.

Stepanenko sat up front closer to coach than the card games.

Yarmolenko held court in the back.

The pilot came on the speaker and sketched out their route through the night sky, heading over Turkey, skirting the coast of the Black Sea, then flying over Romania, Hungary, Slovakia and finally landing in Poland. Folks poured whiskey or champagne into the airline coffee cups. Guys told stories and laughed. The card games heated up. The plane didn't have Wi-Fi so nobody followed war news on their phone. They were truly alone.

Eventually the plane drew even with Crimea, the Black Sea dark and dangerous below them, the waters dotted with Russian warships carrying Kalibr cruise missiles. The crew dimmed the lights and some guys slept. Those playing cards sang together, some Ukrainian folk tunes and a famous old Italian ballad.

Every guy on the plane had a story about what this war has made them abandon. But they'd gained something, too. They'd gained each other. They're not the winningest team, or the most famous team, but they might be the closest team ever assembled, welded by shared trauma and purpose, and none of them will ever forget. They will remember this flight. They will remember the furious noise of beating Scotland and the silence of losing to Wales. They will remember who stood shoulder-to-shoulder with them for both. They will remember drinking duty-free scotch and singing old-fashioned love songs.

Roman Yaremchuk put somebody in a headlock. He and Yarmolenko were the ringleaders in the rowdy back of the plane. When the war began, Yaremchuk found out that his wife's parents were trapped behind enemy lines. He didn't know what to do. His first thought was to call his captain, who was from the city where Yaremchuk's in-laws were trapped. Yarmo, a famous and important man, started working the phones. He used his fame to help a teammate. Soon a military contact organized a mission and the Ukrainian army went in the middle of the night to rescue Yaremchuk's family. Armed men arrived at the door and led them in darkness to a small boat. The soldiers dipped the oars into the water with precision and silently rowed them across a river to safety. Yarmolenko shrugged off even the whiff of praise for his actions, saying that he just did what any teammate would have done for him. The players will remember giving help and asking for it. They will never forget.

The flight attendants announced final approach into Krakow. The plane landed with a little sideways hop and shimmy and the clink of rolling bottles brought on muffled laughter.

"Oh f---!" someone yelled.

What a rare, great night, a chance to forget the games and the war and just enjoy each other, free at 30,000 feet from schedules and news from home, living for a few hours outside the reach of time. The guys looked bleary but happy shuffling through the line at passport control. Finally Petrakov got to a Polish border guard. He held out his documents and smiled.

"Would you accept another Ukrainian in your country?" he asked.

Part III: The Last Dance

The team drove away from their hotel in Krakow to a local team's modern training complex, tucked into a reclaimed patch of forested swamp. Tiny bugs swarmed everywhere. All the players jogged around the pitch. Petrakov dribbled a ball around at the parking lot end of the field and took a shot into the net. The guys chirped at him as they passed.

Eventually they started a 5-on-5 scrimmage. It quickly turned aggressive. The team found a new gear. Everyone felt it. A beast came alive on a random practice field in the rural hills west of Krakow. The Nations League is a considered a farce of a tournament but that's clearly not how Petrakov and his boys saw it. If someone gives them a time and a place they will turn up in their blue and yellow uniforms and show all comers that everything a Ukrainian citizen does right now matters.

"This is not just some routine for us," Yarmolenko said. "This is a chance."

A crowd gathered to watch the scrimmage.

Yarmolenko played for one side. Stepanenko played for the other. They dominated the play. Not so long ago they hated each other. Now they are brothers. Yarmolenko scored first in the scrimmage and blew a kiss in the air. He appeared again young and boundless. Stepanenko marked him, playing on a third of the field, everything full speed.

Petrakov shouted at them joyfully.

Everyone scrapped, grinding and surging, preparing for this last match like a World Cup. They went hard. Nothing in the end is meaningless. Everyone knew about Petrakov's fight to keep his job. Everyone knew the news back home. Sirens in Kharkiv and Kherson. Their air defense net shot down an Iranian drone. The Russians shelled 25 towns and villages along the front. Seven missiles, 22 airstrikes and 67 artillery strikes were reported in the East. Stepanenko's hometown was hit again.

Petrakov sipped from a hot cup of tea and talked with his tactical advisor on the side of the pitch. He knew what to expect from their familiar opponent Scotland, who only needed a draw to win their group in the Nations League.

"They will close down and counterattack," he said.

PETRAKOV LED THE team for the ritual gameday walk through a leafy park on the banks of the Vistula River. He raged as he walked. Two Ukrainian journalists who've been fiercely criticizing him for his decisions seemed to live inside his head. Their news organization is owned by a businessman with ties to Russia, and the old coach, Shevchenko, remains one of the most popular figures in the nation. His critics are, as he says, "burying him alive," and he should know because he sees every word.

"I cannot stop reading," he said.

Standing around the ground floor of the hotel in Krakow he asked if we could switch to Russian. His Ukrainian vocabulary couldn't convey his rage. I said yes. But instead of continuing to rant about the journalists he launched a purple, beautiful screed against the Russians—especially the Russians he once called friends. He has erased them from his phone. The war has destroyed ordinary people's ability to separate their fear and anger into separate silos. Everyone felt everything all the time.

What does this kind of responsibility (and visibility) do to a person? A normal person with a simple life and modest home. When he took this job, he said, he never even asked what his salary would be. For him it was always an act of patriotism. Coaching the Ukrainian national team was the honor of a lifetime, whether his tenure ended Tuesday night or whether he kept coaching for years to come.

"Do you ever think about what your parents would say about you doing this job?"

"Yes, of course," he said quietly.

His dad died in 1989 and never saw a free Ukraine. His mother died in 2011. He was sitting in Poland but thinking about home. His eyes got red and glassy. "My father would have thrown a big banquet and cried with pride," he said. "I often go to their gravesites."

His lip started to betray him.

Standing alone in that cemetery he has made sure they know their son has made good, that he didn't run when his moment of reckoning arrived.

"I talk to them," he said.

THE HOTEL IN Krakow was full of Ukrainian fans. They hung around the lobby and sat in the bar or on the couches down by the elevators. One of them wanted to tell me a story about himself and Stepanenko. He's an old soldier, he explained to me. His name was Oleksandr Kosolapov and his eyes were cold blue. We walked over to the bar and settled into the flimsy and vaguely Scandinavian chairs.

"September 19, 1984," he said.

That's when he got shot in Afghanistan. Thirty-eight years ago.

He smiled at me.

"An American M16 bullet," he said.

The round tore through his chest—he's missing half a lung—but didn't hit anything else. Six days before his 21st birthday he awoke in a hospital. A voice inside told him he must stand or die. He tried and collapsed to the floor. Nurses got him back in the bed. When he was alone, he tried again. This time, despite a wobble, he managed to count one ... two ... three. He knew then he'd survive.

When the Soviet Union collapsed he found himself a veteran with no nation. Technically he lived in Ukraine, but he led a Russian life with the Russian language and Russian customs and identity. "I was absolutely Russian," he said. "My father is Russian. Half my blood is Russian."

He paused.

"My mother is Ukrainian."

He remembered clearly when he first felt Ukrainian. Nearly 20 years ago he traveled to the capital city of his region, Luhansk, and found himself in one of the big squares. Security folks set up barricades and he asked what was going on.

Viktor Yushchenko was speaking.

Yushchenko was running for president against the puppet handpicked by Moscow. He was an underdog with Ukrainian identity at the core of his platform. The old soldier Kosolapov decided it took courage for a man with those beliefs to come to such a pro-Russian region and make his case. He would stay and listen.

"One by one, a nation is formed..." Kosolapov said.

Yushchenko talked about simple things. *This vote was an important moment for Ukraine. Their future as an independent nation was at stake.* All this made sense to Kosolapov. *We must build a new Ukrainian country. We must say to the whole world we are not Russian. We are Ukrainian. We have a culture. We have a history.* But that's not what made Kosolapov decide to turn his back on his political views and follow a new leader. Something else did that.

When the speech ended Yushchenko passed ten feet from Kosolapov. A month before he'd been famously poisoned with dioxin and nearly died.

"When I saw the color of his face..." the soldier told me, going back into his memory, taking long pauses. "I was..."

Old soldiers often end up back on the battlefield in their minds.

"... On October 2, 1983 my commander died in my arms."

When the fighting ended Kosolapov went to see his commander's body. "I remember the color of his face, 40 years after," he said. "It's not color of life but it's not the color of death. It's a middle color. Yellow. Gray. It's a very unique moment two hours after you're killed. I remember this color. When I looked at Yushchenko his face was absolutely the same color."

That changed Kosolapov's life.

"I thought, 'Look at this man,'" he said. "He was almost dead. But he stood up and went forward. This moment ... I decided he's my president."

Ten years after that speech, in 2014, the Russians invaded Ukraine. When the war started, his son said he planned to join. Kosolapov told the boy he'd been with him for his first steps, and his first walk to school, and stood by him at his wedding, and there was no way he'd let him get shot at alone. They went together.

A missile hit their position.

Kosolapov took more than 100 pieces of shrapnel and came a few strands of tissue and skin from losing his right leg. For two weeks, he lingered in a coma but recovered to become a symbol. The football federation brought two star players to visit him. One was Pylyp Budkivskyi (pronounced Phillip) and the other was Taras Stepanenko.

Seeing the players made a real difference. It gave him purpose.

"I was an old man," he said. "I was glad to see young football players."

He caught himself.

"Not football players. Young Ukrainian men."

Pylyp and Taras listened to his story.

"You are the future," he told them. "When we fight, you are our future."

Eight years have passed and he has followed the careers of both players who visited him. Stepanenko is beloved for the fierceness he brings to his Ukrainian club and the national team. Budkivskyi played for a time, as Kosolapov put it, "in f---ing Russia to f---ing play for the bloody f---ing money."

The soldier judges his fellow citizens with severity. There is no context.

"There is much difference between these two young guys," Kosolapov said. "They look like the same guys. They are different men. We are proud about Stepanenko. He is an example in the field. He is fighting. He is a good Ukrainian citizen."

As we talked, Stepanenko himself stepped off the elevator and walked into the bar. He saw the old soldier and recognized him. Came straight to our table. They stepped away from our table and hugged. The national team players go out of their way to pay respect to veterans. They spoke quietly, a football star and an old soldier. "Tiny Dancer" played on the bar stereo. Kosolapov got the chance to tell his story. He gave Stepanenko a warrior's blessing.

"You're a fighter," he told him.

I RAN INTO the old soldier Kosolapov the next day before the match. He grinned and said he'd found a ticket.

"The first time for me seeing the national team on the field!"

"Really?"

"I lived in a small town!" he said and grinned.

His girlfriend laughed, too.

"I really hope we'll celebrate later in the night," she said.

The hotel's energy changed. Everything felt liquid and slow. The unified heavyweight champion of the world waited in the lobby. Fans paced nervously beneath the shimmering lobby chandelier. They held flags and jerseys. Players moved through the lobby from the elevators to their private dining room. Lately they've been considering how they'll be remembered.

Stepanenko told me he wants to personally be known as a man who always tried his best. "I think the most important that supporters will say about our generation," he told me, "is that we were like fighters."

"We will always remember this national team," Yaremchuk said.

The federation president Pavelko said he will remember the bond formed over the past six months. "We are good friends," he said. "We come to each other's help. I am perhaps going to remember this time as a special time indeed, because now, here, with us, new history is being made."

There is, of course, also the history that wasn't made. An unwritten masterpiece, the work left undone. The memory of Ferris wheel turning circles through the hotel window in Wales, a reminder of how they might have been remembered, how close they came to something truly eternal in the history of their nation.

"When I remember Wales, I get so scared," Petrakov said. "God forbid I ever get there again. I'll have unpleasant memories for the rest of my life."

His boss saw a more realistic and nuanced picture.

"He is training them while the war is going on here," Pavelko said. "So he has already inscribed his name in the global history of football."

"Do you think that you'll still be the coach in March?"

Petrakov got a weird smile on his face.

"This will be subject to a decision by the executive committee," Pavelko said. "I cannot comment on this now."

He paused.

"I have my personal opinion," he said.

The hours counted down until it was almost time to leave the hotel and make the short drive to the stadium. Yarmolenko walked through the lobby with a Louis Vuitton dopp kit. The fans gathered by the idling bus. The players went into a conference

room overlooking the valet parking and entrance plaza of the
hotel. Gauzy white curtains hung over the windows giving the
room the feeling of a glowing box. The players looked transparent
almost, like a fading photograph losing pigment and definition.
They sat in neat rows facing their head coach.

Their futures beyond that room were uncertain. People
looked at them through the curtains with awe. They'd made it
to the last game. Even the unsmiling team security guy held up
his phone and took a picture. What I wanted desperately was
for them to stay in that room forever. Then the bond they'd built
over the past seven months would never fade or decay, Petrakov
and these 23 men frozen in time—safe from war and from whatever kind of peace might follow it. The meeting ended and the
glowing room emptied. They marched out together. Coach exited
the hotel last, stepping onto the bus like an admiral boarding his
flagship.

Part IV: War and Remembrance
A cold rain fell on the stadium in Krakow. Ukraine needed an
outright victory to win their Nations League group. Their intensity in the belly of this stadium far outmatched the moment. They
slipped on the jerseys so carefully hung in their lockers. The air
was cold. The stadium speakers shook with war anthems remixed
to heavy house music.

> *Death to the enemy!*
> *Ukraine is in our hearts!*
> *Glory to Ukraine!*
> *Glory to the heroes!*

The public address announcer asked fans from different parts
of Ukraine to cheer when he called out their region. The loudest
cheer came from Kyiv but the occupied areas of Odesa, Donetsk
and Mariupol got cheers, too, letting the world know. *Death to
the enemy! Glory to Ukraine!* The temperature was 53 degrees
Fahrenheit and dropping fast. Rain kept coming down harder.

The Ukraine team took the field. All of them wore their national flag around their shoulders like superhero capes. When the little kids joined them at midfield, the players draped their flags on those shivering kids. The whistle blew and the Scots won an early corner kick. The Ukrainians pressed back, swarming them. Then eight minutes into the match, the young gun Mudryk slipped a perfect pass to Yarmolenko, the new generation helping the old one, and the captain lined up a shot from six yards away with the keeper moving in the wrong direction. A gimme, but a tightly wound Yarmolenko fired the ball over the net into the stands.

Two minutes later, Ukraine missed on a shot from a tight angle against the Scottish keeper. Stepanenko missed a chance to score on a header a half-hour in and then a teammate missed from about the same distance as Yarmolenko earlier. Stepanenko missed again and then half-time arrived.

The Ukrainians controlled the game but remained tied 0-0. The second half began and Mudryk missed a chance to score. The tension felt nearly unbearable. Petrakov stalked the sideline screaming at officials and he seemed almost happy, the water pouring off his nose, soaking through his layers, no punishment without guilt. He looked through the rain with guard tower eyes.

The deluge did something to the acoustics and the stadium echoed with the screams of the Ukrainian fans. Yarmolenko looked exhausted, stopping at the sideline for gulps of water. Stepanenko lined up a clean shot and missed again wide right. Fans threw blue and yellow flares down on the field and the place smelled like gunpowder. Yarmo came out of the game finally and the Ukrainians threw themselves at the anvil of the Scottish defense over and over until they were broken and the referee blew the whistle and the whole thing ended.

A draw, a miserable terrible loss of a draw.

Stepanenko and Yarmolenko changed out of their uniforms. Neither knew how many more times they'd get to play for the national team. Petrakov appeared for his news conference. He looked pale. A microphone went down into the crowd for the first question. A Ukrainian reporter strangely seemed to almost laugh as she asked a question: "I heard there is some issue with your contract?"

"No comment," Petrakov said.

Then he turned and spit on the floor. He leaned towards Alex, the team communications chief.

"Everyone wants me to quit," he whispered.

"Calm down, please," Alex begged. "Calm down."

Petrakov got it together and answered every question and sat on the bus alone as the team showered and loaded their bags. He stared at something we couldn't see. I wondered what he might be thinking. While he waited, a Ukrainian media outlet reported he was no longer the head coach. That news hung in the air of the hotel all night. The next morning nobody seemed to know if he was still the coach. The coaches, staff and families endured a five-hour bus ride to a train station on the border. Kids talked too loud. Adults cringed. Coach sat and stewed. They stopped twice for gas and snacks. The second time he came inside to use the facilities. When he got inside, he stood in line. Eventually he was next. The door to the toilets was mirrored so he had to stand there and stare himself in the face, tired, existentially empty, a man without faith or homeland or harbor. I looked at him, too. I saw him. I saw a fighter, a leader, a grandfather, a coach whose career is the same age as his country, a man born in a nation that disintegrated, a serious, stern man with a dry sense of humor, the father of a DJ, the son of a cog in the Soviet machine, from Kyiv, a Ukrainian, a simple man.

THE CONDUCTOR DIMMED the lights as the train crossed the border into Ukraine. Shades covered the windows. We were now in a war zone. The car swayed from side to side. The football party took up the whole first-class sleeper car, four beds to a cabin. Managers brought on pallets of bottled water because there was none to drink on the train. Staff members peeled hard boiled eggs and poured cheap scotch into coffee cups. The horn blew a long melancholy blast as the train rattled through the night.

I asked Alex about the coach's mood.

"He's frustrated," he told me.

I swallowed hard and, arms out touching the walls to keep my balance, made my way up the train car and stood outside Petrakov's door. He beckoned me to enter. Stepping inside I saw him in the dark, the lines on his face covered in shadow, watching a replay of last night's defeat. He nodded at an empty space next to him on the bed where he sat. The sheets were thin, white with tiny blue lines. An apple and a banana sat untouched on the fold-out table next to his laptop. A glass of orange juice. His phone rested on top of his passport. The screen showed a news story. He rubbed his eyes before closing them and rubbing his nose.

"The only friend left on this planet is my wife," he said softly.

He looked broken. The train took him further and further from Krakow, where some part of him remained. Last night he and the Scotland manager hugged at the end of the match.

"You have an amazing team," Steve Clarke told him.

Petrakov crossed his arms.

"Maybe it's my last game," he said.

The cameras caught the exchange and now the Ukrainian media debated his future. His phone screen glowed. Fans were debating whether he should keep his job.

"There is a poll on the internet," he said.

He didn't tell me the results. I didn't ask.

"It's terrible," he said. "There is war outside. I brought the team together. So much hate towards me, I didn't expect it at all."

"Just make it 48 hours and people will move on," I told him.

He smiled.

"I call it a 72-hours symptom," he said. "You say 48, I say 72."

His voice never rose. No sparks. No flames. The inferno of the past few days settled into smoldering trees. Only ashes and soot. Nine more hours. Soon he'd learn his fate. We rattled slow through the night, a train full of people returning home under the threat of war.

A FEW DAYS later Petrakov walked through the city center of Kyiv, wearing stylish slacks and a tight-fitting magenta sweater. I realized I'd never seen him not wearing a tracksuit. Back at home he's a hero. A random person gave him an enormous hug. Coach looked so happy and relieved. Standing in front of a huge church, across from a plaza filled with the burned-out wrecks of Russian tanks, he breathed in the air of his city. He walked down to the river of his ancestors.

Yesterday he'd retreated to his dacha, a traditional summer house for barbecues, and reconnected with his wife. He sat in the sauna and sweated. He slept. The grass got mowed and the spaniel got walked.

His players started calling.

They remained united in their concern for him. They checked on his mental state as he's so often checked on theirs. Arsenal's Oleksandr Zinchenko, the best active professional Ukrainian player, who was injured for the last few matches, called and said, "Coach, we told our parents and will tell you: 'Don't read stuff on the internet.'"

Federation president Pavelko called and told him to keep working. When his contract ran out at the end of the year, they'd revisit. For now his job was safe. He'd survived 48 *and* 72 hours and he seemed lighter, no matter how hard it was to trust good news during wartime. Recently the papers reported a strange new phenomenon in Kharkiv. The Ukrainians pushed the Russian army back far enough to put the city out of artillery range. People were safe but wouldn't come back aboveground. They stayed mistrustful of the sky.

Petrakov found a café on the wide avenue leading up from the InterContinental Hotel. We stepped into a little bar and the barista spontaneously hugged him.

"Goddamn!" the man exclaimed. "You're the coolest!"

He escorted us to the sidewalk terrace. Petrakov grinned. All this love made him feel good, for sure, but also like the people had never broken ranks with him. He felt justified. Yesterday the cold seemed to be settling in for the winter but today the sun was warm again.

"Indian summer," he said in Ukrainian, and then asked me if we had that phrase. The day felt stolen. We laughed and closed our eyes. It felt good to be warm and happy. I am writing this 53 days later so I can never separate the joy of the afternoon from my knowledge of what was coming. A bomb would seriously damage the bridge from the Russian mainland to Crimea. The Russians would retaliate. Kamikaze drones and hundreds of cruise missiles would fly towards the cities of Ukraine. Day after day after day. The attacks specifically would target power facilities and plunge Kyiv and the other cities in the nation into darkness. Winter has always been the most reliable weapon in the Russian arsenal. It got Napoleon and Hitler and is coming for Ukraine. Kyiv officials warn of brutal months to come, possibly without light or heat. Every privation has made the Ukrainians more determined, and while the war has gone their way, it could turn. Kyiv could still fall.

Survival depends mostly on their ability to keep the world's attention. Lots of official and unofficial ambassadors have done their part. Zelenskyy and Mila Kunis and the Klitschko brothers and, of course, Petrakov and his team. He had done his best and now he sat in the city of his birth and hoped it had been enough. I wondered if I'd ever see him again. He ordered a cappuccino, because he was driving, and at his insistence the waiter brought me and my entourage heavy glasses brimming with three fingers of an Irish whiskey called Writers' Tears. It's been 53 days since that fading afternoon. Just this morning I read a story about Kyiv sitting in snowy darkness, people hoping not to freeze to death on Christmas, and the idea of fighting, even dying, for anything enduring felt like a myth. People have been fighting and dying in this city for a thousand years. Nothing endures but memory and the ever-vanishing warmth of that afternoon remains with me still. We were a strange group: a coach and two Americans and a Ukrainian translator who hosted a cooking show on television before the war and a British SAS commando turned security contractor. We raised our drinks.

"You know what is most important?" Petrakov asked in a serious voice.

We all faced him at the head of the table.

"Now we are sitting in Ukraine but there is a war in the East. People are dying there, but we talk, laugh, alive and healthy."

The city of Kyiv vibrated with life around him, defiant, colorful, loud, free.

"It is a great happiness when there is peace," he said. "I do not understand what people want to achieve by killing. May your families be healthy and your children alive. If we meet again somewhere in this life, we will hug like brothers."

Death to the enemy. Glory to Ukraine.

"Let's drink to this..." he said.

WRIGHT THOMPSON is a senior writer for ESPN. He lives in Mississippi with his family.

10 Eye Surgeries by Age 10. How Julio Urías Beat the Odds to Become the Dodgers' Ace

JORGE CASTILLO

FROM THE *Los Angeles Times* • SEPTEMBER 15, 2022

CULIACÁN, MEXICO—Carlos Urías has a routine before watching every one of his son's starts: He plugs in a *Virgen de Guadalupe* light fixture hanging in the hallway just off the living room and prays.

La Virgen was bright on a recent Sunday morning, colorfully illuminating the dim white space. A few minutes after 10, before Julio Urías took the mound 2,000 miles away in Miami, Carlos approached her. He took off his Dodgers cap, whispered some words and offered the sign of the cross.

"God has been good," he said. "I have a lot to be thankful for up there."

Julio César Urías hasn't spent a summer here in a decade. Not since the boy with the bad left eye and gifted left arm signed with the Dodgers to continue a life already with more bright moments and dark days than most of his peers will ever experience.

The 26-year-old left-hander is a former hotshot prospect who made his big league debut as a teenager, struggled to find his footing with the Dodgers, underwent major shoulder surgery, served a 20-game suspension after being arrested on suspicion of domestic violence, and returned to fulfill the outsized on-field expectations that originally awaited him.

He's the ace on a team with the best record in the majors and World Series-or-bust ethos, starring in Los Angeles as the most beloved Mexican Dodger since Fernando Valenzuela.

"Patience has been fundamental for my career," Julio said. "Being patient and not worrying about when my moment is coming."

The foundation was shaped in this growing city of nearly 1 million people on Mexico's Pacific coast universally associated with drug cartel violence, and in a community called La Higuerita 10 minutes from Culiacán's urban cluster.

It's where Julio grew up, first in his grandparents' house until there was enough money for his family to move into its own home when he was 13.

It's where he was bullied for an eye that wouldn't stay open and where his father firmly demanded excellence on the baseball field. It's where he was celebrated for his uncommon athletic exploits as a boy and where he spends the holidays during the offseason as a man, drawing crowds everywhere he appears in public.

It's where he plans to conclude his career, pitching for the Tomateros de Culiacán in the Mexican winter league, and to invest some of his earnings. It's where he wants to help the people whenever possible. It's where his family will remain.

"I've been here my whole life," Carlos said, "and I'm going to die here."

THE URÍAS FAMILY gathers in their living room to watch Julio's starts, inviting relatives and friends, whenever possible. For this outing against the Miami Marlins, Julio's parents, Carlos and Juana Isabel Acosta, are joined by his brother Carlos Jr. and his grandparents.

As more relatives and friends arrived, Carlos and Carlos Jr. focused on every pitch as the surrounding bustle amplified.

"It's every father's dream to see their son in the big leagues," Carlos said.

Carlos, 50, was a semi-pro baseball player into his 30s.

"I tried," he said.

Julio's slurve, a pitch he unveiled during his breakout 2020 season, was sharp as he plowed through three hitless innings. Then, in the fourth, he left a fastball over the plate to Brian Anderson. Julio didn't bother to see where it landed over the wall, yelling at himself for the mistake. It was the only hit he surrendered in six innings.

"He's not afraid," Carlos Jr., 20, said. "He's only afraid of heights."

Julio's life began with fear. Dread swamped Carlos and Juana the moment they realized their first-born child had an eye problem. Doctors initially couldn't identify the issue until they diagnosed Julio with a tumor when he was 4. Tests found it was benign, but doctors told the family the tumor would aggressively grow through his teenage years and removing it would risk compromising Julio's eye.

Repeated, less invasive, surgeries would be required to keep the eye open. The stress prompted the couple to wait to have another child. Six years later, Carlos Jr. was born.

"The first thing we did when Carlos was born," Carlos said, "was look at his eyes."

Julio's grandfather owned the nine-person household's only car, so Julio and his father would take a 12-hour bus ride to Guadalajara for surgeries whenever the eye was sealing shut. Doctors tied his hands down after surgery so he wouldn't remove the patch or the IV in his arm. He was prescribed medication to hinder the tumor's growth. Carlos estimated Julio underwent 10 surgeries by the time he was 10.

"I think all of that made my son strong," Carlos said.

The rides were usually overnight unless they stayed with the only relative they had in Guadalajara because they couldn't afford a hotel. Eventually, they started taking eight-hour bus rides up the coast to Ciudad Obregón for the procedures.

Once, when Julio was about 9, two passengers robbed everyone on the bus at gunpoint. Nobody was hurt.

"Thank God we didn't have anything," Julio said with a chuckle, "so they didn't take anything."

Children taunted him at school. They called him *tuerto* and *bizco*; one-eyed and cross-eyed. They nicknamed him "four eyes" when he wore glasses. The operations would leave him with a black eye, and children quipped he must've been beaten.

His parents pleaded with him to not fight back when others cracked jokes, worried that a blow could ruin the eye. For a few years, at a doctor's urging, they convinced him to wear a patch over his right eye Monday through Friday for a month at a time to make sure he kept his left one open. He protested. He promised to not close his bad eye. He cried. Carlos and Juana refused to relent.

"He would ask, 'Why am I different?'" Juana said. "I always told him, 'You're not different.'"

There was one place Julio didn't mind being different: for a few hours Sunday on a baseball field, where he was better than everyone else.

He knew he needed vision in both eyes to play. It's what his parents used to encourage him to withstand the name-calling, to endure the long bus rides, to wear the patch. He wanted to play baseball.

"It affected me a bit mentally because I looked in the mirror and I didn't want to see me like that," Julio said. "But, little by little, I came around to understanding and learning, so I think I took out the most positive, and the most positive I feel was this sport."

JULIO OVERCAME HIS first challenge as a baseball player in his grandparents' front yard.

His father built a pitcher's mound in one corner. In another, his grandfather Julián crouched as the catcher and Carlos posed as the hitter. When Carlos noticed Julio was afraid to pitch inside, he started standing with a glove. He begged Julio to not worry about plunking him because he would catch the ball. Julio laughed when his father snatched his first misfires. The anxiety dissipated.

"That gave me the confidence," Julio said.

He dominated the local youth league at every level—as a pitcher and a hitter. He wore No. 7 because his favorite Tomateros player, Darrell Sherman, a star outfielder from Los Angeles, wore the number. He threw changeups by the time he was 7. He smashed jaw-dropping home runs.

"My son was younger than Julio so he would play on the field next to his," said Carlos Rubio, a local businessman who owns a Dodgers-themed barbershop in the city. "And every time Julio was pitching or hitting, I had to watch. He was a phenom."

Julio's dominance earned him spots on national teams, and he represented Mexico in international tournaments in Central America, South America and United States.

"In our 9- and-10-year-old league, they would only let you pitch four innings," recalled Fidel Alba, Julio's youth league catcher. "And he wouldn't allow a hit every time. He would strike out 11 or all 12 batters. And then he would hit two or three home runs a game. As a kid you don't realize how good he is, but everyone in Mexico knew who Julio Urías was."

Carlos coached his son's teams from the time he was 6 until he became a professional. He expected perfection. Julio rarely struggled, but if he did—gave up hits or threw pitches his father didn't like—Carlos scolded him in front of his teammates and ignored him for days. Julio viewed his father as a "military man, like a general."

Years later, the subject was broached between father and son over drinks.

"He told me, 'When you have your children, you do what you want, but I did it that way and look where you are,'" Julio said. "He has a point. There isn't a book on how to raise a child.

He has his reason. It was the best for me because it showed me if I'm going to do something, I have to do it right."

Julio's development didn't wane leading into the summer of 2012. But when it came time to negotiate with major league clubs, Carlos said, teams backed off believing his eye would be a problem. Carlos told teams he had one demand: that Julio be sent straight to the minors in the U.S., not to the Dominican Summer League.

The Dodgers eventually gave the Diablos Rojos del Mexico, the team that owned Julio's rights in the Mexican League, $1.8 million for Julio and three other players. Julio officially signed on Aug. 12, his 16th birthday.

The left-hander spent his first full professional season in 2013 pitching for low-A Great Lakes where he was nearly six years younger than the league's average player. Two years later, while pitching for double-A Tulsa, he underwent another eye surgery. He was back on the mound in two months. He hasn't had an eye operation since.

"Those are the types of things you can call bad, but I don't look at it as bad because it doesn't impede me from anything," Julio said. "I do everything normal like anyone else. That's how I look at it."

One year after the procedure, Carlos received what felt like a random call from his son. Julio asked if there was anyone around. Carlos was at work, coaching children, when Julio said he had news. He was being called up to the majors. They cried.

Carlos rushed home. He and Juana went to La Lomita, to the prominent church overlooking the city atop a hill, with a bouquet of flowers. A family friend surprised the family—Carlos, Juana, Carlos Jr. and sister, Alexia—with plane tickets to New York the next morning to watch Julio pitch against Jacob deGrom and the Mets.

Julio bounced between the majors and minors the rest of the season, posting a 3.39 ERA in 15 starts and three relief appearances. He pitched in two playoff games, but the Dodgers had him open the next season in extended spring training hoping to alleviate his workload. The decision irked him.

"That doesn't happen with a lot of players," Urías said. "But you have to understand they're doing it for a reason."

The next June, he underwent season-ending shoulder surgery, the type of setback Julio had never experienced in his baseball life. He returned to the Dodgers 15 months later, in September 2018, as a reliever and made the postseason roster.

He rode the momentum into 2019 in a hybrid role between the rotation and bullpen. Then his progress came to a halt. He was arrested on suspicion of domestic battery on May 13 after witnesses told Los Angeles police they saw him push a woman to the ground in a parking lot.

Urías and the woman denied the incident was more than a verbal altercation, but authorities reviewed surveillance footage and ruled the woman had been pushed.

Major League Baseball put Urías on paid administrative leave the next day. He was reinstated after seven days and made his next pitching appearance on May 25.

Two weeks later, Los Angeles city prosecutors announced they wouldn't file misdemeanor charges if Urías was not arrested again for violent behavior over the next year and completed a yearlong domestic violence counseling program in person.

In August, Urías accepted a 20-game suspension. He returned in September for the rest of the season.

"It was difficult," he said. "I don't even like to talk about it or remember it because they're very complicated moments in life that you don't want to see yourself or another person in that situation. ... It was a lesson and I feel like if I have a stain, it's that one."

THE URÍAS FAMILY house originally had two bedrooms and a bathroom inside. The kitchen and dining room were outside on a dirt floor. Julio shared a bedroom with his parents and two siblings—the other bedroom was filled with supplies for the neighborhood's plumbing system—until he left for the minor leagues.

They soon added a dining room, kitchen, and living room inside. A second floor was constructed after Julio received his signing bonus.

Upstairs is where Julio's memorabilia and keepsakes reside. The ball from his major league debut. The ball from his first save. The ball from his first World Series appearance. A Guinness Book of World Records that includes Julio for being the youngest player to start a major league postseason game.

The family could afford a bigger, more luxurious space, but this is home.

Everyone in Culiacán understands the city's reputation. The capital of Sinaloa had one of the top 25 homicide rates in the world in 2019. Joaquín "El Chapo" Guzmán, the notorious drug cartel leader, is from a rural community nearby. Narcotrafficking is part of the economy.

Residents, *Culichis*, insist Culiacán isn't the place you see on television. They say it's a place with problems and positives like anywhere else.

They point to the widespread construction, a sign of a city outgrowing its backwoods stereotype. They proudly talk about their food—the barbacoa, the chilorio, and, above all, the mariscos. They share a love for banda music and their celebrated brand of sushi, a breaded twist on the Japanese staple filled with Philadelphia cream cheese. There are people going to school and working hard and living ordinary lives.

Unlike most other places in Mexico, baseball, not soccer, is the prevalent local sport. There's a professional soccer team— Diego Maradona served as manager for two seasons—but this is a Tomateros town.

The city, like the rest of the world, shut down in 2020. Julio, meanwhile, seized a shortened 60-game season to establish himself as an indispensable piece in the Dodgers' machine that went on to win the World Series by beating the Tampa Bay Rays in six games.

Julio was on the mound for the ending, striking out Willy Adames to give the Dodgers their first championship in 32 years. His immediate celebration, a lunge and a howl, has become iconic. His agent, Scott Boras, gifted the family a canvas of it. His father has the image tattooed on his left arm.

That night in Culiacán, family and friends packed the house. Cars paraded up and down the street, honking as they passed. A banda showed up to play in the backyard. People danced until the wee hours.

"It was a special night," Juana said.

Julio returned home that offseason with an idea. After visiting the president of Mexico in Mexico City, he met with the governor of Sinaloa in La Higuerita. They walked through the unpaved streets around his grandparents' home, passed his first school and the neighborhood baseball field his grandfather Julián built with his brothers and friends in the 1960s.

"We all loved baseball," Julián said with a Tecate Light in his hand and a Dodgers cap on his head. "We wanted to play it without having to go into the city. We didn't have cars back then so it was hard."

Julio remembered attending school with his shoes and uniform muddied in the rain. He envisioned an upgraded baseball facility—with grass—for children. As a newly crowned World Series hero, he recognized he had some sway, so he asked the governor if he could have the roads paved and the field remodeled. The governor agreed.

By the following spring, kids played at the renovated Unidad Deportiva Julio César Urías. The field at the complex was named after Paquin Urías, Julián's brother, who led the effort to build the field six decades ago and died of COVID-19 complications in 2020.

Every weekday afternoon, Carlos and other former players, including Alba, work with children at the stadium for free.

"It's a dream come true for me and my family," Julio said. "I've always wanted to help my community, and to do that where my grandfather played is special."

CARLOS JR. IS an aspiring baseball player, too, but his career has been sidetracked. First by the same shoulder surgery Julio endured. Then, in June, by a more serious health scare.

What should've been a routine procedure to remove his appendix became a 21-day stay between two hospitals because of an infection. Julio was in Atlanta, hours from pitching against the Braves, when his family called. Carlos Jr. was scheduled for another surgery. They told Julio to say goodbye to his brother, just in case.

Julio limited the defending World Series champions to one run, striking out nine in a win hours later. His brother survived with a six-inch scar on his stomach. Julio's 2.08 ERA in 14 starts since that day is tied for lowest in the National League.

This season, Julio's stats have vaulted him atop the leaderboards and put him in the National League Cy Young Award conversation.

The Dodgers' World Series hopes might hinge on his left arm. With Walker Buehler out for the rest of the season and Tony Gonsolin on the injured list for an unknown period. Urías is the ace of a rotation featuring Clayton Kershaw, Tyler Anderson, Dustin May and Andrew Heaney. If he stays healthy, he probably will be the team's Game 1 starter for the first time in his career. He's peaking with one season left before he becomes a free agent.

"I think Julio has been throwing the baseball as well as anybody in baseball, gosh, since the break," Dodgers manager Dave Roberts said. "Even before the break, actually."

The success hasn't stopped the eye jokes. Last season, Julio said, a group of Mexican fans taunted him while he warmed up before a game in San Diego. They started with the usual banter. You stink. You're no good. They're going to kill you.

"Thank you," Julio responded. "We'll see a little later. The game hasn't started."

Then one of the men mocked his eye, striking a nerve. Julio turned around.

"I gave it to your team in the playoffs last year and I have a ring," Julio said. "You guys don't have anything. And that was with one eye. Imagine if I had two."

The response, Julio remembered, silenced the group. It's one reason why he doesn't use social media anymore. Why, he reasons, open the door to negativity?

The eye wasn't discussed for his recent start in Miami. The game, an easy 8-1 win for the Dodgers, ended at 1:21 p.m. in Culiacán. The room erupted in applause.

"I can finally breathe," Juana said.

Julio earned the win. His family celebrated with carne asada, mariscos from a local spot and beer.

The next day, Carlos was driving, looking to stop somewhere for horchata de coco, when Julio video called from the visitors clubhouse in Miami. He showed his father a bandage on his left index finger.

"What happened?" the worried father asked.

"You didn't notice it bothering me?" Julio said. "But I'll be fine. It's just a cut."

Five days later, Julio didn't skip a beat, holding the Padres to one run across six innings. Carlos watched from his living room, La Virgen shining in the hallway.

JORGE CASTILLO is a sports reporter for the *Los Angeles Times*. He previously worked for *The Star-Ledger* and *The Washington Post*. The son of parents from Puerto Rico, he was raised in Worcester, Massachusetts, and graduated from Yale. He and his wife, Aileen, live in Los Angeles.

One Night in London: Allegations of Sexual Assault and a Reckoning for Hockey Canada

KATIE STRANG, DAN ROBSON,
AND IAN MENDES

FROM The Athletic • JULY 22, 2022

They arrived in London, Ontario, on June 17, 2018, nearly two dozen young men from all over Canada. They were almost five months removed from a gold medal run at the 2018 World Junior Ice Hockey Championships, an achievement that the *Globe and Mail* called Canada's "hockey glory of the year."

"Drink it in, Canada," a story about the triumph began.

They descended upon London from some of the country's hockey hotbeds, but also its leafy suburbs and far-flung prairie towns, minted royalty coming to a place that, even for Canada, embraces hockey heroes with fervor.

London sits an hour east of the U.S. border just north of Lake Erie. It has 400,000 residents but can feel smaller or larger, depending on the time of year. As many as 45,000 students, most attending Western University, make the city home during the school year. It is also a hockey mecca. The London Knights, a powerhouse junior program, average 9,000 fans a game at Budweiser Arena—an attendance that rivals some NHL teams. In the restaurants and bars downtown, the jerseys of former Knights players hang on the walls.

The players, the World Juniors champions, were brought to London as part of the Hockey Canada Foundation Gala & Golf event. It was a two-day "star-studded" celebration to recognize the champions and others, and it included a lavish dinner and a golf event in which many of the players would participate. Some Hockey Canada executives also attended, as did sponsors and corporate partners, local business leaders and more. Hockey Canada would use the weekend to raise money, and the players were an attraction that would help open wallets.

Most of them would stay at the Delta Hotel London Armouries, the most luxurious accommodation in town. It's a sleek glass-paneled high-rise that emerges from an imposing sienna-bricked building flanked by turrets and framed by crenelated towers. The original structure, built in 1905, served as a militia headquarters for Canadian land force branches. Suspended in the glass arch above the lobby entrance is an antique cannon.

As the players arrived at the hotel and prepared for the festivities, many undoubtedly were excited about the gala but also eager for what might come after, when Hockey Canada's leadership headed back to the hotel to sleep. These were young men in a town filled with college students. Sure, they would soak in the adulation at the official festivities, but the real fun would come at the bars on Richmond Street, where beers are poured into plastic cups, where early 2000s hip hop and dance music is played loud, where they would be surrounded by their peers, feeling like the lords of London.

It was at one of those bars, Jack's, which calls itself "London's premier party destination," where a player and a young woman would connect. After leaving the bar, they would end up back in a room at the Hotel London Armouries, where she says eight players sexually assaulted her. Hockey Canada officials would become aware of the allegations that morning. The London police were notified that evening.

Four years later, Hockey Canada would pay the woman an undisclosed sum to settle a legal claim she brought. After news of that settlement became public, there would be hearings before the Parliament of Canada, which continue on Tuesday, as Hockey Canada officials face questions about those days in London in 2018 and its handling of the alleged assaults.

But that was later.

At the start, there was just the anticipation of a big, celebratory couple of days, the players and Hockey Canada honchos and a hockey-mad populace eager to toast their success, eager to, as the article advised:

"Drink it in."

SUNDAY EVENING, JUNE 17, featured a team dinner. It was a private event limited to players and staff. This was the first time the group had been reunited since winning gold in Buffalo, and the atmosphere was convivial. At some point, a handful of players headed out to join local revelers and to bask in their adulation.

"They were on a tear," said one person who saw them that evening.

At one point that night, a group of five players gathered to take a picture, set against a blank, sterile wall. They're huddled together, arms around each other, subtly grinning. The photo, which was posted on social media from one player's account, according to the person who took a screenshot of the picture, has London, Ontario, tagged as its location. Above that are two emojis: a Canadian flag and a gold medal.

The players' Monday schedule was filled with commitments—media appearances after the announcement of the Order of Hockey in Canada, a press conference about the international sledge hockey event heading to London in December, and the ring ceremony done during a VIP cocktail hour, culminating with the Hockey Canada Foundation Gala that night.

The gala was staged at RBC Place London, the former London Convention Centre, and included the largest attendance garnered to date—roughly 1,000 people. Tickets were sold out well in advance and over $1 million was raised. It kicked off around

7 p.m. Jennifer Botterill emceed the event along with sports broad-caster Rod Black. An itinerary for the evening was superimposed upon a team picture of the World Juniors team. There would be a Local Londoners' Hot Stove, a live auction and recognition of the Order of Hockey in Canada inductees, which included Olympic gold medal-winning coach Mike Babcock, Hall of Famer Danielle Goyette, and Ryan Smyth, who earned the nickname Captain Canada for his bevvy of gold medal finishes representing Canada on the international stage.

Attendees took red-carpet photos and posed in front of banners festooned with some of Hockey Canada's biggest partners; one backdrop showed the logo for BFL, Hockey Canada's insurance broker. One picture taken was of four players from the World Juniors team, posing with their fists outstretched, championship rings on their right hands.

RBC Place was filled with tables covered in cloth and beset with candles and hydrangea-filled centerpieces. A player or staff member was stationed at some tables so attendees could capture a detail from that World Juniors—a funny anecdote about the bus ride in Buffalo, an unknown detail about the power play scheme, a bit of trash-talking exchanged with the Swedes.

Wine was available to the whole table, and it is unlikely anyone would have looked askance if one of the players, who ranged in age from 18 to 20, had indulged in a glass of red to go along with his steak. It was a celebratory event; this was not the environment for teetotaling. (The legal drinking age in Ontario is 19.) One woman in attendance said some players were drinking heavily at the dinner, and that one player commented that she "had a tight a–" in her dress.

The gala concluded around 10 p.m. Many staff members retired early, exhausted from a long day. Some women's hockey players went back to the hotel bar at the London Armouries to catch up over drinks. Some Hockey Canada and London Knights staff members and other gala attendees broke off to go to Joe Kool's, a well-known hockey pub on Richmond Street where Knights team photos and NHL memorabilia cover the walls. Some members of the World Juniors team were there as well, gathered in a back room. One person at Joe Kool's watched as several players in the back room became increasingly inebriated.

"It was carte blanche," the person said.

Several players left Joe Kool's, walking down Richmond Street and arriving at Jack's, a multi-level establishment with security out front, a patio and smoking pen out back and a throbbing mob of college students and young locals inside. Even in June—when many students are away and it's the offseason for the CHL—Jack's signature Dollar Beer Mondays draws a crowd.

"That's the big place (you go)," said one local server.

On a recent Monday night, one woman almost fell down the staircase because the ground was slick with spilled beer. There was vomit in the corner of the landing where she tried to steady herself.

That evening in 2018, the players that were let in—at least one was turned away for being too young to drink, according to multiple people who saw the player return to Joe Kool's—would've immediately been met with a sweaty crush of bodies and the smell of sour beer and cheap lip gloss. Clear cups of beer and shots poured into neon pink ramekins cluttered tables and ledges throughout the bar's crowded first floor.

As packed as it was, they quickly owned the place, and the players kept the rounds flowing through the night, spending freely and handing out drinks to those around them.

SHE ARRIVED AT Jack's that night with a group of friends. As a student at Western University, she was familiar with the popular Monday night scene and the bar's famous dollar beer nights—but she wasn't a regular. Beyond the handful of friends she arrived with, she didn't know anyone else inside the bar.

She was only 18, but she used a fake ID to get inside, joining the sweaty crush of young people, the World Juniors champions among them. (The Athletic, which is not naming the woman at her request, as she fears reprisal, reviewed photos and videos confirming the woman's presence that night and spoke to one of her friends to corroborate details of her story).

The young man she met that night was, initially to her, just a cute stranger in a bar. He told her that he played junior hockey, but she didn't realize at the time that he was among the hockey royalty that had come to town for the gala and golf.

She drank. He drank. Then they kissed several times. He added her on Snapchat. What began as benign, however, turned more aggressive, the young woman says. He urged some friends he was with to kiss her, too. She refused. He asked her to come back to their hotel room. Not to come back to the hotel with him. To come back with *them*. She felt uncomfortable and declined. She had to work the next morning, she told him. Again, he asked her to come back to *their* hotel room. Again, she declined.

As she left a short time later, she felt discomforted. The night started fun. The drinks, the attractive young man, the kissing. But the insistence she kiss others, that she come back to *their* room. It felt wrong.

A different young woman, only two years older, arrived at Jack's with a group of friends at approximately 11 p.m., according to a statement of claim filed in April 2022 in the Ontario Superior Court of Justice.

Shortly after arriving at the bar, she met a member of the World Juniors team who introduced her to a player identified in the lawsuit as John Doe 1. John Doe 1 and some of his teammates bought the plaintiff a number of alcoholic beverages.

According to the statement of claim, the plaintiff got separated from her friends and became increasingly intoxicated through-out the night, exhibiting telltale signs—glassy eyes, slurred speech, stumbling and loss of balance.

Sometime in the early morning, the woman left the bar with John Doe 1. Cabs wait outside the bar regularly, especially on the busiest nights, and it would've been about a five-minute ride back to the hotel. If they had walked, they might have traveled south down Richmond and then east onto a cobblestoned stretch of

Dundas, a roughly 20-minute walk. It is likely they would've had to sidestep other young bar patrons spilling out into the street in the early hours after last call.

Entering the hotel, they would have passed at least one security camera affixed high on the northeast corner of the roof that covers arriving guests. When they entered the lobby, it was about a 17-step walk to the elevator bank. Another security camera on the ceiling just before the elevators would likely have captured their entrance.

As the glassed elevator climbed the tower, the woman could have viewed London. In the distance was Budweiser Gardens arena, situated right next to the stark Ontario courthouse, where the events to come would be detailed in a statement of claim four years later.

Security footage would not have captured the two entering a hotel room—multiple employees told The Athletic security cameras are not present on each floor—but a walk down the hallway would've been lit by wall sconces and guided by an art-deco floor pattern in the carpet.

According to the young woman's statement of claim, at some point in the early-morning hours, she and John Doe 1 "engaged in sex acts" in his hotel room. Then, John Doe 1 invited his teammates to the room without her knowledge or consent.

According to the young woman's statement of claim, they made her touch herself and perform oral sex on them. They straddled her and placed their genitals in her face. They slapped her buttocks, spit on her, ejaculated onto her, and engaged in vaginal intercourse while she was incapable of consent.

At one point, she started crying and tried to leave the room, she said. She was then "directed, manipulated and intimidated into remaining," according to her statement of claim.

Throughout the alleged assaults, the young woman said she feared imminent physical harm. Some players brought their golf clubs into the room. The sheer number of them and the presence of the clubs made her feel intimidated and threatened. As a result, she said she acquiesced to the sexual acts.

"Any reasonable person … would have concluded the Plaintiff was not freely consenting in those circumstances and would have ceased the confinement of the plaintiff and the sexual behaviors toward her," the claim states.

After it was over, the players told her to shower.

According to reports, two videos were made—the first was six seconds long and filmed at 3:30 a.m. and the second was 12 seconds and was filmed at 4:30 a.m. In the videos, the woman, following hours of drinking and what she says were several forced sexual acts, states that all that happened in the room was consensual.

The Athletic reached out to the young woman's lawyer, Robert Talach, on multiple occasions but he declined comment and repeatedly stressed that his client does not wish to speak publicly. It is not clear from the statement of claim what the woman did next, how she got home, but at some point that morning, likely around the time the sun was coming up, she finally exited the hotel.

THE MORNING AFTER, they golfed.

Many of the players teed off at the stately London Hunt and Country Club, a private course set on 267 acres. It was a sunny, clear-skied day. The players wore matching red Nike polos with black collars. They hit balls emblazoned with the Hockey Canada Maple Leaf. There was a 2019 Chevrolet Corvette parked on the 17th hole, and one sponsor set up a tent near the clubhouse, handing out slices of pizza.

At some point that morning, while they were on the course, the then-stepfather of the young woman who said she was sexually assaulted called a Hockey Canada human resources employee, according to Parliamentary testimony by Hockey Canada CEO Tom Renney.

Renney and president Scott Smith were likely in the air already, flying back to Calgary. Once they were on the ground, they learned of the alleged assaults, according to their testimony.

Within a few hours, at approximately 4 p.m. in London, Smith and Renney reviewed the information with Hockey Canada's senior vice president of risk management and insurance, who then contacted someone from Henein Hutchison, a law firm, as well as a representative from Hockey Canada's insurance company.

A couple of hours later, at around 6 p.m., a representative from Hockey Canada contacted the London Police, according to Smith's Parliamentary testimony. By the time that call was made, the players would've been long gone. (Players' luggage was already packed on buses while they were golfing.)

According to Smith's testimony, a "representative of HC" had conversations with someone from Henein Hutchison on Tuesday, June 19. Players were later informed that an investigation would take place. Hockey Canada officials said they recommended that players cooperate but didn't require them to do so. Renney told members of the Canadian Heritage Committee in his testimony that he believed four to six chose to participate. Smith said the number of players was much higher.

Hockey Canada officials have insisted that they did not know then (or now) who the eight John Doe defendants were. Smith said Henein Hutchison, the London Police and Hockey Canada officials all were unable to confirm the identities of the accused. And when the police investigation concluded, no charges were filed and the matter, it seemed, was over.

Four years passed.

Nearly every player from the 2018 World Juniors team went on to play in the NHL, fulfilling their hockey dreams. Hockey Canada continued to collect gold medals in international competition, including another World Juniors title in 2020. It also continued to hold its profitable fundraising event.

The events of June 2018 would have gone unknown to the general public if the young woman involved in the alleged sexual assaults hadn't filed a civil suit with the Ontario Superior Court of Justice on April 22, 2022.

Within a few weeks, Hockey Canada resolved the case on behalf of defendants whose identities officials say remain unknown.

Hockey Canada reached an out-of-court settlement with the young woman for an undisclosed amount. According to Hockey Canada president Scott Smith's testimony last month, the organization liquidated investments to do so. The terms of that settlement are not known, though Minister of Sport Pascal St-Onge testified that Renney told her that the settlement included a non-disclosure agreement.

Renney told the Standing Committee on Canadian Heritage that Hockey Canada didn't "know exactly what occurred that night or the identities of those involved," but found the conduct "unacceptable and incompatible with Hockey Canada's values and expectations," adding that it "clearly caused harm."

Smith said the organization made the decision to pay a settlement based upon the fact that the incident occurred at their "year-end celebration."

"We took responsibility," he said, "because it happened at an event under our control."

A number of players from the Junior World Championship team released statements in the past two months saying they were not involved, were unaware of what went on, or were not present at the event in London. The Athletic made multiple attempts—via email and text messages—to connect with seven lawyers representing some of the players. On July 17, lawyer Tim Gleason wrote in an email that the group would "confer" about a request to supply more information to The Athletic. They failed to respond to later interview requests.

During the Parliamentary hearings that followed the revelations of the settlement, Renney admitted that supervision of athletes during the 2018 event was poor. He said Hockey Canada "fell short." Henein Hutchison offered advice based on the night in question, Renney said, including "how we could ensure more responsible service of alcohol."

Hockey Canada officials' testimony in front of Parliament also revealed that the organization deals with multiple sexual assault allegations every year. (It was later reported, by The Canadian Press and the *Globe and Mail*, that the organization maintains a fund to cover uninsured liabilities, including claims for sexual abuse, which is partially bankrolled by registration fees. Hockey Canada has since said it will no longer use the fund to settle sexual assault claims.)

Following the hearing in late June, Sport Canada froze all federal funding to Hockey Canada. In the weeks that followed, major corporate partners like Scotiabank, Canadian Tire and Tim Hortons, among others, paused or redirected their funding for Hockey Canada.

On July 14, Hockey Canada announced that it would reopen Henein Hutchison's investigation into the allegations, this time compelling all players to participate or forfeit any chance to represent Canada in future programs or international competitions.

The organization also announced that it will launch a third-party review of its governance and has agreed to become a signatory to the Office of the Sport Integrity Commissioner, a governmental agency that is empowered to independently investigate abuse complaints and impose sanctions. It also has committed to requiring all high-performance players, coaches, team staff and volunteers to participate in mandatory sexual violence and consent training—and to create an independent and confidential complaint system.

On July 20, the London Police Service announced in a statement that the department would undergo an internal review of the investigation into the 2018 incident to determine "what, if any, additional investigative avenues may exist."

On Tuesday, Hockey Canada executives will return to Parliament Hill for another hearing. Federal MPs on the Parliamentary committee have demanded more details about how the organization handled the allegations from June 2018—and have subpoenaed the settlement, and the adjoining NDA.

"Hockey Canada is on a journey to change the culture of our sport and to make it safer and more inclusive," said Scott Smith during his opening statement at the first Parliamentary hearing.

Three days later, the Hockey Canada Foundation again held its annual gala and golf tournament. Hockey legends Lanny McDonald, Kim St-Pierre and the late Guy Lafleur were honored at the Niagara Falls Convention Centre, alongside members of the Canadian women's team that won gold at the 2022 Winter Olympics in Beijing and the Canadian men's team that won the 2021 world championship.

Tom Renney opened the gala with emphatic remarks about the recent revelations; he stressed that Hockey Canada had to do better, and that the organization was committed to doing so. It set a more subdued tone for the evening.

There was a gin and tonic station hosted by one corporate partner and wine service at tables for dinner, but the usual open bar that would've been flowing, arming attendees with cold beers and stiff cocktails, was serving drinks for purchase only ... after one complimentary cocktail.

KATIE STRANG is an award-winning senior investigative writer for The Athletic, where she specializes in covering the intersection of sports and social issues, with a particular focus on sexual abuse and gendered violence. **DAN ROBSON** is a senior enterprise writer for The Athletic. He is an award-winning journalist and the bestselling author of several books. Previously, he was the head of features for The Athletic Canada and a senior writer at Sportsnet Magazine and Sportsnet.ca. **IAN MENDES** is a senior writer covering the Ottawa Senators and the NHL for The Athletic since 2021. Previously, he spent seven years as an afternoon talk show host for TSN 1200 in Ottawa and as a contributing writer for TSN.ca. He also worked for 12 years as a television reporter and host with Rogers Sportsnet and has served as a feature columnist for both the *Ottawa Citizen* and *Today's Parent* magazine.

World Cup Villain Luis Suárez Won't Get Taste of Knockout Stage after Rematch with Ghana Goes Sour

BRUCE ARTHUR

FROM THE *Toronto Star* • DECEMBER 2, 2022

DOHA, QATAR—Villains are so rarely given what they deserve. Luis Suárez is one of football's great ones: imperious, unrepentant, vicious, sometimes feral. This was his fourth World Cup, part of a stellar, pockmarked career. He was a man who could wrestle the biggest awards from Lionel Messi or Cristiano Ronaldo in their primes, and be hated all the way. He is 35 now, and this is his final World Cup. And here, the road led back.

"There's been a lot of talk over the years in Ghana," came the question to Suárez the day before, from a Ghanian journalist. "They consider you the devil himself. I spoke to fans yesterday and they are looking forward to maybe retiring you from the World Cup with this game. Have you ever considered apologizing?"

He didn't, of course: In that infamous 2010 World Cup quarterfinal with Ghana, Suárez was given a red card for thrusting his hand up to stop the ball in the box, and the resulting Ghana penalty was stopped, and Uruguay won. Ghana was denied the best African World Cup finish ever. "I didn't say sorry because I did the handball, but Ghana's player missed the penalty, not me," Suárez said. Cold as ice.

He was called El Diablo in Ghana and 12 years later on a Friday night Uruguay played Ghana in their final Group H match at Al Janoub Stadium, as South Korea played Portugal at Education City. Only Portugal was through to the round of 16. Everyone else needed a result.

And Ghana wanted revenge, too. Ghana winger André Ayew was on that 2010 team, and while he missed the Uruguay match due to yellow cards, the Black Stars captain glared at Suárez in the pre-match handshakes like he was going to burn down his house. The day before Suárez had talked about how many of Ghana's players were eight years old in 2010, how many had just heard stories and might misunderstand, life goes on. That glare said history gets dragged right alongside, buddy.

But revenge isn't easy when the villain is great. Five minutes after Ayew missed a penalty, making Ghana the first country to miss two penalties against the same opponent in the history of the World Cup, Uruguay scored first: Suárez got a shot and was stopped, but the rebound was headed in by Giorgian de Arrascaeta. He scored again off a Suárez assist, a clever sand wedgelike flick. At Education City Korea was tied with Portugal, so Uruguay was in position to advance. And Ghana's long-awaited revenge was vanishing into the sea.

Suárez was subbed off in the 66th minute, and his teammates would have to do it without him. His teams have had to do that before, of course. The third time Suárez bit another player during a match—the previous two were during his time at Ajax and Liverpool, respectively—was during the 2014 World Cup, against Italy, and Suárez was suspended for Uruguay's round of 16 loss, then another eight international matches, including an entire COPA America. (He scored against Brazil in his first match back.) That was different than the time Suárez was suspended for racially abusing Manchester United's Patrice Evra—Suárez

and his grandmother tried to claim it was a cultural misunderstanding—and then refused to shake his hand. He's been a piece
of work.

But on this night Suárez was done, and Uruguay just needed
everything to stay as it was. No problem.

The South Korea-Portugal game, however, was maybe 10
minutes ahead, and in extra time South Korea's Hwang Hee-chan
scored a brilliant goal to make it 2-1. South Korea was in position
to advance on goal differential, and Korean fans were weeping in
the stands. For Uruguay to advance, they needed another goal.

Suárez knew right away, and the match became an opera. He
sat on the bench with tears in his eyes, covering his face with his
jersey, looking back up. Uruguay pushed, but Ghana decided: If
we are going out, we are dragging the devil to hell with us.

Uruguay pushed; Ghana pushed back. Uruguay pushed:
Ghanian keeper Lawrence Ati-Zigi kept them out. Suárez looked
like a man watching his country die, his heavy eyes pulled down,
his jersey in his hands. It was 15 minutes of pure hole-in-the-
stomach agony. At Education City, the Koreans were watching the
match on the field, on someone's phone. Ghana would not yield.

One final free kick, the whistle blew, and Suárez covered his
head and sobbed. He stayed there as some of the Uruguayans
harassed the referee like a villain's henchmen. He stayed there as
the field sorted out, as the broadcasts summed it up, as the crowd
started to filter to the exits. This was the end of Luis Suárez and
Uruguay at the World Cup. He wept all the way up the tunnel.

It makes sense that he wept. Think about what drives a man
to compete the way Suárez competed: to put a hand on a ball and
never apologize, to dive so much you become known as a diver in
a sport full of divers, to kick your opponents, to denigrate them,
to refuse to shake their hand, to bite a man, and to do it again, and
again in a World Cup, in a match you need to win. What's it like
to have to let go of that? To have it taken away from you, ripped
away, when football meant so much every time you stepped on
a field that you couldn't always control yourself? Ghana coach

Otto Addo had said of the handball, "If the same incident had happened the other way round ... I'd want every player to do all he can, and even to sacrifice himself." He understood.

So of course Suárez sobbed, and Ghana got to be there, and somewhere Patrice Evra liked an Instagram post of Suárez on that bench. Ghana didn't quite defeat him, but they got to be there when the beast was slain, and this time they got to watch his heart break. See how he likes it. Maybe that was enough for Ghana, this time. They made the devil cry.

From the *Toronto Star*. © 2022 Toronto Star Newspapers Limited. All rights reserved. Used under license.

BRUCE ARTHUR has been a columnist for the *Toronto Star* since 2014, and was named Canada's sportswriter of the year in 2012 while with the *National Post*. Qatar was his first World Cup.

On a Quiet Lake in Rustic Minnesota, Stanford Coaching Icon Tara VanDerveer Runs It Back One More Time

CHANTEL JENNINGS

FROM The Athletic • SEPTEMBER 2, 2022

NORTHERN MINNESOTA—Tara VanDerveer leans back in her Adirondack chair, dogs Enzo and Piper asleep at her feet. She gets quiet, folds her arms and squints past the birch and pine trees as the sun drops toward the tree line across the lake. Pulling out her phone, she confirms what she already knew—the wind, currently breezing at around 4 mph, should fall to 1 to 2 mph in the next hour.

"Perfect," she says.

She puts the dogs inside the cabin; they press their noses against the picture windows facing the lake. They're her only real audience here, and she likes it that way.

VanDerveer, 69, retrieves a wetsuit and pink life jacket from the clothesline and heads into the sauna to change. When she emerges, she still looks like the country's winningest women's basketball coach but also, nothing at all like her. There is, of course, the iconic bob haircut, and perhaps it should come as no surprise that anything she does, she commits to thoroughly (hence, the wetsuit). But her energy radiates like everyone else on the water, the lake junkies who live for these nights with perfect ski conditions, the people who love (truly love) their boats.

She bought this cabin shortly after leading Team USA to gold at the 1996 Olympics. In the previous decade, she had never taken more than two weeks away from the game—the academic calendar was committed to Stanford and her summers devoted to Team USA and recruiting. A worldwide, 52-city tour to grow the popularity of the women's game before the Olympics had taken its toll. But during the team's stop at Old Dominion, on an early morning run along the Elizabeth River, she decided she would buy a house on the water when the Olympics concluded.

Thus began her cross-country search—from Virginia to Idaho to California—to find a refuge. She just wanted a quiet place with a quiet lake. And that's what she found in rustic northern Minnesota.

It was less the summer home of a millionaire coach and closer to a caricature of The Land of 10,000 Lakes, where house numbers are replaced by signs featuring that family's name, where grills are fired up nightly because there are no restaurants within 20 miles and where cabin walls are adorned with lake art with quaint phrases like "A day at the lake is worth a month in the town"—a sign that hangs in VanDerveer's stairwell.

When she got the keys to the cabin, there was no bedroom, no shower and it looked as if it hadn't been updated much since it was built in 1938. But the lot had room for a boat slip on the shore, space to build a garage to store her sailboat and lake views from almost every angle in the cabin.

It was perfect.

For several years, no one seemed to notice the national championship coach and Olympic gold medalist who was spending part of her summers next door. "It's more of a hockey state anyways," her lake friends admit.

For VanDerveer, that was also perfect.

She walks down to the dock, inspects her boat and checks the water temperature—a comfortable 72 degrees. Seven years ago, she bought the used speedboat from a guy in Connecticut who responded to her inquiry email by saying yes, he would sell her the boat, but also, "Do you happen to coach basketball?" Because, of course, her path to the perfect boat would lead her through Connecticut.

When the wind has died down and the sun has nearly set on this warm August evening, VanDerveer finally steps onto the boat. It's 7:50 p.m. A month from now, she'll be back in Palo Alto, Calif., preparing for another run at a national title with Stanford. But tonight, she has a much different kind of run ahead of her, and, save a pontoon idling on the south end of the lake, the water is entirely hers.

She zips up her life jacket and smiles.

"Here," she says, "I am totally at peace."

Six years before VanDerveer won her third national title and seven before she passed Pat Summitt as the winningest women's basketball coach in history, VanDerveer thought she was close to retirement.

In so many ways, that 2014-15 season was like many of the others she had coached at Stanford: The Cardinal upset and lost to top-10 teams on the road and at home, they won the Pac-12 Tournament and ended the season ranked in the Top 25.

But she was different.

"I was just exhausted and I wasn't enthusiastic," VanDerveer says. "When you're not feeling fresh or you're not feeling refreshed, you're not as good as you can be."

And VanDerveer had become as good as she could be by grinding and giving all of her time to the sport. She once consulted a friend (who also happened to be a psychologist) and asked him, "Do you think I should be worried about myself because all I do is work?" He said no, there were seasons to life, and it wouldn't always be that way. But the truth was, it always had.

Now, she was in her early 60s, and she had seemingly accomplished it all: conference championships, national championships, Olympic championships, a Hall of Fame induction. She had molded All-Americans and No. 1 draft picks. She was among the top-10 winningest coaches in basketball history. No one would've faulted her for walking away.

At a dinner after the season, John Arrillaga—a longtime Stanford donor and a person generally in the Stanford-know—approached the coach and told her that he had heard she was considering retirement.

"Don't do it," he said. "Just take the summer off. Get away."

VanDerveer laughed. Coaches didn't just take the summers off. Maybe some did, but *she* didn't. In her three-decade coaching career, VanDerveer had never missed a practice or a game. And even if she wanted to, there was no way Stanford athletic director Bernard Muir would go for that.

She thanked Arrillaga for the conversation, excused herself and drove home.

Fifteen minutes later, her phone rang. It was Arrillaga. He had just spoken with Muir.

"Bernard is fine with it," he told her. "Take the summer off. Go."

So VanDerveer did the unthinkable—for the first time in her career, she would take some time away from the game.

And with a whole summer off in 2015, the first place she went was to her small log cabin in Northern Minnesota, a two-bedroom dream facing westward on a lake with no public access. She had visited for a couple weeks in August every summer since 1998 (after renovations were complete following the purchase in 1996), but she had never really settled in.

She kayaked in the mornings, sat on the back porch for meals, played online bridge with her mom in the evenings and frequently ended her days in the sauna. She water-skied daily behind her jet ski, recruiting friends and visitors to drive her. And in July she left that cabin for another in Chautauqua, N.Y., where she had spent parts of her childhood summers, before returning to Northern Minnesota for the entire month of August.

She didn't recruit. Didn't coach. Didn't think about basketball. For a summer, she hit pause and realized that she didn't need retirement, she just needed *something*. Something different than what she had always done, something different than what had brought about all the success.

Shortly after VanDerveer arrived at Stanford in 1985, longtime Cardinal track coach Brooks Johnson had pulled her aside and told her, "You can do your clinics and tell people how you work, but never tell them how much you rest." And, whenever he'd see her on campus he'd remind her: "Tara, rest is not just a four-letter word."

And VanDerveer had taken it to heart ... for her team.

She had structured her season to have a slow ramp up and a long tapering off period, moving the most intense practices into the fourth, fifth and sixth weeks of the season and starting to pull back on everything else—length, intensity, contact—midway through February. It made so much sense to her that her team needed to make sure their legs were freshest in March, and in order to do that they needed to rest.

But she had never considered that kind of rest for herself. Not until she took that summer off.

Now, she thinks back to 2015, how close she thought she was to walking away, how exhausted she was when she arrived in the summer and how different she felt when she returned to Palo Alto in the fall. That summer changed her and sustained her. That summer, in many ways, is why she still does what she does. Or, why she can, at least.

"You only have so much tread on your tires," she says.

VANDERVEER IS A lake person because her parents were lake people. And while it's not scientifically a genetic marker, most lake people would beg to differ—if you grew up on the water, there's something about a lake's stillness that just hits differently.

Even VanDerveer's sister Heidi, who coaches at UC San Diego and can see the Pacific Ocean from her home, acknowledges the difference.

"The ocean is beautiful, but there's something about a lake that has your soul," she says. "You can take a different kind of breath."

In 1950, VanDerveer's dad, Dunbar, bought a modest one-bedroom cabin on Schroon Lake in Upstate New York. He introduced wife Rita to the cabin shortly after and three years later when Tara was born, she became the first VanDerveer child to spend her summers at the lake. A decade and four more children later, Dunbar and Rita purchased a cabin on Saranac Lake, somehow finding one even more remote than the first.

Because both parents were educators, the entire family had the summers off together. And every year on the last day of school, the family station wagon would be parked facing the street, the family boat hitched on the back. Sandwiches were prepped and bags were precariously stacked and strapped on top of the car. Tara, Beth and Marie would climb into the middle seats; Heidi and Nick would take the back seats, facing the rear toward the boat. Dunbar would make a final call for the bathroom—he'd only stop if they found a gas station on their side of the road (no way were they wasting time crossing over the median).

The cabin had no electricity or running water, which meant the family had to take its small boat across the lake to a natural spring to collect fresh water for the cabin every few days. The place was so quiet and remote that any time another boat came into their area of the bay, it became the highlight of the week. It was here that VanDerveer learned how to swim, fish, and later, how to water ski.

The VanDerveers befriended another family on the lake that owned a speed boat and VanDerveer watched as their kids—avid water-skiers—cut across the water on a single slalom ski. She had snow-skied before, so she felt as though this wouldn't be that different. On her first attempt behind the boat at age 8, she decided to drop one of her two skis, so she, too, could slalom. On her second attempt, she tried to just get up on one ski (something that takes most recreational skiers years to accomplish, if they ever do). She did that, too.

"That, honestly, started the whole visualization process that I use today in coaching," she says.

After a month at the family cabin, they would then head to the Chautauqua Institution on Lake Chautauqua, a 2,000-acre resort in western New York, where VanDerveer's dad ran summer programs for Syracuse and, later, a bed-and-breakfast.

"The Institute," as the family called it, was an entirely different experience. It was busy and loud with hordes of children running around. The VanDerveer kids would spend their days at the Boys and Girls Club, the local sailing club or other educational endeavors. VanDerveer taught swim lessons and competed in sailing competitions, participated in three operas and took flute lessons from a nationally renowned flutist.

After seven weeks, they'd head back to the family cabin to close out the summer, ending their August on a quiet note. They'd close up the cabin the day before school began, pulling into the driveway sometime around midnight. Rita would argue they were getting back too late; Dunbar would say they needed to soak up all the lake time.

"We better still fit into our shoes," VanDerveer says, "because that's what we were wearing the next day."

Six decades later, that was how she decided she would spend her years, again.

In Northern Minnesota, she chooses her ski time based on the weather conditions, but at Chautauqua, it's all about hitting the water before the lake gets too crowded. Her record in a summer is 90 days of skiing, and she thinks—if the weather holds out a bit—she'll hit 75 this year.

"I think I'm just trying to recreate my childhood life," VanDerveer says, shortly after sharing a new and more efficient s'mores technique she learned this summer.

There's a natural perspective that comes with time, but for VanDerveer, that new balance was brought about by her summers at the lake, how it forced her to give up some control and instead, slow down for herself.

"I've known Tara for a long time and she still is obsessed with basketball, but at one point, that was maybe all she did in her career—365 days a year, non-stop," longtime associate head coach Kate Paye said. "This offers a sense of balance, maybe it's healthier, maybe it has allowed her to grow, evolve and learn."

In recent years, those around her have seen her lighter side coming to the forefront. She gladly embraced the nickname "T-Dawg" from her players (and a large fleece jacket embroidered with the name); she danced the electric slide with her team after winning a regional title. After winning the national championship in 2021, she arrived at the press conference rocking a backwards hat, and shortly after, she received a quick phone call from Arrillaga.

"Aren't you glad you didn't retire?" he asked.

She agreed and thanked him. She knows how those moments were rooted in that conversation and her decision to step away for a bit. Because she's not sure if she would still be coaching if it weren't for that conversation.

"Maybe?" she says, "Probably.

"But I don't know if I'd be as happy. I don't know if I'd enjoy it all as much."

JUST BEFORE 8, VanDerveer drops her ski in the water and jumps in.

She grabs the rope and moves it back and forth against the water, getting into her rhythm and shaking out potential knots. The typical ski rope length is 75 feet, but hers—like competitive slalom skiers—is knotted to a shorter length (53 feet, to be exact) so she has greater control in the water.

For a while, it's just her bobbed haircut and pink life jacket visible from the boat, but she quickly pops up from the water and begins her daily therapy.

She starts on her first lap around the lake, the boat drifting right before cutting a sharp left turn at the west end of the lake as VanDerveer flies out onto the glassiest part of the water. The rope slacks and tightens as the 69-year-old careens from left to right, left to right like a metronome on the water.

Her mom used to say that the lake sustained her through the school year when she was a teacher. VanDerveer didn't completely understand it then. She does now.

She no longer takes the full summer off as she did in 2015, but she does make the lakes—in Northern Minnesota or Western New York—her home bases for the summer months. VanDerveer returns to Stanford for minicamps in June and July, goes on recruiting trips to tournaments occasionally throughout the summer and takes calls with her current staff, players and recruits.

But when she returns "home" from those trips in the summer, she returns to the lake. And when she picks up her phone, she's on her back porch looking at the water.

"Could anything be more perfect?" VanDerveer asks.

When she does retire, she doesn't think her summers will look all that different than they do now. But she doesn't know when that will be. She's not ready. Not yet.

The lake is a world away from the basketball courts she'll inhabit in a few weeks and she'll cry when she puts the boat into storage (but, she'll also remind the dogs and herself "it'll be minus 40 degrees here before too long.") But for now the winningest coach of all time is right at home, flying on a 6-inch-wide piece of wood at 30 mph behind a boat, her ski sending spray 15 feet in the air behind her as the sun falls behind the trees.

When the boat finishes its first full lap, she drops down, slowly and controlled, into the water, disappearing under it for a second.

When she emerges, she yells toward the boat, "Let's run it back one more time."

CHANTEL JENNINGS is a senior writer covering women's basketball at The Athletic. She was a 2020 Knight-Wallace Fellow at the University of Michigan and her writing also appeared in the 2018 edition of The Best American Sports Writing. She lives in Minneapolis with her husband, daughter, and dog, and is pretty amused that she was finally able to write a sports story with NORTHERN MINNESOTA as a dateline.

'She Made Us Happy': The All-Star Dreams of Uvalde's Biggest José Altuve Fan

ROBERTO JOSÉ ANDRADE FRANCO

FROM ESPN • JULY 27, 2022

Tess Mata stood beneath the brown awning and threw a yellow softball at the white box that her father had spray-painted on a sugar maple tree. Tess hated practicing out here in the backyard. Every time she missed, she had to chase the ball and walk back to beneath the awning, pushing her glasses up the bridge of her sweaty nose before the next pitch. Do that routine a few times in the heat and humidity of South Texas, and you'd hate it, too.

"It's too hot," Tess finally complained. And so she went inside, got on her knees and whipped a tennis ball against the chimney wall, until one of her pitches strayed. "Hey!" her father, Jerry, yelled, "You're going to break the TV." It was back outside after that.

Tess might have hated the heat and the tree, but she kept throwing because, just like playing softball, pitching was her idea. When she told her parents she wanted to give it a try, her mother, Veronica, worried the position wasn't right for her baby girl, still just 10 years old. Tess had been so timid when she first started school, she'd sneak her baby blanket into her backpack.

"She was always scared that nobody was going to pick her up,"
Veronica says.

But they couldn't tell Tess no; she was too determined. Her
goal was to make the Little League all-star team, and so Tess
watched countless hours of YouTube on her iPad to learn the
pitching mechanics. She refined them at that tree. She kept going
because few things felt better than hitting the target. Sometimes
the ball hit so perfectly, it almost bounced back to Tess.

When that happened, even the neighbors in the Mata's quiet
neighborhood in Uvalde heard the soft thumping of a softball
hitting a tree. Thump. Thump. Thump. Over and over again. Each
time, the ball broke off small pieces of bark. She threw for hours,
and after she was done, Jerry rubbed Biofreeze on her shoulder
to comfort her.

Talking about Tess while standing at the kitchen table, Jerry
says he has video of the first time she pitched in a game for her
team, the Bandits. He pulls out his phone from his front pocket
and scrolls through videos looking for the right one. He stands
there, with salt-and-pepper stubble on his chin and puffiness
under his eyes, wearing a gray T-shirt with the Bandits logo on it.

"Here it is," Jerry says. He holds the phone so I can see Tess
pitching. His back is to the chimney wall, now full of flowers,
balloons and drawings. Further behind Jerry's back is the sugar
maple tree.

"She struck out the first batter she faced," he says.

FOR CENTURIES, THE place that's now Texas was the ungov-
ernable frontier. The place where even if it was a part of Spain,
or France, or Mexico, or its own republic, or the United States,
or the Confederacy, its boundaries and laws were abstractions.
The reality of who controlled the land was different from what
any map said. And no place in Texas was as contested as the
Nueces Strip.

For years after declaring its independence from Mexico in
1836, Texas said its southern border was the Rio Grande. If it even

acknowledged Texas' independence, Mexico claimed the border was further north, at the Nueces River. The land between those two bodies of water, about 150 miles wide and 400 miles long, became the Nueces Strip.

It was a place with no clear owner outside those with a stomach for violence strong enough to hold a claim. A place that seemingly alternated between floods and droughts. At times, with cholera in the water, even trying to quench your thirst in that unrelenting heat could be deadly. That general lawlessness there, mixed with the large and small animals—bears, mountain lions and wolves, and scorpions, tarantulas, snakes and mosquitoes—made the area almost uninhabitable.

Whatever semblance of control Texas gained of the Nueces Strip is largely a result of the Colt revolver. The same year Texas declared independence, Samuel Colt filed a patent for his weapon. Until then, for centuries, handguns were practically all the same: a metal tube that used gunpowder to fire pellet-like projectiles. You took one shot then reloaded. That process could take up to a minute, longer in inclement weather. Often that was the literal time between life and death. In the Nueces Strip, Comanches riding on horseback could shoot as many as 20 arrows in the time it took to reload a gun.

The Colt revolver, which could fire five shots between reloads, was designed to kill more efficiently, and when Texans got their hands on those revolvers, it changed everything; the Comanches stood no chance against them. And because you can't understand this country without knowing how much Texas influences its identity, that gun also changed the United States.

Among the first things the country mass-produced was the Colt revolver. It was a preview of the things the American industrial revolution could make with speed, precision and uniformity. Owning a gun became easier, and if one ever broke, because of its interchangeable parts—hammers, triggers and cylinders—it could be easily fixed compared to when a gunsmith had to repair the entire gun.

"God created men equal. Colonel Colt made them equal." That became a common saying as the Colt revolver's impact spread across the country. Manifest Destiny was the ideology guiding the country's western expansion—from Texas, west to New Mexico, Arizona, parts of Nevada, Colorado, Utah and all of California, then north to Oregon and Washington—and the Colt was the gun used to enforce it.

The Nueces River runs through Uvalde County. The town is on the edge of the Nueces Strip. Mexican long before it was Texan, it's the same place that when preachers brought the good word to the roughest of countries, they often carried a gun next to their Bible. The same place that, today, because it's still surrounded by wilderness, is one of Texas' hunting capitals.

VERONICA AND JERRY thought about moving. Before their oldest daughter, Faith, started school and their family roots grew deeper, they thought about getting out. Not because they disliked Uvalde. Both of their parents were born and raised in this small town of 15,000. Their grandparents, who moved here from Mexico to work, also lived in Uvalde. Jerry still remembers how when his father drank with friends, they'd talk about the places in town where they couldn't go. Despite that, Veronica and Jerry felt safe here. The high school sweethearts only thought about leaving because that's part of growing up in a small Texas town.

Through the years, Jerry, an aviation mechanic, got job offers with better pay in Dallas, Houston, San Antonio, even as far away as Virginia. They'd visit. They'd start looking for a place to live, but it never felt right. "It was just scary to take my daughters to a big city I didn't know," Jerry says, sitting at the kitchen table. So, when it was time to decide, the comfort of home and living in a small town—where you could leave your doors unlocked, ride your bike to the movie theater, and know who your neighbors were—always won.

They stayed, planning for their two daughters to have the same friends from kindergarten to high school, and probably long after that. They'd have the same neighbors, and Veronica, a kindergarten teacher at Dalton Elementary School, would see her young students grow into adults. With time, she'd even teach the kids of her students, too. Faith and Tess would play sports, often with the same teammates, and their lives would, in many ways, revolve around that.

"She was on the softball field since she was a baby," Veronica says of Tess. She grew up watching Faith play so often that Tess would sometimes fall asleep on the grass or stands next to the fields. She spent so much time there that, at first, Tess didn't want to play. "I don't want to do softball," she said, choosing gymnastics and soccer instead. She said that until she changed her mind.

Before she pitched, Tess played second base for two reasons. Because that's the position Faith played, and because her favorite player on her favorite team did, too.

José Altuve this, José Altuve that. Tess talked about the Houston Astros star all the time. Before settling on Oliver, Tess even considered naming her cat José. She talked about him so much that she asked for an Altuve poster and jersey. When Veronica and Jerry bought them, Tess couldn't wait to show Faith.

"He proved that anybody short can play," Jerry says of the 5-foot-6 Altuve. He thinks Tess related to him because of his height.

"GROWING UP, THE schools were divided," Roberto Morales says. Uvalde is nearly 82% Latino, mostly of Mexican ethnicity. The local schools are desegregated today because Roberto's mother, Genoveva, sued the district in 1970. His house is roughly two blocks from Robb Elementary School, and about double that distance from what locals know as *el parque Mexicano*, the Mexican park. "The *Mexicanos*, we were on this side of town," Roberto, 65, continues. "And that's where we stayed because of the gringos. They didn't want you over there."

Over there was the east side of town. It included what the *Mexicanos* know as *el parque de los gringos*. It was in the part of

Uvalde that, when Roberto was a young boy, had paved roads and sidewalks around the big, nice houses with indoor plumbing. On cold nights, that part of town never worried about the gas getting turned off to keep enough pressure in the pipes to heat the other side. That part of town had enough resources for schools. The west side was the opposite of that.

For the schools, that meant not enough textbooks and basic equipment. Not enough organized sports. Not enough Mexican American teachers and administrators who understood the culture. Too many teachers and administrators who guided students toward trade and vocational schools. Too much of a difference between how the white students got treated compared to everyone else.

"You weren't supposed to speak Spanish," Roberto says. When teachers heard anyone doing that, they sent the students to the principal's office. "He had a wooden paddle with a bunch of holes," Roberto remembers. Because of those holes drilled into the paddle, he also remembers the soft whistling sound that came the split second before a violent slap against his body. That type of punishment will make an entire generation, and maybe even the ones after that, lose their language.

"It was bad," says Roberto, a truck driver who delivers asphalt across the state. When he talks, he'll pepper Spanish words or phrases into his sentences, as if he's quietly showing defiance. A subtle reminder that they might have beat him, but they never took those words from him. Roberto repeats himself. "It was bad. *Pero* then, it turned after the walkout. They started hiring *maestros Mexicanos.*"

Roberto was in sixth grade when, on April 14, 1970, Mexican and Mexican American parents and their children, about 600 students, walked out of Uvalde schools. Inspired by a similar walkout in Crystal City, nearly 40 miles south, parents and their children protested. They said the Robb Elementary School principal refused to renew the contract of one of the few Mexican teachers; among other things, those *maestros Mexicanos* translated for parents and didn't enforce the no-speaking-Spanish rule. They also protested the inequalities between their school and the ones on the east side.

At that point, it was the culmination of decades worth of school segregation. Across Texas, school administrators and agricultural growers worried, sometimes saying it explicitly, that properly educating students of Mexican ethnicity would lead to diminishing the state's labor force. In a place like Uvalde—which, like other cities and towns across the country, recruited Mexican labor during the 1930s—there was little incentive to improve schools. There, those of Mexican ethnicity often worked in restaurants, the nearby asphalt mine, in the fields picking cabbage, onions, spinach and cotton, or as sheep shearers. *Trasqueleros*, they called themselves. They stayed in Uvalde until there was no more work, they'd then offer their services to ranchers across the country.

In 1930, Texas' first court case on Mexican school segregation occurred in Del Rio, about an hour's drive west of Uvalde, right on the Rio Grande. The district admitted to segregating schools but argued it was for the students' advantage since many of them traveled with their parents to any field that needed picking or any ranch that needed a hand. They'd have their own pace of learning among those just like them, separate but equal, is what the district said in so many words. A local court ruled against the district. That decision was overturned on appeal, which helped spark the Mexican and Mexican American fight for Texas civil rights. The Uvalde school walkouts were a continuation of that.

Roberto remembers how, as they marched peacefully, singing "De Colores"—the Mexican folk song that became the anthem of the United Farm Workers—Texas Rangers, from atop surrounding buildings, aimed their guns at them. How helicopters hovered above. How even after students returned to class after a six-week boycott, some held back a grade as a form of punishment, others reclassified and drafted into the military, the fight was far from over.

That's when Genoveva, who worked as a cook, sued the school district. Small-town rumors said Fidel Castro had brainwashed her. She got called a communist because she demanded school desegregation. The district court heard her arguments and found nothing illegal. The 5th Circuit Court of Appeals reversed that decision. It ruled that more than 20 years after Brown v. Board of Education outlawed school segregation, Uvalde had exactly that.

Soon after Genoveva's lawsuit, a federal judge ordered Texas to desegregate all of its schools. As a response, in the East Texas town of Longview, two men used dynamite to explode and destroy 36 parked buses that would have taken Black students to the white schools.

In Uvalde, school desegregation came slow. So slow that every April 15, the district had to submit an annual report to the court, showing the changes it made. That went on for decades. So long that, Roberto says, whenever the district hired a new superintendent, their first job was to meet with his mother and ask her to drop the lawsuit, which wasn't fully resolved until 2017, nearly a half-century after it first got filed. "I owe so much to Genoveva," says Dr. Jeanette Ball, who served as Uvalde's superintendent from 2013 to 2018. "It allowed a Hispanic young girl like me to become superintendent." In 2014, the district renamed Uvalde's one junior high school after Genoveva.

With Robb Elementary School, even if it isn't the way it once was, it's still the school on the Mexican side of Uvalde, where almost 90% of the students are Latinx, most of Mexican ethnicity, and a quarter are in a bilingual program. Still the school where just over 81% are classified as economically disadvantaged. Still the school four blocks from *el parque Mexicano*, where, during the walkout, the community gathered to teach the students, trying to make sure they didn't fall behind.

Suffering from dementia, Genoveva is 93 years old. There's a chapter in the book "Revolutionary Women of Texas and Mexico" that's all about her. Roberto keeps a copy in his home and shows it with pride. "God's been good to me, here in Uvalde," Roberto says. "No matter what we've gone through."

"It's been real quiet lately," Jerry says. He has a soft but raspy voice with that Mexican Texan accent of someone who speaks as much Spanish as English. He sits at his kitchen table, in his house a couple of blocks from Morales Junior High School, in a neighborhood once predominately white. It's a house that, until recently, was filled with some sort of sound, most of it coming from Tess.

It was the sounds Tess inadvertently made when trying to keep quiet, sneaking a bag of Takis out of the kitchen before dinner. The sounds she made—those meows—when she played with Oliver around the house. The sounds of her repeated plays of Bebe Rexha's "Meant to Be." That was her favorite song, and when it came on the car radio, she'd have Jerry sing it with her.

"She would make us laugh every day," Veronica says, sitting next to Jerry at the kitchen table. She says even when Tess did something wrong, it was simply impossible to stay upset with her. Like the time they told her not to wear a quinceañera dress for picture day at Robb Elementary because it was simply too much for the occasion. "OK," Tess said. When the school pictures arrived a few weeks later, Veronica and Jerry got the photograph of Tess, smiling while wearing the formal dress better suited for a ball. She'd snuck the dress into her backpack, changed at school, and wore it just for the photo.

That school picture is in the Mata's living room, by the chimney wall, next to the balloons and flowers. It makes them smile when they see it. When they tell the story, it makes them laugh, even now. They're trying hard to get used to all the things that are gone. Trying to get used to no longer hearing the sounds Tess made, the thump-thump-thump whenever she practiced her pitching.

After her first strikeout, she knew she was meant to pitch; even though she'd taught herself to do it, she'd get angry at herself whenever she didn't strike a batter out. And so this spring, Jerry had decided to hire a pitching coach so Tess could work with them during the summer.

"Of course, that didn't happen," Jerry says.

The house is so quiet, you can hear his voice crack.

YOU CAN DRAW a straight line connecting Texas' independence from Mexico in 1836, to the United States' annexation of Texas in 1845, to the United States-Mexico War in 1846, to the United States' westward expansion, to the Civil War in 1860. And along each of these events that physically and philosophically shaped the country, you can trace the spread of the Colt revolver.

The Colt Paterson—the gun patented in 1836—was the weapon of Texas. When Texans decided they wanted parts, if not all, of neighboring New Mexico in 1841, they carried Colts with them. (The Mexican military stopped them at Santa Fe, then forced them to march about 1,500 miles to a Mexico City prison.) From the Colt Paterson, evolved the Colt Walker. The revolver was named after Samuel H. Walker, who wrote letters to Colt, praising the value of his weapon out in the Texas frontier. Walker was a Texas Ranger, the state law enforcement group founded in 1823 to protect the more than 600 white families and their slaves settling in Texas. His letters to Colt also included suggestions to improve the revolver. Colt listened and added a chamber. The six-shooter was born just in time for the war with Mexico.

Those Colts were the weapons Texas Rangers carried as they arrested people of Mexican ethnicity and sometimes made them vanish. It happened so often that loved ones of the missing knew where to look for the bodies, out in the isolated Texas country, among the mesquite trees.

"The history of brutality by the Texas Rangers is one that a lot of Texans know," Dr. Monica Muñoz Martinez says. "It's just that they've seen it intentionally suppressed or worse, celebrated in history and popular culture." A history professor at the University of Texas and a 2021 MacArthur Fellowship recipient, often called the genius grant, Martinez was born and raised in Uvalde. She describes it as "a complicated town" where she made "beautiful and joyous memories."

She attended Robb Elementary School, and her parents participated in the walkouts. She has dedicated her research to uncovering anti-Mexican violence on the Texas-Mexico border, even writing a book about it: "The Injustice Never Leaves You: Anti-Mexican Violence in Texas." Mexican communities across Texas have told her parts of their history got erased or altered. After sharing file folders and boxes documenting the violence done against their families, they thank her for listening to their painful history they refused to forget.

"There are very dark parts of Texas history," says Martinez, who receives hate mail for her work. "But I choose to be inspired by the people who've continued, for generation after generation, to call for justice."

To this day, people sing *corridos*—Mexican songs recounting that history of oppression and tragedy and the folk heroes who waged war when their land got taken from them—about what the Texas Rangers did. They're a sort of oral tradition handed down from one generation to the next. Los Rinches, some songs call the Texas Rangers. Others call them Los diablos Tejanos. The devils from Texas who, in 1855, even crossed south of the Rio Grande looking for runaway slaves then burned down a Mexican town on their way back. The ones who shut down Spanish-language newspapers that wrote about Mexican and Mexican Americans getting lynched, sometimes by Texas Rangers themselves. The ones who blocked school integration. And because the vast Texas land always requires someone to work it, the Texas Rangers were also the ones who brutally broke farm worker strikes.

Just like the Texas Rangers, other law enforcement agencies across the West, including the military, either did little to stop the anti-Mexican mob violence or were part of it. The local, state, and federal government were complicit in all of this; mayors, judges and governors were the ones asking for help in seizing control of their regions from people whose families, in some cases, had been there for generations. And in South Texas, part of this control included dispossessing Mexicans of their guns.

"Well into the twentieth century, the majority-white culture continued to utilize extra-legal violence against Mexicans as a means of asserting its sovereignty over the region," historians William D. Carrigan and Clive Webb write in their academic journal article, "The Lynching of Persons of Mexican Origin or Descent in the United States, 1848 to 1928." Most of that region was the place that'd once been Mexico. "The lynching of Mexicans was one of the mechanisms by which Anglos consolidated their colonial control of the American west."

Some of these lynch mobs carried Colts, too. And at the beginning of the Civil War, before Samuel Colt got increasingly accused of treason, he sold his guns to both the North and the South.

This made Samuel Colt extravagantly wealthy. He'd been buried in debt until Mexico abolished slavery in 1829 and Texas revolted because of it. Until then, he'd been trying to convince the world of the usefulness of his revolutionary weapon. But once Texas, and then the country, and then the world, saw the deadly advantage of firing as many shots in as little a time as possible, Colt made so much money, his mansion—named Armsmear— was the second largest in his home state of Connecticut. Only P.T. Barnum had a bigger home. Colt had so much money that when he died, his widow, Elizabeth, had a church built in his honor in Hartford. Colt Manufacturing Company is still headquartered nearby in West Hartford.

Today, the Church of the Good Shepherd is on the National Register of Historic Places. Elizabeth had the architect incorporate parts of the revolver into the church's Gothic Revival design. Hammers, triggers, and cylinders are there in the archway. Carved into the stone, there's a Colt revolver on the church's porch.

"Sometimes I feel guilty for not being here enough," Faith tells Veronica, sitting at their kitchen table.

Immediately after graduating from high school in 2019, Faith wanted to leave. Her parents convinced her to first attend Southwest Texas Junior College, there in Uvalde.

"OK, I guess," she said. "I'm getting all my basics done in a year, and then I'm leaving." When she did that, she quietly applied and got accepted to Texas State University—two hours away in San Marcos—then told her parents and Tess she was going. Almost immediately, Tess took over Faith's old room.

Moving away for college was hard; you come from a small town, from a small, tight-knit family, and being apart takes some getting used to. To help ease that distance, Jerry and Veronica would send Faith photos of Tess. Photos of her playing softball, of her dancing, of her with Oliver.

"It was like watching her grow through pictures," Faith says, "and not being there for some of the big things that she was going through."

Tess loved whenever her big sister—Sissy, as she called her—came home. She'd be the first out the door to greet her. The one who carried Faith's bags inside. Tess was the one who cried the most when Faith again left home. That's part of the reason Tess and Faith spoke on the phone every day. "She was my mini-me," Faith says.

In addition to inspiring her younger sister to play softball and second base, Faith was the reason Tess wanted to learn how to swim. She wanted to celebrate Sissy's college graduation, about a year from now, by jumping into the San Marcos River that runs through campus. It's a university tradition for graduates to jump into the river that's always 72 degrees.

"She didn't know how to swim," Faith says, "so she was teaching herself."

As Faith talks at the kitchen table, Veronica listens, nodding her head. Veronica says Tess learned how to swim on the Saturday before that Tuesday.

THERE ARE CERTAIN things that happen when there's a mass shooting in your town.

The media arrives and stays for months. Family members of the slain come, too. As do people from surrounding towns, cities and even states. Florists come offering their help. Some of them are from places also broken by a mass shooting, so they know the town's florists can't keep up with the sudden demand.

Hotels are sold out for weeks. And because the infrastructure wasn't designed for this, the streets are congested. There are SUVs from police departments across Texas that, here in Uvalde, because of all the questions of why cops waited so long to act at Robb Elementary, and why they'd waited even longer to give answers, adds to the simmering tension you can feel in your chest and throat.

If you live here, you won't feel as safe as you once did. That feeling of *something like that wouldn't happen here* will be gone. You'll see neighbors change their opinions of guns. Some will embrace them. Others will never want to touch them again. In a similar way, some will find God. Others, being so close to evil and the suffering it brought, will feel lost.

If you're from Uvalde, as clear as knowing the west side of town is where most Mexican and Mexican Americans live, you feel as if time has broken in two. The things that happened before May 24, that Tuesday, and the things that came after. It's in the after that, whenever you tell someone where you're from, they'll almost immediately remember what happened there. They'll ask you about it and, even years later, when you answer, you'll still fight that urge to cry. The wound will always be there. The best you can hope for is that one day it won't hurt as much.

As you drive around, you can see the signs of "Uvalde Strong" and "Pray for Uvalde" just about everywhere you look. On the windows of stores and fast-food restaurants. On decals placed on the back of cars, on T-shirts, and on the sidewalks, written in pastel-colored chalk, near the places of gathering.

Your town is full of people, trying to help by giving away things. A teenager holds a sign near a coffee shop on Main Street that says, "Free Carne Guisada." At Town Square, across from the county courthouse whose front lawn has a granite monument saying Uvalde's main street was once Jefferson Davis Highway, a boy walks around offering free bibles. A sign in Spanish, taped to a light post, near there, says there's free therapy for the survivors.

Someone will write a *corrido* about the tragedy. Your eyes look swollen from the lack of sleep and the nightmares when you do sleep, but mostly from the crying. From the sadness of hearing mariachis, who traveled from San Antonio, sing and perform "Amor Eterno." That song of loss and longing that makes it feel like your soul is being cut apart by a dull knife.

You hear the pain and anger in the voice of Jorge Barrera Lopez, the Brown Beret who, along with other members of the Chicano civil rights organization, traveled from San Antonio too. He tells you about Pharr—another small Texas town, right on the Rio Grande—and what happened there on February 6, 1971. Mexican and Mexican Americans gathered to denounce police brutality. During the protest, a deputy sheriff shot and killed 20-year-old Alfonso Loredo Flores. Nothing ever happened to the cop who pulled the trigger. Shot in the head, Flores died with his hands in his pockets.

"It just never ends," Lopez says.

When there's a mass shooting in your home, there will be a main memorial. Here, it's at Robb Elementary. There, you see parents, holding their child's hand, walking toward the school. With bloodshot eyes, they stare at the victims' photos surrounded by wilted flowers and stuffed animals whose color has faded from being so long beneath the sun. Some visitors try to clean them as best as they can before the town manager tells them to leave it alone.

At that same memorial, someone places a Happy Meal box in front of each of the children's photos. Because of the heat, some balloons next to those photos have popped. They once flew next to handwritten signs offering condolences and lamenting everything that's happened.

"I'm sorry we all let you down," one of those signs reads.

It's a shattered town full of what sounds like people trying to catch their breath. You wonder if the person with loud screams and cries has lost a family member or friend. You can smell the burning of wax candles that, when the sun sets, try to brighten the darkness of this small South Texas town.

They can't.

"JUST MOVE," FAITH tells Veronica and Jerry. They're sitting in their kitchen, which is full of food and bottled water that friends and family have brought them.

Move from Uvalde is what Faith wanted. Maybe to San Marcos, to be with her as she finishes college. After a few years, maybe they can all move to the Dallas area or somewhere around Austin. Maybe even away from Texas. Move to a place where they don't know where everything is. A place where people won't know their name and everything that they've lost.

"I can't," Veronica answers. "This is where we brought Tess home. This is where I raised her."

Inside Tess' room are the things one would expect from a 10-year-old-girl that was deeply loved. A corkboard filled with thumbtacked photos of the two sisters and Tess with her friends. "I love you, Faith!!!!" Tess wrote in black marker on the lower left corner of the corkboard's wooden frame.

The room has trophies and medals from sports she played. A bag full of softballs is on her dresser, next to her glove. Stuffed animals—a teal-colored octopus, a purple owl and a pig the size of a pillow—lie on her bed, atop a comforter full of butterflies in all colors and sizes. Tess' softball bat pack rests on the floor in front of the closet full of the clothes she once wore. The money she earned selling bracelets with beads is still in the jar. She was saving money to visit Disney World again. Not far from that is a picture of Tess with her cousins from the day she learned how to swim.

Her Altuve jersey has been turned into a pillow and put inside a protective plastic. The family says they'll carry it with them from now on, whenever they travel. They also say the Altuve poster will stay on her wall. It's next to a floral arrangement made with Houston Astros colors.

Some things inside that room, they'll give to family and some of Tess' friends. They've been asking for things that were once hers. Things that, if they hold to their nose and take a deep, deep breath, still smell like her.

For now, this is Tess' room, as close as possible to how she left it. Oliver, who, Faith says, is the reason Tess also wanted to attend Texas State and become a veterinarian, often lays in the middle of the bed. He lays there most of the time, like he is waiting for Tess. The family says they know it sounds crazy, but they think Oliver can still see her around the house.

"This is where our heart's at," Jerry says of Tess' room, and their home, and their small South Texas town next to the now waterless Nueces River.

"After all this, I don't think I can live here anymore," Faith says.

She wants to leave and take her parents with her. Veronica and Jerry say they can't. Everything that's left of Tess is here.

OF THE 11 deadliest mass shootings in this country, five of them have happened in Texas. The first of them, from atop a tower on the University of Texas campus in 1966, is considered the country's first modern mass shooting. The second, inside a Luby's Cafeteria in 1991, helped change the state's strict gun laws. For years after that shooting in Killeen, one of those survivors, Suzanna Gratia Hupp, traveled the country telling her story. How she watched her parents die. How she'd left her gun in her car, afraid that if caught carrying it, she'd lose her chiropractor's license. How the gunman wouldn't have killed so many had she had her weapon. How she wasn't upset at that gunman as much as she was at lawmakers who didn't allow her to defend herself and her family. In 1996, Hupp was elected to the Texas House of Representatives as an unflinching proponent of gun rights.

The year prior, Governor George W. Bush signed a bill allowing Texas citizens to carry concealed handguns. In 1997, Bush signed an amendment removing that same law's prohibitions against carrying concealed handguns at churches. Since then, and increasingly more recently, Texas gun laws have loosened. In 2021, Governor Greg Abbott signed a law that allows Texans to carry a handgun without a license or training. He called the bill the "strongest Second Amendment legislation in Texas history." According to the Pew Research Center, there are 588,696 registered guns in Texas, the most of any state, and 45.7% of residents own a gun, which ranks 27th.

Three of Texas' deadliest mass shootings have happened in the past five years: at a church at Sutherland Springs in 2017, at a Walmart in El Paso in 2019, and at Robb Elementary in Uvalde. At the Sutherland and Uvalde shootings, the gunman used an AR-15. Colt bought the production rights to that weapon in 1959. Colt's patent expired in 1977, and other companies now mass-produce similar models.

As Veronica and Faith walk onto the baseball field, near the eastern town limits of Uvalde, they hold each other's hand. Along with Jerry, who walks beside them, they've been doing more of that recently. Holding each other, trying to figure out how to live through the days.

They wear matching gray T-shirts with the Bandits logo on them. Three weeks and two days after that Tuesday, they line up next to the other families along the first-base line. All of them here, at an all-star game ceremony, to honor the lives of the 19 students and two teachers killed at Robb Elementary. That number is higher if you count the husband who died of a heart attack two days after his wife, who was Tess' teacher, was killed.

Even higher if you count those still here, though a large part of them is gone.

"That day has never ended," Veronica says. She wears a button with a photo of Tess over her heart. Tess is smiling. "She was happy," Veronica says. "She made us happy."

In the past 17 days, Uvalde has held 21 funerals. Most were held in the same two churches. Most of the dead were buried in the same cemetery 3½ miles from the baseball fields. The same procession route, the same families, the same worthless attempts to turn off the bad thoughts.

The last of the funerals was at 10 in the morning on the day of this ceremony. "It's hard," Veronica says, "but we'll get through this." She wears dark aviator sunglasses. She says Tess wouldn't want to see her cry.

Uvalde Little League officials considered canceling the all-star tournament. That was around the time when teams across the country, as far away as Hawaii, filled the league's Facebook page with pictures of kids playing in honor of the Robb Elementary students and teachers. They wore Uvalde patches on their jerseys and stickers on their helmets. They said prayers and observed moments of silence.

In small towns like Uvalde, Little League binds the community. That's why Uvalde officials ultimately chose to continue the tournament as planned. Maybe it could, for at least a game, bring people together. Maybe, again, kids could run around and play until they got tired and fell asleep next to the fields. Still, it felt jarring to play games in a town wrecked by grief. A town that is broken by unanswered questions.

Long after Robb Elementary has been destroyed—which it will be because there's no need for a physical reminder of the time when kids called for the police to help them and they didn't come—those questions will linger.

If this was the school on the white side of town, would the police have acted differently?

That's the main question. It hardly matters to those asking it that a sizable percentage of Uvalde police officers are Latino. Because of the painful history: That's why that question will haunt this place. It'll be here forever. In the same way, those who were at the Uvalde civic center that night will say they'll never forget the agonized screams of people who just found out they'd lost so much.

"She left us a lot," Veronica says of Tess. She sometimes holds a small piece of cloth that's been folded over several times. It's what's left of the baby blanket Tess snuck in and out of her backpack so often the thread started to run. She kept it, hoping to give it to Tess whenever she became a mother. "We can hear her voice every day," Veronica says.

In the days after, the Matas found a TikTok account Tess kept hidden because she wasn't allowed to have one. The account had over 200 unpublished drafts of Tess smiling and talking, dancing and laughing. Along with the selfies she took on Veronica and Jerry's phones when they weren't looking, Tess left them a sort of digital diary that they can look at whenever they miss her too much.

Jerry thanks God for that. He says that's helped. He says they'll probably always have anger about the police, and the lack of gun control, and everything else, but that won't bring Tess back. They hold each other. They laugh and smile whenever he, or Veronica, or Faith, talk about Tess. But because some moments are easier than others—moments when all of them think leaving might just be easier—sometimes those same memories make them cry.

"We want to celebrate her," Veronica says.

That's why they're here, for the ceremony in this park where, since it hasn't rained since the day after that Tuesday, the palm trees look dry and the grass is browning. It's going to be a long, hot summer, and already just over half of Texas is under an extreme drought. Just some 20 miles up the road in Concan, the town has shut off its water from midnight to 6 in the morning, trying to conserve what they have. With climbing temperatures, there's the ever-present threat of rolling blackouts, as Texas' power grid struggles to meet the energy demand.

But those problems, right now, feel distant. One of those things that come after trying to survive. Right now, Uvalde is here, on this field, in this aching moment. Standing here, it's hard to say this is a moment of healing. Even long after these games have ended, healing will not come. There is something horribly familiar in this truth, something horribly familiar about Uvalde. I felt it as soon as I arrived. It's in all the spoken parts: the connection forged by our shared Spanish language, letting me closer to all the pain, the pain that I recognized from my own home in El Paso. It's in all the quiet parts too: the past that's never gone, and the deep, unsaid fears that your broken home might never recover, the worry that Texas, and this country, will eventually rip the hope right out you.

None of this had to be this way. That's what it feels like, standing here. Not the past, not the present, and not the seemingly inevitable tomorrow. It all could have been different. Avoided. We didn't have to grow up alongside the Nueces River, listening to songs and stories of the violence all around us. But we did.

The ceremony continues, and a man, standing in front of the pitcher's mound, plays the national anthem on his melancholic trumpet. About a half-mile to his right is the hospital where some of the victims died. The Border Patrol station is a half-mile toward his left. Behind him, just past the center-field fence, the United States flag flies at half-staff.

"We would like to remember the 21 individuals who we lost that day," a voice over the PA system says.

Nevaeh Bravo. Jackie Cazares. Ellie Garcia. Uziyah Garcia. Amerie Garza. Jayce Luevanos. Maranda Mathis. Alithia Ramirez. Maite Rodriguez. Annabell Rodriguez. Layla Salazar. Jailah Silguero. Rojelio Torres. Irma Garcia. Eva Mireles.

"And our 2022 Little Leaguers," the voice says.

#6, José Flores Jr. #13, Xavier Lopez. #2, Makenna Elrod. #2 Alexandria Rubio. #3 Tess Mata. #4 Eliahna Torres.

Each of their Little League photos hangs outside the dugouts. All of them in uniform, holding a bat. All of them smiling. All of them just 10 years old.

"You've got to remember their names," Veronica says, holding onto her Faith.

As the Matas walk back to their car, the mother of another victim is carried back to hers. Her family tries to comfort her, tries to quiet her high-pitched cries. They can't. Her face and body shake violently and uncontrollably.

"It's painful," Jerry says. He forces a smile. "But we can never forget."

If there's a more unjust, heartbreaking scene than this, may we all be spared of it.

ROBERTO JOSÉ ANDRADE FRANCO is a feature writer at ESPN. He's been a finalist for the National Magazine Award and the Dan Jenkins Medal for Excellence in Sportswriting. He lives in the El Paso–Juárez borderland.

A Legacy of Exclusion

JERRY BREWER

FROM *The Washington Post* • SEPTEMBER 21, 2022

Fritz Pollard died waiting for the NFL to change. He lived until he was 92, and that was not long enough. For his last 65 years, he yearned to see another person like him: a Black man, valued and empowered, with the title of head coach.

In 1921, when the star running back also coached the Akron Pros, professional football seemed ahead of the racist times. It chose not to stay that way. Sixty-eight years elapsed before Art Shell became the second African American to hold the position in 1989. Pollard had succumbed to pneumonia three years earlier, in pioneering solitude, never witnessing that dreamy day when Black minds would be as appreciated as Black athleticism.

"He was waiting for the time the NFL became fully racially unbiased," said his grandson Stephen Towns, a periodontist who lives in Indianapolis. "He was waiting for leadership that reflected what he saw on the field. But it never happened. It was a real sore spot for him."

He was Coach Pollard 26 years before Jackie Robinson burst through baseball's color barrier. Yet more than a century later, the NFL has trusted just 26 Black men to direct its teams, a total inflated by five interim coaches. As the 2022 season unfolds, the sport is enmeshed in a racial discrimination lawsuit and fails to meet the most meager standards for coaching diversity.

The NFL never integrated. Not fully, at least. Not properly. Unlike baseball, there is no clear before and after in its history. It took a winding path of organic integration, segregation and reintegration that can be trimmed to a truth: With its actions, the NFL has always placed conditions on inclusion. Exclusion has always been the point.

It is the tormenting legacy of a league that could have set a standard for inclusion. When Pollard joined what was then called the American Professional Football Association in 1920, he endured racist taunts from the crowds and cheap shots from opponents. But he also was the sport's highest-paid employee, earning $1,500 per game. For a while, his speed and intelligence prevailed over bigotry. Then the fledgling league, which was struggling to compete for relevance with baseball, boxing, college football and horse racing, aspired to become what it is today: a massive and indomitable force, this nation's greatest sporting addiction.

The NFL kept out African Americans from 1934 to 1946, a capitulation to White players who complained that the handful of Black players in the league were taking away jobs. After World War II, it reintegrated while reinforcing classic, biased beliefs about who could play where on the field and strengthening a Whites-only leadership sentiment, amplifying old prejudices as its profile rose. Those decisions combined with a tradition of inheritance and nepotism to create a caste system that still plagues progress 101 years after Pollard provided a model for equality and meritocracy.

His obituary began exactly how he feared it would: Frederick Douglass Pollard, the only Black head coach of an NFL team ... He was a trailblazer who never saw fresh footprints on his path.

The NFL was ahead and thought it was behind. Now it's just an aloof giant with one foot in the segregation era and the other in a courtroom.

"Until we understand the past, I don't think we're really going to understand the future," said Hue Jackson, the former coach of the Oakland Raiders and Cleveland Browns. "We're going to continue to put Band-Aids on it because we don't really want to have those hard conversations about where all of this started."

FOOTBALL HISTORIANS REFER to it as a "gentlemen's agreement," peculiar phrasing for a pledge that team owners made to ostracize Black talent. In 1933, two African Americans, Ray Kemp and Joe Lillard, played in the league. There would not be another until 1946, when Black media members and activists criticized the Rams, who had relocated from Cleveland to California and sought to play in publicly funded Los Angeles Memorial Coliseum. Competition from the All-America Football Conference—which had recruited Paul Brown, a White coach who was a seminal figure in pushing for the sport's desegregation, to lead its Cleveland franchise—also persuaded NFL owners to abandon the color ban.

It took 16 years for every NFL team to reintegrate, with Washington owner George Preston Marshall finally ending his obstinance in 1962. Even then, doors were merely cracked open across the league. Diversity had to squeeze through, one audacious soul at a time.

The NFL didn't have a Black official until 1965. Marlin Briscoe, the first Black starting quarterback of pro football's modern era, didn't get an opportunity until 1968. The long and arduous journey of minority quarterbacks is well told, but linebacker, center and guard were among the other "thinking positions" once considered unattainable.

Aspiring leaders had it worse. In 1957, Pittsburgh hired Lowell Perry as the first African American assistant coach of the modern era. Twenty years later, when future Hall of Fame coach Tony Dungy began his career as a player with the Steelers, there were just 10 Black assistants in the league. In 1985, *The Washington Post* reported there were just 32. The league lasted without a Black general manager until 2002, when the Baltimore Ravens promoted Ozzie Newsome.

This problem is not old history. It is a morphing reality that floats in the current of societal progress and embeds systemic racism even as times change. Undoubtedly, things are better, but they have never been right. The NFL is rooted in selective integration, a largely unacknowledged sin that rots its soil. Nothing can grow.

"It's all related to who they were," said Louis Moore, an author and history professor at Grand Valley State University whose work focuses on the intersection of race, sports and politics. "It's all related to the owners and their gentlemen's agreement to keep people out. It still impacts the NFL today because, post-World War II, when football becomes modern and grows in popularity, you have this tradition of what can be integrated and what can't be. The quarterbacks and coaches are the people who are the face of the league, and the NFL has always been reluctant to let a Black man be that face. It influences every perception about the game."

Perhaps if the NFL had more turnover in the ownership ranks, it would be harder for these relics of prejudice to persist. But this is a legacy league, full of families that bought in long ago and established a troubling ethos buttressed by the sport's economic dominance. The NFL has grown from an afterthought to a 32-team behemoth that prospers from a predominantly Black labor force. It has not progressed, though. The real power exists in a White billionaire clique that keeps getting more exclusive and refuses to evolve. The same kind of person who governed a team in the 1930s still runs the show now, only with a much greater wealth advantage over the average American and an even more cloistered lifestyle.

The descendants of four owners who were part of the Black exile still control franchises. George Halas paid $100 for the Bears in 1920. Tim Mara spent $500 on the Giants in 1925. Charles Bidwill put down $50,000 for the Cardinals in 1932. Art Rooney was charged a $2,500 fee for an expansion Pittsburgh franchise in 1933. Although they made Black players disappear for a dozen years, they left their families with integrated teams now worth billions.

While it is unfair to hold their descendants responsible for decisions made—or unchallenged—decades ago, decency and self-awareness should dictate a stronger commitment to breaking the chain. Instead, these families often minimize or deny the ban, deflecting responsibility for its residual effects.

Of that group, only the Rooneys have been a consistent leader in the minority hiring discussion. Throughout the league, negligence abounds—and coaches suffer the most.

"Minority coaches are frustrated today more so than maybe any time I've ever seen," Dungy said.

WHEN HE STARTED coaching, Dungy sported a beard. It was his signature look in the 1980s, along with a mini-Afro, groomed much like a young Mike Tomlin. One day, Dungy ran into George Young, who was the New York Giants' general manager for nearly two decades.

"If you really want to succeed in coaching, you need to shave your beard," Dungy recalled Young telling him.

Dungy, in his mid-20s, was confused. Facial hair? Really? Were his hopes and dreams dependent on a razor?

Dungy consulted Dan Rooney, the Steelers' president. "Is this true?" he asked. "Am I not representing you the right way?"

"No, we want you to be who you are," he remembered Rooney saying. "Don't worry about that here with the Steelers."

Dungy spent 16 years as a defensive assistant and interviewed for several openings before the Tampa Bay Buccaneers hired him in 1996. He was the NFL's fifth Black head coach. He was 40 and full of gratitude, having outlasted scrutiny of his personal style and mild-mannered demeanor.

He did not yell like a coach. He was not White like a coach. He was unsure whether any owner would embrace him.

"The owners are telling me that I might have to change, and maybe you can't be as close to the players," Dungy said. "Maybe you've got to come across as more determined or more forceful.

Maybe you've got to change who you are. And I just really started thinking: 'Do I do that? Do I come across differently in order to get a job?'"

Dungy refused. He kept in mind what Rooney had told him. At the time, he was with Minnesota, not Pittsburgh. But the memory of an organization that truly saw him boosted his conviction. To the detriment of the sport, few organizations seek or appreciate original talent. Rather, they attempt to copy what worked in the past. And the past was so exclusive, so limited, that mythologizing it hindered vision.

IN EARLY FEBRUARY, during another deflating hiring cycle, Tomlin was the NFL's lone Black head coach. It was 2002 again, when Herm Edwards stood alone for a short time. It was 1989 again, when Shell stepped into history. It was 1921 again.

"It's more disappointment than hurt," said Towns, 75, who gave an acceptance speech in 2005 for Pollard's posthumous Pro Football Hall of Fame induction. "You move on, but you always feel that animosity of what could have been. If my grandfather were alive, I think he would be extremely militant and extremely outspoken about the whole hiring process."

On Feb. 1, Brian Flores filed a racial discrimination lawsuit against the league and its teams. He included tanking allegations against Miami Dolphins owner Stephen Ross and details of what he considered a sham interview with the Giants. Two additional coaches, Steve Wilks and Ray Horton, later joined the class-action suit. It should be a cloud hovering over this season, but the league's popularity makes all skies look sunny. The initial public outcry subsided, and while Flores awaits his day in court, the matter seems to be merely another nuisance for the NFL to crush.

In the league office, Commissioner Roger Goodell has attempted to prioritize diversity with new strategies, revised programming and multiple expansions of the Rooney Rule, which requires teams to interview minority or female candidates for head coaching and top front-office openings. However, these initiatives amount to a veneer of concern, shielding the serial indifference of the clubs that perpetuate the inequity. There has never been a policy powerful enough to force the owners to change. They won't allow such accountability. It's their league, so it's all about their whims and their comfort level with the candidates.

"No one is going to force them to do anything with their team that they don't want to do," said Marc Ross, a former executive with the Giants and Philadelphia Eagles. "… Any initiatives or pressure [don't matter]. It's what they want to do."

The NFL is a small, elite world. It doesn't matter who you are as much as *whose* you are: which family, which friends, which coaching or general manager tree, which offensive or defensive tradition.

For aspiring Black head coaches, the world is even smaller. Examine the ones who made it, and there are maybe a dozen pathways to recognition. The bulk of them come from the Steelers, the Dungy tree or the Bill Walsh tree. It's symbolic that late Raiders owner Al Davis—who hired Shell and Tom Flores (the first Latino head coach) as he championed diversity throughout his organization—was often considered a pariah.

"It's extremely scary to think that we're in 2022 and these conversations are even happening," said Brian Levy, a White agent who represents several prominent Black coaches. "That's, to me, the scariest thing. The results are what they are, and they speak for themselves. You're walking up a down escalator."

ANTHONY LYNN, AN assistant head coach for the San Francisco 49ers, did not want his son to follow him into this profession. He tried to steer D'Anton toward Wall Street. But D'Anton loved football too much.

D'Anton was a defensive back who played his final game at 24, much like Dungy. In 2014, he took an internship with the New York Jets, where his father worked. Since then, he has taken assistant jobs with the Buffalo Bills, the Los Angeles Chargers, the Houston Texans and now Baltimore. D'Anton was on his dad's staff when Anthony was the Chargers' head coach, but he has moved around on purpose to learn from as many great minds as he can.

"I've wanted to coach since I was in the seventh grade," said D'Anton, now 32 and teaching the Ravens' safeties. "After playing, I missed being on the field, the energy, the creativity. I just knew I had to get back on the grass."

The Lynns are one of those cute father-son coaching stories, but they come with an asterisk. Long ago, Anthony prepared D'Anton for the realities of being Black in this business.

"He gave me the twice-as-good-to-get-half-as-much talk when I was 8 years old," D'Anton said. "Then he gave it to me again as a coach."

D'Anton remains an idealist as he rises in the profession. He's earnest. He stays in the moment, giving his best at every stop. In the NFL, many coaches begin with this mentality, only to see their spirit diminished by the pressure to win and the struggle for equal opportunity.

The NFL allowed Black players before its peer leagues, and it reintegrated just before the others opened their doors. But that whiplashing exposed a transactional ruthlessness: Exclusion is the preference. Diversity is a constant negotiation.

D'Anton inherited persistence rather than privilege. It is a requisite trait in the Black struggle for opportunity in America, an injustice that only the powerful can correct with intentional action.

NFL owners wasted a century making Black coaches—and the game itself—wait for better. The obligation falls on them, if they ever recognize it, to see that D'Anton walks a path more stable than the one Anthony has traveled.

JERRY BREWER is a sports columnist at *The Washington Post*. A graduate of Western Kentucky University, during his career he also has worked at *The Courier-Journal* in Louisville, Kentucky, the *Orlando Sentinel*, and the *Philadelphia Inquirer*. He lives with his wife and two sons in Seattle.

The Keeper

JULIET MACUR

FROM *The New York Times* • AUGUST 31, 2022

To begin her goodbye, Fatima stood inside her family's walled-in courtyard in Kabul, Afghanistan, shovel in hand, and pierced a patch of soil with the tip of its sharp blade.

Fighting back tears, she began to dig.

In the shade of a grapevine, with the sweet smell of rose bushes hanging heavy, she made a hole about two feet deep and just as wide, and placed some items into it.

Four soccer jerseys lovingly tucked into a plastic bag. Five golden trophies in the shape of a goalkeeper's glove. They symbolized her accomplishments as the goalkeeper for the Afghanistan women's national soccer team, and she adored them, once even telling her mother, "These are the things that keep me alive."

But on this day in mid-August 2021, they might get her killed.

Just days before, in a whir of trucks and rifles, the Taliban had conquered Kabul and begun searching for anyone considered an enemy. Government workers. Human rights activists. Judges. The targeted groups, now rushing to hide and save themselves, included female athletes like Fatima, who, according to the Taliban's fundamentalist views, had defied Islam by playing a sport in public. The jerseys and trophies would identify her as a traitor.

If the Taliban found them, she and her family could be tortured and killed.

Just 19 years old, Fatima struggled to comprehend that her life, her country and all the gains Afghanistan had made in the 20 years since the Taliban last ruled were collapsing.

She feared that she would never finish her bachelor's degree in economics, never open a business as she had hoped and never return to the soccer field or help bring about the day when Afghan women could thrive as equals to men.

Even more terrifying was the thought that she was about to die after barely having lived.

As she dug the hole in her backyard, she felt like she was digging her own grave.

The Family Helper

Growing up, Fatima—who is called Fati (pronounced FAH-tee) by family and friends—was faced with constant reminders that women in Afghanistan had limited options. (At the request of Fati and her teammates, *The New York Times* is not using their last names because they fear retribution from the Taliban.)

Like many Afghan women, Fati's mother never learned to read or write. She was engaged to be married at 13 and had the first of her five children a few years later. While raising her family, she moonlighted as a seamstress, sewing cushions that Afghans use as seating.

Seeing how her mother was forced to live, Fati, the second child, set out to do more and be more. She read and wrote for her mother. She tended to Kawsar, her youngest sister. She recalled once fixing the electricity in her house by fiddling with the wires as her mother stood by, holding her breath and whispering prayers.

Fati became proficient in English when she and her sister Zahra binge-watched Marvel films. Her father, who worked as a night guard in an apartment building, was so proud of Fati that he often called her his son.

At school, some students teased her because she was Hazara, an Afghan ethnic minority that is overwhelmingly Shiite Muslim and remains a prominent target for Sunni militants like the Taliban. Fati bristled when they called Hazara people useless and stupid. She grew tough inside.

"If you are strong and hard, no one can beat you," she recalled thinking, "and then you can always find your way."

Then one day, three classmates waved her over and invited her to play soccer.

"You are so tall!" shouted Bahara, one of those girls. "Come join us. You will be a good goalkeeper!"

Finding Her Power
Until then, Fati was not even aware that women in her country played organized soccer.

For Afghan girls, playing sports in public had long been risky. Religious hard-liners say women violate the Quran when they play soccer because men can still see the shape of their bodies even if they wear hijabs, long sleeves and pants. They call them prostitutes and threaten their fathers and brothers, saying they should be punished for letting a family member dishonor them.

But among more progressive Afghans, particularly women who had seen their rights curtailed under the Taliban's first rule, from 1996 to 2001, there was a persistent push to allow girls and women to think and behave in ways once forbidden.

Fati said later that she basked in the moments on the soccer field when she could be aggressive, diving to save a shot or walloping the ball with a thunderous goal kick. She found it exhilarating to show her power by staring down an opponent who dared to think that scoring on her was a possibility.

Fati's mother supported Fati's love of soccer, telling her: "I don't want you to be like me. Don't rush to get married and end up kind of like a slave in the house." She convinced Fati's father that soccer was a worthy endeavor for a teenager who had aspirations of life beyond the kitchen.

Fati rose quickly in the sport.

After a national team scout saw her play at a high school tournament, he invited her to practice with the national squad. There, she learned to be agile and fearless, but most of all to be a leader. In a country that had been at war her whole life, Fati finally felt free, safe and in control.

Six months later, she was promoted to the senior national team, joining her friends Bahara, Mursal and Somaya on the squad.

They were the girls who had first invited Fati to play the game, and their relationship would reach much further and deeper than what happened on the field.

Searching for Inspiration

It wasn't long before soccer became a mooring for Fati's whole life. It gave her the confidence to chase her goals.

Mornings, she worked at an organization called Good Neighbors, where she taught English to girls and women. Evenings, she studied economics at a university. Her older brother, Khaliqyar, feeling a duty to protect her, often escorted her there.

Other times, she remembered, she walked alone by moonlight, her hands shaking with nerves because the route was unsafe even in daylight. To go unnoticed, Fati dressed like a boy, wearing sneakers and baggy clothes, and covered her head with a hoodie.

The rest of her time was devoted to soccer. It was too dangerous for her team to play at home, so it traveled to countries like India, Tajikistan and Uzbekistan, facing squads that practiced more, on better fields, with better coaches. Fati's team lost again and again. Commenters on social media said the team was bad because Afghan women weren't meant to play soccer.

The pressure to prove critics wrong became so great that once, after losing to Uzbekistan, Fati went back to her hotel and considered flinging herself off the fourth-floor balcony.

A teammate soothed Fati as she pleaded: "God, why aren't there results? I want to win just one time."

Back home, she looked everywhere for inspiration. Scouring YouTube for documentaries, she was moved by the story of Colonel Sanders, the founder of Kentucky Fried Chicken.

"He tried so much to be accomplished, make his business bigger and make his recipe taste just right," she said. "It really motivated me to try harder."

Her team won its first game, finally, in 2019. Fati never wanted to let go of the feeling.

On social media, positive comments began to appear. She and her teammates were interviewed on television, becoming role models for other girls.

Her family was delighted. The soccer federation was paying Fati $100 a month to play on the national team and she received another $150 to head the women's grass-roots effort and help manage the under-15 team.

Yet even as her life seemed on an upswing, a fault line was spreading throughout Afghanistan.

Terrorist attacks increased, with the violence reaching hospitals, schools and wedding halls. Hundreds of people, including many members of the Hazara community, were killed by both the Taliban and the Afghan branch of the Islamic State.

In the spring of 2021, President Biden announced the U.S. military would withdraw from Afghanistan. But when Fati heard about the Taliban making advances in the provinces, she told her teammates not to worry. The Taliban would never take over Kabul.

'They Are Going to Kill the Athletes'

One day in August, Fati was working inside the women's soccer department of the Afghanistan Football Federation when an employee from the president's office burst in, shouting that the Taliban were closing in on Kabul. Gather every document they could find, he said, and put the paperwork in a pile. They needed to destroy anything the Taliban could use to target female athletes.

"Hurry!" the man said. "We're going to burn everything."

Fati said she and a half-dozen other female workers began opening drawers, grabbing all the papers they could, sometimes stacking them to their chins as they carried them away.

Registration forms. Girls' photos. Uniform order forms. Travel documents. The entire history of the women's national team program, which began in 2007, soon lay in an unruly heap.

When Fati and her co-workers were done, they stopped to take a breath. It dawned on them: Their lives were really in danger.

Before leaving, Fati grabbed some passports and ID cards that players had left behind and slid them into her backpack. She knew those girls would be stranded in Afghanistan without them.

Three days later, Fati was headed to a final soccer practice for her local club when her phone began sounding off. Frantic messages were popping into the team's group chat.

"Go home, training is canceled."

"Don't go outside, girls."

Bahara, her former high school classmate who became a defender on the national team, shared a video she had made of the Taliban arriving in one of Kabul's squares. She had been on her way from dental school when she saw trucks flying white Taliban flags, with soldiers honking horns and shooting guns.

"It's real, girls," Bahara wrote in Dari, the players' native language. "They're here."

The city became almost unlivable, especially for women.

Stores and schools closed. Women shut themselves in their homes. The Taliban roamed the streets with paint cans to cover any evidence of shops like beauty salons.

Every day on Facebook, Fati read about killings and more killings. It was impossible to know what was true. Social media posts showed bloody images stamped 24 hours ago. And then one hour ago. And then one minute ago.

Fati and her teammates knew they needed to leave Afghanistan.

"Just be united and let's see how we can get out of here and find a way," Fati said in a text to her team. "Inshallah, there will be a way."

One evening, the team received a text from a veteran player named Nilab. She was a team captain known for being outspoken about women's rights.

She had received an anonymous text: *Somehow if we see you, we will capture you and tie you up like a dog and we will not release you. We will kill you.*

Nilab warned the group: *Girls, you know they are going to kill the athletes. They will kill them and hang them from the goal in the Olympic Stadium, just like the Taliban did with people before.*

Fati, who was at home, felt a chill go through her body as her family slept in the adjacent room. Nilab sounded scared. And Nilab, who several times had been abducted and beaten by militants who tried to silence her, was never scared.

Looking for help, Nilab tried to reach leaders of the Afghan Football Federation and FIFA, the international governing body of soccer, but they didn't respond.

At last, a breakthrough. Perhaps the team's only hope.

Nilab received a text from Khalida Popal, a former captain of the Afghan women's national team who had fled the country because of death threats prompted by her activism. In 2018, she had exposed a sexual abuse scandal involving Afghan soccer officials who were molesting members of the senior national team, which at the time was the level above Fati's.

"I'm a little worried about you," Popal wrote to Nilab in Dari. "Are you OK?"

Nilab responded with a harrowing voice message: "No, Khalida, I swear to God, we are locked in the house. You know that enemies are on every side of our house."

She ended by saying, "We have no way to escape. If you can do anything for us, please help us."

Within hours, Popal was added to the group chat and introduced herself.

I'm sorry for you girls that you can't play soccer anymore. I am in contact with you from Denmark. I am going to try to find a way for you to get out of Afghanistan. I'm trying to get you out.

And wherever you end up, the U.S.A. or wherever, after that you can help your family.

But not now.

Forced to Go Quiet

As the Taliban closed in on Fati's world, Popal was in her apartment north of Copenhagen, pulling together a trusted group of lawyers, sports officials and human rights activists who could help get the national team out of Afghanistan. She had worked with many of them, including Kat Craig, a British human rights lawyer, on the sexual abuse case.

The first task was to convince governments that the team needed saving.

Popal and the former Afghanistan women's coach Kelly Lindsey rallied current and former players living outside Afghanistan to talk to the news media and spoke to reporters about the urgency of getting the girls to safety.

"Now our players are totally helpless," Popal told CNN. "The biggest nightmare is that they are identified and they are taken by the Taliban."

She told the girls to burn their national team jerseys and delete or lock their social media accounts. After years of encouraging them to speak out for the right of women to play sports, she was begging them to go quiet.

At the same time, Popal's soccer connections searched for a country that would take the players. Maybe the United States. Or Canada. How about Germany or Belgium?

Nikki Dryden, an Olympian and immigration lawyer in Australia, called Craig Foster, a human rights activist and former captain of Australia's national soccer team. Foster had connections in the Australian government. On a video call, he told a group that included Popal, "I'll get Australia to take the players."

Within days, Fati and her teammates received a thrilling text from Popal.

"We have a country," it said.

Fati had no idea how far Australia was from Afghanistan. It seemed like another planet. But she was grateful to go anywhere that wasn't under Taliban rule.

Popal issued instructions to the players: *Start packing. Bring only what you need. Your passport and cellphone. Water. Some biscuits for a snack. A power pack to charge your phone.*

Crucial documents would need to go along too.

Jonas Baer-Hoffmann, the general secretary of FIFPRO, the international union for professional soccer players, supplied a letter titled, "EXTREMELY URGENT: Request for Airport Access for Women Football (Soccer) Player," saying that the Australian government had agreed to take national team members on its next flight out of Kabul.

Fati had everything she needed to get out of the country. She just had to wait for word from Popal that she should go to the airport.

A Solemn Pledge

Fati asked her old high school friends Bahara and Mursal to come over and collect their passports, which Fati had taken from the soccer federation. The two players arrived with Somaya, their former classmate.

Fati dragged a rug from the house to her backyard, beneath the grapevine where she loved to read and study, so the friends could sit and talk, drink cold water in the heat and eat Afghanistan's famously delicious apples—for maybe the last time.

As military flights out of the country roared above them, the friends made a promise: If one of them made it out of Afghanistan, that person would work her whole life to save the rest.

"You will have the responsibility to help the others," Fati said, as they all nodded. "You should do your best. I want to make that clear."

Looming over them, Fati and her friends recalled, was the fear that there was no hope for any of them. They treated their goodbyes as final.

"We should have this last hug," Mursal said, and they embraced.

Fati led her friends to the door and watched them depart. In their black dresses and full hijabs, they looked like dark floating clouds that slowly faded into the distance.

Fati went inside, grabbed her soccer trophies from the top of the refrigerator and headed to the backyard. The spot under the grapevine was a perfect place to dig.

After many restless hours, she fell into a deep sleep. At about 8:50 a.m., Bahara called, shouting into the phone: "Fati, wake up! Didn't you get the messages? We have to be at the airport at 9 a.m.!"

Escape From Kabul

On the day she would leave her old life behind, Fati could hardly think because she had a headache from lack of sleep. But within minutes of Bahara's phone call, it was like a bomb of energy had exploded inside her brain.

She opened her blue school backpack and began tossing things in. A handful of markers. A necklace and earrings given to her by her closest friends. Old soccer credentials from tournaments. Photos of her family.

With each item she shoved into the bag, she could feel her heart pounding.

Her parents and siblings gathered around, flooding her with questions. Where are you going? Can we go with you? Popal had said she could not guarantee that any family member would be let into the airport, especially without a visa application. But she said the players could at least try.

Like a platoon commander, Fati began shouting orders.
"Everybody get ready to go!" she yelled. "Forget worrying
about what to bring. Right now your life is the most important
thing."

Her mother started crying, and Fati told her to focus. Her
mother's assignment was to get cash and important documents,
like Khaliqyar's driver's license and everyone's ID cards. Fati's
brother Ali Reza, 15, sprinted to a store to buy food. Fati's mother
shoved pounds of provisions into her own bag, including choc-
olate chip cookies and juice boxes.

Zahra, 18, asked what she should wear. Fati told her to find
the longest, darkest dress because they didn't want to anger the
Taliban.

Fati's sister Kawsar, 4, repeatedly asked in her lilting voice if
they were really going to Australia. With a forced smile, Fati said
yes while combing Kawsar's hair.

Fati put on a Spider-Gwen T-shirt she loved because it
represented girl power. Over that, she donned a long robe-like
covering she had bought at a secondhand store.

This was no abaya, the traditional Muslim dress. This was
more like a black cloak Harry Potter would wear. Fati fastened
it with a pin at the chest. The hood was so huge that when she
draped it over her head, she couldn't see.

Fati and her family were ready.

Before heading out the door, Fati said, she toured her house
and courtyard one last time, examining everything so she would
remember the details.

Goodbye, grapevine. Goodbye, jerseys and trophies, now
safe beneath the ground. Goodbye, dreamy-looking mountains
in the distance.

Goodbye, childhood.

As their taxi drove off, Fati turned to see her aunt, who had
stayed behind. In the Afghan tradition of bidding people good
luck when they take a trip, the aunt was splashing water onto the
road with a watering can.

This time, more than ever, Fati would need all of that good luck.

A Born Leader

Hidden under one baggy sleeve of Fati's cloak, written in blue ballpoint pen on her arm, was the phone number of Haley Carter, a former assistant coach of the Afghanistan women's program who was at home in Texas.

Carter, a former Marine Corps officer who served two tours in Iraq, had inside information to help players navigate Taliban checkpoints. Fati became her contact because she spoke the best English.

About a week before, the two had connected on WhatsApp.

From the start, Carter could tell Fati was a born leader because Fati was already coordinating logistics for some of her teammates. That put Carter at ease. She knew that the best partners in life-or-death situations were the ones who calmly take charge.

Before leaving for the airport, Fati thanked Carter for her help.

Carter responded: "There's no reason to thank me. You are a player and I am a coach. It's my job to work to make sure you are protected."

When the national team players convened at their meeting place, a gas station outside the airport, they laughed. The group of mostly teenagers had never seen one another so hidden in fabric. Nilab looked like a spy in her abaya, gloves that covered her tattoos and sunglasses. Fati and the others were dripping sweat beneath their layers.

All around them was chaos, with thousands of people clambering to get into the airport and onto the final planes leaving Afghanistan.

Taliban soldiers repeatedly beat people with whips and electric cattle prods as the sound of gunshots echoed. Children wailed. A faint smell of gunpowder lingered.

Blood in the Dirt

For two days, Fati joined a group of players and some of their families—more than 100 people in all—on a miles-long trek around the airport, trying to find a way in. Her teammates asked: "What's the plan? Where are we going?" Fati kept answering: "We're close right now. Don't worry. Almost there." Carter was sending maps that showed the location of entry gates and Taliban checkpoints.

During the day, the temperature soared to the 90s, making the players and their families woozy with dehydration. Though some of them brought water, there wasn't nearly enough. A national team member lived nearby, so some girls headed to her house to drink or use the bathroom.

At night, the temperatures dropped to the 60s and the group crowded together to stay warm and nap. But Fati stayed awake. She wanted to be alert when Carter texted her with instructions.

The North Gate was completely blocked, so at Carter's suggestion, Fati led the group back to the gas station where the team had first assembled. From there, she and her brother Khaliqyar, 23, decided to check out the Abbey Gate, a different airport entrance. A player named Farida joined them.

Fati's mother began to sob as they parted, saying, "Don't go, why can't someone else go?" and Fati almost cried, too.

"Please stop, you are making me weak," she told her mother, handing her backpack to her because it had gotten too heavy to carry. She promised to return soon.

Players began texting the group chat, asking for directions to the best gate of entry.

We cannot do this much longer.

The Taliban is beating me.

Popal, coordinating the evacuation from Denmark, saw the desperate messages and insisted that everyone calm down. Writing in Dari, she told them to pretend it was the Champions League soccer final, but one without fouls or red cards. *Use your elbows! Punch and hit people! Do anything to get to the gate!*

To get inside the airport, Fati would have to pass through two Taliban checkpoints and a Taliban-laden area just before the main entrance.

Approaching the first checkpoint, she wasn't sure how she would move even a single foot ahead. Two young girls, crushed by the crowd, gasped: "We don't want to go here. We just want to be alive." They reminded Fati of her little sister, Kawsar.

Fati yelled, "Give them air, don't push them, they are just little!" as she used the hood of her cloak to fan them. Khaliqyar put one of the girls on his shoulders.

One Talib shot his gun so close to Fati that her ears rang for 15 minutes. Everything went black. Khaliqyar ran off to buy water from a vendor and revived Fati by splashing it in her face.

After a few minutes, they waded back into the crowd and pushed past the first checkpoint. Fati said she felt men's hands groping her as she struggled to protect herself. She lashed out at one man, slapping him hard.

"This is embarrassing for you, look at yourself, you animal," she said. "Our country is almost done and this is what you choose to do?"

The second checkpoint was even harder to pass. Two cars were parked nose-to-nose in the road, with Taliban soldiers standing guard. One man in the crowd recognized Fati and yelled, "Hey, that's the national team player!"

As the Taliban edged toward Fati with their guns pointed at her, the crowd surged forward. The force was so powerful that one Talib was knocked down and trampled, splayed on the dirt beneath a sea of stampeding feet. Fati could see his bloody head as she passed. The other Taliban fighters began shooting toward the crowd.

In the confusion, Fati and Farida slid across the hoods of the cars, past the checkpoint. But Khaliqyar was stuck behind. A Taliban soldier slammed the butt of a rifle into Khaliqyar's shoulder, knocking him down.

With 20 feet between them that now seemed like 20 miles, Khaliqyar made a choice. "Just get out of here, go! Save yourself!" he said, urging Fati forward.

He waved goodbye and then pointed to the sky, looking up to God.

Surging Past the Taliban

Popal had texted the players, urging them to push ahead on their own if they were to make it to the plane. Many were already separated from their families. Fati, now alone in the crowd, realized that she hadn't said goodbye to her parents and siblings. She hadn't even kissed Kawsar's little cheeks.

Her body and mind were numb. Her parents, sisters and younger brother were who knows where, with her backpack. And Khaliqyar, her brother, friend and loyal protector, was also gone.

The voice in her head was relentless and harsh: *It was such a long journey for nothing, and now your family will be in danger because of you. You're a failure. You are the weakest person in the world.*

Fati felt a hand on her shoulder. It was Farida, telling her not to cry.

Embarrassed, Fati snapped back into tough-girl mode.

"I'm the decision maker here. I'm stone-hearted," she repeated to herself after stomping away. "I should listen to my sixth sense that's telling me to go forward."

Two checkpoints down. One last effort to get to the airport gate.

Fati's group grew to six after she and Farida bumped into other women they knew. Nilab, their fearsome friend, was among them. The whole group looked ready for a fight, with dirt caked onto their hair and clothing, and hands black with filth.

The women forced their way through the crowd inch by inch, crouching low and scurrying forward, just as Nilab had learned in military school. Fati briefly separated from the others and was punched and kicked in the back by a Taliban fighter.

Now close to the gate, they stood and waved empty water bottles at American soldiers inside the airport. Those soldiers beckoned them forward. But Taliban fighters wouldn't let them through.

So the women held hands and formed a chain, each player grasping so tightly that it hurt, and bulldozed their way toward the door.

Somehow they made it. An Australian soldier greeted them: "This is the end of the road for the Taliban and the end of the danger."

Trapped in a Sewage Ditch

All around her, Fati saw teammates, many with at least one family member. Standing there by herself, she didn't feel happy to have conquered the crowds. She felt crushed.

After keeping her phone off to save a dying battery, she turned it on and called Khaliqyar. When he answered, she exhaled.

Her big brother had gone home after parting with Fati at the second checkpoint. Their parents and Kawsar were already there. Khaliqyar said they had given up trying for the airport gate after the Taliban beat Fati's father with a cattle prod as he clutched a screaming Kawsar in his arms. Fati's teenage siblings, Zahra and Ali Reza, were still outside the airport somewhere.

Fati told Khaliqyar he should come back and described the best way to get in. "Oh God, just come," she told him.

She checked her messages. A group of players and family members, including Bahara and Mursal, were stuck just outside the gate, standing in a sewage ditch, knee-deep in watery muck, as American soldiers stood guard atop the high wall.

In her voice messages, Bahara was crying and begging for help, saying she couldn't get in touch with any teammates. Mursal would later describe how she had tried to show a soldier her visa letters, only to have him kick her, point his rifle at her and threaten to shoot her.

Safe inside the airport, Fati remembered the promise she and her friends had made to one another. She had to try to save them.

After pleading to soldiers that she needed to leave the airport briefly to help her friends, she found an Australian officer to accompany her outside.

With her Harry Potter cloak flowing behind her, Fati walked along the outside wall to look for teammates. They found her first.

"Fati! Fati! We are here!" they shouted. When the people nearby heard those calls, they also started shouting, "Fati, help *me*! Please help *me*, Fati!" She tried her best to tune out those other people as she pointed to five teammates and at least three of their family members, whom the soldier lifted out of the river of sewage. To Mursal, it was as if an angel had come for them. She had been sure that Fati, whom she called her "bestie," would never leave them behind.

And then, a miracle. Behind those girls, standing tall and looking stunningly clean because he had gone home and showered, was Khaliqyar. He had made it to the gate after following people to the sewage ditch, as Fati had instructed him to do. The only items he carried for himself were two sweatshirts and an extra pair of pants.

And he had her backpack.

A Flight to Dubai

After spending a day in a processing area, the group of around 80 national team players and family members, smelling of sewage and sweat, boarded a military plane and huddled together inside its giant metal belly. They were bound for Dubai, the first stop before heading to Australia.

Carter, the former coach and Marine Corps officer, had demanded photographic proof that Fati and her teammates had boarded the plane. So Fati texted her a snapshot of the mass of passengers in front of her. The image made its way to thousands of people after Carter shared it on social media.

During takeoff, Fati and other players recalled, the sound of weeping rose above the sound of the engines. The next day, at a processing center in Dubai, Fati and Khaliqyar cried again when their teenage siblings, Zahra and Ali Reza, unexpectedly showed up. The two had been in the sewage water for more than a day before Alison Battisson, an Australian lawyer who was part of Popal's group of helpers, got them out of the country, coordinating with a soldier to identify Ali Reza, who was wearing a mustard-colored vest that made him stand out in the crowd.

Fati was finally able to talk by phone to her mother, who thanked her for saving Khaliqyar, Zahra and Ali Reza.

"You saved my children when I could not," her mother told her. "Take care and be strong."

Those words echoed inside Fati's head throughout the 14-hour plane ride to Australia.

When she arrived at her hotel in Sydney, Fati closed the door of her room, put her back against it and sank to the ground.

"Finally," she said to herself. "I'm safe."

A Fractured Soul

Seven thousand miles from her family's home in Afghanistan, Fati tried to distract her siblings and make them smile.

She brought them to her window to show them what Australia looked like, telling them it would be a wonderful place to live. They weren't buying it. The city was on lockdown because of the pandemic—a zombie apocalypse, as Fati later described it—and they were still struggling to process what they'd been through.

Ali Reza had seen his father beaten with a whip and Zahra was devastated by the news that 130 people, including one of the Marines who had helped her out of the sewage ditch, had been killed in a suicide bombing. She was so overwhelmed with grief that she had been fainting during long sessions of sobbing.

Moya Dodd, a former member of the FIFA executive committee and former national team player from Australia, helped provide support.

"Could you bring Zahra some coloring books?" Fati texted Dodd, hoping that the distraction of coloring would make Zahra "stronger and fresher."

But even Fati sometimes sat alone and asked why me, and why did all of this happen? She asked God for mercy.

"Sometimes I feel so much broken," she said.

Head of the Household

In Australia, Fati hoped to become the woman and soccer player she had always wanted to be, free of a Taliban regime that would deny her and all women their humanity.

But those bigger goals would have to wait. First, she would need to be the head of a household, a surrogate mother to her siblings, a breadwinner, a translator.

Because of her English skills, she became an unofficial spokeswoman for the refugee group. One of her first tasks was compiling clothing sizes for everyone so that Dodd's soccer charity, Women Onside, and other nonprofits could buy those items. Fati also fielded requests from her teammates and their family members. Like for more pistachios. Or body spray. Or oil made for curly hair.

A lot of people wanted to help the team after its escape made news around the world. Asma Mirzae, a former Afghan refugee on the board of Women Onside, was one of them. She drove more than 500 miles from Melbourne to deliver food to them made by her mother and others in her Afghan community.

Fati said that the first whiff of Mirzae's dish of rice with raisins and carrots transported her back to dinnertime with her family. While she and other players ate, tears dripped from their cheeks onto their plates.

To thank those who rallied around the team, Fati drew an Afghan girl on sketch paper Dodd had given to her. The girl was dressed in a blue burqa, with a soccer ball in her hands and a broken heart. To one side was the Australian flag.

Fati was grateful to be in Australia, but essentially still had no home. From Sydney, most of the Afghan national team players moved to Melbourne, where they began their long wait for permanent visas so they could stay in the country.

After three months in a hotel, Fati chose a four-bedroom house in a suburb with a thriving Afghan community because her siblings wanted to be near other Afghans. Bahara left Kabul with no family, so Fati invited her to live with her. Paying bills was hard, even though everyone in the house received subsistence money from the government. Several times, Fati fell behind on rent and utilities, with her bank account once dipping to just $5.

Each morning, she woke to a colorful collage of sticky notes on the wall next to her twin bed. It was her to-do list, and it grew by the day.

Fill out school forms for Ali Reza. Help Khaliqyar find a job. Call her refugee services case manager to answer yet more questions, hours of questions, about herself and her siblings as they awaited their visas.

"I left my childhood back in Afghanistan," Fati said one day, choking up but quickly composing herself.

Life in a new country was especially hard for Fati's younger siblings. Back home, she and her family—like many Afghan families—slept on the floor in the same room. Now, on many mornings, Fati would nearly step on Zahra, who was sleeping on the floor next to her bed. And if Fati heard rustling at night, it would often be Ali Reza dragging his comforter downstairs, where he would set up camp on the living room floor.

Fati did her best to make her house a home. She stored the dining table in the garage because many Afghans prefer to eat while sitting on the floor. On top of the two Persian-style rugs she had received from a local soccer referee, she spread out a vinyl tablecloth so her family and friends could share meals the way they did in Kabul.

To break the day's Ramadan fast one night in April, Bahara whipped up roast chicken and vegetables from a YouTube recipe. Fati made a batch of firni, an Afghan custard.

During the meal, Fati leaned on one of the donated couches in her living room and lamented that this didn't feel like home because Afghans don't use couches. They sit on large cushions, the kind Fati's mother made.

When Bahara said they could eventually buy cushions for the house, Fati quickly said no.

"My mom will make them for us when she finally comes here," she said, as the room grew quiet.

Fearing for Her Sister

Fati and her teammates had access to mental health experts who could help them process the trauma of being ripped from their country. But she and many others decided that holding unofficial, friends-only therapy sessions was a better idea.

In those sessions, they reminded themselves that it was a miracle they were alive and safe. But they felt guilty that so many people in their country—so many of their friends and relatives— were still suffering.

Mursal shared that her brother who was in the Afghan special forces was kidnapped, but managed to run away from his captors. Bahara, whose forearms were Popeye-level strong after working in her family's sandal-making business, shared that she missed her family so much that her chest hurt.

"Did you hear about the bombing at the mosque?" Bahara said one day as she scanned her social media feed. Dozens of people, including many children, were killed or wounded when a roof collapsed on worshipers. The mosque was in an area where many Hazara lived, and Fati rushed to call her mother to see if everyone was OK.

Fati was sick about her little sister Kawsar, who had no future in Afghanistan beyond becoming a housewife. There was no school for girls after the sixth grade. No sports for girls and women. All the rights that Fati and her teammates had fought for had disappeared.

Yet during the daily calls with her mother and Kawsar, Fati remained upbeat. Her mother did, too, though Afghan life had grown arduous because food, jobs and money were now scarce. They put on a strong front for each other.

"Now that you are in Australia you can laugh, and I like that," her mother told her one night, when Fati had friends over who were making a ruckus. "Remember those days back here when you had to wear a scarf and sit in the corner? It's good that you are not here."

But Fati felt torn inside. She had a recurring nightmare in which Taliban fighters were searching her home in Kabul, and her mother and Kawsar were frozen with fear. In the dream, her sister screamed, and Fati tried to scream, too, but nothing came out. When she awoke, she was soaked in sweat and shaking.

One day, Kawsar jumped into the frame of Fati's video call with her mother and showed off drawings she had made in kindergarten.

"A fish!" the little girl said in Dari, pointing to a little blue fish. "The number 2! Another fish! The number 1!" She stopped and stared at Fati. "When can I show you these in person?"

"Soon, my darling, soon," Fati said, changing the subject as she felt the tears coming. "Hey, what color do you like the best?"

Erased From Her Family History

In Afghanistan, Fati had been somebody. As the national team's starting goalkeeper, she was often in the news. When traveling internationally for matches, she promoted a woman's right to participate in sports and society.

In Australia, the new Fati was in blueprint stages.

As one of the national team's captains, she was given opportunities to speak publicly about the team's dramatic exit from Kabul, including addressing one crowd at the Australian Open and another at a human rights conference. Yet she was caught in a typical refugee limbo, unsure of where her life was going.

Twice a week, she and her sister Zahra worked at an Indian restaurant. They slipped on hairnets and long rubber gloves to spoon concoctions of curry into plastic bags for hours. The jobs allowed them to send money to their family. But as with so many refugees, those jobs took up their time when they needed to be studying English, crucial to success in their new lives.

Popal, the former player responsible for rescuing Fati and her teammates, continued to check in with the players. During one of those calls with Fati this spring, she noticed that Fati looked unsettled, so she asked how she was doing.

"If you want me to say a lie, I am good," Fati said.

After the team left Afghanistan, the Taliban continued to search houses for anyone considered a traitor to the new regime. Days before Fati's conversation with Popal, it had been Fati's family's turn.

When the soldiers asked how many people were living in the house, her father answered: "Three. We are just three. Always three." They didn't find anything incriminating.

Her mother told Fati that as a precaution she had deleted all of the photos of Fati from her phone. All evidence of Fati's existence in the house was gone. Fati felt shattered.

She stopped sleeping. She ate junk food. Once again, she felt useless to do anything to help her family, and her mind started to swim with anxiety and remorse.

At least one thing could boost her mood, and Popal made it happen.

Popal had been hosting Sunday night video calls with the players to talk about things such as how to fit into Australian culture (don't go swimming with all of your clothes on, for example). But Popal had made another call that ended up bringing Fati and the rest of the team much-needed joy.

She had called Foster, the man with so many Australian connections, and said, "It's time that the team starts playing together again."

'Be Like a Lion'

Fati didn't know anything about Melbourne Victory, the club that stepped up to sponsor the Afghan women's national team. But she quickly learned that it was a top-notch business that set out to give her and her teammates the best of everything.

Melbourne Victory assigned the players a coach who had just won the women's championship for the club, bus transportation to and from practices and games, and trainers to get them back into shape after not playing an official match since early 2021.

One day, the club invited the team to a jersey presentation held at a soccer store.

Fati had never felt so appreciated. She and her teammates posed for photos, taped video interviews and received a pile of equipment, including cleats that cost more than $250. "Ooh, so professional," she whispered to Bahara before they were given game jerseys that were branded Melbourne Victory but also honored their home country.

When Fati discovered a small Afghan flag on the back of her jersey, she ran her finger over it and remembered how proud she had been to represent her country.

After the ceremony, John Didulica, director of football for Melbourne Victory, said the club supported the team playing together again because it would be "the ultimate act of defiance to the Taliban."

The team had its first game, against ETA Buffalo soccer club, in late April in Melbourne. That morning, Fati and her teammates received a text from Popal, in Dari:

I wish you success in the season. Be like a lion when you go on the field. Show all of them your power and your unity as Afghan women. Inshallah, you will be a success and success will be ours.

FIFA had not recognized the squad as a national team in exile, so the Afghan players were left to play in a state soccer league. About 75 fans, most of them supporting the other team, lined up against a chain-link fence that surrounded the field. A backdrop of chirping from white cockatoos and green lorikeets broke the pregame silence.

To the Afghan players, the game was as important as a championship final. Most were playing on empty stomachs because they were fasting for Ramadan. Yet they remained aggressive and fierce, relentlessly pushing the ball up the field. After one shot ricocheted off the opposing team's left post, Fati yelled, "Why is this happening?"

The score was still 0-0 in the second half when an attacking Afghan midfielder took the ball on a breakaway run and sent it flying into the net. The players erupted in cheers, jumping on one another in celebration.

The sound of the referee's whistle broke their hearts. An Afghan player had been offside. The official trotted to the team's bench, saying, "I can't sleep if I allow that."

The game ended, 0-0. Coach Jeff Hopkins told the team he was content with the result, particularly because the players hadn't had much time to practice together. Fati translated.

"No sad faces, OK? No sad faces," he said to a group of players with sad faces. "It's so good for us just to see you out there playing football."

Fati was the last to board the bus back home, greeted by applause for her performance in goal.

"Our Batman!" Bahara shouted because Fati had fended off every shot that came her way. Fati laughed, waving off the compliments.

In the months after that day, Fati remained fractured, her soul in two places. Her parents and Kawsar were still a world away, and she worried that she would never see them again. No one knew when, or if, they would get visas.

But on this day, on the bus after her first soccer game in her new country, among her teammates, Fati saw new possibilities.

"It was powerful for us to play together again," she said, propping her knees on the seat in front of her. "I feel like we are here and alive."

She paused before adding, "I have the power to be me again."

JULIET MACUR has been a sports reporter and columnist for *The New York Times* since 2004, and has covered 12 Olympics since graduating from Columbia University's journalism school in 1997. She worked at the *Orlando Sentinel* and then the *Dallas Morning News* before joining the *Times*, and in 2014 wrote a bestselling book about the cyclist Lance Armstrong. A proud daughter of Polish immigrants, she grew up in New Jersey and now lives in Washington, D.C., with her husband, daughter, and Labrador retriever.

On Punches

HAMILTON NOLAN

FROM Defector • DECEMBER 27, 2022

It only takes one punch to change your whole perspective on things. One punch can bring you to the instant realization that what you had thought to be true was in fact untrue. What you thought was easy was actually hard; what you thought was enlightenment was just a waiting room in a very long tunnel. It can instill the virtue of humility in a much faster and more profound way than any course of study ever could. As humility is the gateway to wisdom, a punch can open wisdom's door.

There are really only two kinds of punches: regular, and bad. This is from the perspective of the person being punched. There's no way to know anything about a punch except to be hit by it. The puncher is the chemist refining the drug, but the punchee is the one shooting it into his veins. The knowledge lies on the receiving end. You can tell a man who beats you up things that he could never know about himself. A small consolation, but something.

Regular punches come from a regular person hitting you regularly. These punches fall within the normal realm of boxing experience. They fall within the bell curve, not on the long tail. They feel like things that you have felt before. Which is not to say they feel good, or they feel like nothing—they feel like being punched in the fucking face. They may be light, medium or hard; they may slide off easily, or give you a momentary rattle, or make your head ring like when you walked into the top steel bar of the jungle gym in second grade. What makes them regular is not that they are something to be welcomed or shrugged off, but that you experience them as a human being, punching you with a fist that is inside a glove. This of course can be a jarring experience. But on the bright side, it could be much worse.

Bad punches do not feel like a man hitting you with a fist. Bad punches feel like a machine, perhaps a malicious robot, hitting you with a 2x4, the end of which has been covered with a small boxing glove as some sort of awful joke. Other times they feel like being hit with a boxing glove that has been filled with concrete and allowed to harden. Other times they feel like being hit with a cannonball that someone has carefully painted the image of a boxing glove on, like the WW2 fighter pilots who painted angry teeth on the front of their P-40 Warhawks. A bad punch seems unreal. As soon as it touches you, you instantly understand that you cannot allow another one to touch you again. While regular punches can be blocked, bad punches travel right through the hand you are blocking with and deliver a shockwave that resonates deep in your chest, making you fear your heart might just stop from surprise. Like people instinctively raising their hands to protect themselves from being shot, it quickly becomes clear that you might as well not bother. The only thing to do is to not be there when it arrives. Bad punches turn what is supposed to be a back-and-forth contest into a desperate scramble for survival, the difference between a sparring match and a person fleeing a baseball bat attack. More fundamentally, they make you ask yourself how much you want to be doing this at all.

THE ABILITY TO throw these otherworldly type blows is dependent purely on the person, not on the technique. Regular people throw regular punches. These regular punches can certainly be improved; they can get faster, and harder, and more precise, and then they will be fast, hard, precise regular punches. Bad punches are a gift from god. Or maybe from the devil. The expression in boxing is that someone has "heavy hands," an expression whose descriptive accuracy cannot be improved upon. Some of us punch with hands, and some punch with bricks. But everyone is expected to fight each other like it's fair. It's not fair.

BOXING'S APPEAL LIES in its simplicity. Two hands, and no kicking. With two hands, it is only possible to throw a few different kinds of punches. The closer you look, though, the more fractal each of these kinds of punches gets, branching out into entire kingdoms. A book, an interminable book, could be written about the jab. To jab, get in a boxing stance, with one foot back, and shoot your lead hand directly off the shoulder and into the mouth of the person standing across from you. That is a fair enough description of a jab.

To round out the description, though, you would have to explain that you can also bend at the waist and slide your front foot forward and stab your jab into that person's bellybutton, your head descending to a level that in theory is just below the height of the counterpunch that will be coming back. Or you can start with your lead hand low, by the waist, and fire an up jab that does not come straight forward at chest level but instead is flicked upward with your shoulder muscle like you were cracking a whip backhand, rising directly through the middle of your opponent's raised guard and smacking him on the chin, which is also called a shotgun jab, because of its similarity to being blasted in the face with a wounding but not lethal dose of buckshot. Or you can start with a jab to the body and bring it straight up to the head, or start with a jab to the head and immediately collapse down as if sitting on a rock and sink the jab to the body. Or you can double jab, which is a tap-tap rapid-fire jab to the face, which, if you want, can be a soft lead jab designed just to move your opponent's guard followed by a harder second jab; or, when he expects the double jab, you can triple the jab instead, drawing his hands tighter around his face with each tap until all his defense is in the middle and none on the sides, so you can bring the hook. Or you can just keep up a steady, poky jab that is not even designed to hit a guy so much as to keep him busy doing something besides hitting you. Or the feint to the body followed by a sharp jab to the head, or vice versa, or you can jab, then feint the right hand, then jab again. Or the hook off the jab, which is another full chapter in itself.

Hard jabs involve stepping in, just a tad, just enough to create the momentum of your body going forward, which makes the jab carry the weight of all of you and not just the little bit of flicking action that you can generate with your shoulder. That almost imperceptible forward movement in the hands of a master can endow a little jab with the power to stagger men and break noses. A hard jab is dispiriting, because you know that the jab is the weakest punch of all. If you put your hand up to catch a jab and the jab carries your hand back so that you hit yourself in the face, you are in for a bad day. If getting hit with the jab causes your head to snap back, your near term future can feel very dark. There are only worse things to come.

The jab is called "one," as in "give him the one-two." The two is the straight right hand (or left hand, for southpaws) that comes immediately behind the jab. The straight right is sometimes called the cross, but I prefer straight right, because the straighter it is, the better. When the average person wants to throw a very powerful punch they typically throw a wild hook, because this is the thing that naturally feels hardest to us, the wild haymaker that you will see in any bar fight or first day of sparring. This is one of many cases in which your natural instinct is the opposite of what you should actually do, in boxing.

Ideally your hardest punch should be short. It should travel in a straight enough line that you could shoot it down a pipe in front of you without touching the sides. Your jab hand comes off your front shoulder, and your straight right comes from your back shoulder, so it goes farther and carries more power and also takes more time to get there and therefore is more challenging to land. Its power begins in your back foot, which rotates and pushes off the floor, which rotates your hip, which rotates your shoulder. The arm is just the delivery mechanism. You can do a million curls and get huge arm muscles and you will punch slowly and weakly. You will be beat up by a smaller, skinnier person who is able to turn their hips. Punching power begins in the center of the earth, which you push away from. It comes from torque, which comes from rotation. Take your right finger and touch your right hip bone, the pointy part of it in the front. The rotation of this point 90 degrees forward is what gives your right-handed power punch its power. Imagine an iron rod running from this point up to your right shoulder. These points are connected. They turn together, propelled by the back foot. When both the hip and shoulder have rotated so that your chest is facing your opponent, you let your fist go in a straight line. This is a properly executed power punch. This is the one that knocks someone out. Any punch thrown without this rotation is just a glorified jab. There is nothing morally wrong with it, but it is nothing to brag about.

The one-two exists because it is difficult to stand in front of someone who is looking right at you, who is a decent boxer, and hit that person with a straight right hand, blammo. It is too easy to see coming, and it comes from too far away. It is too unlikely, too abrupt. It is like trying to fuck without foreplay. The jab is the kiss that precedes the fuck. The jab is fast, and easy to land, and you can pop it into someone's face, temporarily blinding them, and as soon as you pull it away, they find that the right hand has arrived. One two. Bang. A good one-two that lands sounds like BAPBAP, with almost no pause between the two. Men have made millions of dollars and risen to fame and glory by perfecting these two movements alone. Both punches can come perfectly straight, down the middle, and land on the chin, or only the jab can be straight, drawing the opponent's hands together, and then the right hand can be looped just enough that it comes around the outside of the opponent's left hand, cracking him on the temple.

It is a very basic motion that with many years of practice can become lethal. Perfecting it is easier said than done. Everything in boxing is easier said than done. There is nothing more worthless than a long discussion of what someone would do if they were in a boxing ring. The combined total value of everything you will read here is less than the value of a single black eye.

After the one-two comes the three. The three is the left hook. It is a pleasing testament to the fluidity of human anatomy to find that each individual punch in the one two three flows naturally into the next. You shoot your left jab; as you pull it back to your chin, you rotate your shoulders and fire the straight right; and then, as you pull that back to the other side of your chin, the shoulders turn again, back the other way, and you crook your arm and pull your elbow parallel to the ground and sweep the left hook straight through. Each punch puts you in position for the next. All you have to do is throw it. Unlike the jab and the right, the left hook comes from the side. Some people throw their hooks short and tight, which captures the power of the body best and carries it in the punch, but other people, with longer arms, can throw hooks that loop out to the side far enough that they reach outside their opponent's peripheral vision, meaning that if you are not paying very close attention the punch may arrive on the side of your head without you seeing it coming. This is the reason why the proper boxing stance includes your back power hand carried flush against your jaw, always, unless you are punching with it. You keep it there so that if the left hook arrives unannounced, it hits your glove instead of your jaw. The moment that your right hand strays from your jaw, whether from laziness or just the urge to freelance, your jaw becomes a very attractive target. When learning to box, it is useful to imagine sticking that glove to a piece of velcro on your jaw and carrying it there wherever you go. Your feet will move, and your body will move, and your head will move, but one thing that will remain the same throughout all of those movements is your right hand, which is held right up by your jaw, so help you god. If you look closely you will see many boxers, when they finish punching, bring their hands back and tap their gloves against their face, a physical cue that verifies for you that, yes, your protection is in place. Proper hand placement should be taught by a coach; if not, it will be taught by getting punched in the jaw. You will learn it or stop boxing.

If you hold your left tightly by your jaw on one side, and your right hand tightly by your jaw on the other side, and you pull your elbows together so that they are almost touching, and squeeze your forearms in front of you, you are in a defensive shell that will catch most punches. In theory a fighter can just shell up like this and be safe, a turtle whose head and legs are all pulled in. This would not make for a thrilling fight. The best demonstration of boxing's inherent balance is the fact that in order to punch, you must, by definition, open yourself up to be punched. You cannot hit someone while also keeping your hand against your face. This keeps things interesting. No matter how defensively skilled a fighter may be, every time he throws a punch it is absolutely certain that there will be a moment when his arm is extended away from his body, and the parts of his body and head that are usually protected by that arm are at least briefly unprotected. Every punch can be counterpunched. A successful counterpunch, however, must be delivered so that it arrives at its target between the time the opponent starts his punch and the time he brings his hand back into position after the punch. We are talking about a fraction of a second.

This is why boxers are obsessed with timing, a quality that is distinct from speed or quickness or agility. Timing is the ability to see a punch coming and, before it hits you, to throw your own punch through the opening that has been created, the wormhole in the spacetime of someone's defense. The whole concept sounds impractical, considering how fast these things are happening, but it is helped along by the fact that certain punches are intrinsically matched to certain counterpunches, like proteins sliding into their own special cell receptors. A jab, for example, can be countered with a right hand thrown over the arriving jab. This is the single most straightforward counterpunch. It is a wonderful one, because the right hand is always harder than the jab, so that someone who may have just been probing you gently receives back a shattering and demoralizing blow. That will teach them. The straight right, if you can slip it, can be countered with the left hook to the jaw that has been vacated by the punch in question. Or the left hook to the body, dug under the unprotected ribs. Every hook can be countered by a straight punch, which should arrive faster than a curved punch if thrown at the same time. Any punch that causes someone to lean forward can be countered with an uppercut; as soon as you see someone's chin leave the line of their center of gravity, which is halfway between their feet, and creep forward over the front foot, it is time to start looking for a chance to throw the uppercut. It is nearly impossible to land unless someone is pushing their chin forward, in which case it can land with ruinous effect. The uppercut is the natural equalizer against a fighter who wants to come forward and apply pressure. But it is tricky, and if you throw one and miss, your hand will fly upwards, leaving your arm extended vertically, and you can be countered in turn by a vicious left hook, or really by anything else. Most body punches leave your head open to be hit; most punches to the head leave your body open to be hit. The harder you punch, the greater your risk of being out of position when you miss, and the harder the counterpunch you can eat in return. People spend decades acquiring the speed and timing and muscle memory and expertise to minimize their chances of being hit in a boxing ring, but there is no way to eliminate that risk. Getting it to zero would require not punching, which guarantees that you will lose a fight. In the physical universe, time slows as your velocity approaches the speed of light; in the boxing universe, risk to yourself increases with your own aggression. Both laws keep their respective universes in harmony.

Getting punched hurts. But pain in boxing comes in a variety of flavors, a palette appreciated by perverse connoisseurs. The only punches that really "hurt" in the traditional conception of pain—the kind of sharp, sudden, stabbing pain you feel when you stub your toe or slice your finger open chopping vegetables—are punches to the gut. Body shots. Body shots body shots body shots. Without freakishly long arms it is impossible to cover your entire body and head in a defensive position, so there is always a certain tradeoff between guarding your face and guarding the area from your waist to your neck, and most people tend to err in favor of covering their face, which is where your eyes are, which see the punches, which are scary. This is a long way of saying that you will often be hit in the body, because that is what's open to be hit. Boxers do all of those situps and ab exercises not to look good or out of a wellness philosophy centered on the importance of a "strong core" but instead to build a literal layer of armor in their midsection to withstand punches. Your abs are a Kevlar vest for your internal organs. If you are in shape and haven't skimped on your workouts, you will find that you can let most body punches bounce off your stomach, no problem. You don't even feel it, at the moment. After you finish up and take a shower and go home and lay down on the couch you will find that you feel like you have a stomachache. Sometimes you can't figure out why.

However. There are certain spots on your body that, if hit just right, will send an immediate electric shock through your stomach and liver and spleen and kidneys and cause your entire being to seize up as if your nervous system just detected that it had ingested poison. These are the bad ones. The difference between a bad body shot and one that bounces off harmlessly is just an inch of distance. You may absorb the first 99 punches to the belly in a perfectly carefree manner and then, with the hundredth one, which happens to land on that little, invisible pressure point, collapse in a heap and pray for death. The reaction to a bad body shot is indistinguishable from someone being shot with a pistol, and, for a brief time at least, the two experiences are equally incapacitating. Being knocked down by a body shot is not so much a sign of a broken will as it is an uncontrollable physical response.

Even very determined fighters who stay on their feet after one of these punches undergo an instant transformation from athlete to broken old man: a grimace, a half-hunch over, a hopeless shuffling step away from the source of the pain. No matter where your hands were before you took that body shot, after you take it, your hands will fall down to protect your body. There is not a single worse experience that you can imagine in that moment than taking another punch in the same place that the last punch landed. Boxers hurt to the body will drop their hands and leave their face exposed and then be knocked out with a punch to the face and ultimately go home happy, because at least they didn't take another punch to the body. This is not unreasonable. Before judging someone for succumbing to a single well-placed underhook to the stomach it is useful to imagine the feeling of having very bad food poisoning—and, while you are feeling that feeling, having to participate in a fistfight. I suppose someone in this world may be able to drink a gallon of curdled milk and then run a marathon, but it should not be the baseline expectation.

Punches to the head are different. "Painful" is not quite the right word for them. A flat punch to the front of the face is jarring; shocking; somewhere on a sliding scale that runs from enraging or terrifying, depending on your personality. A really hard punch to the head makes your head ring, which is not a fanciful expression but a literal one. "Ding!" it says inside your skull. Just as you could feel your shin break from a baseball bat to the leg, so too can you feel your brain breaking, just a little. Hard head shots stun you, even if you feel that you are still processing things as usual. Your brain scatters, then takes a few moments to pull itself together again. In those moments, you may get hit and stunned again, and again, and that is how singular bad events build into an entire temple of doom.

Apart from the violent dissolution of your functional mind, punches to the head are bothersome more than devastating. A punch to the nose will make your eyes water; a punch to the mouth will split your lip, leaving you dripping blood in a most theatrical way, though with little pain; a hook that sneaks around and lands directly on your ear hole will force an explosion of air into your eardrum, leaving you deaf for a week or two, or for life if it's not your lucky day. Even a soft punch to the thin-skinned area right under your eye will raise a welt and give you a telltale black eye and cause you to say "you should see the other guy!" with a forced smile for days to come. Scratches and cuts, black eyes and busted lips, flat noses and brows thick with scar tissue— the most visible signs of fighting are the least bad. If they were all that you had to worry about, boxing would be much more popular as a pastime.

Punch someone who has never boxed before dead in the face and they will experience a shot of adrenaline that will activate both their fight and their flight reflex, paralyzing them for a moment and then sending them into a wavelike series of paroxysms of intense anger and dread, pooling together into confusion. Punch someone who has boxed for years dead in the face and, unless the punch actually hurts them, it will just slide off. Like walking through a raindrop. There is something to be said for becoming inured to extreme situations. Much of boxing comes down to purging yourself of the natural panic reaction that nature has instilled in us all. When you spar with new guys, you know that the first solid shot to the face will fill them with all of those overwhelming emotions and that they will start swinging like they are in a bar fight, and this will tire them out in about a minute. Then you can do whatever you want. This is just one of the many normal human reflexes that will get you hurt if deployed in a boxing ring. You naturally want to pull your head back from a punch. This will get your jaw broken. Instead, you need to duck under the punch, like a surfer dipping under a roiling wave. You naturally want to move away from the source of a beating. This will just keep you forever on the end of an advancing attacker's punches. Instead, you need to move counterintuitively forward into the violence, where you can smother the punches that need space to pick up their power. You naturally want to grimace in pain when pain strikes you. A boxer learns, from experience, to carry a poker face no matter what—not because he has stopped feeling the pain, but because he has come to understand that there is no sympathy to be found where he is. No outward expression of suffering will gain you any benefit. No one will come to save you. One imagines that an astronaut cut loose on a spacewalk, drifting irretrievably into the void, will eventually stop screaming for the same reason.

Every fighter is at all times under assault by two forces, one visible and one invisible. The visible one is the person across the ring, trying to beat you to death with fists. The other, equally ferocious opponent is fatigue. Everyone watching a fight from outside pays attention only to the fighters, but the fighters themselves must always pay attention to the specter of fatigue, stalking them from behind. If you allow fatigue to catch you, it will kill you just as certainly as your opponent will. To become tired first in a fight is to lose. Experienced boxers are masters at managing energy. They grab moments of rest for individual body parts. A boxer may take a step back and drop his front hand, just to rest his shoulder muscle for a few seconds. He may start showily bouncing on his toes as a distraction from the fact that he is letting his arms rest. A good defensive shell can be deployed while you lay back on the ropes and take punches on your forearms as you catch your breath. As fighters grow more refined, all extraneous motion is purged, leaving master boxers with no movement that does not serve a purpose. Twitchy, aggressive fighters wear down fast. Calmness is everything. Even if you are getting beaten to death, you may as well be calm about it. That way you can think. Getting all excited will just invite your doom in more quickly. The classic aspects of boxing training—the running, the jumping rope, the endless rounds on the heavy bag—are all just to get you in shape to do the rounds without collapsing. They don't actually make you a good boxer. That's a whole other set of training. Boxers must sweat and grind and torture themselves just to be able to beat the fatigue. Beating the other fighter is an entirely separate matter. Yet you can't ignore either one. The visible and the invisible dangers are equally fatal.

"Toughness" is a concept that is often held up to explain fighters, but it does not capture the deal that is really being struck. The popular conception of toughness is some intrinsic quality that people possess that allows them to wade through fire that is too hot for most, a sort of metaphysical callus that protects its owner from the world. That is a myth. People who do things that are very hard, like fistfighting at its most extreme, are not separated from everyone else by a quality; instead, they are separated by a decision. The decision they have made is to not care about the consequences of what they are doing to themselves. This is the price of entry to being a real fighter. Of course it requires hard work and persistence and struggle and the willingness to walk through an absurd amount of pain, but none of that can proceed until the primary decision to disregard death, disfigurement, and dementia has been made. There is no guarantee that all of these things will come a fighter's way, but it is probable enough that worrying about them, like a normal human, is an insurmountable obstacle. You can't give too much of a fuck in boxing. The person who gives less of a fuck about life will always go harder, and the person who gives more of a fuck will lose. This is why most professional boxers had hard lives before they ever started boxing. If you have anything nice to look forward to, it is hard to get excited about fighting for a living.

I have always thought of boxing as a ladder stretching from the ground all the way into the clouds. You begin on the bottom rung. Through pain, and pain, and study, and study, you ascend. Years go by. You can look down and feel superior to those beneath you, until you look up and see that the ladder continues rising far, far above you. Farther than you will ever climb. There is no absolute judgment of anything in boxing; there is only what you can do with the one person standing in front of you that day. There will always be a million more behind that. The reward for progress in boxing is just a scarier monster to play with.

Punches are the only absolute. Punches mark your time. Punches tell your story. Punches are your teacher, and punches are how you teach. The boxers, all of us, got together and punched each other as long as we could, then spent the rest of our time trying to remember what it was like. Add up all the punches we took and subtract all the punches we gave, and you end up back where you started. Wiped clean. All the memories are knocked out of us. We're ready to be reborn.

HAMILTON NOLAN is a journalist who writes about labor, politics, and boxing. He's written for Gawker, *The Guardian*, *In These Times*, and elsewhere. He lives in Brooklyn.

Untold Stories of Harvey Updyke's Last Confessions—and the Plot to Kill Auburn's Iconic Oak Trees

BENNETT DURANDO

FROM THE *Montgomery Advertiser* • NOVEMBER 20, 2022

AUBURN—Stickers disguised the color of the car but made it twice as memorable. Through the office window, elephants and various sizes of the cursive Alabama "A" were visible. They were layered on top of one another in a slapdash arrangement, like a scrapbook collage. Maybe the car was crimson. Maybe it was white. It was clearly a clunker, though. Receptionist Erin Walker imagined the stickers probably made up for missing patches of paint.

Its driver stood within two feet of Walker's desk. At eye level from her seat, his belly was hanging out of his T-shirt. It was January, but he wore Bermuda shorts.

"I want to kill out a couple acres' worth of trees," he announced. Five or six TruGreen Lawn Care employees occupied the small Opelika office that day. One stood and asked for details.

The customer explained his situation. He and his wife lived on Lake Martin. She was away on vacation. He was shopping for Spike 80DF, an aggressive herbicide that withers trees by being absorbed through the roots, then flowing into the foliage. "She wants a better view of the lake from our house," he said. "So I'm taking it upon myself to get rid of these things."

They didn't have what he needed. TruGreen didn't sell chemical products; it provided services. A manager explained several better treatment methods and offered to send someone out to the house for a cost estimate.

He declined, but Walker asked him to leave a name, phone number and address anyway. He signed his name, "Al," and left.

Harvey Updyke didn't know when to lie and when to tell the truth. It vexed him for the last nine years of his life. His one-man criminal operation required careful planning for which he didn't have the patience. In just 10 minutes at the Opelika office where he failed to acquire his weapon, he revealed precise details about his life: His wife was on vacation visiting their daughter. His daughter did just have a baby. She did live in Louisiana.

But his explanation for the Spike 80DF pursuit was pure invention. And at his next stop, he changed his story to a different lie.

The truth? Updyke wanted to poison the sacred Toomer's oak trees on the campus of Auburn University, located about nine miles from the TruGreen Lawn Care office. He wanted revenge after Auburn won the 2010 national championship with a team he believed had been assembled by cheating. "I wanted Auburn people to hate me as much as I hate them," the Alabama fan told CBS News in 2019, one year before his death following a years-long battle with congestive heart failure and coronary disease.

He wanted to commit the most notorious act of football fan villainy of all time. And he wanted the world to know about it.

Maybe that's why Updyke—a former Texas state trooper—didn't cover his tracks that day in January 2011.

More than a decade later, AU is in the process of regrowing the trees at Toomer's Corner, where generations of Auburn football fans have gathered to celebrate wins by draping toilet paper over the branches—they are approximately 40 feet tall now. When the original 80-year-old oaks were cut down and removed in

April 2013, Updyke was in jail. It brought an end to "the biggest story in the state," says Paul Finebaum, whose call-in radio show provided the sound byte of Updyke's infamous confession.

It remains possibly the biggest story in the history of the Iron Bowl rivalry as well. That rivalry will be renewed Saturday when Auburn visits Alabama (2:30 p.m., CBS).

But most of the full story is unknown. The Montgomery Advertiser interviewed more than 20 people involved in the ordeal, reviewed dozens of pages of court filings and consulted television and radio interviews from the time to track down the untold saga. It's part tragedy, part absurdist comedy, part whodunnit and part parable about the perils of sports fandom gone too far.

Herbicidal maniac

The person who sold Updyke the poison does not wish to be named. He understands it was a perfectly legal sale. And that there was no way to know what Updyke planned to do. But he is an Auburn fan with a family of Auburn alumni. He has only told relatives and coworkers about it. About 10 people in total. Being the individual who handed the culprit his weapon extracts a heavy emotional toll.

The timeline between Updyke's whiff in Opelika and his next stop is unclear. He might have driven the hour to Montgomery that same day.

He called AgriAFC—a retail store that sells agricultural products for crop protection, fertilizer and more—first. Proprietary sales manager Val Ivey didn't usually answer the phone, but his secretary was out of the office. "I was calling down there to see if you had something that would kill an oak tree," Ivey remembers Updyke saying. Then before Ivey had time to respond: "I live up on Lake Martin."

Updyke explained that his house was about 800 square feet but in a neighborhood with more exclusive homes. He wanted an addition, but two oak trees blocked the space where he hoped to build.

Ivey's first thought was, "Why don't you just cut them down?"

"Oh no, I can't do that," Updyke said. "My wife wouldn't stand for that. She's kind of an environmentalist." But she was in Texas. If he poisoned the trees while she was away, they would begin to die when she returned home—but she would never know why. No choice but to chop them down.

"Let me ask you this," Ivey said. "There are products that will definitely kill those trees. But when it rains and water flows, it's going to kill everything in sight where it flows. What's the terrain like?"

Flat as can be, Updyke insisted.

Ivey directed Updyke to the company's warehouse down the street. Soon he arrived in his beat-up car. He told the retail worker his new story. He answered the same question about why he couldn't simply cut down his trees. He traded cash for a four-pound bag of Spike 80DF and signed an illegible name on the purchase log.

"You think this will kill the oak tree?" the salesman remembers Updyke asking before he left.

"You could kill a lot of oak trees with that," he replied, chuckling.

In the next few days, TruGreen in Opelika consulted territory manager Jake Formby, who was familiar with Lake Martin. He hadn't been in the office when Al visited. He relied on coworkers' descriptions.

Formby noticed the house number Al wrote couldn't be real. The house numbers on Silver Hill Road weren't even close to that. He tried calling the phone number Al left. It didn't exist. Formby was stumped. Then he noticed something. The fake phone number started with "259." That could realistically be a house number on Silver Hill Road.

Formby went exploring.

"Just trying to get a sale," he says.

That and he wanted to test whether his investigative sixth sense was correct. As he drove past the "259" house, he spotted the stickers.

"I still swear today, it's a red car with a bunch of Alabama stickers on it," he says. "And when the detectives were asking me questions, they said, 'Are you sure it was a red car?' And I'm like, 'Are you kidding me?' Now I don't know. It might have been a white car. I can't remember, but all that I remember is it had a bunch of Alabama stickers all over it. Places where you don't put stickers."

Formby parked and put on his door-to-door salesman face. It was about 11 a.m. He knocked. A dog barked. Formby waited.

Finally, Updyke answered. He was shirtless. "I woke him up," Formby says.

He explained he was there to work up an estimate for Updyke's ground cover. Updyke didn't know what he was talking about. Formby reminded Updyke of his visit to the office.

Updyke denied ever going to the office. Formby was caught off guard. He apologized and returned to his car.

He called the office. Back in Opelika, they described Al's car. Formby looked to the driveway. "I know I'm at the right place," he said. So he hung up and knocked on the door again. By this point, he had no idea if he even wanted a sale. He just wanted to know what was going on.

"Are you sure you didn't come to our office and didn't ask for an estimate?" Formby asked.

"He didn't threaten me or nothing," he remembers. "I'm kind of surprised now that he didn't give me, like, 'Get the hell out of here.' Nothing like that. Just totally denial."

The call

Ivey happened to be driving to Birmingham, listening to "The Paul Finebaum Show" on his car's radio. His first thought: "This guy knows what he's talking about. I believe there's some legitimacy here." The reality of where Al had bought the poison didn't cross his mind.

The warehouse salesman was listening live, too. His first thought: "I hope we don't have Auburn fans thinking, 'We need to find out who sold this stuff.'"

Police and the state Department of Agriculture would be in the office the next day, tracking down the purchase. In the Opelika TruGreen, employees crowded around a computer and listened to the call.

Everyone knows the call by now. "Arguably the most famous call in sports radio history," Finebaum says. "Al from Dadeville" told Finebaum that after Auburn's comeback from a 24-point deficit to win the 2010 Iron Bowl, he saw a Cam Newton jersey on the statue of late Alabama coach Paul W. "Bear" Bryant in Tuscaloosa. His blood boiled, and he poisoned the trees for retribution.

An Auburn student called a campus police officer, who called a campus official, who called Gary Keever, a horticulture professor who would become Auburn's Lorax: the spokesman for the trees.

Early one morning, DoA inspectors Ray Marler and Jerry Haynes arrived at Toomer's Corner with sampling tubes. Students walking between classes surrounded them. It was almost a goofy sight. "We didn't want to make it obvious," Marler says. "We kept it down low, like we were doing other things." They took the samples to a pesticide residue lab on Wire Road. There had been a fire in the lab the previous December, limiting AU's resources to process the samples. The school would have to send it off for testing at a Mississippi State lab.

The martyr and the cryptic voicemail
Stored in a professor's laptop on Auburn's campus, a memento of Updyke remains. At least, Scott McElroy thinks the voice is Updyke's. It sure sounds like him. But police never gave the

once-scorned Auburn professor confirmation. Never closure. Maybe the voice was an actual witness, telling the truth.

"I'm really hesitant talking about this, just because it was so difficult to handle at the time, and I'm glad it's over," McElroy acknowledges. "But then again, it's part of Auburn history. So we don't need to forget that it happened, or stupid stuff like this could probably happen again."

He also wants to set the record straight.

Many large-scale controversies involve a martyr. In this story, McElroy was Auburn's. One decade later, he still keeps a file of the most baffling voicemail that barely anyone has ever heard.

His story goes like this: When Updyke called Finebaum, McElroy was in Puerto Rico for a weed science conference. He teaches principles of weed science, an AU undergraduate class where students learn 40 to 50 types of herbicides and how they're used; how to identify more than 100 weed species; the history of herbicides and the impact of weed management on human development dating back to prehistoric times.

"Weeds are mentioned in the Bible, for goodness sakes, and parables," McElroy says. "They've been around since humans have been around."

He got his undergraduate and master's degrees from Auburn. He was on the University of Tennessee faculty for four years before returning to AU, where he also researches herbicide resistance. Few people know herbicides like McElroy.

Somebody told him about Updyke's radio call the morning after the show. A man named Al had poisoned the oak trees. He did it with Spike tebuthiuron. And crucially: He told Finebaum he did it after the Iron Bowl.

It was Jan. 28. McElroy's mind raced. Tebuthiuron is a photosynthesis-2-inhibiting herbicide. If this was true, the obstruction of PS2 would be evident by now, after almost two months.

McElroy had a research blog at the time. When he returned to Auburn, he grabbed a ladder and his fluorometer and visited the trees. He didn't tell anyone. This was a simple test that didn't require much fuss. He climbed into the canopy of the trees and pointed the fluorometer at a leaf. "It flashes a light then reabsorbs the emitted light and gives you a reading," he says. "From that class of herbicide, you can instantly tell if photosynthesis is being inhibited."

It wasn't. McElroy scoffed. He checked other locations. Same result.

So he blogged about it: The Finebaum caller was a liar. The trees were safe.

McElroy gave several interviews about his findings. Finebaum's show picked up his blog as Auburn sent soil samples to Mississippi State for more thorough, formal testing. The buzz died down.

Mississippi State's lab handles countless samples of potential chemical misuse. Sometimes the cases go to court after testing. The lab's biggest case involved the Gulf of Mexico oil spill in 2010. Usually, though, it handles relatively minor dust-ups: A farmer sprays pesticides, and the wind blows it off the property and onto a neighbor's crops.

This was different. "Normally an inspector might drop the samples off in evidence bags," says Gale Hagood, who is retired from the lab now. "This was a significant misuse. State car. Bit more security involved." Multiple unmarked black SUVs pulled up as though they were carrying the president. The evidence bags held soil, bark and leaves.

Chemist Cindy Foster analyzed the samples. The high profile made it a priority case, so testing took less than a week. Foster relayed her results to Hagood for review. Hagood was responsible for communicating the test's verdict back to Alabama's Department of Agriculture. She was one of the first to see the truth:

"Those trees were never coming back."

It was two weeks after his semi-viral blog that McElroy got the call. He was in Orlando for another conference. AU hadn't announced it yet, but the tests were back: fatally high levels of tebuthiuron in the soil.

"Immediately, I had egg on my face," McElroy says.

He rushed back to Auburn. The coming weeks would be miserable. Auburn reprimanded him for going over university leadership's head. A team of experts was selected to handle PR. McElroy was not included. He wasn't credible anymore.

Message boards slaughtered him. McElroy couldn't look away. He had never been in a public spotlight. He read conspiracies that the university itself had poisoned the trees to distract from Heisman-winning quarterback Cam Newton's 2010 eligibility scandal. The same online dwellers who invented that idea crucified McElroy; in interviews, he had referred to tebuthiuron as a pesticide. "He doesn't even know what a pesticide is," McElroy remembers reading. "A pesticide kills pests. This is an herbicide because it kills weeds."

The professor fumed. The U.S. Environmental Protection Agency defines a pesticide as any chemical that kills insects, diseases, weeds, anything. "It's an umbrella term," he insists. "They had no idea what they're talking about, yet they're calling me an idiot."

Meanwhile, Auburn's team, led by Keever, started the long process of setting up a grid system across Samford Lawn to test the depth of poison penetration at different areas. It was an arduous mapping process. Keever deflected frightened parents, who were concerned the chemicals had seeped into the water supply. That theory even earned brief attention from the Department of Homeland Security regarding whether Updyke's crime constituted a terrorist attack. Auburn brought in an engineering firm to validate that the water was safe.

The whole time, McElroy agonized over one question: How was I wrong? Eventually, he grew to understand what had happened: Updyke didn't poison the trees after the Iron Bowl, like he said on the radio. He did it after Auburn won the national championship, more than a month later. When McElroy performed his bootleg test, only a week had passed. It takes time for Spike 80DF to move through a tree's vascular system—its bloodstream of sorts—to the leaves.

"I was assuming that a person who would poison trees just to upset a rival sports opponent would be honest about when he did that," McElroy says. "Which was dumb on my part. I met him at his word. Why would you take somebody at their word who would commit a crime?"

But the cryptic voicemail, which he played for the Montgomery Advertiser, is the last remaining mystery. McElroy will never know for sure who it was. But when the professor rushed to his office the morning after his incorrect blog was exposed, he found a 17-second recording on his work phone.

"I just want to tell you that you're full of (expletive). That I know the guy that poisoned the trees. I saw him do it on the webcam. You can take your fancy little meter or whatever it is and tell all your Auburn buddies anything you want to. Your (expletive) trees aren't poisoned? I hope they rot and die in hell, you cheating (expletive)."

'Why have you been seeing my wife?' The search for Al from Dadeville

Jay Sewell was in the right place at the right time, or maybe the wrong place at the wrong time. "I jokingly say it was bad luck," he says now. He was 27 years old, just five years out of school. He had missed his graduation from AU because he was at the police academy, and he drove a patrol car until his 2008 promotion to Auburn Police Department detective. There were the detectives who kicked in doors, and then there was Sewell. He was an ambitious, analytical investigator. The brains, not the brawn. His sergeant, Scott Mingus, called him Jimmy Neutron.

Sewell was in the office Jan. 27 when a concerned citizen called about Updyke's call. "I was there and got the tap on the shoulder, I guess," he says.

Tommy Dawson was the opposite in some ways. He was police chief at the time, a confident 26-year APD veteran with a big personality that made him an effective interviewer. He says he's the sixth generation of his family to graduate from Auburn. He grew up in Lee County and attended Beauregard High School.

Sewell ran with the case, even though he felt skeptical about the call. First he called the Alabama Department of Agriculture to learn more about the herbicide. He learned power utility companies sometimes pour Spike 80DF on power lines to prevent trees from growing. Its anti-arbor purpose is specific.

While he waited like everyone else for the test results from Mississippi State, Sewell contacted Finebaum's producers and acquired a recording of the call. He used a law enforcement database to search for driver's licenses with a first, middle or last name similar to "Al" in Tallapoosa County and surrounding areas. "It was a needle in a haystack at that point," he says. Albert, Alex, Alan.

Updyke's middle name was Almore.

Sewell used phone records to form a list of numbers for the potential Al candidates. In stepped Dawson with a unique method: He says he cold-called the numbers, "trying to strike up a conversation with the folks on the phone to see if we could recognize the voice."

Dawson needed a tactic to keep them talking long enough. "Were you down at Walmart today?" he remembers asking someone, feigning anger in his voice. "Were you the one who bumped into me at the store?"

It only took the chief a couple of tries to strike gold. Here's how Dawson remembers the call:

"Is this Harvey Updyke?"

"Yes."

"Well, why have you been seeing my wife?"

"I ain't seeing your wife!"

Accusations of adultery worked like a charm.

"He went on and on about 'I don't know who you are,'" Dawson says. "We had to get him to talk about something. ... We were relatively certain after talking to him in that conversation that he was the guy. Listening to the voice. We didn't have to get a voice expert."

Still, it was only a lead. Nothing concrete. Sewell was contacting telephone providers, trying to access phone records of who called into Finebaum's show that day. "Again, needle in a haystack," he says. "It's a tedious process. Being a call-in radio show, there are dozens of people calling in at any one time. So we would get these numbers, and then you have to get a subpoena. And send it off and request account information. So that's taking weeks."

They didn't have weeks when the soil tests returned positive. As Auburn held a press conference Feb. 16, citizens were encouraged to call APD if they knew anything.

Administrative assistant Drucilla Cooper was working the phones the next day when a man called, asking to speak with a detective. He knew who poisoned the trees. She put him on hold and quickly jotted down the phone number in case he hung up. Then she tried to connect the call to a detective. All the lines were busy.

"I can't get in touch with anybody, but if you leave me your name and number, it's confidential and I'll be glad to ask a detective to call you back," Cooper told the caller. She remembers feeling suspicious about his reply: "Well, I don't want to give my name."

Cooper was experienced. She was cool under pressure. She kept him on the line with small talk for five minutes. Then, "let me try again." Still, no detectives were available. Cooper took the caller off hold, wondering if she could casually catch him off guard. "I'm sorry, what was your name again?"

She'll never forget the way he answered, like James Bond.

"Updyke. Harvey Updyke."

She scribbled the name, hung up and ran her note to the detectives. They were able to convince Updyke to drive to the office that day for an interview, at which point Updyke admitted to making the call but not to poisoning the trees. Sewell couldn't believe his luck; he guessed it would have taken potentially months to track down the suspect if he hadn't essentially turned himself in. Sewell contacted the Tallapoosa County Sheriff's Office and started putting together a search warrant for the house where Updyke was living on Lake Martin. It was a friend's place.

Dawson and Lorenza Dorsey questioned him. Dorsey is one of the most celebrated public servants in Auburn to this day; he's retired but still works part-time for APD, and he was not permitted by the current police chief to comment for this story. Dawson doesn't remember much—because he says he didn't last long in the interrogation room.

Dawson claims Updyke came in blithering about Alabama football and using language that offended Dawson.

"I can put up with a lot of things," Dawson says. "I'd been a police officer for 26 years, and I can take most cursing. But if you're going to take the Lord's name in vain to the degree he was taking the Lord's name in vain, I don't do well with that. So I said, 'Harvey, before the Lord strikes you dead and I get killed because I'm close to you, I'm going to leave you in this room by yourself.'"

That left Dorsey to deal with Updyke. The chief trusted Dorsey more than he trusted himself anyway. Dorsey had a way of relating to anyone. Sewell obtained the warrant, and a group of investigators drove to Dadeville with Updyke riding in a patrol car. Dawson stayed behind.

It was dusk by the time everyone arrived at the house. The Auburn PD entourage was accompanied by Bill Hough and David McMichael from the Tallapoosa County Sheriff's Office. They were there to stand outside as a courtesy, in case neighbors had questions.

Investigators brought Updyke inside to ask questions during the search. McMichael, an Alabama fan, thought about the case as he waited out front. "It's sort of like when something happens in law enforcement," he says. "No matter where it happens, if there's something that's bad, it puts a black eye on the whole profession. He put a black eye on the Alabama fanbase."

After a while, the Auburn detectives sent Updyke outside because they were tired of listening to him talk. McMichael and Hough babysat. Updyke talked about his son, Bear Bryant Updyke, and his daughter, Crimson Tyde Updyke. He didn't mention the case. He did go on about Nick Saban's Alabama team.

"We didn't ask him any questions. Bill and I would cut eyes at each other, like, 'Good gosh,'" McMichael says. "He never asked me my name or anything, and I never offered it to him."

Inside, police were focused mostly on finding Updyke's laptop. They suspected there would be a search history revealing Updyke had researched his poison options. How else would anyone know what Spike 80DF tebuthiuron was? The computer was nowhere to be seen. "We never found that, and we thought that was kind of suspicious," Sewell says. "Whether he had taken it somewhere else or threw it in the lake."

It would have been a nice bonus. But Sewell's team had already built a case. Updyke had admitted to making the call in which he confessed to the act of poisoning the trees. That alone was enough to handcuff Updyke in his front yard. Later, Haynes from the DoA would gather swab samples from the car's steering wheel and dashboard, both revealing traces of Spike 80DF.

Before he was taken into custody, Updyke only requested one thing: He wanted his Alabama letterman jacket that was inside.

The investigators loaded him back into the patrol car. Just before they slammed the door and began the trek back to Auburn, one declared, "War Eagle."

'Can you help me get a lawyer?'

A few days after the arrest, Finebaum answered the first of many unexpected private calls he would receive from Updyke. Their complex relationship was in its early phases. Eventually,

Finebaum would be the only media member granted a visit with Updyke during his incarceration. They would talk from time to time, publicly on Finebaum's show and privately, before Updyke's death. Finebaum wasn't afraid to call

Finebaum is a former newspaper columnist who possesses the self-awareness and media literacy to understand that his name will forever be entangled with Updyke's. He often jokes that Updyke's radio confession will be in the first sentence of Finebaum's *New York Times* obituary someday. Knowing that, he has always been open about the tale.

There's just one detail he has never publicly shared.

In a matter of days, two court-appointed defense attorneys had backed out of representing Updyke because of their Auburn fandom. Now a third lawyer, Jerry Blevins, was preparing to file a motion to withdraw over "irreconcilable conflicts." It was Feb. 21.

"I need to talk to you. They're trying to screw me over with this lawyer," Finebaum remembers a nervous Updyke saying on the phone.

He didn't know where to turn. It was clear that any local court-appointed attorneys would follow others' footsteps and withdraw: Either they would be Auburn fans or cognizant of the ramifications of representing Lee County Undesirable No. 1.

"He was ranting and raving," Finebaum says.

Updyke needed to find his own defense team. "Can you help me get a lawyer?" he asked Finebaum.

"Harvey, I'm not really sure I want to get in the middle of this," Finebaum said. But his mind was racing. *It's not a bad idea to maintain a relationship with this guy. Maybe we can get him back on our show. He didn't know what to do.*

He says his first call after getting off the phone with Updyke was to Richard Jaffe, a prominent Alabama defense attorney who has helped exonerate death row inmates and famously represented Olympic Park bomber Eric Robert Rudolph. "I don't know what to do with this guy," Finebaum told him. Jaffe, an Alabama graduate, declined to take the case, according to Finebaum.

Finebaum eventually received a recommendation for Glennon Threatt from Birmingham. Threatt confirmed that Finebaum called him asking if he would be willing to represent Updyke. Finebaum passed along Updyke's number.

After calling Updyke, Threatt agreed to take on the case for free.

"I knew the case had very high publicity value," he says. "I was looking for something to further my career, and I thought it was a cool case to be involved with."

Finebaum still ponders the ethics of his involvement. He thinks there's an important distinction.

"As a newspaper columnist, there's no way I would have gotten involved," he says. "But I'm like, ehh, I'm a talk show host. I don't know what lines I'm crossing, but I think everyone should be entitled to reasonable counsel. So Glenn got the job."

On Feb. 22, Threatt filed a notice of appearance. The first time he met Updyke was in court. Updyke wore an Alabama football tie.

"Harvey, what are you doing?" he said. "You're going to piss off the judge. We're in Lee County."

Updyke shrugged. "Gotta represent."

The Iron Bowl of court cases: Jordan-Hare Stadium or neutral site?
Building a defense was difficult. Evidence was overwhelmingly stacked against Updyke, and taking the case to trial would be like Alabama playing the Iron Bowl in Jordan-Hare Stadium with referees who were raised on Auburn's Bodda Getta cheer. The jury would be a selection of Lee County residents, and Updyke's attorneys feared Judge Jacob A. Walker was an Auburn fan. Walker turned down an interview request for this story.

Everett Wess joined the defense team. He and Threatt had worked together on capital murder cases before. The district attorney offered a 10-year sentence. Updyke was insistent with his lawyers: Plead not guilty, and go to trial. He was 62 with a list of health issues. He didn't expect to make it to 70.

"The way Harvey looked at it, he said, 'If I'm convicted for 10 years, I won't live,'" Wess says. "'That's like the death penalty for me.'"

The only problem: Updyke kept getting in his own way.

As the seasons changed, Threatt often took Updyke to Zaxby's for fast food in Auburn. During their lunches, he would advise Updyke on how to handle the case's publicity: Do not speak to media. Do not appear in public. And above all, do not attend Alabama football games.

"He was a great guy. He was the kind of guy you want to spend an hour with and have a beer with," Threatt says. "He was funny. Real likable and salt of the earth. He was sincere and genuine. There was nothing fake about him at all."

But …

"He lived for the publicity, man."

After a preliminary hearing April 20, Updyke claimed he was assaulted at Tiger Express gas station on U.S. Highway 280. The assailants got away, he said. Photos of his bruised face were entered into the court records. But security camera video showed no evidence of an assault. When Threatt asked Updyke why, he said it happened in the back of the gas station. "What were you doing back there?" Threatt asked him. Updyke never answered that.

"I think he did it to himself," Threatt says now. "I think he hit himself in the head and pretended to be attacked."

Updyke was on his way from the hearing to Birmingham to appear in Finebaum's studio for a live interview when the alleged attack happened. Finebaum had recently made a comparison between Updyke and Tommy Lewis, a figure of Crimson Tide legend. Lewis was on the sideline in the 1954 Cotton Bowl when an opposing running back raced past Alabama's defense and toward a 95-yard touchdown. Nobody was in his way until Lewis ran off the bench and illegally tackled him at midfield. Lewis explained himself by saying he was "just too full of Alabama."

"Harvey, you've heard that story," Finebaum told Updyke in a conversation off-air. "You're just too full of 'Bama."

Finebaum was led to believe the purpose of the interview was for Updyke to apologize to the Auburn fanbase. Meanwhile, Threatt had ordered Updyke not to do it. "It never helps a defendant to talk to the media," he reiterated.

Updyke called into the show April 21 anyway. He said he no longer wanted to appear in person, fearing for his safety after the gas station incident.

The conversation lasted 45 minutes. Updyke never explicitly apologized to Auburn. He did, however, steal Finebaum's line. Near the end, when Finebaum asked if there was something he wanted to say to Auburn fans, Updyke referenced Tommy Lewis: "They asked him, 'Why'd you do it?' He said, 'I just have too much 'Bama in me. Too full of 'Bama.'"

After he ended the call with a "Roll Tide," Finebaum thought to himself "for about the 15th time," he says now, "I'm done with this guy. We're done."

Threatt was furious. By the end of May, Updyke had been indicted on two counts of criminal mischief, two counts of desecration of a venerated object and two counts of vandalism of a crop facility. He continued to plead not guilty, but now he did so by reason of mental disease or defect.

Then a new football season arrived. Updyke went to an Alabama game. He snapped selfies with fans. On Sept. 29, he called Finebaum's show again. This time he did apologize to Auburn fans "for what I have been accused of doing." It was a subdued, remorseful side he had never shown before. He had recently been hospitalized. He was dealing with chronic heart disease and back ailments.

Threatt says he told Updyke after the September Finebaum call, "If you're not going to take my advice, you need to get another lawyer."

"Well, I guess I will," Updyke responded.

On Oct. 6, 2011, Threatt became the fourth defense lawyer to withdraw from the case.

Wess stayed. A trial loomed in Lee County. Wess asked the judge to step down from the case because of potential ties to AU. Walker declined. Wess tried to reduce the charges to misdemeanors. He filed a motion to set the monetary value of the trees to $20, and he argued that poisoning trees should not qualify as desecration of a venerated object. "Usually you think about messing with a cross at a church or desecrating a grave," Wess says now. His attempts failed.

But in a case filled with odd twists and turns, the motion Wess wrote requesting to change the location of the trial is the most amusing and encapsulating.

"The University of Alabama and Auburn University have one of the most intense and passionate intrastate rivalries in this country. This passion arguably has been known to cause mental and physical health problems for fans of the universities and their respective athletic programs. ... For many years because of the aforementioned intensity and passion, an important football game called the 'Iron Bowl' was played in Birmingham. ...

"The defendant argues pretrial publicity has prejudiced the community of Lee County as it makes it reasonably certain that a fair and impartial trial cannot be had. It makes sense to meet at the historical meeting place of Birmingham where many disputes involving Alabama and Auburn have been decided."

The last confessions of Harvey Updyke

The motion for a change of venue was denied. At last, it was almost time for a trial in summer of 2012. Witnesses were receiving subpoenas. Jury selection was set to begin June 19.

But Updyke wasn't done bragging.

"So one night Harvey calls me," Finebaum says. "He would just have these late-night calls. And he called me one night, all upset."

Finebaum told Updyke they couldn't talk anymore. "I have been subpoenaed to testify against you."

He remembers the conversation unraveling in a matter of seconds.

"Well, what are you going to say?"

"Well, I'm simply going to respond to questions about the phone call you made and tell the truth."

"Tell the truth about what?"

"My only involvement in this whole case, Harvey, is you called in as Al from Dadeville, and you said you poisoned the trees. I don't know whether you did or not."

"Of course I did it," Updyke said. "You know that. I went to the store—"

"Harvey, please don't say anymore, OK?"

Finebaum felt obligated to call the district attorney the next morning and report Updyke's latest confession. The DA laughed and told Finebaum the trial would be fairly cut and dried. Evidence was already overwhelming. This latest admission barely mattered.

That was Updyke's last confession that was never publicly shared. Then came the final one that went viral.

Andrew Yawn had only written a few stories for the *Auburn Plainsman* student newspaper. He was inexperienced. His dream job was to cover the New Orleans Saints. But on June 19, he had a crash course in covering hard news. He had been assigned to cover the jury selection. He was in the reporters' booth at the courthouse, watching Updyke as the charges were read. Updyke's head was drooped, "chin kind of almost hitting his chest and kind of resting there," Yawn remembers. There had been rumors about Updyke's health issues.

Yawn posted his observation that Updyke appeared unwell on a new social media conveyance called Twitter. An older reporter admonished him for speculating: "What are you, a doctor? You can't say that."

"Well," Yawn thought, "I guess I'll go ask him."

He was a student. He didn't know that wasn't protocol. At a break in the action, Yawn approached Updyke and his wife. They started a conversation. Yawn was from Louisiana. Updyke had family there. They talked for almost an hour. Updyke confirmed his health issues on the record.

Eventually, Yawn gathered up the courage to ask: "Harvey, what really happened that night?"

Updyke looked both ways out of the corners of his eyes. "Did I do it? Yes," he said. Yawn was taking notes. Updyke didn't seem to care. He kept talking. Only at the very end does Yawn recall him saying slyly, "Don't tell anyone."

Yawn called his editor and described what had happened. "What are kind of the ethics there?" Write the story, he was told.

The *Plainsman* published Updyke's confession. The next day, Yawn gave several interviews before police handed him a gag order.

Wess tried to discredit the word of the student journalist. But the confession had stirred more controversy just as the case was finally nearing trial. Two days after Updyke spoke with Yawn, Judge Walker delayed the trial, deeming that media coverage and public interest rendered it too difficult to empanel an impartial jury. In September, Wess motioned to withdraw as counsel.

"I liked him. He was a nice guy," Wess says. "Just when it came to Alabama football, I guess he had the potential to lose it a little bit."

Judge-appointed defense lawyers had to carry Updyke to the finish line. On March 22, 2013, nine days after Walker granted a change of venue to Elmore County, Updyke pleaded guilty. The case never went to trial. He was incarcerated for 76 days for poisoning the trees. On April 23, Auburn removed the dying oaks.

If Updyke had never called Finebaum in the first place, Keever estimates Auburn wouldn't have detected visible signs of death for months. He has no guess as to how long it would've taken the university to discover what the problem was.

But Updyke called.

"He was proud of it," Threatt says.

The moment that made Updyke proudest, though, he managed to keep a secret. During one of the many meals he shared with Wess while Wess represented him, Updyke indicated that he had researched herbicides on his laptop. Police did a thorough search of the house on Lake Martin, he told Wess. Investigators looked everywhere—"every room, in the attic, under everything."

Except for the place where Updyke had hidden the evidence: inside his barbecue grill.

Epilogue: The sour taste of iron

Police never found out the exact night Harvey Updyke poisoned Toomer's Corner. Sewell even looked through the live webcam footage, finding no "smoking gun moment." But Updyke did it after dark, between Jan. 14 and Jan. 26, 2011. He mixed the herbicide chemical with soda and poured his drink unevenly around the dirt.

Updyke died in 2020 with close to $800,000 in restitution unpaid. The case was closed.

Sewell left the Auburn PD two years after taking on the case. He enrolled in law school and is now an associate at the Birmingham-based firm Lightfoot, Franklin & White. His first day of law school, everyone was prompted to share a fun fact about themselves. Sewell's fun fact was that he had led the Harvey Updyke investigation. "The first guy after me was like, 'I can't follow that,'" he says.

Dawson, the former police chief, received an apology via one of Updyke's lawyers months after storming out of the interview. "We were kind of looking forward to hearing the case," Dawson says, "because we had a bucketload of evidence."

McElroy keeps his copy of the voicemail. He plays it for students in his class but otherwise seldom shares it. "Fair warning, it gets pretty crass," he tells his class before pressing the button. "It's my party trick."

Finebaum was catapulted to national prominence with help
from Updyke's call. His show expanded from radio to television.
His voice is the ethos of the SEC these days, and he still takes
callers on SEC Network. In fact, the moment he found out the
soil had tested positive, he was in Atlanta, talking to a network
about syndicating the show on TV. "The irony of it," he chuckles.

Ivey's retail manager who sold Updyke the poison still feels
guilty. Ivey doesn't. He stands by it being an ordinary sale. Ivey
lives in Birmingham now. His granddaughter is an Auburn
student, the fourth generation of his family to attend AU. "You
know, in all the time I was at Auburn, I never rolled the trees,"
he says. "I never did. Anyway, shame it happened. That guy's a
lunatic."

Most people interviewed for this story seldom attend Auburn
football games since the incident. Updyke's crime left a sour taste
in their mouths. It was a cautionary tale against taking sports
too seriously.

"Like I said, he was one of the most vile people I ever met in
my life," Dawson said in August. "I used to really enjoy Auburn
football, but with people like Harvey, it's hard to enjoy it sometimes. Of course, he's definitely not the worst person ever. I'm not
trying to say that. I've met some other folks who were a whole
lot worse than Harvey, just in different ways. Harvey was just—I
don't know what. A grown man acting 12 about a sport."

Then Dawson paused as the conversation ended.

"So, think Auburn's going to be any good this year?"

BENNETT DURANDO is from St. Louis, Missouri, where he grew up reading
the *St. Louis Post-Dispatch* sports section. Currently covering the Colorado
Avalanche for *The Denver Post*, he has previously written about SEC sports
for the *Montgomery Advertiser* and other *USA TODAY* Network papers; the
Columbia Missourian; and his hometown *Post-Dispatch*. Durando's first byline
was in the *Avery All-Star Action*, his grade school newspaper. He enjoys hiking
and spending time with his cat, Bowie.

King of the Hill

JANA MEISENHOLDER

FROM The Atavist Magazine • JULY 2022

1. The Acceleration

On a Thursday night in August 2021, hundreds of people gathered along the banks of the Okanogan River in the small town of Omak, Washington. The air was thick with smoke from recent wildfires and shot through with tension. The crowd craned their necks to see the top of a nearby hill, which on one side plunged straight into the river. At the hill's crest, illuminated by floodlights, more than a dozen men sat on horseback wearing helmets and life preservers. An ambulance was stationed below. Some spectators began to pray.

In Omak, the second week of August is synonymous with Stampede, an annual four-day rodeo featuring saddle bronc riding, steer wrestling, and Native American drumming and dancing. Stampedes like the one in Omak are common across the American West, but the big draw here—the grand finale of each day's festivities—is unlike anything else in the country. Riders like the ones atop the hill spur their horses to top speed, fly over the crest, and charge down a precipitously steep dirt track. After crashing into the Okanogan, they cross to the opposite bank and— if they make it that far without serious injury—dash 500 feet to the Stampede's main arena. The thrilling, grueling spectacle is known as the Suicide Race.

The jockey with the best showing over four days earns the coveted title King of the Hill. There are men who have won once, twice, or several times, making them local celebrities. Omak sits on the edge of the Colville Indian Reservation, and the vast majority of riders are Native. Competing in the Suicide Race is a matter of pride: Many riders' forefathers "went off the hill," as locals say, and the event echoes Native traditions dating back centuries.

In 2021, most of the riders were repeat contenders or past winners, but one man was both an outsider and an underdog. Around Omak, which has a population of fewer than 5,000 people, Andres Beckett was known as "the rookie." Twenty-nine years old and Mexican-American, Andres mostly worked construction. His forebears didn't go off the hill, and he had to fight for years to get to the race's starting line—a streak of white paint hastily sprayed onto the ground. Jockeys in the Suicide Race need skill and grit, but even more important is mentorship. The tight-knit community of legacy riders know the course in detail—how to train for it, survive it, master it—and they don't share that expertise with just anyone. Wannabe racers have to prove themselves, earn the privilege of learning from the best.

Andres had done that, enduring setbacks and humiliations before securing the guidance required to compete. Now he waited impatiently for the starting gun to go off. Between his legs was the muscled mass of JD, his horse. Andres's boots were taped into the stirrups of his saddle—falling off was not an option. He knew JD could sense his nerves; whenever he gripped the reins, the horse's ears twitched. "Let's have some fun, JD," Andres said. "Let's get it." In his head he heard music, the eerie melody of a song by a Russian electronic band he'd listened to while preparing for the race. It made him feel close to death.

Bang.

Fuck it, Andres thought.

He hollered at JD, and together they galloped for the edge.

ANDRES'S ORIGIN STORY is fraught, which is to say it's quintessentially American. His maternal grandfather, Crecencio "Chencho" Ovalle, left his wife and children in Mexico in the 1980s to find better economic opportunities in the United States. Ovalle was caught trying to cross the border several times and sent back. When he finally made it through, he continued as far north as he could get, finding work picking fruit in the apple, berry, peach, and plum orchards around Omak, which is less than 50 miles from the Canadian border. Ovalle was one of only a few Mexican immigrants in the area. Soon he sent for his wife, and together they saved enough money to pay a coyote to smuggle their two daughters and the girls' aunt into America.

One of those girls was Andres's mother, Adela. She was 18 at the time. She gave birth to Andres almost exactly nine months after she arrived in Omak. Right from the start, he was different from the rest of the family. "My hair was blond, my eyes were blue," Andres said. In the early 2000s, during a family trip to Denver, Andres threw food across the dinner table at his cousin and ignored the adults who told him to stop. His uncle George looked at the rambunctious ten-year-old and said, "You're going to be crazy, just like your dad."

Andres was confused. The man he believed was his father, José Muñiz, was reserved and disciplined. Muñiz had crossed from Mexico into the United States with his best friend, only to watch the friend be crushed to death as the two of them hid under train cars to evade Border Patrol agents. "I'm talking about your real dad," George explained, "your white dad."

Here was the truth: In the spring of 1991, a 23-year-old named Tony Beckett, who had spent a few years in the Navy, got on a Greyhound bus in Nashville that was bound for Seattle, where his mother lived. Adela, recently arrived in America, boarded the same bus—she was headed to Omak to reunite with her parents. Tony, who was athletic and had blond hair and blue eyes, asked if he could sit next to her. Adela didn't speak English, and Tony didn't speak Spanish, so they communicated through hand signals and smiles. In the several days it took to drive across the country, their romance blossomed. When they arrived in Seattle, Tony wrote his phone number on a piece of paper and gave it to Adela.

But she didn't call him, not even when she learned she was pregnant. In fact, she told no one about the baby, wearing loose dresses and covering her stomach with pillows, fearful that her family would reject her if they knew. Only when her water broke did Adela finally share her secret. She asked José Muñiz's sister-in-law, María, to drive her to the hospital. Andres would later credit this decision with the closeness he felt with his aunt María his whole life. "She watched me be born," he said.

Adela's family was baffled: Where had this baby come from? Who was the father? She finally contacted Tony when Andres was two months old, but made it clear she was in a relationship with Muñiz, who would raise Andres as his own. Still, Tony insisted on meeting his son. Uncle George, who later would let the truth slip to Andres, picked Tony up at the bus stop in Omak.

During his visit, Tony made a deal with Adela: She could raise Andres until he was ten, then the boy would live with his father until he was ready for college. Adela, an undocumented immigrant at the time, felt like she had to agree. Back at the bus stop, Aunt María assured Tony, "I'll look after Andres and make sure he grows up good."

After Tony left, Adela panicked. She didn't want to give up Andres—not ever. A relative suggested a place where she could raise her son and remain hidden if Tony ever came to take him: a secluded 35,000-acre property in the mountains owned by a man named Ben Whitley, who was looking to hire a ranch hand in exchange for lodgings. Muñiz became that ranch hand, and Whitley, who was in his fifties at the time, was like a grandfather to Andres. "He could tell that I was the outcast of the family, so he took me under his wing," Andres said. "Every day I hung out with Ben." It was Whitley who taught Andres how to drive a tractor and ride a four-wheeler, Whitley who showed him how to prepare steers for auction at the county fair.

Andres was a curious, active kid, with a fondness for unorth-
odox pets: a rattlesnake, scorpions, a nest of baby mice. "I either
connected with the animal or I didn't," he said by way of explanation. Muñiz taught him how to shoot a gun when he was just
a toddler. As he got older, Andres helped with tasks around the
ranch, bucking hay bales, changing sprinklers, and assisting with
the birthing of calves. Every year he and his family went to the
Omak Stampede. He was mesmerized by the Suicide Race and the
hero's welcome the jockeys received from spectators. When the
Stampede wasn't happening, Andres and his friends took turns
tumbling down the Suicide Race's legendary track. But his first
love was bull riding: men holding on for dear life to massive,
undulating beasts, and somehow making it look elegant. He
wanted to be just like them.

One day at a local coffee shop, Whitley asked his friend Larry
Peasley, a Colville tribal elder known for his work at rodeos, to
teach Andres how to ride. They used a mechanical bull and
started out slow, going over the fundamentals, working on body
positions. "He was a quick learner," Peasley said. Andres's best
friend, Jerid Peterson, came over to Peasley's ranch to practice
with him. "Sometimes we pretended to be world champions,"
Andres recalled.

Peasley saw natural ability in Andres. "He was doing well,"
Peasley said, "and then I don't know..." He trailed off.

"One of the opportunities I pissed away," Andres chimed in.
There was a tinge of guilt in his voice.

2. The Drop

When Andres learned about his biological father, it brought on
an identity crisis. Sometimes he wondered if he was the progeny
of a bad man from a bad family. In other moments he considered
what life would have been like had he grown up with his dad.
Destitution is a reality for many people in Omak, where a quarter
of the population lives below the poverty line. Andres's mother
and stepfather struggled to make ends meet; sometimes all they

had to eat was deer that Muñiz had shot himself. "That was our grocery store right there," Andres said. When he thought about a childhood in Seattle with Tony's family, he imagined wanting for nothing. "What if they're just really good people, and I could have a good, normal, white-people life?" he said.

Andres got angry when he learned that his mother was throwing away child support checks Tony sent to Omak. Why was the family eking out an existence when there was money right there to be deposited? "I don't need anything from him to raise you," Adela said. Tony had never demanded that Adela make good on the deal they'd struck when Andres was a baby. Still, she worried he might.

In 2009, Andres's sophomore year of high school, his mother and stepfather announced that the family—which by then included Andres's three younger siblings—would be moving to Wenatchee, a town two hours from Omak and about six times the size. Right before they left, Andres was hanging out with his friends, saying goodbye, when he spotted a dark-haired girl in volleyball gear getting out of a car. Her name was Indra Renteria. He approached her and they exchanged numbers. She was also the child of first-generation Mexican immigrants. Andres was smitten.

He left with his family, but he didn't last long in Wenatchee. A year later, he moved back to Omak by himself, to be closer to his friends and to the girl he now loved. (Renteria wasn't allowed to date in high school, so she had to sneak out of the house to see Andres.) His mother and stepfather were so furious they cut off contact for a while. At 17, Andres was responsible for paying his own bills, plus monthly rent to the extended family he was staying with in a dilapidated mobile home. Despite their circumstances, Andres noticed that his hosts never seemed to worry about finances the way his parents did. "Money wasn't an issue," Andres said. "They would eat really good. I knew something was up. They wouldn't tell me what it was until later on, when they saw they could trust me."

Their secret source of income was drugs, namely cocaine and methamphetamine. One day they tasked Andres with driving up north to meet a guy who they said would give him a bag. Andres was instructed to bring it back, and was paid in cash for his efforts. After several of these trips, his relatives began teaching him more of the business: how to weigh out the drugs in twenties, grams, eight balls, halves, and by the ounce. Before long he was dealing.

His popularity at Omak High School skyrocketed, especially among the juniors and seniors who, as enrolled members of Native tribes, had each received a lump-sum payment on their eighteenth birthday. (Known as "18 money," these payouts from trust accounts are common in Native communities.) Andres started wearing Nike Air Force shoes and other expensive clothing. "I was constantly rolling up with a fresh hat and shit people would trade me for drugs sometimes. I had a chain and a little ring," he said.

In the fall of 2010, there was a drug bust in a nearby town, and local suppliers got spooked. Andres was instructed by a family member to hide duffel bags filled with pistols, assault rifles, and shotguns. Then they rushed together to the storage units where the family kept their drug supply. They grabbed everything they could, along with a few bottles of bleach and a knife. Back home, Andres cut open the pink and white bricks and flushed their contents down the toilet. He didn't want to get caught, didn't want to go to prison.

Before 7 a.m. the next day, the authorities turned up and banged loudly on the door. They arrested one of the relatives Andres was working for, cuffing and detaining him on the front lawn just as a school bus full of kids pulled up to the house. The police didn't have anything on Andres, so they let him board the bus like it was any other day.

After the raid, word got around that Andres was no longer dealing, and his life came crashing down. His popularity evaporated. He wasn't making money. "I didn't even have enough to invest in an ounce of weed I could turn around and flip. I was so broke," Andres said. "This is when I found out who my friends really were." Renteria stuck by him, as did his childhood buddy Jerid Peterson. Still, he fell into a deep depression.

When he found someone willing to front him an ounce of cocaine, he jumped at the chance. But the remaining family members he was living with were trying to rebuild their lives after the bust, and they kicked him out. His aunt María, the one who was in the delivery room when he was born, and her husband, Ramón, agreed to take Andres in. They lived in a small, run-down house in Eastside, a neighborhood a mile south of Omak's Stampede grounds. Andres rented a storage shed from them, where he slept and dealt drugs—without his aunt and uncle knowing. Andres described María and Ramón as "really good, innocent, humble people that the whole town knew and liked." He didn't want to hurt them.

Gang violence had increased in recent years on the Colville Reservation, which poverty, limited law enforcement, and jurisdictional challenges made an easy target for criminal enterprises. "By far the highest incidence of known gang activity occurs in the Omak district," Brian Nissen, a member of the Colville Tribal Council, told the Senate Committee on Indian Affairs in 2009. Some of the gangs were Native; others were Hispanic. "Much of the violence associated with gang activity on the Colville Reservation appears to be focused on recruitment of new members and the gangs' defense of their prospective territory," Nissen said. "These territories are important to the gangs in part due to drug distribution."

Andres saw firsthand what gangs were like—not because he was affiliated with one, but because he sold them drugs. His operation had middlemen and regular customers in the Native Gangster Bloods (NGB). In retrospect he described the group as "a bunch of sketchy motherfuckers," and said he believed that one of them, whose father also happened to be a cop on the reservation, broke into his shed. "Stole my coke, stole all my cash, stole all my jewelry, anything that I had that was worth anything he stole," Andres said.

After that he was back to zero, and he still owed money for the ounce he'd been fronted. He started looking for legitimate work and approached Dan Yaksic, the co-owner of a local glass repair business. With his first paycheck, Andres paid off his debt. With his second and third, he invested in more drugs. Once word spread about Andres's new workplace, he began dealing out of the shop behind Yaksic's back.

Members of the NGB broke into Andres's shed again, this time with guns and pit bulls. They also followed his aunt María around. In response Andres bought an AR-15 rifle. He also begged Yaksic to front him cash, but instead his employer sat him down for a talk. "I know what you are. I can tell what kind of shit you do," Yaksic said. He warned Andres to avoid doing anything drastic, because it would end one of two ways: He'd either die or go to prison. "Let all that go," Yaksic said, referring to Andres's life as a dealer.

Andres didn't listen to Yaksic's advice, at least not right away. He was offered an opportunity to move $25,000 of cocaine into Canada, a windfall. He planned on trekking over the border on a mountain trail, wearing a camouflage outfit and carrying the brick of coke in a backpack. But Andres couldn't shake what he called a "bad feeling." Ultimately, he let someone else take the job. He later heard that the person who'd replaced him was murdered. After that, Andres decided to leave drug dealing behind for good.

But that wasn't the end of his troubles. Around the same time, he met his biological father for the first time and learned that Tony had schizophrenia. Because the condition tends to run in families, Andres began to worry he might develop it, too. Then, in 2014, Aunt María fell into a coma after developing an infection while recovering from open-heart surgery. Andres slept on the couch in her hospital room every night. One day he noticed his aunt's feet were changing colors. María had gangrene, which required a double amputation. Eventually she died from post-surgery complications.

Andres considered filing a malpractice lawsuit with the help of a local attorney whose lawn he had mowed for pocket money as a kid. But Andres didn't follow through. Instead he daydreamed of confronting the doctor who had operated on his beloved aunt, following him home from the hospital and gunning him down. Andres went as far as to wait outside the doctor's office one day, pulling on a bottle of Maker's Mark behind the wheel of Aunt María's old car. But when the doctor drove off after work, Andres didn't move. "I broke down crying like a fucking kid," he said. "I realized I couldn't do that."

What followed was "a dark, dark stage," Andres said—"a year or two where I didn't care about anybody, I didn't care about nothing." It was bookended by yet another tragedy. In August 2016, right around Stampede time, Jerid Peterson was killed in an accident while apprenticing as an electrical lineman. He had just turned 23. Renteria attended Peterson's funeral with Andres, and afterward she noticed a change in her boyfriend. "He just wants to do everything and anything, and that definitely picked up," she said. "I think Andres feels like he has to live his life like it's going to end tomorrow."

With his best friend gone, an idle dream Andres sometimes indulged in as a kid started to coalesce into a plan. Peterson had shared the same fantasy. "We always promised each other that we'd do the Suicide Race together," Andres said. Maybe now he could run it for them both.

BEFORE THE ARRIVAL of European colonizers, the Columbia Plateau, which forms swaths of present-day Washington, Oregon, and Idaho, was home to several Native tribes, including the Nez Perce, Wenatchi, Palus, and Colville. Foreigners brought with them disease and destruction. They also brought horses. "It was probably the best gift the white man ever gave us," the late Stampede organizer and horse trainer Eddie Timentwa told author Carol Austin, who wrote a book about the Suicide Race in 1993.

By the 1700s, horsemanship had become an integral part of Native culture. The animals assisted in transportation and territorial expansion. "Mounted war parties could strike enemies at greater distances and with greater force than ever before," writes anthropologist Deward Walker. Horses also led to larger traditional gatherings, allowing more people from a wider geographical range to come together. During salmon-spawning season, plateau tribes would meet at the confluence of the Sanpoil and Columbia Rivers to harvest and dry the coming winter's supply of fish. Horses served as entertainment and objects of sporting competition. Riders paraded horses adorned with tribal regalia and beaded stirrups and bridles before running perilous mountain races.

After the plateau tribes were forced onto the Colville Reservation, the tradition of horse racing continued, and people wagered on riders. Stories of these events were most often passed down through oral tradition, but in 1879, Erskine Wood, a U.S. military officer, wrote of one horse race, "It did not take long for the excitement to grow and soon the bets were showering down and the pile swelling visibly with such great rapidity that it was marvelous how account could be kept. Blankets, furs, saddles, knives, traps, tobacco, beads, whips, and a hundred other things were staked." (Wood wrote positively of many of his encounters with Native tribes, but also participated in the violent removal of the Nez Perce from their ancestral land.)

In the 1920s, Hugh McShane, a white man married to a Colville woman, introduced a mountain race at the rodeo in Keller, Washington. The race, described by Austin as "a half mile, pell-mell down a nearly vertical, boulder-strewn chasm in the face of a mountain," quickly became a crowd favorite. But it wouldn't last: The construction of the Grand Coulee Dam in the 1930s flooded Keller, forcing residents to relocate. In Omak, about 60 miles northwest, Claire Pentz, a furniture salesman in charge of publicity for the town's rodeo, heard about McShane's event and decided to stage one of his own. Locals brainstormed what to call the starting location, a precipitous incline on the Okanogan's southern bank. Murder Hill was floated, but organizers settled on Suicide Hill. "The suicide race draws only the most nervy riders," *The Omak Chronicle* declared.

In 1942, a jockey named Bev Conners drowned in the river during the race. Since then, according to various sources, no other jockeys have died. But injuries are common, including grievous ones. Larry Peasley, who taught Andres how to ride a mechanical bull, has two adult children who were nearly killed in the race. In 2002, his daughter Naomie—one of only a few women to ever run the race—suffered a skull fracture and flatlined on the way to the hospital. Doctors were able to revive her. A few years later, Peasley's son Tyler went somersaulting off his horse and was trampled by oncoming riders. He fractured his ribs and suffered a broken pelvis and hip.

It's not hard to see what makes the race so dangerous. There's the hill itself, more than 200 feet of earth pitched at a harrowing angle—according to one race organizer's measurement, it's steeper than the Great Pyramid of Giza. Riders charge down the slope at full gallop, reaching speeds up to 30 miles per hour by the time they hit the river. Then there's the lack of any hard-and-fast rules about how the race should be run. Horses aren't lined up in an orderly fashion at the starting line. What happens on Suicide Hill is a free-for-all, with mounted jockeys jostling each other, fighting for a competitive spot. The aggression only escalates during the race. Riders violently whipping other jockeys in the face with their crops, attempting to throw them off balance or slow them down, is a common tactic, and often a successful one.

The best Suicide Race jockeys are adrenaline junkies, as athletic as they are knowledgeable of the event's 1,260-foot-long course. They've meticulously mapped out the quarter-mile and know what to do when: Lean back before this point, lock your knees here, sit forward just after that section, pull back the reins there. Riders have incredible core and leg strength to help them stay in the saddle, and they know how far their bodies can tilt sideways if need be, to avoid injury or inflict it on a competitor.

In 2002, the race's all-time reigning champ, Alex Dick, passed away at the age of 83. He had 16 King of the Hill titles to his name; his obituary in a local newspaper noted that Dick, who was Native, "set a record that will probably never be broken." So far it hasn't been. Yet if there's a first family of the Suicide Race today, it's the Marchands. Three brothers—Loren, Francis, and Edward—have followed in the footsteps of their grandfather, Jim, an endurance racer who died after a horse fell on him in 1990, and an uncle, George, who holds three Suicide Race titles. Loren, now 34, has been crowned King of the Hill seven times, most recently in 2015. Francis and Edward have never won the overall title, but they've come close.

As the dominant force in the Suicide Race, the Marchand brothers have a wealth of tips and tricks, and they know all the best places around Omak to practice. But the race is a tradition most often shared among kin, and the Marchands are notoriously wary of letting people who aren't blood, or at least Native, into their inner circle. They also reject weekend warriors and wannabe jockeys who are in it purely for the exhilaration. "The Marchands don't fuck with anybody," said Conner Picking, a Suicide Race jockey and a great-grandson of one of the founders of the Omak Stampede.

That didn't stop Andres from trying to get their attention.

3. The Scramble

By the summer of 2018, Andres, now 26, had cleaned up his life and was working construction and picking up jobs as a handyman. He was also holding fast to his desire to learn from Suicide Race royalty, looking for a way in to their good graces. One day he accompanied a welder to a small ranch in Eastside owned by Preston Boyd, a Colville elder renowned for breeding and training thoroughbreds for flat-track racing. Boyd needed the men to fix his broken horse walker, a motorized machine that leads horses in a circle. While Andres worked, Boyd took a good look at him.

He noticed Andres's height—just five feet six inches. He probed the young man about his weight.

Boyd was searching for a new rider to exercise his racehorses, because his usual guys were getting too busy. Among them was his great-nephew, Francis Marchand. Francis was helping Boyd break some new horses that summer, but his schedule was increasingly packed with rodeos—a formidable horseman, Francis regularly competed in saddle bronc and bareback riding. Andres's specs were promising for the kind of rider Boyd needed. Sure, he couldn't gallop a horse yet, but he could learn. Boyd told Andres he might fit the bill.

Andres knew he was being given a rare opportunity—a chance to get to know Boyd and one of the Marchands, and to show that he had what it took to run the Suicide Race. But months went by and nothing happened. Boyd never followed up with Andres about exercising his horses.

Omak is the kind of place where everybody knows everybody, and sometimes Andres bumped into Francis at social gatherings. He would bring up Boyd's suggestion that he was rider material as casually as he could, to see if Francis knew anything about his great-uncle's plans. Andres also asked about going off the hill— what it felt like, what it took to win. Francis recognized Andres's ambition, and in early 2019 he told him to stop dithering and get to the point: If he wanted to become a rider, he should go to Boyd and say so. "You want to do this? Look him in the eyes," Francis said. "In any culture, you grab a guy, shake his hand, and tell him you want this."

Andres took the advice to heart, but he didn't want to seem desperate. He waited until he ran into Boyd at a gas station one day, then asked if he could help exercise his horses. Boyd said sure, and Andres showed up at 7:30 the next morning to start learning.

Unlike bull riding, which Andres took to easily as a boy, riding racehorses was challenging. Though short, he was stocky and muscular; working construction had made him strong, but he wasn't nimble or quick to respond to a horse's stride. Montana

Pakootas, a seasoned jockey who helped out on the ranch, had to constantly remind Andres not to yank the reins, but to pull them gently, if he wanted to slow a horse down. "Use your wrist, not your whole arm," Pakootas said. Otherwise, when a horse was going full speed, Andres risked throwing it off balance.

Andres's riding improved, and by the summer of 2019 he was exercising Boyd's newest racehorses for several hours most days of the week. Boyd expected his riders to stick to a routine, for the horses' sake. "I take Wednesdays and Sundays off to let their muscles, if they get sore, to give them a little rest," he said. On training days, it was Andres's job to guide horses to a trot around a local track for a quarter of a mile, getting their blood pumping and helping them build stamina. Eventually he would get them up to a gallop. As a horse became more aerobic, Andres learned to increase its speed against its pulse, maintaining a low heart rate even while the horse worked hard over varying distances. After weeks or months of training, when a horse was comfortable running at top speed around the track in Omak, Andres took the horse to Emerald Downs, a race facility in Seattle, not to compete but to get acquainted with crowds and the whirring sound the starting gates make when they open.

Andres exercised Boyd's horses for free, and he and Renteria, who was selling Amway products at the time, sometimes struggled to cover the bills. Andres picked up odd jobs where he could, but not anything that took away from his time with Boyd's horses. The Suicide Race was never far from his mind. He watched videos of past races over and over, studying them. "He'd always say, 'I hope I go down the hill one day,' but I never thought he would actually be in it," Renteria said. Sometimes Andres was surprised he still had a girlfriend at all. "He told me that he thought I'd break up with him since all he did was ride," Renteria said, smiling.

One day, when Andres had been working with Montana Pakootas for a while, he decided to tell him about his ultimate goal. Pakootas, who had run many Suicide Races and was crowned King of the Hill in 2004, was hosing down a horse at the time. In response to what Andres said, he turned and sprayed him in the face. That's how the hazing began. Another time Pakootas dumped a boot full of water on Andres's head. "You scared of getting wet? Because that water fucking feels like it just whips you in the face," he said, referring to the dive into the Okanogan River. Andres was humiliated, but he kept showing up, kept taking shit.

When Boyd asked him to come along to Emerald Downs for an official racing event, Andres jumped at the chance. At the Downs, Andres awoke every morning at 4:45 to feed the racehorses, then got them ready for the day's competitions. Francis Marchand and his brother Edward were there, helping care for Boyd's horses, and they picked up Andres's hazing where Pakootas had left off. "Edward wasn't easy on me, that's for sure," Andres said. The eldest Marchand brother, known for his success in the extreme sport of Indian relay racing, in which a rider changes his mount mid-competition, seemed to notice every mistake Andres made while warming up the horses. "It's almost like he waited for me to fuck up," Andres said, "just so he could go off on me and drive me away."

Andres persevered, and over margaritas at an Applebee's one day, he felt bold enough to say it to Edward straight—what he wanted, what he was sure he was capable of. What did he need to do to go off the hill? Edward, who had placed second overall in the 2018 Suicide Race, shook his head in response.

"You don't have what it takes," he said.

"What's it take?" Andres asked.

"It doesn't matter. You don't got it."

ANDRES HAS A generally calm disposition, and he looks younger than his years, almost childlike. He is always clean-shaven. Most days he wears a purple trucker hat and a belt with a bottle opener on the buckle. He almost always has a piece of green or blue chewing gum in his mouth. But his comportment and appearance belie a rash streak, a tendency toward recklessness.

Like the time he yanked on the wheel of his car and did a U-turn in traffic to come alongside a disheveled man he saw walking at the side of the road, with a small, scruffy dog trailing behind him. Andres pulled up to the man, jumped out of the car, and got in the stranger's face, reprimanding him for letting the dog wander so close to traffic without a leash. It turned out the dog didn't belong to the man, so Andres grabbed it. "Fuck, man. That heated me up," he said. "The fact that he was just gonna let it get hit."

Andres drove to Renteria's sister's house and left the dog there—never mind that she wasn't home at the time. He took a shot of apple-pie-flavored moonshine, got back in the car, and ignored Renteria's sister's phone calls until the next day. When they connected, he explained what had happened; eventually the dog was reunited with its owner.

The thing about Andres's impulses is that they're almost always in service of what in his mind is the right thing to do. "He does have some trauma, obviously, but he has the kindest heart," Renteria explained. "He really does." Maybe that's why Andres didn't lash out at Pakootas whenever he was hazed, or at the Marchand brothers when they rejected him. But just as important as Andres's hard-won goodness and maturity are the adults in his life—parental figures who have helped ground him. When asked why people seem so keen to nurture him, Andres replied, "Because I do right things while doing wrong things."

Preston Boyd is high on the list of people Andres credits with giving him a leg up, and more. Though approaching 70, Boyd can toss a hay bale over a fence and carry a bag of horse feed slung over his shoulder with the ease of a younger man. When he isn't working on the ranch, he's watching the news, college basketball games, or televised flat-track races, always with a pen and a notebook in hand. He wears glasses he peers over when talking, and he smokes Marlboro Reds. The fourth of 12 siblings, Boyd never had kids of his own, but armed with master's degrees in education and social work, he worked for many years as the program manager of

Children and Family Services on the Colville Reservation, helping place kids in foster care. After the Marchand brothers' mom died unexpectedly when they were young, Boyd took in Edward, who was then a wayward 16-year-old. Nearly two decades later, the two men still have dinner together every night. Edward's four children with his partner, Carmella, are Boyd's surrogate grandkids.

Once Andres was exercising his horses, Boyd took him under his wing, too. They started meeting for breakfast regularly at a restaurant called Appaloosa, where Boyd knew Andres loved the homemade raspberry jam. Andres took to affectionately calling Boyd "P-Word." Sometimes when Andres shot a deer, he brought the tenderest, most coveted cuts of meat to Boyd's home and left them in the freezer.

Renteria could see what the blossoming relationship meant to her boyfriend. "I like Preston because he has a lot to teach—to be a hard worker, be on time," she said. "I feel like he sees something in Andres, or he just feels something for Andres." Boyd encouraged Andres to become a better horseman and find his way into the Suicide Race, even when hurdles appeared in his path, ones that went well beyond the struggle to secure a mentor. Andres had hoped to finally persuade someone to train him for the event in 2020, but then it was canceled, because of the COVID-19 pandemic, for just the third time in its history. That November, Andres's uncle Ramón succumbed to the virus. Faced with yet another devastating personal loss, Andres mourned, but he also continued riding. He kept his eyes trained on the hill.

The following May, almost two years after Andres's conversation with Edward Marchand at Applebee's, a racehorse named Tiz that Andres had bought and trained himself won a flat-track race at Emerald Downs. With that accomplishment under his belt, Andres decided it was as good a time as any to make another play for the Suicide Race, which organizers had recently announced would return that August. This time he managed to do it with all three Marchand brothers present, including Loren, the ultimate

King of the Hill. He wanted to know if one of them would train him.

Loren laughed and asked if Andres had ever been on a horse. Then he leaned in, bringing his face close to Andres's. "I'm talking about a real horse," Loren growled, "not just a fucking tame *racehorse.*"

Loren instructed Andres and his brothers to jump into his truck. He drove them all to Boyd's ranch, where Loren was stabling his own Suicide Race mount, Augustus, a beefy animal. The horse had only a halter around his head—no reins, no saddle—but Andres jumped on the horse's back without a second thought. Augustus immediately began spinning. When Andres started to slide off one side, Loren reached over and grabbed his other foot, twisting and stretching his ankle until it hurt like hell. "Let go! Let go!" Andres begged him. Loren did, and Andres dropped to the ground.

"Fuck, let me on him again!" Andres yelled.

He mounted Augustus once more, and the horse panicked tenfold. He started running, then tried to turn, but his hooves slid and he fell forward onto the ground. Andres didn't let go, absorbing the tremendous shock of the landing through the animal's neck and chest. The Marchand brothers sprinted over and caught the horse before he—or Andres—got seriously hurt. Once they'd calmed Augustus down, everyone took a moment to catch their breath.

"Fuck, that felt good," Andres said. He told the Marchands he could feel Augustus's heartbeat between his thighs.

"That was the first time anybody rode him bareback," Loren said.

A few weeks later Francis finally agreed to train Andres for the Suicide Race. Most riders prepare for at least a year before the event. Andres would have only the summer. What he was attempting would be difficult, Francis warned. "You can't just show up and ride, you know?" he said.

Andres knew. He also knew he needed to find the right horse—his own horse.

4. The Stretch

Some Suicide Race horses are caught in the wild on the Colville Reservation. Others are rescued from slaughter. Still others are purchased from reputable breeders. What riders look for is a rare combination of traits: responsiveness, sure-footedness, strength, and bravery. After all, the horse has to be willing to charge off a cliff again and again. "A suicide horse is a study in diversity," Carol Austin writes in her book. "It walks calmly through bustling crowds of onlookers and weaves through vehicles like a police horse. It gallops into the rodeo arena before thousands of screaming fans, a seasoned performer. It waits patiently for more than an hour on top of Suicide Hill while loudspeakers blare.... It possesses the speed of a racehorse, the courage of a charging cavalry mount, and the savvy of a wild mustang."

Horses can sustain injury or, worse, die as a result of the Suicide Race, a fact that draws scrutiny from animal rights organizations, some of which have attempted to shut the event down for good. According to the Progressive Animal Welfare Society, a Washington nonprofit, "Since 1983, at least 22 horse deaths have been documented. In 2004, three horses were killed in the first heat alone." PAWS lists "heart attacks from overexertion, broken bones from shocking collisions and tumbles, and even horrifying death by drowning" as a few of the race's many offenses. The event has been the target of protests, angry editorials, and even bomb threats. "If you go on any video on YouTube and you start reading the comments, it's nothing but hate," Andres said.

Race supporters maintain that riders love their horses, bond with them, and become so attuned to their movements that man and animal practically move as one. To ride in, or better still win, the Suicide Race is to hearken back to a time when horses carried Native Americans to other kinds of triumph. Eddie Timentwa, the late race organizer, once described the event as "symbolic of the warrior that rides first into battle and receives recognition from the tribe and the elders."

Once a horse can no longer run the race, often after several years of competition, it receives a dignified retirement. It's released into the nearby mountains to run free, resold as a working ranch horse, or allowed to live a life of leisure in a pasture. A horse's premature death is always a tragedy. After Coors Boy, a veteran rider's horse, was killed during the Suicide Race, a public memorial service was held, and people from all around Omak paid their respects. Some riders bury their horses in their own backyards.

Andres didn't have much time before the 2021 race to find his horse. Nor did he have much money to pay it. (Typically, a jockey either owns their horse or runs one owned by a trainer in the area.) But the Marchands had an idea: A few years prior, Loren had been given a chestnut-colored quarter horse, so called because the breed is fast over short distances. Francis had noticed the horse's spunky personality and had plans to use him in ranch work. "He ain't going to get tired on me," Francis said. The horse wasn't broken to ride, and he didn't have a name. One night, after hours of drinking and chasing wild horses on the reservation—tribal authorities offer a bounty per horse caught—Loren proposed a bet: If Francis could ride the horse bareback, he could have him. Francis did it, and the brothers named the horse Drunk Deal, soon shortened to JD. (The letter j, they agreed, sounded like the d in "drunk.")

Francis sold JD to Andres for cheap. When he first met the horse, Andres was shocked by how skittish he was. "He was wild as shit and would kick at us," Andres said. Every day, he would approach JD inch by inch, letting the animal know he wasn't a threat. Sometimes it worked, sometimes it didn't. "He was so crazy, we couldn't even get shoes on him," Francis said. Eventually JD got used to Andres, who would grab the horse by the head and baby-talk to him, assuring the animal that everything was OK. Before long Andres was riding JD. "It was green on green," Boyd said. "The horse and him were both going through a new experience."

There are four distinct stages of the Suicide Race, starting with the acceleration at the top of the hill, across a 150-foot flat. That's followed by the drop—a moment of weightlessness after which horse and rider descend the steep dirt track to the river. Then comes the scramble, the effort to get across the river—a sandy-bottomed incline littered with rocks—and onto the opposite bank. Finally there's the stretch, during which a horse must sustain a full gallop beyond the length of a football field. Each stage requires a different training method.

Francis had Andres start by running JD on the rugged land behind his house seven days a week. They practiced galloping at full speed on flat land and on slopes, both during the day and at night—the first three runs of the Suicide Race take place after the sun has set, which means both horse and rider need to be accustomed to running in the dark. Sometimes Francis glimpsed Andres atop JD on his property after midnight, silhouetted against the mountain range in the distance. Francis sent video of the training sessions to Loren, who offered feedback about how Andres was holding his reins, sitting in the saddle, or wielding his crop.

Once JD was comfortable on land, Andres introduced the horse to water. First he sprayed JD in the face with a hose, just like Montana Pakootas had once done to him. Then he took the horse to Omak Lake with the Marchands to practice. The first time Andres and JD hit the water together at full speed, the horse reared his entire body back and his head smacked Andres in the face so hard he got a black eye. But in time JD got used to the water, and the sensation of running through it.

One day as August approached, Andres had breakfast with Boyd and Larry Peasley. Andres took the opportunity to apologize for taking Peasley's training and guidance when he was a boy for granted: "I let you down because I fucking gave it up." Peasley told him not to worry about it. "We all do that at one point or another," he said. When Andres said he was planning to go off the hill, Peasley started showing up to practice sessions to give advice.

Andres took to putting his chest against JD's every day when they were alone in the stable. "We're going to fucking do this," Andres said. He felt JD's muscles tense in response. By early August, they were ready to go through the steps of qualifying for the race. Elimination runs are held on Suicide Hill and usually draw a small crowd of onlookers. If a horse accelerates toward the drop and balks, it's immediately disqualified. There is also a veterinary check, to determine if the horse is in good condition, and a swimming test in the river. Andres and JD met all the criteria.

When the race lineup was announced, Andres was hanging out with Edward Marchand at the horse barn on Boyd's property. Edward hugged Andres and told him he was proud. "Let me hear your war whoop," he said. Andres, feeling shy, let out a small cry.

Edward slapped his back. "Come on, really fucking do it!" Andres tried again, louder.

"Fuck that—this is how you do it," Edward said. The man who once told Andres that he didn't have what it took threw his head back and let out a long, deafening wail. To Andres it sounded like acceptance.

THE OMAK STAMPEDE is cacophonous. There are screaming teenagers strapped into carnival rides and deep fryers sizzling with french fries and corn dogs. Enthusiastic voice-over announcements compete with Top 40 country played at full volume. The cheering at rodeo events is a dense, steady roar, while at the Native encampment the pounding of drums provides a rhythmic pulse for traditional dancers.

The Marchands took Andres away from all the noise the morning before the first run of the Suicide Race. They drove deep into the Colville Reservation, to a sweat lodge in the mountainous Desautel Pass. There the brothers let Andres join their private prerace tradition, a smudging ceremony in which they burn sage. The rite is intended to purify the spirit and proffer good luck.

Back in Omak, Jerid Peterson's uncle handed Andres a necklace strung with a single AK-47 bullet casing holding some of

Jerid's ashes. "I felt safer knowing Jerid was with me," Andres said.
He also wore his uncle Ramón's pants, his aunt María's wedding
ring, his favorite hat, and black cowboy boots Renteria had bought
for him. Edward immediately cut holes in the boots with a knife
so they wouldn't fill up with water.

During race betting, which happens four hours before the
starting gun, at least one person put money on Andres after they
found out that the Marchands were in his corner. Just after sunset,
all 22 Suicide Race jockeys entered the main Stampede arena on
their horses and jogged around in a circle as an announcer called
out their names one by one. An AC/DC song pumped through
giant speakers, and the crowd screamed and stomped their feet.
Andres could tell JD was nervous. "He was flaring his nostrils. I
could start to feel it myself," Andres said.

At the trailers where riders dress for the race, Andres scram-
bled to put on all his gear. Life jacket, gloves, helmet. Wait—his
whip. Where was his whip? Then he remembered that JD's legs
hadn't been wrapped, which is important to protect a horse from
injury. Andres grabbed a pair of scissors. But where was the tape?
Edward ran over to help him. "He had my back big time," Andres
said.

When Andres joined the other riders to prepare to go up
Suicide Hill, he didn't talk to anyone. Instead, he watched carefully
to make sure no one messed with JD—some jockeys were known
to loosen competitors' saddles or commit other forms of sabotage.
Andres also attended to his feet. Loren had told him to use thick
rubber bands to keep them in the stirrups, but Andres decided on
Gorilla Tape. He wrapped three layers around his boots. "When I
go down that hill, I'm ready to die with JD," he said.

The jockeys were escorted to the hill by police. As they
approached the starting line, they all went silent. "I looked around
and could see the looks on some of the cowboys' faces," Andres
said. "You could tell they were scared." He had heard that the first
night's run was always the worst.

Andres's family was in the crowd to support him—even his mom and stepfather, who had moved to Nashville several years prior, had come out to see him race. Larry Peasley was filling his usual duties as one of the race's outriders, which meant that he would be waiting at the bottom of the hill to help if anything went wrong during the most dramatic part of the event. On top of Suicide Hill, Andres lined up next to Montana Pakootas, who wore an eagle feather in his helmet for protection. Loren Marchand was at the other end of the starting line. Andres was glad some of his mentors were there, even as his competition.

In the distance, Andres heard the drum circle at the Stampede's Native encampment—the sound would go all night. "Before the race," Carol Austin writes in her book, "the riders share a feeling that they are related, and in fact many are brothers, cousins, nephews, fathers, and sons. But as soon as that pistol pops it will be every man for himself." Andres remembered what Francis taught him: Think what your horse thinks. "We got this," he whispered to JD.

The gun went off. Jockeys immediately started whipping each other. Andres yelled as loud as he could, an exhalation of fear as much as a command to his horse. It was just him and JD now, against the world. They galloped across the flat—it was pitch-black ahead. "It was like dark, dark, dark, then drop," Andres later said.

Andres and JD flew over the edge, and for an instant they hung in the air. Andres felt his guts go up into his chest, as if he were on a rollercoaster. His lungs froze. "I couldn't breathe for a second," he recalled.

When they landed on the slope, JD kept his balance. Dust clouds exploded around them as one by one the riders made the treacherous descent. Andres saw a horse's hooves in the air and a rider wreck in front of him. But there wasn't time to assess what was happening, who was up and who was down. He and JD just kept hurtling down the hill.

The river hit violently, as Pakootas told Andres it would. Sharp rocks under the water's black surface sliced open one of JD's front legs. Andres held on to the reins. "Head up, JD! *Head up!*" he screamed. But instead he felt the horse going down, and himself going down, too, pulled by the tape keeping him in the stirrups.

Thousands of pounds piled on top of Andres and JD as jockeys who'd been behind them on the hill crashed into the river. Water was in Andres's mouth, then his lungs. I'm going to die right here, he thought. Instinctively, he protected the back of his neck with his hand.

Then, as suddenly as it had started, it was over. Other riders and horses swam by and made it onto the far shore. Andres and JD had survived, but they couldn't race—both were injured. They finished the race, straggling across the finish line, but there would be no more runs that year.

"I never wanted something so bad before," Andres said. "We trained all fucking summer. We did all this to just fucking have it end tonight."

5. The Reprisal

On the Colville Reservation, there is a formation known as the Omak Rock—a huge boulder, estimated to weigh some 40 tons, that appears to balance precariously atop a much smaller rock. It has stayed in this position through numerous natural disasters, including the 1872 North Cascades earthquake. The boulder is the thing people talk about, what tourists come to see, but without the smaller rock the formation would be just another chunk of granite.

Andres knows that both he and his ambitions would be nothing special without the people who hold him up: the Marchands, Pakootas, Peasley, Boyd, Renteria. After he washed out of the Suicide Race, his circle of support gathered to dissect what went wrong, and to think ahead to next year. Andres would heal; JD would, too. There would be another Suicide Race to run.

In early 2022, with several feet of snow on the ground, the Marchands invited Andres to bring JD and go horse chasing with them on the reservation. It would be good training, they told him, since it would help improve JD's stamina and confidence in the wild. Plus, being part of a pack would hone his competitiveness. But JD lost his footing in the powder and ended up reopening his leg wound. Andres feared this meant he couldn't go off the hill again come August, that he'd have to wait another year for a second shot at making a name for himself.

Francis had a solution. He said he would help Andres train and ride Frank Cartel, an eight-year-old dark-brown horse that Francis had recently bought from Boyd's cousin. Andres met the horse but didn't feel a connection. Frank Cartel had only run flat-track races and wasn't used to the terrain of the Suicide Race. Plus, he didn't have JD's untamed nature, something Andres identified with. "I just trust JD more," he said. "I've got a better bond with him. He's crazier."

During the first half of that year, Andres continued to exercise Boyd's horses between construction jobs in Oregon. He started a honeybee farm, hoping to sell honey, candles, and lip balm at the local farmers market. He also bought and renovated a mobile home with plans of renting it out. But these were just things he did while he waited. The Suicide Race was the organizing principle of his life, the thing everything else revolved around. The hill had never abandoned him, and he wouldn't abandon it.

After six months of healing, JD was ready to be checked out by the Suicide Race's official veterinarian. In early summer, she gave the all clear for the horse to run. Andres was ready—he had everything he needed. Together, he and JD could charge toward the precipice once more.

JANA MEISENHOLDER is a Taiwanese-Australian-American journalist and writer based in the San Francisco Bay Area. Her non-fiction writing has appeared in *The Wall Street Journal*, *Rolling Stone*, The Atavist Magazine, *Taipei Times*, and other publications. She focuses on longform narrative features and is always on the search for any story that spotlights memorable characters—often underdogs and outsiders.

The Phillies' Andrew Bellatti Made a Fatal Mistake as a Teen. A Tale of Remarkable Forgiveness Followed.

ALEX COFFEY

FROM THE *Philadelphia Inquirer* • DECEMBER 21, 2022

Lynette Reid doesn't like clutter. She keeps a tidy home in western South Dakota, and is quick to toss out anything she doesn't need. But for the last 12 years, she has held on to an old cardboard box in her garage.

She isn't sure why. Inside it are files that lay out, in painstaking detail, the worst day of her life: Jan. 22, 2010. Her husband, David, and her son, Garrett, were driving home from the movies. They were approaching Steele Canyon High School, near San Diego, when a red Ford Mustang suddenly collided with their Dodge Caravan.

The driver of the Mustang, 18-year-old Andrew Bellatti, was not drunk. He was not on drugs. He was just running late. As Bellatti approached the high school, a car pulled out of the entrance. It was a rainy day and the roads were slick, so he didn't want to hit his brakes. As he accelerated, and veered across the double yellow line to pass, he lost control of his car. Garrett broke several bones. David died at age 50.

Lynette, 59, has shuffled through that box maybe two or three times since the accident. But one night in late June, she found herself shuffling through it again, and came across a letter that Bellatti sent her from jail. The first thing she noticed was his cursive. It was remarkably neat for a teenager. Every word was carefully crafted in pencil, with not a comma or a period out of place.

The second thing she noticed was his empathy. It wasn't just that Bellatti was apologizing profusely; it was that he made an attempt to put himself in her position. He told her he couldn't sleep because of what he had done. He told her it would live with him for the rest of his life.

"You don't deserve this at all," Bellatti wrote. "I can't imagine how my mom would feel if my dad was gone."

When Lynette first read Bellatti's letter, in 2010, she was moved. Initially, he was facing vehicular manslaughter charges that could have sent him to prison for five years, but she knew that wasn't what David would have wanted. So, she asked the judge to reduce Bellatti's sentence. She wanted him to be home by Christmas.

"It was just bad luck," she said. "It was a bad accumulation of things. The placement of the high school, the rain. There was no malice, it was just an accident. He was a baby. I wanted him to have a life."

As Lynette read Bellatti's letter again, in 2022, she wondered what he was up to. She knew that he was playing minor league baseball in the Tampa Bay Rays organization at the time of the accident, but didn't know where his career had gone from there. She asked her husband, John, to look into it. He returned a few minutes later.

"You're not going to believe this," he said.

A new Phillies fan

When the Phillies signed Bellatti to a minor-league contract in November 2021, the transaction was announced with little to no fanfare. Major League Baseball was about to go into a lockout, and once that was over, Phillies fans turned their attention to the free-agent signings of Kyle Schwarber and Nick Castellanos. But Bellatti, then a 30-year-old journeyman with just 20 games of big-league experience, quietly proved to be a reliable reliever. He was called up in mid-April, and stayed with the Phillies for the rest of the 2022 season, posting a 3.31 ERA in 54⅓ innings. Bellatti became someone manager Rob Thomson could trust in high-leverage situations. And that was how he was used on June 26, when Lynette came across his letter.

The Phillies were playing in Petco Park earlier that day. Thomson called on Bellatti to close the game, and he did just that, earning the save with 14 pitches, no hits and no runs. When John relayed this to Lynette, a few hours later, she was filled with pride. She had no idea that Bellatti was still in the big leagues, let alone pitching in their hometown San Diego.

"To come back from that nightmare, and to be able to pitch for a major league team, *and* get the save, it was just amazing," she said.

Lynette started tuning into Phillies games regularly from that point on. She'd check their box scores and look at highlights online. During the playoffs, she watched the Phillies on her living room TV in South Dakota. Whenever she saw Bellatti warming up in the bullpen, she'd run into the kitchen until his outing was over.

"I would get so nervous for him," she said. "It's sort of like watching your kids play."

John would tell her when it was safe to come back, and then would provide a summary of Bellatti's outing. It was often a good summary. In his first career MLB postseason, Bellatti allowed just one earned run and one walk in seven innings. He was as locked in as he'd ever been.

And Lynette loved to see it. She'd watch clips of his postseason outings, laughing with delight as batter after batter tried, and failed, to hit Bellatti's slider.

"They were all over the place," she said. "A foot away from the ball."

By the end of the Phillies' postseason run, Lynette had fallen thoroughly in love with baseball again. Growing up in western Nebraska, she spent her summer nights keeping score for a local team. After graduating from the U.S. Navy's basic corpsman school, she was stationed in San Diego as an ultrasound technician, and began going to Padres games.

Lynette was a regular at Jack Murphy Stadium, where she watched Tony Gwynn, Trevor Hoffman, and Ken Caminiti in the prime of their careers, but became disillusioned after 1998, when the Padres traded away some of their best players.

Decades later, it was Bellatti—the man who went to jail for taking her husband's life—who reignited her love for the game. There are some who can't understand why she is so forgiving. She feels those people are missing the point.

"They don't understand the whole situation," she said. "His age, the slippery road, they just don't get everything. It's easy to be judgmental when you don't understand the circumstances.

"Of course, watching him is a little bittersweet. But I'm very proud of him. I think everybody screws up when they're young, and to be able to come back around, on that grand of a scale, and make something of your life, it's commendable."

'A light at the end of the tunnel'
Bellatti still remembers the pride he felt when he first drove that red Ford Mustang. It was not just something he wanted, but something he earned. After the Rays selected him in the 12th round of the 2009 MLB draft, he used some of his $100,000 signing bonus to buy the car. It was pristine.

Until Jan. 22, 2010, when it turned into a piece of scrap metal. Bellatti was in disbelief. How could something that once brought him so much joy suddenly cause so much pain?

He would never receive an answer to that question, or any of his other questions, but he had plenty of time to think about them while sitting in county jail. Because the jail was overcrowded, he spent his first month in a maximum security cell. He shared his 6-by-8-foot room with two other men, all of them in locked inside for 23 hours a day.

That was his lowest point. Bellatti wondered if his life was over, let alone his baseball career. For a while, he had a recurring nightmare. He'd see himself flying down that hill by Steele Canyon High School, just seconds before he made impact with David's Dodge Caravan. And then he'd wake up.

He eventually realized that there was no sense to be made of a senselessly cruel situation. So he ripped off a piece of paper, grabbed a pencil, and wrote Lynette a letter. He never received one back, but heard about his reduced sentence from his agent, Jonathan Weisz. Her forgiveness allowed him to forgive himself.

"It meant everything to me," Bellatti said. "She had all the right in the world to be angry or wish me harm or anything you can think of. But her gesture made me feel like everything was going be OK. There was a light at the end of the tunnel."

Bellatti spent the next two months in a low-security cell. Instead of having to stay in his room for 23 hours a day, he was allowed to work various jobs. At first he was a barber, then he joined the laundry service, and then the janitorial staff. He exercised at the gym in his spare time.

The Rays assured Weisz that there would be a spot waiting for Bellatti upon his release, and they made good on their promise. Bellatti was released early, in 2011, because of good behavior. By June, he was pitching for the Rays' low-A affiliate in the New York-Penn League. By August, he had a full season in the books, allowing just 21 earned runs in 72 innings.

A long road to the Phillies

Bellatti steadily climbed through the Rays' minor league system from there, making his big-league debut in 2015. It was a short stint. After just 23⅓ innings, he was diagnosed with right shoulder tendinitis and was sent on a rehab assignment. Despite his injury setback, he pitched well overall, and expected to make the Rays' opening day roster in 2016.

It did not pan out that way. Bellatti suffered another shoulder injury early in the minor league season, and was designated for assignment in June. He got calls from almost every team, and negotiated a deal with the Dodgers but failed to pass his physical. The Dodgers had concerns about his elbow, but according to Weisz, Bellatti had never felt elbow pain before. That deal fell through, so Bellatti signed a minor-league contract with the Orioles in 2017. A few weeks later, he injured the flexor tendon in his pitching arm in spring training.

The injury required a full repair, which cost him the 2017 season. In 2018, Weisz held a tryout for Bellatti at a local college in San Diego. There were about 10 scouts in attendance, holding up radar guns, but when Bellatti threw his first pitch, it clocked in at 85 mph.

Weisz looked up and saw that Bellatti's eyes were starting to water. He tried to throw a few more pitches but felt his elbow crunch. He walked off the mound without acknowledging any of the scouts.

"My elbow," he told Weisz.

"OK," the agent said.

An MRI revealed that his ulnar collateral ligament was as "loose as a rubber band," in Bellatti's words. He underwent Tommy John elbow surgery in February but had no job lined up. While he was rehabbing, his wife, Kylee, started working a day shift at Bloomingdale's and an overnight shift stocking shelves at Victoria's Secret. She got Andrew a job at Bloomingdale's, too, where he sold men's sports gear, women's shoes, women's handbags, and men's suits.

Because Bellatti hadn't thrown in 2½ years, Weisz suggested he pitch in the independent league after he was done rehabbing. Bellatti was skeptical at first, but he found a sense of freedom in unaffiliated baseball. He wasn't stressed. He didn't have to worry about being released. He could just pitch.

After he went through a brief spring training, and one relief outing for the Sugar Land Skeeters, the Yankees signed him to a minor-league contract. He spent the 2020 pandemic season refining his craft, and signed with the Marlins in 2021. He had only 3⅓ innings worth of experience with their big league team but thrived at triple-A Jacksonville, posting a 1.52 ERA in 29⅔ innings.

By 2022, he was back in demand. The Phillies weren't initially on the top of Bellatti's list, but after talking to pitching coach Caleb Cotham and director of pitching development Brian Kaplan, he was convinced.

"It was the perfect marriage," Bellatti said. "It wasn't just their knowledge of me, but their mantra. After I heard that—PHAH—I was like, I have a few more Zoom calls to go, but I know where I want to be."

The Phillies' pitching mantra (the heck with all hitters, to say it in a family-friendly way) resonates with Bellatti because it is about fearlessness. His journey hasn't been direct, but it has provided him a unique perspective, one that makes any obstacle seem paltry in comparison.

"I don't remember the last time that I was scared to face anybody," he said. "And I know you don't need something like this to happen in order to have that mindset. But I think my path has just provided me with this feeling of, 'I don't care who's in the box, I don't care what team we're playing.' I *want* to play the best team. And that mindset can only help you."

The power of forgiveness
Lynette Reid and Andrew Bellatti have never met. They've never talked directly. They might never meet, or talk, and that is OK. There is no right or wrong way to process trauma, and Jan. 22, 2010, was traumatic for everyone involved. But nevertheless, they do have a connection.

Bellatti throws his changeups and sliders and four-seam fastballs with gratitude. He knows that if it weren't for Lynette's forgiveness, his life could have turned out very differently. She has pushed him to be a better ballplayer and a better man, and 12 years later, he has become one.

Lynette knows that. And when she sees him up on that mound, striking out the side, making batters look foolish, she believes he's honoring her late husband.

"I just sit back and let him do his thing," she said. "It's wonderful to watch. He's just doing his job. They put him in to get three batters out and he does it. He's just a grown-up doing his job, and I want him to know how proud I am."

ALEX COFFEY has covered the Phillies for the *Philadelphia Inquirer* since 2022. She began her journalism career in 2019, covering the WNBA's Seattle Storm and then the Oakland A's for The Athletic. She is a proud second-generation sportswriter.

The Pain May Never Fade for Delaware State's Players. I've Been There, Too.

KURT STREETER

FROM *The New York Times* • MAY 13, 2022

At first, Pamella Jenkins, the head women's lacrosse coach at Delaware State University, wasn't worried when Georgia sheriff's deputies pulled over her team's bus.

Her team, around 70 percent Black and representing a historically Black college with roots that stretch to the 1890s, had been enjoying the trip home after playing in a tournament in Florida. They were doing nothing wrong. The team's chartered bus was not speeding as it eased north on Interstate 95. It made sense when she heard a deputy tell the driver that he had the bus in the left lane and needed to be in the right.

But it was not long before the mood shifted in a way that feels all too familiar—a mood I can relate to as an African American who once played college sports and plied the same Georgia interstates while competing in the low levels of professional tennis.

Suddenly Jenkins's team was being accused of having drugs on board. More deputies arrived. A drug-sniffing dog circled. Jenkins, who is Black, shared her athletes' feelings: shock, fear, anger and frustration.

Video footage, which contradicted the Liberty County sheriff's account of the stop, shows a group of white deputies rifling through luggage. One of them took a package and asked whose it was. When the player responded that it was hers and didn't know what was inside because it was a gift from family, the deputy met her with suspicion. Jenkins said the deputy found nothing more than a jewelry box inside.

"I'm sitting there, and I'm trying to stay calm, but at that moment, I'm so upset and scared and frustrated at what is happening to us," Jenkins said of the April 20 incident in a phone interview this week.

"Unfortunately," she said, "these situations can escalate." And then the worst can happen. So she led by example and kept her stress under wraps. Her athletes followed suit.

The deputies did not find drugs. The driver—who, no surprise, just so happened to be Black—did not receive a traffic citation. An officer came aboard and said the team could go.

Think about what they went through.

Think about all Black athletes crisscrossing America for competitions, from youth basketball and football teams to college players. Some travel alone. Some with teams. Some in small groups. If you think that fear of encounters like this is not part of the mix, think again.

I have my own stories. If you've read my columns for a while, you may know that I was once a serious tennis player, one of the few Black nationally ranked juniors in the 1980s—a starter on a top-ranked team at the University of California, Berkeley. After college, I played for a few years in the minor leagues of professional tennis, traveling to every corner of America and good parts of the globe.

I was profiled by the police after playing in one of those tournaments in the early 1990s, when another Black player and I had made the doubles final at an all-white country club in Birmingham, Ala. To say that we were an astonishing sight to the club members—and to the all-Black grounds crew that cheered us at every match—would be the mother of all understatements. We lost, but we were jubilant. We'd made a statement by going as far as we did.

But while driving our rental car to the next event, set to be held in Augusta, Ga., we were pulled over by a highway patrolman in the rural stretch between Birmingham and Atlanta. I remember his wide-brimmed hat and his invasive questioning. What were we doing in this car? Where were we going? The next thing I knew, he was looking through our bags.

Why were we pulled over and searched? My partner had been driving well within the flow of traffic. We were just two young Black guys in a shiny rental. It didn't help when the patrolman asked for our identification and saw we were from California.

It has been three decades, so I don't recall all the details about what took place next, but somehow, the deputy hauled my partner off to the local, small-town police station. About an hour later, my partner walked out. As I remember it, he didn't get so much as a ticket. He was unscathed but shaken. I drove the rest of the way.

That wasn't the only time I was profiled during my short time at the basement level of pro tennis. The worst instance came in Europe in 1992, when I traveled from Paris to London after playing in France. At London's Heathrow Airport, customs officials pulled me out of the line and began asking pointed questions.

They asked, sternly and accusingly, why I was in Europe playing tennis. Prove it, they said.

I stood helplessly beside them as they rifled through my tennis bags. They found clothing, rackets and my journal, which they read with a seemingly voyeuristic interest. Then they led me to a windowless room and left me there without saying when they would be back. I wasn't alone in that room. I was with about a dozen Black travelers from African countries.

I sat for one hour, then two, then three. After eight hours of confinement, a guard came in and let me go. He never apologized.

There is an unseen burden Black people carry long after such encounters. It's a shroud. You question yourself. "What just happened? Did I do something wrong?" You struggle to make sense of what just took place. "Was that officer, that shopping mall security guard, that customs agent, really just doing their job? Or was I treated this way because of my skin color?"

The uncertainty is its own terror.

We are left with doubt, rage and tears. We become well versed in stuffing emotions deep down and moving on. Or at least we try.

And now, through no fault of their own, the young Delaware State lacrosse players must deal with this kind of pain.

After the stop, Jenkins said, the trip home was unusually quiet and even somber. Shock does that.

The full force of the incident did not hit for days, until a player wrote a story about it in the campus newspaper and word of what happened began to spread.

"It was re-traumatizing all over again, reliving the whole thing," Jenkins said. "And that's when we realized, 'Whoa, this was really bad.'"

KURT STREETER writes the "Sports of The Times" column for *The New York Times.* He has a particular interest in the connection between sports and broader society, especially regarding issues of race, gender, and justice. In 2020, his work earned best column writing awards from the Associated Press Sports Editors and the Society of Professional Journalists, two of the highest honors in sports journalism. Before coming to *The Times* in 2017, he was a senior writer for ESPN. He was also a general assignment reporter at *The Baltimore Sun* and spent 15 years at the *Los Angeles Times*, where he wrote about everything from crime to education to religion and was a front-page feature writer. He was the first African American to serve as a captain on the U.C. Berkeley men's tennis team and helped lead the Golden Bears to a national indoor title in 1989.

After Surviving a High School Shooting, He Was 'An Empty Shell. No Emotion.' Now What?

MICHAEL ROSENBERG

FROM *Sports Illustrated* • DECEMBER 29, 2022

Keegan Gregory loved his first high school diving practice so much that choosing a swimsuit for the next one took on outsized importance, like picking an outfit for the first day of school. *This is what I'll wear. This is who I'll be.* He stuffed all three of his Speedos into his backpack, along with his laptop and school supplies and a winter coat he borrowed from his mom, and decided he would choose a swimsuit before practice later. Later never came.

Keegan had stopped in a bathroom to pee before biology class when he heard gunshots. He opened the bathroom door slightly, to see what was happening outside, and saw students running through the halls. He quickly closed the door and at 12:52 p.m. he texted his family:

HELP
GUM SHOTS
GUN
IM HIDING IN THE BATHROOM
OMG
HELP
MOM

Keegan had just turned 15. He was 5'4" and 105 pounds. A freshman. He thought he was alone in the bathroom, but when he turned he saw another boy.

Keegan did not know the boy's name but he recognized him. He was a senior named Justin Shilling. A few months earlier, Keegan had seen Justin at a freshman orientation called Link Day. He was sitting in front of Keegan with a fanny pack full of Smarties, throwing them out to other kids.

In the bathroom, Justin pointed for Keegan to go into the lone stall. He told Keegan to sit on the toilet, with his feet up on the seat, so nobody would see he was there. Justin tried to hide behind the partition. He told Keegan that as soon as they had a chance, they would run.

They heard another gunshot. This one was so loud, Keegan thought it must have come from the girls' bathroom, next door. It was actually in the hallway, and it left the school's biggest football star, 16-year-old Tate Myre, dying on the floor.

Keegan and Justin heard the bathroom door open.

At 12:55, Keegan texted his family again:

he's in the bathroom

Ethan Crumbley was once a boy in his mother's arms, and then he was a quiet, troubled kid who played video games online and walked to school alone in ratty shoes—another American son left to his own devices until one of those devices was a gun. Now, police would later say, he had assumed the only role he would play in the town of Oxford, Mich., forever: the shooter.

The shooter had allegedly already shot 10 people, including fatal blows to Tate, 14-year-old Hana St. Juliana and 17-year-old Madisyn Baldwin. He kicked open the stall door and stared at Keegan and Justin.

Keegan looked back at the shooter. They had gone to Lakeville Elementary and now Oxford High together, but Keegan did not know who he was. The shooter was skinny, and when he spoke he mumbled. All of his authority came from the SIG Sauer SP 2022 9-mm semiautomatic handgun he held near his schoolmates.

Keegan had never seen a real gun before. It would be months before he would stop seeing this one.

At 12:56, Keegan texted his parents:

i'm with one other person

he saw us

and we are just standing here

He thought about texting his parents that he loved them, but that felt too much like goodbye.

The shooter backed out of the stall.

Justin and Keegan were not sure what to do. Maybe the shooter had spared them and Keegan could pick up his backpack near the sink and go back to the diving team and the rest of his freshman year; and Justin could walk out with him, finish his final high school bowling season and go to his senior prom, graduate and head off to Oakland University to study business ...

Justin opened the camera app on his iPhone and held it near the floor, at an angle. He motioned for Keegan, who was still crouched on the toilet, to look at the phone and see whether the shooter was still in the bathroom. Keegan quietly told Justin he could not see the screen.

Justin leaned over and looked at his phone. He saw a pair of feet. The shooter walked back to the stall and motioned for Justin to come out. At 12:59, Keegan texted his family:

he killed him

OMFG

The shooter turned to Keegan, pointed to the wall and told him to lean up against it.

MEGHAN GREGORY MISSED the text messages from her oldest child because she was busy protecting her youngest one. The FDA had just approved COVID-19 vaccinations for kids under 12, which meant that her 8-year-old son, Sawyer, was eligible.

Meghan had seen the virus take an aunt of her husband, Chad; one of her distant cousins; and the parents of a few friends—and so she and Chad had been extremely cautious with their five children. Even after Oxford reopened its schools in August 2020, following the first wave of the pandemic, the Gregorys kept their kids home for remote learning all year. No one in the family had gotten the virus.

Now, as Meghan and Sawyer left the pharmacy at Target, fire alarms went off. Meghan would never know why. She looked at her phone, saw Keegan's texts, jumped in her car and raced toward Oxford High, like hundreds of other parents. Sawyer asked his mom why she was sobbing. He thought about the fire alarms and wondered: "Did Target burn down?" Meghan had no answer for that, or for anything else. She was so rattled that she missed her exit on the highway. She got off at the next one, turned around and saw a fleet of police cars speeding toward her son's high school.

CHAD GREGORY WAS in a meeting at his office in downtown Detroit when Keegan's texts came in. He responded to his son right away, repeating the only advice he could think to give:

Just stay down

We can't come to you but just stay down, quiet and calm

Stay down and don't move or engage. We love you

Chad, who works in event hospitality, told the two colleagues in his meeting that he had to go. He bolted for his car in the parking structure across the street ... 41 miles away from home. He and Meghan had chosen to raise their kids in Oxford, instead of the suburbs closer to Detroit, for serenity. They lived in a house on a lake. They went out on their pontoon to catch bass and pike, and they sat on the deck and watched meteor showers. They let their kids walk to two nearby parks without an adult—as long as they asked for permission first. Chad had turned down jobs in other cities so they could stay there.

Oxford, Meghan liked to say, was the safest place they could be.

AT HOME, SAWYER Gregory looked out a front window at a suddenly terrifying world. A neighbor had lain on the floor in the fetal position, bawling. Something had gone tragically wrong, and if the adults couldn't process it, what chance did an 8-year-old have? Chad arrived, glared at the neighbor, picked up Sawyer, put him on a bathroom counter and said: "Listen. Keegan's O.K. Everybody's just upset. We're safe. You're gonna be O.K."

Keegan had texted his family to let them know he had survived. But when he came home that afternoon, his parents looked into his eyes and still didn't see him. Meghan says her boy was "an empty shell." Chad says he was "stone. Absolute stone. There was no emotion."

They all walked downstairs to Keegan's bedroom, where he started crying. He told them about the other boy who had looked out for him and was then killed in front of him, and about how the shooter pointed for Keegan to lean up against the bathroom wall. Keegan had believed he faced two options: He could follow the shooter's instructions and get killed. Or he could run and get killed.

He had decided that if he ran, at least they would know he tried. He bolted past Justin, past the backpack with the Speedos in it, out the door and down the hall, past a teacher performing CPR on a kid—who turned out to be Tate Myre—running so fast and so frenetically that his arms flailed, his body an emergency helicopter desperately trying to take off. He ran and screamed and turned a corner and ran through the cafeteria, past the performing arts center and then to the school's front door.

That's where he first saw a police officer.

Keegan held his chest as he talked to the cop and pointed back down the hallway he had just left. The officer told him to go outside. Keegan paced back and forth and sat down on a curb by the snow.

Oxford's dean of students, Nicholas Ejak, came out and walked Keegan back into the building. The shooter had been apprehended, but Keegan did not know that. Many students were still in the school. Keegan was still holding his chest. He remembered that the assistant principal's office had a door that automatically locks when closed, so he went inside. Another administrator gave him a bottle of water. Police kept Keegan in the school for more than two hours before finally allowing him to go home.

That night, Oakland County Undersheriff Michael McCabe announced that "Police arrested the suspect five minutes after the first call," which he said came in at 12:51 p.m.

IF KEEGAN WAS sure of anything in those first uncertain days, it was that his community needed him.

Oxford vowed to do what American towns are supposed to do when a local teen kills his classmates. It would be #OxfordStrong. Keegan wanted to be strong, too. He got moving, moving, moving. He and his friends tied ribbons of blue and gold, their school colors, onto flag posts. They helped make T-shirts. Keegan slept at friends' houses, or they slept at his.

Two days after the shooting, a student at nearby Lake Orion High was arrested for threatening to shoot up his school if he got a gun. One day after that, Keegan, Meghan and Chad attended a vigil downtown where somebody collapsed. It was just a fainting episode, but the citizenry panicked, fearing another attack. The shooter's parents, it had been reported, were on the lam—had they come back and started shooting?

The people of Oxford sprinted in all directions. Meghan says she saw a friend lift a double stroller *with kids in it* over his head and start running. Keegan lost a shoe. Meghan ducked into a restaurant owned by friends, which set Keegan off: *How can you go inside?* He was worried about being trapped in a crowded room with another shooter, but he and Chad followed Meghan inside.

Keegan thought he heard a gunshot.

Pop.

Then another, and another …

Pop pop pop pop pop-pop-pop-pop-pop—

"Do you hear them?" Keegan asked his mom. "Do you hear the gunshots?"

Meghan looked at him and said, "There are no gunshots, bud."

TWENTY-TWO YEARS AFTER Columbine, nine years after Sandy Hook, three and a half years after Parkland and 175 days before Uvalde, the Oxford shooter pinned his town on America's map of shame.

Hana, Madisyn, Tate, Justin. What do you say to a family that loses a child, or to a town that loses four? "My heart goes out to the families enduring the unimaginable grief of losing a loved one," President Joe Biden said hours later from Minnesota, where he was touting a bipartisan infrastructure bill. Keegan's diving coach, John Pearson, says he received more than 500 cards from people in the diving community.

Hana, Madisyn, Tate, Justin. Their deaths dominated the national news, but by the crude, inhumane measurement of body count, the tragedy was not large enough to hold America's attention for very long. Gun violence is now the leading cause of death for children in the United States. A 2018 Pew research poll found that most teenagers worry about a shooting at their school. A generation of students has been conditioned to believe the unbelievable: that school shootings are the cost of doing business in America.

Hana, Madisyn, Tate, Justin. In death, as in life, most people were drawn to Tate. He was the school football star, the kid who managed to be popular while still being nice to everyone. One of Keegan's teammates, swimmer Kamari Kendrick, a sophomore at the time, told *The Washington Post* that Tate Myre was his "idol" and said "everybody knew him and everybody loved him."

Days after the shooting, an Oxford football and wrestling coach, Ross Wingert, told the *Detroit Free Press* that Myre had tried to stop the massacre: "I was told that everybody in that school was running one way, and Tate was running the other way." At the Big Ten championship game, four days after the shooting, Michigan's football players wore patches with four stars, for the victims, plus the number 42, for Tate. A Change.org petition to rename Oxford High's football stadium after Tate Myre said he had been "killed in an attempt to disarm the shooter" and that "his act of bravery should be remembered forever." More than 300,000 people signed the petition.

Hana, Madisyn, Tate, Justin ... and nearly Keegan, too. But he had survived, and so he did what Oxford survivors did. He went to their funerals. At Hana's, he looked around and wondered: *If something were to happen here, how do I get away?* At Justin's, he saw the casket from a distance, exclaimed, "It's open!" and sprinted away. Keegan eventually made it through the funeral, and at the end he asked his parents whether he could go up to Justin's casket by himself.

"I just want to talk to him one more time," he said.

That day Keegan signed the guestbook with a teen's penmanship, a freshman's grammar and all the appreciation in his heart: *Thank you Justin. If it weren't for you, I wouldn't be standing right now. I can't thank you enough. I pray and pray your doing good up there + I'm sorry.*

Keegan walked out of that funeral to a life he had no chance of resuming. Forget dreams; the Gregorys couldn't even make plans. For Christmas break, Meghan and Chad decided to drive the kids to Nashville, go to a Titans game, then surprise them with a trip to Saint Martin. But Keegan heard fireworks at the Titans game and panicked; and he saw cops in the stadium with guns in their holsters and worried somebody would steal one. The family left shortly after the opening kickoff.

In their Nashville hotel Keegan saw a man bleeding and had flashbacks to the school bathroom. He had a nightmare in which the shooter came into their room and killed his siblings, and Keegan was just standing there, unable to save them. He told his parents he did not want to fly to Saint Martin, because if something happened on the plane, he had no way out.

The Gregorys canceled their trip and went skiing in Northern Michigan instead. Keegan tried a jump, a ski fell off and he cut his right leg down to the bone. In the hospital, he gestured toward the front desk and asked his mom, "Did you see that? He looked just like Justin."

Meghan looked. There was nobody there.

Justin was gone. In a way, so was Keegan. He told his dad he saw the SIG Sauer SP everywhere. At night, while the rest of the family slept, Keegan lay awake in bed, covered in fear. Every creak of the floor could be an intruder, every hour could bring death. As the oldest child, Keegan had the coolest room, on the lower level, with sliding doors that opened out toward the lake. One night, he had a nightmare where somebody pulled up on a boat and started shooting bullets through his windows. He tried to soothe himself with music, but when he put on headphones he thought: *Well, now I can't hear if something happens.* He took the headphones off and stayed in bed, alone, until morning rescued him from the night.

When he got out of bed, Keegan was too exhausted to do anything but sit on the couch. He still wanted to sleep, but he couldn't. He needed to keep his brain active, but he wasn't sure how. He started cuddling on the couch with his mother, watching movies and shows he'd enjoyed as a little boy, like *The Lorax* and *Yogi Bear*. At one point he went to the bathroom, and while he was away fireworks went off on the TV. Keegan darted out, terrified, even though he said he knew it was just a show.

"I don't know what's wrong with me," he told his dad.

What was wrong was that he'd witnessed a murder on his way to biology class, and now his amygdala—the part of the brain that processes fear and trauma—was swelling. If something burned on the stove, Keegan freaked. Any sudden sound triggered him, and a house with two parents and five kids and a dog is an arena full of sudden sounds.

The Gregorys were living on tiptoe. They adopted a second dog to keep Keegan company at night. Meghan, who usually does the grocery shopping for the family, simply stopped doing it. Chad took over and wondered whether Meghan even noticed that food kept appearing in their kitchen. It didn't matter to Keegan. He had no appetite. He was living on a bowl of cereal a day. In the middle of it all, Chad's boss called. "I know it's a rough time," he said, but he had some good news: Chad was being promoted. Chad thought back to a world where that was a big deal. The whole family was trying to cope with Keegan's trauma, and nobody was quite sure how to do it.

Keegan tried going to church, but his thoughts kept interrupting his prayers. Where were the exits? How would he flee from an attack? One night when Meghan came home, Keegan heard the front door open, so he ran out the sliding door of his lake-facing room and from outside called his parents on his phone: "I escaped out of the house! Someone's in there! I'm in the neighbor's yard!"

With no prompting or immediate context, Keegan would tell his parents the percentage of *it* happening in a grocery store or on a plane. He didn't have to say what *it* was. He spent his nights researching shootings. He was statistically unlikely to be trapped in a bathroom at school with a shooter, but it had happened. Therefore, in his mind, anything that was statistically unlikely would probably happen. The kid who used to bounce giddily from one friend's house to another's had nowhere to go, because wherever he went he was doomed.

PROSECUTORS, POLICE AND local news outlets started to release details about the shooting, and most of it made other people look awful.

Police said the shooter's parents had bought him the gun on Black Friday. Prosecutors implied that the school was culpable: A teacher, they said, had spotted the shooter searching online for ammunition, then called his parents. Afterward, the shooter's mom texted him: *LOL I'm not mad at you. You have to learn not to get caught.* Ejak, the dean, and school counselor

Shawn Hopkins had met with the shooter the morning of the
attacks, after a teacher found a picture he'd drawn of a person
who appeared to have been shot, along with the words, "The
thoughts won't stop. Help me." Ejak and Hopkins had advised
the shooter's parents to seek psychiatric help—but they had not
checked his backpack. If they had checked, prosecutors would
say in court, they would have found the SIG Sauer SP, along with
a hardbound black journal with the shooter's name written on
top of it and a vow inside:

I will cause the biggest school shooting in Michigan's history
I will kill everyone I f---ing see

Days after the shooting, the district declined an offer from
Michigan attorney general Dana Nessel to investigate, choosing
to hire an outside law firm instead. A lot of strong people in a
strong town in the strongest country in the world were getting
suspicious.

The Gregorys say they kept contacting the school district to
figure out a plan for Keegan to resume his education. Chad says
that when he called, "the answer was always, 'Just let us know
what you need.' We're saying, 'We don't *know* what the options
are.' I don't think they knew, either." He says that when Meghan
emailed administrators, "we were ghosted—not even responses.
… We're getting no email that says, 'Here's the counselor. Here
are options for a revised curriculum.'"

Oxford High reopened for business on Jan. 24—almost
eight weeks after the shooting. The day before, Principal Steven
Wolf posted a three-minute-and-41-second-long video telling
"Wildcat Nation" that "we have been through so much to get
to this moment" and that "we are reclaiming our high school.
We have been reminded again and again," Wolf said, "of one
important fact: Our community is strong." The first day back
would be "a great day to be a Wildcat, and that's because we're
#OxfordStrong."

Four words Wolf did *not* utter: Hana, Madisyn, Tate, Justin.
The school closed off the bathroom where Justin was killed. A

temporary memorial for the victims was taken down before school started; the surviving children were told that this was so they could heal. Three days after school reopened, the families of Tate, Justin and Keegan, plus two more students, sued the shooter's parents and the school district, arguing that administrators had ample reason to know the shooter was a threat and had failed to act.

CHAD SENSED A change in town. The victims' families were asking questions: *What did the district know? Why wasn't there a transparent, independent review of the school's protocols?* Some other parents did not want answers—their kids were back in school, and they didn't want to relive the day of the shooting. Others spread ridiculous stories. Parents told Meghan and Chad that they'd heard there were actually *three* kids in the bathroom when the shooter walked in. Or that Keegan was in there, Justin came in, and the shooter asked who wanted to die first. "Everyone," Chad says, "had their own version of their own truth."

After the victims' families sued the school district, Wolf finally responded to the Gregorys' emails. "I'm sorry I'm just replying this evening," he wrote on Jan. 30. "I've spent most of today just going through emails trying to get caught up. Your request is important." The principal offered Keegan the option of in-person, Zoom or online classes.

Keegan started to take the online classes, but even those were more than he could handle. He stopped after less than a month. He was wading through the shrapnel of his old existence, searching for his new one.

Jokes that were funny to him before were not funny anymore. Before the shooting, he loved anime—but now it was too gory. Art, in general, felt too free-flowing. Keegan needed control. He stopped fishing, which depends too much on the whims of the fish, and started playing ukulele. *If I play these chords in this order, this song comes out.*

His mind was a book that alternated between narrators: one first-person, one omniscient. The omniscient narrator understood that he was a 15-year-old kid who had seen what no child should ever see, and that it had traumatized him. The first-person narrator was irrational and short-tempered.

Meghan and Chad would lay out a schedule for the next day, and pragmatic Keegan would agree to it. Then morning would come and he'd snap: "I never said I would do that!" He raged at any surprise, no matter how trivial. "You told me you were buying Minute brown rice!" he screamed when the wrong brand showed up in the kitchen. He was learning to drive, but he'd lost his ability to stay calm and concentrate. He would pull into traffic without looking; his parents would say, "*Keegan!*"; and he would yell, "I didn't see them!"

The rest of the family watched Keegan try to hold off his anger, to react like the boy he used to be. Then he would lose the battle with his new self and explode.

The Gregorys had fended off COVID-19, but Keegan's trauma spread through the family like a contagious disease. Sawyer told his mom, "I'm never going to Target again." Bentley, then in fourth grade, who always wanted to be Keegan, defended his brother's explosions: "Remember, his brain isn't working right." Piper, an eighth-grader, made herself busy so she wouldn't have to deal with it all. Peyton, a seventh-grader and the middle child, called her house from school in the middle of the day, worried about her big brother: "Is Keegan up? Is he O.K.?" Sometimes she asked to stay home. She would miss 27 days of school and her grades plummeted—a crisis dwarfed by a much larger one.

Meghan, who was coaching gymnastics six or seven days a week, took what she thought was a temporary break, but eventually she closed her gym. She started making her kids wear tennis shoes everywhere, so that if anything happened they could run. She heard other parents talk about how brave their kids were for going back to school, and she wondered: Do they mean that Keegan is somehow less brave because he stayed home?

Meghan and Chad tried to make sense of the new Keegan. Crowds scared him. School scared him. Would diving scare him? Diving practice was after school, with fewer kids. His team sometimes practiced at another campus, nearby Lake Orion High, because Pearson, the coach, led both teams, and so Keegan decided to attend a workout at Lake Orion. Pearson could tell Keegan was nervous. Pearson usually stands while he coaches, but he sat on a bulkhead and had Keegan sit in a chair next to him, a small but welcome act of tenderness.

Pools can be loud—boards bouncing, words echoing off walls—but diving itself gave Keegan the control he craved. If he had played a free-flowing sport like hockey or basketball, he would not have gone back. But dives are scripted and independent: *stand, jump, flip, enter the water, swim to the edge of the pool.*

Keegan's first meet was on a snowy day in Berkley, a Detroit suburb. Beforehand, he sat on the bus with his headphones on, staring at the Waze app on his phone. The ride strayed from the route, and Keegan called his mom in a panic: "The bus is going the wrong way!" The driver had just taken a wrong turn, but that was the last time Keegan took the bus.

He started to find that he could enjoy diving meets as long as he sat on the side by himself, wearing noise-canceling headphones, when it got too loud. Then diving started to give him bits of what he needed: "You're all hyping each other up, even though we're against each other," he says. "I love the community." The sport even got him to walk back into Oxford High for a few practices. He entered through an emergency-exit door right behind the diving boards, never seeing the rest of the school.

Keegan made it all the way to Michigan's state championships, where he finished 23rd in the boys' one-meter, quite an achievement for any freshman, let alone a severely traumatized one who was barely sleeping.

Watch him on that board, and you might think Keegan Gregory was himself again. His coach knew better. On inward dives—when athletes start by facing away from the pool—Keegan used to jump up and spin within two feet of the board, as he was supposed to do. After the shooting, he jumped five or six feet away from the board, his mind pushing his body toward safety.

IN MARCH, KEEGAN went back to school during the day—for one class, with only a few students in it. He says it was O.K., because "I knew every single person since, like, kindergarten." He got there late, left early, survived it all and decided he wouldn't be doing that again.

IN APRIL, A terrorist threat was made against three nearby high schools—including Lake Orion, where Keegan practiced diving. A teenager in the United Kingdom was arrested for what was apparently a sick joke. Keegan became even more steadfast: He was never going back to school.

IN MAY, THE office of Oakland County Sheriff Michael Bouchard awarded valor citations to two deputies for responding to the Oxford High shooting "without hesitation," for entering the high school "without waiting for additional backup" and for apprehending the suspect "within seconds."

"Your actions, while risking your own safety," Bouchard said, "were why the senseless shooting stopped. Had it not been for the two of you, the shooter probably would have exhausted his last 18 rounds. The students, faculty, their families and the community are forever indebted to you both."

THE SHERIFF WAS telling the world his officers were heroes. Parents were suing the school district. The district was shielding itself with lawyers. The shooter had pleaded not guilty to four counts of murder. Prosecutors charged the shooter's parents, James and Jennifer Crumbley, with involuntary manslaughter; they also pleaded not guilty. Hana's sister, Reina, was pushing the school to erect a permanent memorial to the victims (without success). Keegan was seeing two therapists.

One therapist was conventional; the other specialized in eye movement desensitization and reprocessing, a method that helps patients process trauma. The EMDR therapist told Keegan's parents that he was starting to disassociate from reality—disconnecting from his own thoughts and memories. (He knows it, too. For this story, Keegan said that if his parents remembered something and he didn't, it's fair to say that it happened.) Part of that EMDR therapy meant closing his eyes and reliving the day of the shooting, until he hit what his therapist calls a "point of disturbance" and what Keegan describes as "all of a sudden, in my stomach, an anxiety feeling … *boom*." He closed his eyes and saw the shooter kick open the stall door, saw blood all over the bathroom, saw Justin's face as he lay dying at age 17…

"I hate therapy!" he told his parents.

They asked whether he wanted to quit.

"No," he said. "I know it's going to make me better."

Keegan knew he needed therapy to have any chance of getting from here to there—of forming a social life when he was scared of crowds; of going to college if he never went back to high school; of being the big brother that his siblings missed. But it all seemed so far off. He was downing Tums like they were popcorn, 20 to 30 tablets a day, just to survive 24 hours in Oxford.

He told his parents he wanted to start working out. They took him to Planet Fitness, but he dismissed it as "a soccer mom gym." Keegan wanted to add *real* strength. He started going to Building Your Temple Fitness, in town, where serious weightlifters went.

In June, Keegan went to visit his mom's family in Ohio, and he felt freer than he had since he fled the bathroom. Then he came back home, and anxiety choked him again.

"I hate Oxford!" he told his parents.

He used to feel so free in his town. Now he felt trapped in it. His parents were getting increasingly frustrated with what they felt was obfuscation from the district and with the portion of the community that they thought was lying to itself.

County prosecutors, along with the lawyer for the victims' families, produced what they say were a slew of warnings that the shooter would become the shooter. On a math worksheet he drew pictures of people being gunned down and wrote, "My life is useless," "Blood everywhere" and "The thoughts won't stop, help me." He had gone to school with a baby bird's head kept in a jar. But some people rushed to defend the district. (Attorney Timothy Mullins, who represents the district, did not respond to repeated interview requests for this story.)

The Gregorys felt their truth was being dismissed—and their son marginalized—because people didn't want to know what had really happened. By Michigan law, Keegan wasn't even technically a victim.

At a meeting with Michigan's attorney general, Meghan asked why the proper timeline hadn't been released. She had the text messages. She knew there was no way the cops came in and arrested the shooter within five minutes, because Keegan was still trapped in the bathroom with him after that. Another parent told her she had it all wrong—they had personally checked with the sheriff and confirmed that the sheriff's timeline was correct.

Meghan started asking Chad, *Can we move?*

"But I don't mean *move to another state*," she says. "I mean *move to another country*. It's not like you can move to Colorado and you're not going to have [this] happen."

Chad says he remembers watching news coverage of the Columbine High shooting, in the spring of 1999, and how it was all about the police—"whatever they did or did not do to save lives"—and the victims, and the shooters. He says: "Personally, I don't f---ing want to know about the shooters, right? How does this get stopped? Where's the bold sort of overarching authority that comes in and says, 'This is not acceptable?'"

School shootings are clearly not acceptable, yet they are just as clearly accepted. CNN found that in one stretch covering 2009 to '18, there were 288 school shootings in the U.S. In that same time, Canada, France, Germany, Italy and the U.K. combined for *five.* So much has changed about American life since then, but not that. According to the U.S. Naval Postgraduate School for Homeland Defense and Security, 110 children have been shot to death on school grounds in the last two academic years. Another 287 were wounded, and 39 suffered minor injuries.

Those are facts. So is this: America has more guns than adults—by far the highest rate of civilian gun ownership in the world. Connect those two facts, and you are accused of playing politics, of having an agenda, of being anti-American, even when you are trying to protect children, even when the child is your own son.

The sadness in Oxford runs so deep and so wide that a lot of people prefer to look away. Chad understands. He is embarrassed to admit this, but it's true: By the time Sandy Hook happened, in 2012, he had already stopped watching news about school shootings. It wasn't that he didn't care. He cared so much that caring overwhelmed him, and so he took steps to care less. He had been desensitized by choice.

Meghan watched for days. Even after a shooting took four of her town's children and wrecked the life of her own, Meghan searched inside herself, looking for empathy for the shooter and his parents. She has none anymore. She copes by accumulating facts about the case, and Chad worries she is stifling her emotions.

Chad walls off, and Meghan worries he is being avoidant. He still can't look at Keegan's text messages from the bathroom. But they need to give each other the space to cope in their own ways or their marriage will crack. They get up every day determined to be supportive spouses, good parents and thoughtful citizens of an angry nation.

THE DIVER SOUGHT control, and not just over a sport. Keegan started waking up early, working out five or six days a week and monitoring everything he put in his body. He cooked lean, protein-rich meals for himself and drank protein water. In the Gregorys' kitchen this summer, Meghan casually mentioned that when Chad travels for work she stays up late and sleeps late. Keegan sternly told her to take melatonin at 10 p.m. and put her phone away. Then he made himself a meal of ground turkey and rice. He will never get to be a typical teenager, so he has stopped trying.

"Most people my age will stay up till 3, sleep until 1 and do nothing," he says. "But I feel good about myself when I get up, I go to the gym, I eat good foods."

Keegan has the speech patterns of somebody who was thrown from childhood into adulthood in less than an hour, dropping "whereas" and "body dysmorphia" into conversation but describing the diving community as "the funnest thing ever." This summer, he still couldn't fathom going back to school, but he had started making other plans. He intends to compete in a powerlifting competition in Ohio in November, part of a five-year plan to become a bodybuilder. He says he likes the discipline and purpose it gives him.

His parents see something else: Nobody else would protect Keegan, so he started adding layers of armor to protect himself.

The Oxford school district maintains that it did all it could reasonably be expected to do. The shooter's parents say the media and prosecutors have unfairly held them responsible for the shootings. The sheriff's office says the shooter was arrested within five minutes of the first call for help, but the time stamps on Keegan's text messages say otherwise.

Thousands of people were understandably touched by the story of a beloved high school football star dying while trying to stop a shooter. There is no doubt that Tate Myre was beloved. But there is no indication he was trying to stop the shooter. The Myres' lawyer, Ven Johnson, acknowledges that Tate was shot from behind, from a considerable distance. What kind of society needs a dead teenager to be a superhero? Does that mean the kids who fled were selfish for trying to save their own lives? Why isn't being a great kid enough?

As for the sheriff who commended his officers for stopping the shooter before he exhausted his last 18 rounds: The truth is that after Keegan ran out of the bathroom, the shooter walked out on his own and did not fire another shot. He got on his knees and surrendered, and *then* police found and arrested him. It's all on the security footage. Meghan and Chad have watched it.

The stories we tell ourselves rarely include the shooter stopping on his own. But that is what happened in Oxford. "He was done," Chad says. Why? Maybe Keegan's sprint surprised the shooter and jolted him out of his murderous trance. Maybe he was already coming out of it when he entered the restroom, and that's why he took several minutes to execute Justin. Maybe we will never really know. Maybe you don't want to hear any more about the shooter.

But maybe you do care that in July, when Meghan, Chad and the victims' families' lawyer watched the video footage from the day of the shootings, they saw what appeared to be a security officer open the bathroom door while Justin, Keegan and the shooter were inside. The officer then closed the door and walked away. When the lawyer went public with it, the school board's response was not outrage or remorse; it was self-defense.

School board president Tom Donnelly, a pastor at Firmly Rooted Ministries, responded immediately in an email to the community, writing that "isolating a single moment in a video—out of context—does a disservice to our staff members. ... These attempts to sway public opinion with speculation before the investigations are complete are counterproductive and designed to divide us."

At an Oxford school board meeting two days later, Meghan spoke.

"I am here trying to understand tonight how we got to this point," she said. "We have always trusted Oxford schools with our children. ... I'm trying to understand, as patient and quiet as we have been, why you have chosen to turn this personal. How unprofessional to try to place blame on us for the community divide."

She got a standing ovation.

Oxford was broken.

"People can't listen to each other right now," says Pearson, the diving coach, who skipped the school board meeting because he loves the Gregorys but is sympathetic to the school board. "They can't talk to each other because of the emotion. It's torn the community apart."

The Gregory family walks on both sides of that divide. Their lawyer is slamming the school district, but four of their kids keep going to district schools. They shop among those who don't understand them, and they commiserate with friends who do. They have decided to stay in Oxford for now, because at least in Oxford the shooting does not have to be explained. In packs people argue, but one on one they get it.

Then there is Keegan. In August, he sat on his back deck wearing an OXFORD SWIM AND DIVE T-shirt and a camouflage Detroit Tigers hat, with the sun and lake behind him and a bottle of protein water in front of him. He plans to dive again this winter, but he has built his life more around the gym and health food, isolating himself as a survival mechanism. He wants to hang with people, but not in crowds. He doesn't want to go back to school, but he wants *to want* to go.

"I could go in for one class," he said. "And I think I'm gonna start doing that and see how I feel. Because, to be honest, I have no idea how I'm gonna feel when I'm actually in the school. Because I could think that I'm gonna be fine—and then it's horrible. Or I could think that it would be kind of bad—and then I'm fine."

YELLOW SCHOOL BUSES line up on Oxford Road. The sun has yawned itself awake. Another school year has begun. Kids stand outside Oxford High on August 25, carrying the clear plastic backpacks they were given after the shooting, waiting to go through their school's newly installed metal detectors—seniors and freshmen, athletes and artists, best friends and future romantic partners ... and standing in line with them: a sophomore named Keegan Gregory.

He has decided the best way he can beat anxiety is to stare it in the eye until it blinks. His schedule is stacked with morning classes. He says he will "knock out those" and then go home before lunch. His parents were skeptical right up until this morning, when Keegan got up early, listened to music, took an anti-anxiety medication called buspirone and found the courage to walk into the building where the shooter wrecked his life.

"He was like a ghost—I'd never heard of him, I'd never seen him, not even in the halls," Keegan says of the shooter at one point. "I'd never seen that face. So there's also that side thought: How do we know there's not *someone else* I don't know about in school who could be a bit crazy?"

He convinces himself that the metal detectors, the clear backpacks and the ID checks will protect him, and he points out that "the majority of the time, I'll be in a classroom, which will be good. Nobody in a classroom really got injured." Since the day of the shooting, he has grown from 105 pounds to 138, and most of that new weight is muscle. He is #OxfordStrong.

He also has a new tattoo on his right forearm. His mom and dad got the same one: the date of the shooting, in Roman numerals, with four hearts at the bottom. The first three hearts are for Hana, Madisyn and Tate. The fourth, for Justin, has a halo over it.

Keegan walks into school. He does not know that his mom is sitting in the parking lot, in her Kia Carnival, with the engine running, in case he texts and says he wants to go home.

The front door of the Kia opens and Jill Soave, Justin Shilling's mother, climbs inside. She and Meghan did not know each other before the shooting, but now they're close friends. They went back into Oxford High in January, before it reopened, and prayed together. In May, the Shilling family joined the Gregorys and the

Myres in suing the district. Jill does not resent Meghan because her child got out, and Meghan does not feel guilty for it.

Jill places a white to-go cup of Bigelow chamomile tea above the dashboard. She is wearing a pink shirt to honor Justin, and she is thinking about her youngest son, 14-year-old Clay, who is, like Keegan, a sophomore at Oxford. The last time Clay saw Justin alive was in school that morning; their paths crossed in the same place at the same time every day. When Clay went back to school last spring, he skipped a class so he wouldn't have to go to that same spot. On many days since, he has gone into school, called his mom and said, "O.K., panic attack," and she has picked him up and taken him home.

Clay "feels a sense of pride to not run from it," Jill says. "But that doesn't always last."

The sun continues to rise. Other kids' parents keep texting Meghan: *We hear Keegan's at school!* There are signs that Meghan's life is getting easier. Jill's is getting harder. People want to move on, and she never will. She says that at a recent open forum for parents at Seymour Lake Park, one woman complained, "I don't think it's fair that the victims get to see the video [of the shooting] before us." Jill says, "Desperate, needy people are drawn to these things." Another parent said that she needed to know, for her own mental health, that the school did not intend to do anything wrong. Jill thought: *If I can keep my composure and my kid is dead, and you can't keep your composure* ... But where would arguing lead her? To bitterness? Anger? Who wins then?

"You become what you're opposing," Jill says.

Together, the mothers try not to let casual indignities rob them of their grace. They don't have the time or energy for every fight. Jill says, "Certain days, I can't leave the house. It's hard to think and function."

Jill looks out at the school where her son was killed, in the district she is suing, and she says, "If I had it in me, I'd volunteer in the lunchroom."

Jill and Meghan keep looking through the windshield at their town. A Coca-Cola truck is parked next to the football stadium. Jill points to the apartment building across the street from the high school. In April, a single father and Army veteran named Dennis Kendrick was shot to death there by a man he had never met, in what police say was a case of mistaken identity. Just a few months after telling *The Washington Post* that Tate Myre was his idol, Kamari Kendrick had lost his dad, too. Jill says, "My heart just broke." She donated $500 to the GoFundMe campaign for Kamari.

"Every time something happens, it's always the same thing on the news: 'This is just pure evil,'" Jill says. "It's like a movie with the same script. I just don't understand why so many people have so many guns."

At 9:04 a.m., Keegan texts his mom:

I might try and do lunch

Meghan is stunned. Jill is so happy for her. Keegan ends up staying and eating lunch in a courtyard outside with his friends. When he goes home, he asks his mom to text his EMDR therapist, to let her know that he made it through the day and that he is grateful for her. Then he takes a long nap.

Keegan will go back to school the next day, and the next week, and he will go to Oxford football games with his friends, and he will keep going back to school until one early September day when he sees a fellow student in a trench coat and panics. He asks his mom to get him out of school safely. On Sept. 11, before he is ready to go back, Oxford High emails the community to say there has been a vague threat from an unknown person on Snapchat. The school remains open, but Keegan stays home. That week, two members of the Oxford school board resign, including Donnelly, the board chair. The following week, Keegan starts going back to school again.

LAST YEAR, ON Nov. 30, Keegan Gregory went home from school and told his parents the story of the bathroom, the shooter and the other boy.

Justin was in the hospital, being kept on life support so that doctors could harvest his organs. But Meghan and Chad didn't know that. All they heard was that the other boy's name was Justin Shilling, and he was in the hospital, alive. They told Keegan.

Keegan did not believe them. They had not seen what he had seen. He knew.

But he wanted to believe.

He thought about Justin, the last person he met in his last moments as a child—how Justin told him to crouch on the toilet, so nobody could see him, and how Justin said that when they had a chance, they would run.

Keegan asked his parents a single, desperate question.

"Does he know I'm alive? He wanted me to *live*."

Keegan is trying, Justin. He is trying so hard.

MICHAEL ROSENBERG is a senior writer at *Sports Illustrated* and the author of the critically acclaimed *War As They Knew It: Woody Hayes, Bo Schembechler, and America in a Time of Unrest*. He lives in Michigan with his wife, Erin, and their children: Audrey, Max, and Eli.

The Secret MVP of Sports?
The Port-A-Potty

RYAN HOCKENSMITH

FROM ESPN • JANUARY 5, 2022

It's 12:31 p.m., and Ben Cansdale has been staring at five port-a-potties for a half hour. Cansdale is a member of a five-truck Modern Disposal Services crew, based in Buffalo, that is dispatched on game days to do what they call a "half-suck" when a home game kicks off.

From the driver's seat, Cansdale, 31, describes the mayhem that is about to happen once the Nov. 21 Bills-Colts game begins in 30 minutes. As he talks, drunk people wobble past, pointing and waving at him. One woman stands in front of the truck and tries to get Cansdale's attention so she can take a picture of him.

She laughs and points like he's a carnival exhibit, but Cansdale shrugs it off. "People treat us like a joke sometimes," he says. "But I take great pride in doing my job. I don't think these people want to see what happens if we're not here, cleaning up after them."

Cansdale's job isn't glorious, but sports couldn't happen without people like him. From college football cathedrals on Saturdays to raucous NFL stadiums on Sundays, with thousands of kids' soccer fields in between, the port-a-potty is an unsung hero for most outdoor sporting events in the U.S. If you trace the rise of big-time sports in America and the boom of the port-a-potty business over the past 50 years, it's like the two things are dancing together. The portable bathroom business is at $17 billion and rapidly growing, largely because of the constant need at sporting events. And that makes toilet cleaners like Cansdale essential workers at our nation's sports fields.

He doesn't have time to let his pride take a hit, anyway. A half-suck is the Olympics for the Modern crew—the six men, riding in five trucks, have about 90 minutes to take care of 196 port-a-potties spread over the public parking lots outside Highmark Stadium.

For each port-a-potty, Cansdale must replace two rolls of toilet paper from a latched holder, suck out as much as possible from inside the bowl and clean the seat with water and a scrub brush. He gives a quick hand sanitizer check but has never had to refill one at a Bills game. "The truth is, nobody's washing their hands," Cansdale says. "They just want to get in and get out."

The Modern drivers call it a "half-suck" because the goal is speed and just to get the stalls usable for after the game. They'll do full sucks and total cleans starting Monday morning.

The half-suck math is daunting: At about 40 toilets per guy, with people streaming in and out of the port-a-potties as they try to do their jobs, the cleaners will have less than three minutes per toilet, all while trying to navigate giant trucks through tiny windows of crowded parking lots. On top of that, the weather report says some wicked Buffalo wind and rain is about to roll in right around kickoff today, with temperatures expected to drop down into the 30s.

About 10 minutes before kickoff, Cansdale opens the truck door, and there's a light in his eyes. "It's go time," he says. "Buckle in, this is going to be a wild, smelly ride."

THE FIRST PORTABLE bathroom is believed to have been invented by the ancient Egyptians around the 14th century B.C. It was discovered in the Kha tomb and was simply a wooden stool with a hole in it and a piece of pottery underneath for collection.

The concept of mobile restrooms evolved slowly over the years, with centuries of civilizations essentially just doing small tweaks on the chamber pot. The need for portable bathrooms rose in the late 1800s as more and more American jobs drifted into large-scale mining and building projects. An abandoned copper mine in northern Michigan from the turn of the 20th century was recently discovered in remarkably preserved condition, including a wooden box that had been used by miners as their underground bathroom. For miners and construction workers who desperately needed bathrooms while on the job all day, finding a tree or a wooden box often was the best they could do 100 years ago.

That changed around 1940, when the first formal port-a-potties were developed for World War II ships docked off the California coast. The new ships didn't yet have bathrooms, so supervisors grew frustrated at the productivity loss from workers leaving to find facilities on shore. They built temporary early port-a-potties, made with a wooden outer shell and a large metal storage tank underneath a wooden toilet seat.

The concept of port-a-potties spread quickly to construction sites in the coming years, then to fairs, festivals and sporting events. It's impossible to overstate how seismic the addition of portable bathrooms has been to society, especially sports. "Large public gatherings for sports, especially football, have become an integral part of our society only over the past 75 years or so," says Dr. Laura Walikainen Rouleau, a social sciences senior lecturer at Michigan Tech and author of an upcoming book, "Private Spaces in Public Places." "You couldn't do that without an evolution of the bathroom that included portable facilities."

But in interviews with bathroom experts—yes, there are brilliant minds devoted to the topic—and even port-a-potty companies themselves, it's remarkable how little of portable bathroom history has been recorded. "That's a reflection of how people view and treat port-a-potties as a whole," says Alison K. Hoagland, author of "The Bathroom: A Social History of Cleanliness and

The Body." "They're a last-ditch, worst-case-scenario moment for most of us. So it's a field that has barely been studied."

This much we know: By the 1950s and 1960s, most large events had begun to hire companies to bring in temporary bathrooms for outside stadiums. Tailgating had become a new American tradition, with attendance at college football games alone surging from 18.9 million in 1950 to almost 30 million in 1970, and a need for portable bathrooms was inevitable. "In all our research, there are two main things that people always have cared about when they tailgate," says UC Irvine professor Tonya Williams Bradford, who has studied and written extensively about tailgating in the U.S. "One is that they want a spot where their friends will know how to find them. The other thing they talk about is port-a-potties—they want them close, but not too close. They just want to be able to make a beeline for them if they need to."

But back then, organizers usually didn't devote much attention or money, so long lines and disastrous facilities were the norm. Many events appear to have aimed toward one portable toilet for every 500 or so attendees. (Nowadays, port-a-potty companies recommend about one stall for every 50 people at an event. And if alcohol is being served, that number drops to 1 for every 40 attendees.)

Legendary San Francisco-area sports writer Art Spander, who recently retired at age 82, has attended more than 40 Super Bowls and 50 Masters, and at least 30 Wimbledons, US Opens and men's Final Fours. He's especially well known for attending 68 straight Rose Bowl games, home to one of the largest collections of portable bathrooms in the world—around 1,100 for the Parade of Roses, with 1,700 at the game itself. So he's seen the critical rise of the sports port-a-potty. Talking with me about them recently, he says, he's come to a realization: "You know, thank god for port-a-potties," he says. "I don't know how sports could have kept growing in this country the way they have if we didn't have those things."

He tracks a big jump in the number of sufficient port-a-potty facilities to the mid-1970s. "Decades ago, there were never enough," Spander says. "People would just have to go behind their cars or try to hold it until they got in the stadium. You used to see people just go off to the side of the road on the way into games. It was pretty disgusting."

There's a very good chance that that is a direct result of sports organizers watching the biggest port-a-potty disaster in human history: 1969's Woodstock. That's when 500,000 people showed up at a farm in upstate New York and had to use 600 toilets—an absurd 1 bathroom for every 833 people. In his Oscar-winning documentary, "Woodstock," one of filmmaker Michael Wadleigh's most memorable sequences is when he captured a jovial man named Thomas Taggart of the Port-o-San company cleaning out a row of portable toilets. His happy disposition, contrasted with the epic chaos and grossness of a half million people in the mud and sewage of Woodstock, became an enduring image.

One striking thing about the Woodstock footage is how little port-a-potty technology has progressed. Taggart, at a music concert in 1969, and Ben Cansdale, at a Bills home game in 2021, walk into nearly identical plastic shells, with toilet paper latched into holders on the side. Taggart uses a long hose and tank to suck out a shallow porcelain bowl, which closely mirrors Cansdale's process. The only notable difference is the bowls of 2021—they're made of plastic, much wider and can hold about 10 gallons.

"The formula seems to work, and at the toilet conferences I've been to, I don't see port-a-potty innovations coming in the future, either," says University of Illinois architecture professor Kathryn Anthony, a bathroom expert who has testified in Congress about the need for equality in American restrooms. "You just need the basics, so you can get in and get out."

BEN CANSDALE GRABS his gloves. The Modern crew is supposed to wait until the Bills-Colts game kicks off, but every second counts when it comes to cleaning 196 portable bathrooms in 90 minutes.

Cansdale gloves up, then walks around to the compartment outside the truck that holds a few dozen rolls of toilet paper. He uses the same assembly line system as many of his teammates—he does all of the TP replacement down the row, then five straight half-sucks, then scrubs all of them. It's much faster than if he tried to do each one completely before moving on to the next.

A roar rises from inside the stadium as the Bills run onto the field. Cansdale takes that as his starter's pistol. Fireworks blast off overhead and a military jet buzzes past the stadium as Cansdale takes off, carrying a mound of toilet paper rolls. He makes it through the first two stalls when he throws open Door No. 3 and finds a Bills fan in red, white and blue Zubaz pants peeing, oblivious that he forgot to lock the door.

Cansdale smiles and shakes his head as he closes the door. He'd said on the ride over that people have no qualms about using a toilet during the cleaning process, and that's exactly what plays out over and over again for the next hour and a half. "They gotta go ... so they go," Cansdale says.

Now it's time to get rid of "the volume," as Cansdale calls the contents of the port-a-potties. He has a big vacuum tube connected to an empty 500-gallon tank on the trunk—it looks like if a Ghostbusters proton gun and a leaf blower had a baby. Cansdale warns in advance that of all the gross things he sees and smells in his job, nothing compares to the initial blast of air that comes out of the vacuum before it reverses flow.

It's so much worse than he described. The wave of warm air is like opening up a 450-degree oven that has been baking full baby diapers all day. When it hits, a guy standing nearby gets a whiff and immediately dry heaves and starts half-jogging the other way.

For the next hour, Cansdale moves with surgical precision as he sucks out each toilet. They're much shallower than you'd think—an empty stall looks a lot more like your kitchen sink than a bottomless pit.

He hangs up the hose at around 1:10 p.m., and now it's time for the grand finale: scrounging up any cans and debris, pouring five gallons of water back into the toilet to refill most of it, and giving a quick scrub all around the seat. When it gets a little colder, he'll fill his truck with salt water so it doesn't freeze.

He grabs discarded White Claw and beer cans with his gloved hands and throws them away. As he works his way down the line, Cansdale's hose begins to clog, so he reaches down with his gloves and pulls out ... somebody else's gloves. Later, he fishes out two iPhones floating at the top of separate stalls.

When he gets done with the last one, he walks down the row and drops in a small blue dye pack. The plastic packs have some deodorant in them, but their job is mostly to color the water so people can see as little as possible of what lurks beneath.

Cansdale flings open the first door, gives a quick scan, drops in a pack and lets the door slam shut behind him. Then he checks toilet No. 2, then 3, then 4. When he gets to the final one, he pulls the door open and finds the guy in Zubaz—yep, he's back—who didn't lock the door again. He shrugs and heads for the truck, on to the next row of port-a-potties on the other side of the parking lot.

Cansdale throws his bucket on the truck, climbs in and looks over with the devilish smile of someone who has, literally, seen some s---. "Welcome to the port-a-potty disposal business," he says as he revs the engine.

Would you believe that the bathrooms of tomorrow might look a lot like ... port-a-potties?

Terry Kogan is a University of Utah law professor and a founding member of Stalled!, a group of architects, legal experts and LGBTQ+ advocates who are pushing for more inclusivity in restrooms around the world. Over the past century, Kogan says, many of society's most important conversations about diversity and inclusion have ended up centering on the bathroom.

"Sexism, racism, access for those with disabilities ... we don't have the best track record when it comes to public restrooms," Kogan says. "I wouldn't want to make it too radical and say that the bathrooms tell the story of a nation. But you can tell a lot about a society by how it configures its bathrooms."

And now, in the middle of a national conversation about gender, bathrooms again have often become a focal point. Kogan and his colleagues believe we still send discriminatory messages with men's and women's restrooms, usually with images of a person in a skirt or a person with pants that signals what a man or woman is. Stalled! also believes that our current men's/women's construct isn't age-inclusive because it often limits parents and caregivers of different genders.

On the Stalled! website, Kogan & Co. present detailed 3D visuals of what futuristic, inclusive bathrooms could look like—and they sure seem like really fancy, clean, indoor port-a-potties.

For a stadium restroom, Stalled! suggests building a wall that separates a large space from the main traffic flow outside. On the other side of that wall, there'd be an open area for anybody, regardless of gender, with mirrors, benches and sinks. And in the back, there'd be rows of closed-off stalls, with no visibility into them, where you'd have no idea who was in the bathroom beside you, and it'd be noisy enough that even sheepish people wouldn't have to worry about the sounds associated with using a restroom.

As prehistoric as their design can feel, portable bathrooms are, oddly, where society may be headed. "In that way, port-a-potties are a great equalizer," he says. "They're private, anybody can go in them and people seem to get over their fears about who will use the stall beside them."

Stalled! advocates to basically wipe out all gender labels to make what Kogan calls all-gender, multiuser stalls, similar to the way most rows of port-a-potties make no distinction.

But in Buffalo, one of the most popular places for Bills Mafia members to convene is Hammer's Lot, where owner Eric "Hammer" Matwijow considers it a perk that he labels two stalls for women only. He's a gruff, 64-year-old roofer with a lifetime of port-a-potty experience, and he spends $2,500 per season to have six total port-a-potties (two for women, four for whoever wants to use them) serviced by Modern Disposal.

On the day of the Colts game, Hammer spends a large chunk of his morning barking at lot workers about the bathrooms. "Make sure there are no guys going in the women's port-a-potties," he yells.

In conversations with more than 20 women outside the Bills' stadium, cordoning off restrooms got a unanimous thumbs-up. "It's a huge factor—I like the idea of women having their own toilets," says one woman who politely declines to give her name for a story about port-a-potties. "I don't want to have to hide behind a car, and I don't want to go in something disgusting. So you gotta have 'em, and you gotta make sure they're not a mess, too."

That can be an issue in private lots. Almost half of the 380 total Modern port-a-potties near Bills home games are in private lots, but the drivers can't squeeze their trucks into smaller lots like Hammer's when they're full of cars. So by 5 p.m. on the day of the Colts game, a Hammer's Lot worker had declared one out of commission and put two trash cans blocking the front of it. (Cansdale had to clean that one the next day, and says he needed a power washer to clean barf off the sides of the walls.)

Across the street in another lot where port-a-potty maintenance seems to be less of a concern, a couple walk up to two stalls holding hands. Near the doors, they release their hands and open their respective doors ... only to look at each other and turn away in horror.

"No way," the guy says, and they leave seconds later.

Sometimes the cost of having to hold it isn't as bad as the price of getting to go.

THERE'S SOMETHING ABOUT portable bathrooms that seems to really bring out our inner Johnny Knoxville.

On Nov. 6, Iowa State band director Christian Carichner was having a quick lunch at Jack Trice Stadium before the Cyclones played Texas. The band warms up on game days, then has a tradition of scattering around the tailgating lots to play the fight song. As Carichner mowed through a soggy cheeseburger, a friend approached and showed him a viral clip of his band. About 50 members had hidden near 10 port-a-potties, waited until they were sufficiently occupied, then jumped out and started blasting the 25-second fight song.

The clip shows kids putting fingers in their ears as perplexed toilet users meander out into the blaring noise of "ISU Fights." A few hours later, the band put on a remarkable halftime performance in which it paid homage to a history of video games and e-characters, from Super Mario Brothers up through Pokémon. "And yet, the thing that goes viral is our band members at the port-a-potties," Carichner says. "But hey, nobody wants to go into a port-a-potty. If you're going to be in there, don't you think it's a little nicer with some music playing in the background?"

There's also a horrifying subgenre of YouTube videos featuring people trying to run across the top rows of port-a-potties. The most infamous examples seem to happen at Triple Crown races— especially the Kentucky Derby—where daring adults attempt a toilet sprint. Many videos feature fans throwing full beer cans at the runners, and eventually most either fall down on top of the toilets or down through the ceilings. The roofs of port-a-potties are quite thin and can support only about 100 pounds of pressure before they collapse.

The day of the Bills-Colts game, Cansdale and other crew members stand around at Modern's local headquarters and rattle off an endless stream of stories about port-a-potty shenanigans.

The rundown, of course, begins with the tipped-over port-a-potty. "The funny thing is, if you tip one over backwards, it's usually fine—everything stays down in the bowl," says Dan McKenna, the crew supervisor. "But if it goes over frontwards ..."

McKenna doesn't finish his sentence, and he doesn't have to. The crew members all nod their heads, a solemn remembrance of what makes for the longest, darkest moments of any port-a-potty cleaner's day.

The whole crew sighs in unison when one of them mentions how at almost every construction site, some clever worker puts on his best Cousin Eddie voice and yells down at them, "Hey, is the s---ter clogged?"

McKenna then mentions that lately they've had a few instances where people either light port-a-potties on fire or blow them up entirely.

Uh, *blow them up?*

He gestures for us to follow him, and he walks back between a few dozen port-a-potties surrounding the garage area that have been returned, sucked out but are in need of a full clean.

McKenna stops in front of a stall that will soon be going to port-a-potty heaven. He approaches one with side walls that are still mostly upright, but the entire middle, including the toilet seat and bowl, was blown to pieces by either dynamite or a significant amount of fireworks. Somebody from Modern put a fluorescent green traffic cone at the bottom that serves as a temporary tombstone for this poor fella.

"Rest in peace," one guy says, and everybody laughs.

By the time the Bills limp into the locker room trailing the Colts 24-7 at halftime, the entire crew of Modern is on the road back to headquarters five minutes away. The five trucks have successfully half-sucked almost 200 portable toilets, and the guys are exhausted.

Their "volume" is emptied into one big tanker, which then takes it over to the Buffalo sewage treatment facility. They'll repeat the same thing the next three days, this time with a meticulous full-suck of the private and public lots. Two weeks later, during the windy Monday Night Football game in which Mac Jones throws only three passes, Cansdale and his crewmates do the suckiest half-suck anybody can remember. The wind is so strong that multiple port-a-potties blow over and zip around parking lots like big plastic sailboats, sending terrified Bills fans running. The only thing that keeps them anchored is following up the half-sucks by filling the bowls as high as possible with extra gallons of water.

But when Cansdale heads home on game days—even the port-a-potty-calypse of Bills-Patriots—he's way happier than you'd think a person could be after vacuuming out plastic toilets at a football stadium. Before taking this job earlier in 2021, he'd been making $15 an hour as an electrician. He's now above $25 an hour, with significant bonuses for working Bills games. He's still pretty much a rookie, but his veteran teammates talk about him like he's the Micah Parsons of the 2021 port-a-potty business: gifted, fast, relentless, unafraid of the fray.

Before he took this job, he was scraping by while he and his pregnant girlfriend, Lindsay, rotated between which bill they could skip that month. He dropped out of the punk-rock band he'd been in for 10 years and desperately tried to come up with a way to buy a ring and propose to Lindsay without getting the lights to their small home shut off. Then she had their son, Silas, 11 months ago and things got *really* tight. He had to look for another job.

He posted a résumé on a job-search site and got 17 reach-outs right away. One was from Modern Disposal, asking him to become one of the 750 people who take care of much of Buffalo's trash and portable toilets. He felt some initial embarrassment about possibly being in the waste business, but then he heard about the salary and benefits and applied to be a garbageman. Within a week, he was at Modern Academy, where the company trains the trash collectors and port-a-potty half-suckers of tomorrow.

There's a pretty clear hierarchy at Modern Academy—most people with a commercial driver's license would prefer to do garbage rather than sewage. So solid prospects with no real preference, like Cansdale, often get courted for the port-a-potty track.

"When it comes down to it, I find no shame being able to take care of my family," he says. "I make good money and have good benefits, and I live stress-free right now. I don't see any shame in that."

He comes home from mad dashes, like he had on Sunday, exhausted and smelling terrible. He calls Lindsay from outside the house so she can distract Silas while Cansdale flies inside and jumps right in the shower. When he gets out, he plays with his son for a bit before dinner, then everybody preps for bedtime.

Cansdale still tries to play his acoustic guitar a few minutes every day, usually right before they put Silas to bed around 7 p.m. On the day of Bills-Colts, when he starts strumming an original song, he hears the pitter-patter of tiny feet trodding toward him. His son surges into the room and listens to his dad play.

It's a silly tune Cansdale developed one night during a particularly messy diaper change. Silas loved it the first time his dad sang it, and Cansdale loves that it's the last thing he'll do on this day. The lyrics are nonsensical and interchangeable, except for the one-word title, which Cansdale thinks is just the perfect chorus: Stinkybaby.

After graduating from Penn State in 2001 with a journalism degree, **RYAN HOCKENSMITH** got an internship at *ESPN The Magazine* and has never left. He transitioned from writing into editing in the mid-2000s as part of the magazine's award-winning run in New York City. When the magazine relocated to ESPN headquarters in Bristol, Ct., in 2011, Hockensmith served as a senior editor before taking a job as a deputy editor at espnW from 2014–16, then with the ESPN.com college football team from 2016–18 before moving back to the magazine. From 2018, he gradually wrote more and more, culminating in moving full time to a writer role in March 2022. Hockensmith is a survivor of bacterial meningitis, which caused him to have amputations on both feet. During his 20-plus years at ESPN, he has emerged as a proud advocate for coverage of those with disabilities and addiction issues. He and his wife, Lori, have three daughters.

How the Texans and a Spa Enabled Deshaun Watson's Troubling Behavior

JENNY VRENTAS

FROM *The New York Times* • JUNE 7, 2022

The accusations have been frequent and startling: more than two dozen women have said the football star Deshaun Watson harassed or assaulted them during massage appointments that Watson and his lawyers insist were innocuous.

Two grand juries in Texas this year declined to charge him criminally and, while the N.F.L. considers whether to discipline him, he has gotten another job, signing a five-year, $230 million fully guaranteed contract to play quarterback for the Cleveland Browns this coming season.

It is time, Watson and his representatives say, for everyone to move on.

Yet a *New York Times* examination of records, including depositions and evidence for the civil lawsuits as well as interviews of some of the women, showed that Watson engaged in more questionable behavior than previously known.

The Times's review also showed that Watson's conduct was enabled, knowingly or not, by the team he played for at the time, the Houston Texans, which provided the venue Watson used for some of the appointments. A team representative also furnished him with a nondisclosure agreement after a woman who is now suing him threatened online to expose his behavior.

Rusty Hardin, Watson's lawyer, said his client "continues to vehemently deny" the allegations in the lawsuits. He declined to respond in detail to *The Times*'s questions, but said in a statement, "We can say when the real facts are known this issue will appear in a different light."

The Texans did not respond to specific questions about Watson's use of team resources. They said in a statement that they first learned of the allegations against him in March 2021, have cooperated with investigators and "will continue to do so."

A spokesman for the Browns said the team had no immediate comment. An N.F.L. spokesman declined to comment, saying the Watson matter is under review.

Watson has said publicly that he hired about 40 different therapists across his five seasons in Houston, but *The Times*'s reporting found that he booked appointments with at least 66 different women in just the 17 months from fall 2019 through spring 2021. A few of these additional women, speaking publicly for the first time, described experiences that undercut Watson's insistence that he was only seeking professional massage therapy.

One woman, who did not sue Watson or complain to the police, told *The Times* that he was persistent in his requests for sexual acts during their massage, including "begging" her to put her mouth on his penis.

"I specifically had to say, 'No, I can't do that,'" said the woman, who spoke on condition of anonymity to protect her family's privacy. "And that's when I went into asking him, 'What is it like being famous? Like, what's going on? You're about to mess up everything.'"

An Appointment with an Acquaintance

Before Watson was drafted by the Texans 12th overall in 2017, he was a championship-winning quarterback at Gainesville (Ga.) High School and Clemson University.

N.F.L. teams widely viewed him as a prospective franchise quarterback with no known character issues, and he seemed to be living up to his billing. When Hurricane Harvey walloped Houston in August 2017, before Watson's rookie season, he donated his first game check to stadium cafeteria employees who were affected by the storm.

Since the first wave of suits were filed against Watson last year, the main allegations against him have become familiar. Women complained that Watson turned massages sexual without their consent, including purposely touching them with his penis and coercing sexual acts.

It's not clear when he began looking for so many different women to give him massages. Hardin has said his client needed to book appointments "ad hoc" when the coronavirus pandemic began, though Watson began working with numerous women before then.

Not all of the women who gave Watson massages between October 2019 and March 2021 have detailed their interactions with him. Some who have shared their experiences say they had no problems with him. Others describe troubling—and similar—behaviors.

The 66 women are:

- The 24 who have sued him, including two who filed suits within the last week. In the most recent suit, the woman said Watson masturbated during the massage.
- A woman who sued but then withdrew the complaint because of "privacy and security concerns."
- Two women who filed criminal complaints against Watson but did not sue him.
- At least 15 therapists who issued statements of support for Watson at the request of his lawyers and gave him massages during that period.
- At least four therapists from Genuine Touch, the massage therapy group contracted with the Texans.

- Five women identified by the plaintiffs' lawyers during the investigation for their civil suits.
- At least 15 other women whose appointments with Watson were confirmed through interviews and records reviewed by *The Times*.

A deeper look at the civil suits, including a review of private messages entered as evidence, shows the lengthy efforts by Watson to book massages and the methods he used to assure women that he could be trusted.

One woman who sued Watson was a flight attendant who began taking massage therapy classes during the pandemic. She and Watson were in the same social circle, but Watson acknowledged in a deposition that they had never really spoken except to say hello.

In November 2020, after a friendly exchange on Instagram, Watson saw that the woman was a massage therapist and sent a message asking for an appointment. As they struggled to work out a time, Watson told her, "Just tryna support black businesses," a message he repeated later.

Watson regularly presented himself as an ally to businesswomen. In the suit filed this week, the therapist alleged that he told her that he "really wanted to support" Black businesses, and on another occasion, he left a woman perplexed when he purchased 30 bottles of her $40 skin cleanser.

In messages to the woman, whom he knew from his social circle, Watson asked to meet at The Houstonian, an upscale hotel and club where the Texans had secured a membership for him. She said she wasn't comfortable going to a hotel because she knew Watson's girlfriend—and indeed had once babysat her and her younger brother. The woman told Watson she wanted to keep things "professional and respectful."

"Oh most definitely always professional," he texted. "I even have a NDA I have therapist sign too." He was referring to the N.D.A. he had received just days earlier from a member of the

Texans' security staff. Watson didn't explain in the text how the woman would benefit from signing a document meant to protect him.

Finally, the woman suggested they meet at her mother's home in Manvel, a 30-minute drive for Watson. He responded, "Damn thats far," but agreed to make the trip.

In the civil suit the woman filed against Watson last year, she said she was uneasy with his directions to "get up in there" during the massage, but chalked it up to her inexperience and agreed to work with him again. When he ejaculated during the second appointment and then asked her for another massage later that day at the Houstonian, she first agreed, then told him she could not make it. She eventually blocked his number.

Initiating Sex
Most of the women Watson saw for massages did not sue or call the police. But even some who did not complain said Watson came looking for sex.

The woman who sold bottles of cleanser to Watson had a few appointments with him during the summer of 2020. This aesthetician, who spoke on condition of anonymity to protect her privacy, told Watson when he booked an appointment that she was licensed only to give him a back facial. But she said in an interview with *The Times* that he got fully undressed and directed her toward his groin. While she said there was no sexual contact, she believed that he was seeking more than a professional massage.

Watson and his lawyers have said he was only seeking massages. The lawyers have acknowledged that Watson had sexual contact with three of the women who have sued him. But the sexual acts took place after the massages, they said, and were initiated by the women. Asked whether he was asserting that Watson never had sexual contact with any other massage therapists, Hardin didn't respond.

Another woman who spoke to *The Times*, a physical therapist who did not sue Watson, said he initiated sexual contact in all three of their appointments.

This woman, who spoke on condition of anonymity to protect her privacy, said in an interview she began by working on Watson's back. But when he flipped over, she said his demeanor and voice changed, and he began aggressively dictating where he wanted her to touch him. In their first session, she said he got into the happy baby yoga pose—on his back with his feet in his hands—and asked her to massage between his testicles and anus. She laughed off the request but said he grabbed her wrist and put her hand there.

The woman said Watson twice initiated sexual intercourse, once by pulling down the scrubs she was wearing. She and Watson knew each other from around town and were on friendly terms, and she admitted she let him proceed with these sexual acts. "I just didn't know how to tell him no," she said.

Hardin said in a statement: "It would be irresponsible and premature for us to comment on vague details put forth by anonymous individuals."

A $5,000 Payment
In June 2020, Watson began frequenting a spa in a strip mall off Interstate 45, at least a 30-minute drive from his home or work. He had found A New U Spa on Instagram and sent a message. The owner, Dionne Louis, became a resource for Watson, able to connect him with multiple women for massages.

She looked out for him, she said in a deposition, sometimes arranging for a security guard when Watson came in, concerned the expensive cars he drove might make him a target for a robbery. She also got things from him. In November 2020, Watson paid her $5,000 through an app, she said, to buy spa equipment. Louis told one of her employees in a text, "I told you I'll show you how to get money from men that's my specialty."

Louis and her lawyer did not respond to requests for comment.

During the months Louis and Watson worked together, she set up appointments for him with several women who worked there, none of whom was licensed in Texas to perform massages.

One was the woman who said Watson begged her for oral sex.

She described how he tried to build up to sexual acts, starting with his request that she work on his behind and go higher up on his inner thighs, which put her hands uncomfortably close to his testicles. When he flipped over, she said, he was exposed with an erection, but she refused his requests for oral sex.

That woman did not sue Watson, but four other employees of A New U Spa did. They all said in their lawsuits that Louis gave him special attention.

In June 2020, one woman said in her suit, Louis drove her to a hotel to meet Watson for a massage, during which he groped her and touched her hand with his penis. Louis was not in the room, but in text messages she later sent to this woman, she appeared to refer to Watson treating her employees poorly: "I been talking to Deshaun I just told his ass off he got it now." Louis added in a second message, "I told him he can't treat us black women any kind of way." (In her deposition, Louis denied sending these messages, though evidence in the civil suits indicates they were sent from her number.)

Nia Smith, who also worked at A New U Spa, filed a lawsuit against Watson last week, the 23rd of 24 civil cases. Smith said that during their first massage, Watson asked her to put her fingers inside his anus, a request she said she told Louis about afterward. She said in the second session he asked her if she wanted his penis in her mouth, and that he repeatedly requested sex in their third and final massage. Smith also claimed that Louis knew Watson was seeking sex and told her she needed to keep Watson happy. In a deposition, Louis denied she knew anything about Watson's sexual desires.

In early November 2020, after Smith stopped working at A New U Spa, she posted text messages from Watson along with his phone number and his Cash App receipts on Instagram. She included the message, "I could really expose you," adding an expletive.

Help From the Texans

Days later, when Watson went to work at the Texans' stadium, he found an N.D.A. in his locker. He later said in a deposition that Brent Naccara, a former Secret Service agent who is the Texans' director of security, put it there after Watson told him about Smith's Instagram posts.

Watson began taking the N.D.A. to massages that same week, giving one to the woman in Manvel, who signed it, and another to a woman who said in her lawsuit that she ended the session after he suggested a sexual act. Watson told her she had to sign in order for him to pay, so she did, according to her filing. Watson said in a deposition that he used this N.D.A. only for massage appointments because he had lawyers and agents who handled his other business.

It's unclear whether the Texans knew how many massages Watson was getting or who was providing them. But their resources helped support his massage habit away from the team. Watson acknowledged in a deposition that the Texans arranged for him to have "a place" at The Houstonian. He used the fitness club, dined there and also set up massages in hotel rooms.

At least seven women met him at the hotel for appointments, according to interviews and records, including two who filed civil lawsuits and two who complained to police.

The Texans weren't aware of the massage appointments at the hotel "that I know of," Watson said. He also said that his access to the property was not under his name. One woman who gave Watson a massage at The Houstonian said she was told the room was registered to a member of the Texans' training staff.

A Well-Connected Lawyer

To preserve his reputation, his career and possibly his freedom, Watson hired Hardin, now 80, a veteran defense lawyer whose clients have included the former pitcher Roger Clemens, the evangelist Joel Osteen and, in the Enron case, the accounting firm Arthur Andersen.

Hardin has said the women who have accused Watson of sexual misconduct are lying. He had ample opportunity to make his case to the district attorney's office. Through a public records request, *The Times* reviewed the communications between Hardin and the prosecutors in Watson's criminal cases. These messages revealed extensive communication between the two sides and demonstrated, at the least, the value of a well-paid and well-connected lawyer.

In early 2022, Hardin, a former prosecutor himself, began a regular dialogue with Johna Stallings, the Harris County sex crimes prosecutor handling the Watson investigation. In the two months before two different Texas grand juries heard the criminal cases against Watson, Stallings and Hardin met at Hardin's office, spoke over the phone 12 times and exchanged more than two dozen text messages, according to public records.

Some of their exchanges were peppered with congenial remarks about cases they were trying. Others were more opaque. One day, Stallings asked Hardin if he could chat. He said he was in trial, then asked, "Any problems?" They spoke over the phone twice that day.

The amount of contact between the prosecutor and the defense was noteworthy, said Njeri Mathis Rutledge, a former Harris County prosecutor who is now a professor at South Texas College of Law Houston.

"There are some well-known defense attorneys like a Rusty Hardin that may have gotten a little extra real estate in terms of time, but even given the fact that it was Rusty, that's still a lot of time," Rutledge said.

The Times also reviewed communications between prosecutors and the lawyers for the women suing Watson. There was just one exchange: In March 2021, Tony Buzbee, the plaintiffs' attorney, alerted the district attorney's office to the allegations in the civil suits. The district attorney asked if his clients had made reports to the police, and eight of Buzbee's clients soon did. The prosecutors had some direct contact with these women, rather than going through Buzbee.

In a statement, Hardin said it is "a standard practice" for lawyers to work directly with law enforcement and prosecutors.

The Harris County district attorney's office did not respond to specific questions about their prosecutors' contacts with Hardin and lawyers for the women. In a statement, a spokesman for Kim Ogg, the district attorney, said prosecutors "vigorously examined all the evidence and spoke at great length with accusers."

In March 2021, Stallings prepared to present her cases against Watson to the Harris County grand jury. She and Hardin exchanged more than a dozen calls and messages during the week of the hearing. Instead of putting his client in front of the grand jury, Hardin created a slide presentation arguing for Watson's innocence and gave it to Stallings along with other documents he deemed important.

"We will let our submissions to you on our client's behalf serve as our presentation to the Grand Jury," Hardin told her in an email. The grand jury declined to charge Watson, and a Brazoria County panel followed suit.

Amanda Peters, a former Harris County prosecutor who teaches law at South Texas College of Law in Houston, said such submissions, known as grand jury packets, are not the norm for the average person facing charges. They are more commonly introduced in high-profile cases in which the client can afford an elaborate and costly defense.

The N.F.L.'s discipline is likely the next step. Watson has been shuttling between Cleveland, where he is training with his new team, and Houston, where he met with N.F.L. investigators and is giving depositions in the lawsuits. The civil cases, if not settled, will be tried after the football season.

Through it all, Watson has been adamant that he did nothing wrong. In a deposition on May 13, he was asked about the text message he sent to Ashley Solis, one of his accusers, immediately after their appointment in March 2020. "Sorry about you feeling uncomfortable," he wrote to her. Watson acknowledged that Solis was "teary-eyed" at the end of their session, but testified under oath that he still does not understand why.

"I don't know," Watson said. "Like I told you at the beginning of this depo, I'm still trying to figure out why we in the situation we are in right now, why I'm talking to you guys, why you guys are interviewing me. I don't know. Do not know."

Deshaun Watson agreed to be suspended for 11 games and pay a $5 million fine after the N.F.L. appealed his six-game suspension.

From *The New York Times.* © 2022 The New York Times Company. All rights reserved. Used under license.

─────────
JENNY VRENTAS is a sports reporter for *The New York Times*, working on enterprise and investigations. She previously covered the NFL for *Sports Illustrated*. She is a 2006 graduate of Penn State University and earned a master's degree from Columbia University's Graduate School of Journalism in 2007. She is also a proud member of the New York Times Guild and the local chair for the NewsGuild of New York, standing beside her fellow journalists to raise standards for workers across the industry.

Remembering Roger Angell, Hall of Famer

DAVID REMNICK

FROM *The New Yorker* • MAY 20, 2022

In recent years, as his odometer headed toward triple digits, Roger Angell became known around our office for the way his cheerful longevity complemented his talent. He was not only the greatest of baseball writers; he had also lived long enough to see Babe Ruth, of the Yankees, at one end of his life and Shohei Ohtani, of the Angels, at the other. Age conferred authority. When Roger covered the Yanks in their late-nineties heyday, Joe Torre, the team's heavy-lidded chief, would sometimes interrupt one of his avuncular soliloquies to a clutch of young reporters and look to him for affirmation: "Roger, am I getting that right?" Sitting in his office, Roger, much like Torre, held court, telling stories about playing Ping-Pong with James Thurber, editing William Trevor and Donald Barthelme, and watching ballgames with the Romanian-born artist Saul Steinberg, who would put on a flannel Milwaukee Braves uniform before sitting down in front of the TV. I once came to him complaining about how hard it was to find writing that was truly funny, and Roger, as if recalling a recent Tuesday, replied, "Harold Ross said the same thing."

And yet Roger was hardly stuck in the past. When the Internet came along and climbing stadium steps no longer held much allure, he watched games late into the night and filed twenty-four-karat blog posts. Although he was insistently modern, he knew what some were thinking when they dropped by his office to see him, natty as always in crisp khakis, a blue Oxford shirt, and a Paul Stuart blazer: Holy shit—he's still vertical! When at ninety-five he published a collection of personal essays and other writing for this magazine, he gave it a characteristically wry and self-knowing title, "This Old Man: All in Pieces."

No one lives forever, but you'd be forgiven for thinking that Roger had a good shot at it. Like the rest of us, he suffered pain and loss and doubt, but he usually kept the blues at bay, always looking forward; he kept writing, reading, memorizing new poems, forming new relationships. When another versatile, sports-minded writer, Budd Schulberg, reached his nineties, he gave away his star-studded address book to a younger writer. He had no use for it: "Everyone in it is dead!" Roger kept replenishing his address book, and his life, with new and younger friends. He went to spring training in Arizona and Florida, full of hope, always on the trail of new prospects. His thirst for the sensation of being alive survived the worst. Roger was married for forty-eight years to Carol Rogge Angell, but when she was dying she told him, "If you haven't found someone else by a year after I'm gone I'll come back and haunt you." After Carol died, Roger followed her instructions, and his heart. He began a long and wonderful love affair with Peggy Moorman, whom he married in 2014, and who was by his side until the end.

"Getting old is the second-biggest surprise of my life, but the first, by a mile, is our unceasing need for deep attachment and intimate love," he wrote in "This Old Man." "I believe that everyone in the world wants to be with someone else tonight, together in the dark, with the sweet warmth of a hip or a foot or a bare expanse of shoulder within reach."

Roger died on Friday. He was a hundred and one. But longevity was actually quite low on his list of accomplishments. He did as much to distinguish *The New Yorker* as anyone in the magazine's nearly century-long history. His prose and his editorial judgment left an imprint that's hard to overstate. Like Ruth and Ohtani, he was a freakishly talented double threat, a superb writer and an invaluable counsel to countless masters of the short story. He won a place in both the American Academy of Arts and Letters and in the Baseball Hall of Fame—a unique distinction. The crowd of friends from the magazine who drove four hours north to watch him receive the J. G. Taylor Spink Award at Doubleday Field, in Cooperstown, wore custom jerseys declaring themselves Roger's "Angells."

Roger was born to a very particular sliver of twentieth-century American society. His father, Ernest Angell, was a Harvard-trained lawyer who went on to lead the American Civil Liberties Union. His mother, born Katharine Sergeant, was educated at Bryn Mawr and became this magazine's first fiction editor, a close editorial partner to Harold Ross. After divorcing Ernest Angell, she married another founding eminence at the magazine, E. B. White. Mrs. White, as she was known at the office, neglected to tell Roger the news of her wedding; Roger, who was nine at the time, heard about it only a couple of days later, through a relative who had read about it in Walter Winchell's newspaper column. In a marvellous portrait of Mrs. White by Nancy Franklin, called "Lady with a Pencil," Roger made it plain that, though both mother and son felt the pain and the disruption of the divorce, he relished the hours he spent listening to her talk about the office in midtown and witnessing her limitless devotion to language and to her writers: "It was the main event of her life—*The New Yorker*, and *New Yorker* writers, and what was in the magazine. It wasn't a matter of power. It was about what was on the page or what could be on the page if something worked out." Roger followed suit. As a kid, he read endlessly and developed a mean party trick, memorizing the caption of every cartoon published in the history of the magazine.

After graduating from Harvard, Roger served in the Army Air Corps. He spent much of the Second World War stationed in the Central Pacific, where he was the managing editor of a G.I. magazine. He also found time to write fiction. In March, 1944,

The New Yorker published a very short story called "Three Ladies in the Morning." The author's byline, which came at the end of the piece, was "Cpl. Roger Angell." After returning home, he spent a long apprenticeship at *Holiday*, a distinguished travel magazine of the mid-century, and finally came to *The New Yorker* as an editor in 1956, after the Whites had moved to Maine. Eventually, Roger led the fiction department; he was, as he often said, "doing my mother's job in my mother's office." Some of the writers Mrs. White had brought to the magazine—Thurber, Nabokov, Updike—eventually became her son's writers. Roger, who may have carried on one of the longest engagements with psychotherapists in the city's history, once said that a shrink told him his inheritance was "the greatest piece of active sublimation in my experience."

As an editor, Roger was devoted, open-minded, and some-times hard-knuckled. He did not just ladle out the superlatives. His proofs were littered with ziggy cross-outs, querulous question marks, aggressive arrows, and the occasional hard-won "Yes!" As a writer he was a "taker-outer," not a "keeper-inner," as he said, and that urge carried over to his editing. Clarity above all. Nothing thrilled him more than to bring in someone fresh and promising. In the early seventies, he knew to be patient when the work of a young graduate student named Ann Beattie was plucked from the "slush pile." Even as he rejected story after story over nearly two years, he kept writing her encouraging, sometimes instructive, letters. He kept Beattie in the game. Then came this:

> Oh, joy . . . Yes, we are taking "A Platonic Relationship," and I think this is just about the best news of the year. Maybe it isn't the best news for you, but there is nothing that gives me more pleasure (well, almost nothing) than at last sending an enthusiastic yes to a writer who has persisted through as many rejections and rebuffs as you have. It's a fine story, I think—orig-inal, strong, and true.

Angell was also writing for the magazine: humor pieces, Talk of the Town stories, and the annual holiday poem, "Greetings,

Friends!" In 1962, he and the magazine's editor, William Shawn, discussed the idea of his writing about baseball. Mr. Shawn was no baseball maven, but he was always curious. When Roger described to him the intricacies of the double play, his cheeks, Roger recalled, "grew pink with delight." Thus encouraged, Roger set off to Florida for spring training, and began writing the pieces that would form his first baseball book, "The Summer Game."

In the office and elsewhere, Roger was a complex character. The weather of his moods varied. He was funny, encouraging, vulnerable, but he was not without pride or temper. In his prime, he walked the halls jingling the change in his pockets like Molly Bloom's lover, Blazes Boylan. Was he steamed or jolly? Not always easy to know. Put it this way: you didn't want to disappoint him. He always had our affection *and* our respect.

On the page, Roger created—he *threw*—a voice that was utterly joyful, as buoyant as a lottery winner. He hated the poetical and the hard-bitten. The Roger Angell of the baseball pieces was a man at liberty, delighted to be in the stands on a long-shadowed afternoon, part of a vast community of fans. The sentences were ebullient but never decorous. An ur-Wasp, he was tickled to learn the Yiddish word for "over the top": *ungapatchka*. He took it as an immense compliment when a friend told him that he admired the "un-*un-gapatchka*-ness" of his work. Roger's best baseball prose—his early piece on the struggles of the fledgling Mets, "The Old Folks Behind Home"; his profiles of the fearsome Bob Gibson, the vanquished Steve Blass, the submariner Dan Quisenberry; his chronicle of the epochal Boston-Cincinnati World Series of 1975, "Agincourt and After"—radiated a sense of wonder at the complexities of the game and those who play it. His enthusiasm for baseball was so immense that it could not be confined to a singular loyalty. In a given season, he was capable of giving his heart to anyone. He was a Mets fan, a Yankees fan, *and* a Red Sox fan. In anyone else, this would have been unforgivable.

I had the privilege of witnessing Roger's joy in the game more than once, but never more so than in October, 2000, when we went together to Shea Stadium to watch the fifth and final game of the World Series, a Subway Series dominated by Torre's Yankees. Sitting in the left-field stands, Roger held forth on everything from Torre's understated generalship to the "premature decrepitude" of Shea to the best kind of notebook. (Mead notebooks: "They take ink perfectly.") He recited a Homeric catalogue of his favorite baseball names: Hack Wilson, Napoleon Lajoie, Mookie Wilson. They spanned the age—the age of Angell. I could have sat in the stands listening to Roger (and, incidentally, watching the Yanks and the Mets) forever. But there would be no extra innings that night. Mike Piazza's towering attempt to tie things in the ninth fell short and into the glove of Bernie Williams.

"That's it," Roger said, and led the way to the Yankees clubhouse. The Bombers were winners again. Roger entered the room under great arcs of foamy champagne. Happily soaked, he made his way to Torre, and listened in on yet another soliloquy to the young scribes. On some point of historical interest, Torre paused, and looked Roger's way for confirmation. Roger, sagely, nodded assent.

After a while, Roger said, "We should check in on the losers. The story's in there, too." We hustled over to the home-team clubhouse, where the Mets picked gloomily at a sad array of snacks and made the customary remarks about next year. Roger wrote that down, as well.

His Mead notebook now sufficiently inked, he led the way past the revellers and the mourners along the ramps and made it out to the parking lot. We found his Volvo station wagon and climbed in. Another gaudy night in Queens. Roger got behind the wheel and, driving alarmingly fast on the Grand Central Parkway, he talked about next year. Spring training was four months off.

DAVID REMNICK, a former staff writer for *The Washington Post*'s sports section, has been the editor of *The New Yorker* since 1998. He won a Pulitzer Prize in 1994 for his book *Lenin's Tomb: The Last Days of the Soviet Empire*. His most recent book is *Holding the Note: Profiles in Popular Music*. He lives with his family in New York City.

The Qatar Chronicles, Part I

GRANT WAHL

FROM Fútbol with Grant Wahl • SEPTEMBER 15, 2022

DOHA, QATAR—They're everywhere here in Qatar, even if nobody acts like they see them.

The authoritarian Persian Gulf nation that will host World Cup 2022 has 2.1 million migrant workers, who make up 95 percent of Qatar's workforce and 73 percent of its population. If you spend any time at all in Qatar, you'll see sprawling groups of blue-clad, neon-vested laborers, largely from the Indian subcontinent, toiling in the sun on construction sites and roadsides. If you stay at a gleaming new hotel, chances are the valets, the security guards and the staff cleaning your rooms and serving your food are from somewhere in East or West Africa.

In my experience, which has included weeklong trips to Doha in 2013 for *Sports Illustrated* and in 2022 for this story, migrant workers are treated by Qataris as though they are invisible—unless locals in the planet's wealthiest nation per capita are unhappy with, say, their service at a restaurant or private hotel cabana, when they can be bracingly cruel to the waitstaff.

Looming over everything are Qatar's migrant worker death toll (often related to long hours in the infernal heat) and its apathy toward investigating the cause of those deaths. Last year, *The Guardian*'s Pete Pattisson cited government sources to report that more than 6,500 migrant workers had died in Qatar in the decade since the country was awarded the World Cup in 2010. (A total of 38 deaths have been directly tied to World Cup stadium construction, though nearly all of Qatar's infrastructure growth has some connection to the World Cup.)

For its part, Amnesty International cited data from Qatar's Planning and Statistics Authority that an even higher number— 15,021 non-Qataris of all ages, occupations and causes—had died in Qatar in the past decade. (Qatari officials claim the migrant mortality rate is within the expected range given the workforce size.) Just as troubling, Amnesty says Qatar has failed to properly investigate up to 70 percent of its migrant worker deaths, noting that "in a well-resourced health system, it should be possible to identify the exact cause of death in all but 1 percent of cases."

When the World Cup starts on November 20, the primary focus for billions of fans around the globe will be the soccer on the field. The same will be true for thousands of visiting sports media, including me. But I didn't feel right about covering the soccer in Qatar without first visiting and doing independent reporting, speaking to migrant workers about their experience there. And I thought my readers would want to know: What is life like on the ground for these workers? What has Qatar actually done to improve conditions for its workforce since it got the World Cup 12 years ago?

By the time I arrived earlier this year, World Cup stadium construction was basically complete. And so for Part I of The Qatar Chronicles, I traveled to Qatar in late February and trained my energy on migrant workers in the hotel sector. In Part II, I'll detail what U.S. Soccer has been doing behind the scenes to prepare for the non-soccer aspects of a World Cup in Qatar, including educating its players and doing due diligence on its hotel and vendors, as well as addressing LGBTQ+ rights in a country that represses them.

My plan for Part I: to visit all 14 of the FIFA-affiliated hotels in the main sections of Doha in the West Bay and The Pearl (including where the USMNT will be staying), and speak to at least one migrant worker at each one.

Promising them anonymity for their protection, I wanted to hear their thoughts. How were they being treated by their employers? And was the new set of worker-protection laws announced by the Qatari government to its own great fanfare in 2019 actually being followed on the ground?

There was a reason I didn't publicize my Qatar visit on social media and didn't say anything publicly about it until I had left the country. The fact is that journalists can get detained in Qatar—including two reporters for the Norwegian TV World Cup rights holder last November—and I wasn't hoping for a repeat of that during my time there.

More importantly, risk is ever-present for workers, too. Malcolm Bidali, a Kenyan who worked as a security guard in Qatar and wrote a human rights blog under a pseudonym, was detained for five months last year (often in solitary confinement) by the Qatari authorities and eventually deported for spreading "fake news," creating a chilling effect across the migrant worker community.

But independent reporting on Qatar is important. In early September, the Qatari government spent a large sum of money to provide first-rate travel and accommodations to journalists from around the world who visited Doha, with the expectation that they would report favorably on Qatar's readiness to host the World Cup. Not surprisingly, many did. Accepting thousands of dollars in free travel from the people you're covering is a violation of ethics for reputable media organizations. Nor is it independent reporting when Qatar's Supreme Committee organizing the World Cup hand-picks migrant workers to speak to the media.

For me, the only way to do truly independent reporting was to use GrantWahl.com's money (your paid subscriptions matter, so consider subscribing) and travel to Qatar, spend two days in a state-mandated COVID hotel quarantine, deal with a government-required COVID phone app that doubled as a surveillance tracker, and then introduce myself to random migrant workers at those 14 FIFA hotels. I had to earn their trust in 90 seconds, explain who I was, give them my business card and ask them questions about their experience.

I was also well aware that I shouldn't arrange any interviews in Qatar with government- or World Cup-affiliated groups. When I did that during my trip in 2013 for a *Sports Illustrated* story, the Qataris made sure to fill my schedule with so many meetings that they knew I wouldn't have time to do any reporting on my own. This time, I waited until *after* I returned from my visit to contact Qatari authorities and FIFA for their perspectives.

In the end, the only thing I wanted to do on this trip was to interview migrant workers. And that's all I did. Several of them have stayed in touch since then via WhatsApp. For their honesty and trust I am grateful. I also recorded some audio tracks as I went through the reporting process in real time:

Which laws have changed for migrant workers in Qatar since December 2010, when it won the right to host the World Cup? In 2019, after years of pressure from human rights organizations and global trade unions, Qatar announced sweeping labor reforms that it said marked the end to the kafala system, common in the gulf states, which required migrants to have sponsors who controlled their exit visas and could thus prevent them from leaving the country.

"For the first eight, nine years, there had been no progress, and the ongoing abuses and exploitation of migrant workers continued because there was a bit of a denial from both Qatar and FIFA about the need to do any reforms," May Romanos, a lawyer and Amnesty International Gulf researcher on human rights who has worked in Qatar since 2017, told me. "Qatar finally agreed [to reforms] I think because of the ongoing pressure and the spotlight it came under because of this World Cup. They signed an agreement with the International Labor Organization [ILO] committing to a reform program and started to introduce some important legal reforms."

"Three years after the start of this program, we have seen some important legal reforms being introduced," Romanos went on. "Now migrant workers can leave the country and can change jobs without the permission of their employer. There is a new minimum wage"—1,000 Qatari riyals a month, or $3,296 a year—"and new labor committees that are supposed to expedite the access for justice for migrant workers. So the legal framework is better, but the implementation and enforcement are weak. And there have been also ongoing loopholes in the system that allow abusive employers to continue exploiting migrant workers."

According to the new laws, it is now illegal in Qatar:

- For employers to keep the passports of their workers,
- For employers to prevent their workers from changing jobs inside Qatar if they so desire, and
- For workers to pay a "recruitment fee" (sometimes $2,500 or more) to agents in their home country or in Qatar to secure employment in the country.

But are those new Qatari laws being enforced on the ground? The only way to find out for yourself is to go to Qatar, walk around Doha and talk to the workers themselves.

At first, I was really, really bad at that! Because I was staying at one of the 14 FIFA hotels in Doha's West Bay—all of which are high-end international brands—I was able to station myself on a relatively quiet beach chair near the outdoor swimming pool. Over at the bar, hotel guests were ordering beers and cocktails, which are a lot easier to find in Doha today than they were when I visited nine years ago.

When a worker from the pool staff walked by, I stopped him, introduced myself, gave him my business card and explained my story, adding that I would look forward to interviewing him when he wasn't on the clock if he wanted to send me a message. (I wanted to respect that he was busy doing his job and would probably prefer a more discreet location.) He smiled and took my card, and quite reasonably I never heard from him again.

By the time I recorded my second audio track the next morning, you could hear some anxiety in my voice. Time was running out on my stay in Doha, and I needed to start getting some interviews done. I resolved to continue being discreet (it helped not to have TV cameras with me), but from now on I would try to strike up a conversation the moment I met someone.

In the end, I spoke to a total of 20 workers at all 14 FIFA hotels in Doha's West Bay and The Pearl, and I did interviews at all but one hotel, which happened to be the one I was staying at. Long story short: The vast majority of the migrant hotel workers in Doha are men, so I wanted to interview at least one woman. When I introduced myself to a woman working in the lobby of my hotel, she asked to bring me to their corporate communications head. I explained I was speaking to workers themselves. She asked for my name, and I gave her my first name before racing upstairs, packing my bags and checking out immediately. By that time, thankfully, I was well on my way to completing my interviews.

By the time I was done, I had a mixed bag of responses in a few areas, but some clear patterns emerged about which new laws were being enforced and which weren't.

Passport confiscation. The majority of the workers I spoke to at FIFA hotels said they had possession of their passports. But multiple respondents told me their employers had control of their passports, in clear violation of the new Qatari law. "It has now been three years without my passport," an East African security guard who said he works seven days a week, 12 hours a day, told me. "I'm supposed to ask the company for my passport when I finish."

At another FIFA hotel, an East African bellman who works six days a week, 12 hours a day, told me his employer "kept my passport for three months. When I finished three months, I was qualified. They returned my passport to me and gave me a Qatari ID."

The workers I spoke to who didn't have their passports did not work directly for their hotels, but rather for subcontractors who have agreements to provide laborers for the hotels. I quickly learned from speaking to workers that subcontractors are far more often in violation of Qatari laws than the hotels themselves are with their direct employees. But that doesn't absolve the hotels of responsibility; the subcontracted employees are still working at their properties.

"Passport confiscation is illegal, but it's still happening," Amnesty's Romanos told me. "You will find it with many migrant workers, including domestic workers. You rarely find a domestic worker in possession of her passport."

Sharan Burrow, the general secretary of the International Trade Union Confederation (ITUC), was one of Qatar's most vocal critics before the legal reforms were announced in 2019. When I interviewed her in 2014, she told me: "Qatar is a country without a conscience," as the ITUC demanded that FIFA take a revote for the host of World Cup 2022.

But when I interviewed Burrow eight years later for this story, the global trade union leader had done a near-180 on the Qatari government's stance toward migrant workers. What happened? Well, these days she and the ITUC, as well as the ILO and several other global trade unions, are working with the Qatari state, following their negotiated agreement in 2019.

"We got to the point [in 2014] where I was totally frustrated with [Qatar's] lack of interest in the issues, in talking to us or indeed the International Labor Organization in dialogue, to look at how to fix the problems," Burrow explained to me. "So as the workers, the union, took a complaint to the ILO, the highest form of complaints is called an Article 26. And it's basically heard before the governing body of the ILO. Its ultimate end could be in sanctions, but we were determined to continue to offer the route of negotiations, because we wanted to change the laws and change the country, not to actually just see the country punished. And at a certain point [Qatar] decided to negotiate, and so the ILO and the ITUC, represented by myself and my legal team, sat down, and we negotiated an agreement for legal changes that would be effected over three years. And they were. And so those changes are in place."

You can't help but notice the tensions these days over Qatar between the global trade unions (which have joined forces with Qatar following the settlement) and human rights organizations like Amnesty International (which continue to release reports about the new laws not being enforced on the ground). Perhaps that's not surprising given the structural differences between unions and human rights groups.

"Unions were probably one of the main critical voices when it came to Qatar in 2014," Amnesty's Romanos told me. "They brought a complaint accusing Qatar of forced labor, which eventually pushed the country to agree to this reform process. Since then, many of the unions backed the reform process, supporting Qatar and the ILO to deliver on these reforms. They considered the progress that has been made as one that should be celebrated for improving workers' rights and conditions in the country. Whereas for us, we see our role as a human rights organization that should continue to monitor the situation and acknowledge progress, but also point to the gaps and continue to push the government to reform the system. As long as we continue to document human rights abuses, we will continue to speak up and ask for more."

As for the ongoing confiscation of workers' passports inside Qatar, Burrow spoke like someone who's now a Qatari government insider. "If you're still in touch with those people and they don't have a passport, suggest they ask for it back," Burrow told me in an interview. "And if they don't, then I'd love to help them, because one phone call and I could fix that."

Recruitment fees for agents. About half the workers I spoke to at the 14 FIFA hotels, including several who had moved from their countries to Qatar *after* the new laws had been announced, said they'd had to pay recruitment fees to agents, which is illegal.

"In our country we paid agents," an East African security guard who works six days a week, 12 hours a day, told me. "They told us we are supposed to pay, so we paid. It was around 5,000 riyals [$1,373]." That put the worker in a hole of debt that he had to start digging out from the moment he arrived in Qatar.

"The payment of recruitment fees is just a rampant issue," Amnesty's Romanos says, even after the new Qatari laws were announced. "Over 70 percent of low-skilled migrant workers in the country would have paid recruitment fees to come to work in Qatar."

The ITUC's Burrow, who's working with the Qatari government, says: "The recruiting fees remain a problem. And you can't actually blame the Qatari government for this one, because they're deregistering any recruitment agency in Qatar where they have the power. They did like 20 in the last couple months which are not indeed heeding the laws. But it's the countries of origin that we have a problem with. And even though in some of those countries the Qataris set up their own visa center, there are still agents that are charging to get people through the door. So it remains a real problem. It's not just limited to recruits to Qatar. It's recruits to almost every Gulf state."

The ability for migrant workers to choose to change jobs inside Qatar. One of the watershed aspects of the new Qatari laws was supposed to be workers' ability to choose to leave their job for another one inside Qatar without needing permission from their employer. But a clear majority of the workers I spoke to said that was not possible with their employers, which is illegal.

Here's a selection of what workers told me: "You can't change your job. If you need to, they send you home and you come back with a new visa for a new company." ... "It's very difficult to change jobs. For our company, they don't allow it." ... "The transfer from one company to another company is the main issue. It's almost not possible, because they require permission from your employer, which most of the companies aren't giving." ... "I would change my job if I could, but it's not possible." ... "I got another [job] offer, but my company doesn't allow changing."

When I informed the trade union's Burrow how many workers in Qatar told me they couldn't change their jobs, she said: "Well, they can. And 242,000 workers did change jobs from October 2020 to October 2021. The problem is no longer with the laws."

Yet clearly there is a major problem if so many workers told me it wasn't possible. Amnesty's Romanos said: "On paper, you can change jobs because you don't need the permission of your employer. But then your employer can retaliate by filing absconding cases against you and canceling your Qatari ID to block your job transfer, meaning that you are then at risk of being forced to leave the country or be deported because you ran away from your job, which is still considered an offense."

Wages. One new law that appeared as though it was being followed was Qatar's new minimum-wage law of 1,000 riyals a month (or $3,296 a year). None of the workers I spoke to said they were being paid below the minimum wage, and none said they were failing to be paid on time.

That's not to say that it doesn't still happen. "The issue of unpaid salaries remains rampant, with thousands of cases being heard in court," Amnesty's Romanos told me.

On wages, the ITUC's Burrow, who works with the Qatari government, said: "There's a minimum wage that is evidence-based, and it has a capacity to be reviewed regularly. It includes not just a wage base but an allowance for food and accommodation. And the minimum wage not only raised wages for about 300,000 workers, it ended the apartheid system of wages where some nations, like Nepalis, were paid less than Indians. It is also applicable to domestic workers and probably the only country in the world where domestic workers are guaranteed the minimum-wage equivalent to any other worker."

What do you see when you look at Qatar's minimum wage? Progress or outrage? Qatar is the richest country on the planet measured by GDP per capita. The new minimum wage works out to about $1.25 an hour. That's shockingly low by Western standards. But it's also an improvement over what used to be the case.

At the end of every interview I did with a migrant worker, I asked a question: *Do you regret coming to Qatar?* I heard plenty of criticism about living conditions and work hours and day-to-day aspects of their jobs. But it was admittedly striking that nobody I spoke to said they regretted coming to Qatar. A lot goes into that answer, obviously, especially the conditions in the countries where those migrant workers come from.

"From the job side, it's cool," a West African security guard told me. "I work 12 hours a day, seven days a week. They say all work and no play make Jack a dull boy. So I'm dull. For real."

"Do you like it here?" I asked.

"Not really," he said. "But you know, I don't have a choice. The reason is I'm saying if you compare it to my country, here I've got a job. So it's OK, but not really. I mean, I don't like it here like I want to stay here forever. But because of the job, that's why I'm here."

When I told Amnesty's Romanos none of the workers I interviewed said they had regrets about coming to Qatar, she said she wasn't surprised.

"That's exactly what I was expecting the answer to be," she told me. "I think this stems from why they come to Qatar in the first place. They just come in search of better job opportunities. They tell you, 'I'm here to work so I can send my kids to a good school so that my kids don't have to go through what I'm going through.' That's why migrant workers migrate in the first place. They want to make a better future for themselves, for their families back home and their kids. And I think this remains the ultimate reason that pushed them to leave their home countries."

"For many it's not necessarily the harsh working conditions that push them to complain," Romanos went on. "It's just the way they are treated. All they ask for is: 'Treat us humanely and pay us our money, because that's why we're here.' They're not asking for much, right? They understand that they're not in Qatar on a vacation. It's not a job where you're going to have fun and enjoy it. But it will be enough to pay your recruitment loan back home and support your family somehow. That's why we say don't use people's vulnerability to allow for your system to exploit them. It's not OK to say: They come from different or less privileged backgrounds, so whatever we offer them here is better than what they get back in their home countries. Qatar, like any other government, has an obligation to ensure that every person on its territory is enjoying their human rights, including being treated fairly and paid on time and not suffering any labor abuses."

The message came from David (not his real name) in Qatar on WhatsApp in May, in reference to FIFA inspections and the subcontractor he works for:

David: Hey brother

I'm David in Qatar one day you did for us interview

Me: Hi David, it's good to hear from you. How are you?

David: I'm good brother you are still in qatar

Me: Good to hear. I am at home in New York now. I'll be in Qatar for the World Cup in November and December.

David: OK I want you to come in our company yu see how we live cause this people are lies they brought other people to interview in accommodation and they lock us inside another accommodation for us to not talk with fifa people

Me: I'm so sorry to hear that. Are you OK?

David: My company is called ----- it is very bad we pass alot off staff but people are afraid to say that why I look for your number

Me: Thanks for contacting me. I'm writing a story soon on worker treatment in Qatar. Would you be OK speaking to me again? I wouldn't use your name.

David: This is how we live six people per room

People working in hotel are living good two people per room but us supply company we pass alot of staff and your fifa people are hide alot of things. If you work in hotel they will give you good place to live most people are suffering from this contract company they treat us like animals

I still get regular WhatsApp messages from some of the workers I interviewed in Qatar. Most of them are questions about whether I can help them obtain work visas for the United States. It's difficult. There's almost nothing I can do in that area.

When I visited Qatar in February, as I mention in the audio track below, it did not appear that FIFA was doing due diligence on hotels and subcontractors supplying those hotels with laborers. But as FIFA mentions in its statement below, it has since conducted an audit of Qatari hotels. Based on the WhatsApp message I received above, it's fair to ask if those FIFA audits are being corrupted by some of those being audited.

Here's the statement FIFA sent to me for this story, including links to its workers grievance mechanism and video on labor reforms:

FIFA STATEMENT

FIFA is steadfast in its commitment to ensure respect for internationally recognized human rights across all its operations and events in accordance with FIFA's Human Rights Policy and the UN Guiding Principles on Business and Human Rights. FIFA does not accept any abuse of workers by companies involved in the preparation and delivery of the FIFA World Cup 2022.

With that in mind, FIFA is implementing an unprecedented due diligence process in relation to the protection of workers involved in the FIFA World Cup Qatar 2022 in line with FIFA's responsibility under the UN Guiding Principles on Business and Human Rights. This work, which is implemented in partnership with the Supreme Committee for Delivery & Legacy (SC) and involves collaborations with trade unions and other independent monitors, focuses on companies building FIFA World Cup infrastructure, including stadiums and training sites, as well as service providers involved in the delivery of the competition, such as in the hotel, security, or transportation sectors. In the hospitality sector alone, FIFA and the SC implement a comprehensive audit and inspection programme covering 159 hotels in Qatar.

Hotels, as well as any other service provider associated with the FIFA World Cup, who fail to ratify issues identified through the FIFA and SC audit and inspection programme will have their contracts terminated. Any worker who feels their rights are being violated should contact the SC Workers' Welfare hotline or FIFA's Human Rights grievance mechanism for the FIFA World Cup.

Besides these measures aimed at workers involved in the preparation and delivery of the World Cup, FIFA has actively pushed for the implementation of broader labor reforms that apply to all companies and projects across the country and benefit all workers in Qatar. We would also like to highlight this video on the wider labor rights reforms in Qatar since being selected as host for the FIFA World Cup 2022 in 2010.

And here's the statement sent to me by the Qatari government:

QATARI GOVERNMENT OFFICIAL:

Qatar is committed to ensuring that everyone who comes to work in our country has a positive experience. In the last five years, Qatar has introduced extensive reforms to strengthen and protect the rights of all workers. This includes a new national minimum wage, the removal of exit permits, the removal of barriers to change jobs, stricter oversight of recruitment, better access to justice and compensation, better accommodation, and improved health and safety standards.

The government has also worked with labor-sending countries to combat exploitative practices before workers arrive in Qatar. Through the establishment of Qatar Visa Centers (QVCS) in labor-sending countries, Qatar has created a unified visa system that expedites the recruitment process and prevents unregistered recruiters from engaging in illegal practices.

In conjunction with the reforms, Qatar has taken major steps to increase its enforcement capacity. Working in cooperation with international partners, the government has introduced stricter punishments for rule-breakers and made it more difficult for unscrupulous employers to break the law.

Qatar has strengthened the capacity of its labor inspectors who carry out thousands of inspections each year at work and accommodation sites across the country. Violations of the law are recorded, and penalties are handed down through the courts.

The number of rule-breaking companies has and will continue to decline as enforcement measures take hold and voluntary compliance increases among employers. Individual cases of wrongdoing are dealt with immediately, but these cases do not represent an underlying fault with the reforms that have been introduced.

With new laws in place, the responsibility also rests with companies, both local and international, to ensure they comply with the law. Several initiatives targeting the hospitality sector have been launched by the government to ensure hotel operators understand their legal obligations, and all hotel operators contracted by the Supreme Committee now implement the SC's Workers' Welfare Standards in their operations. Qatar has repeatedly said that systemic reform does not happen overnight and shifting the behavior of every company takes time. The reality is that no other country has come so far so quickly.

Qatar will continue to ensure that its reforms are effective and long-lasting, and that the rights of every worker in Qatar are protected.

In May, Amnesty International issued a new report and a public call for FIFA and the Qatari government to create a fund for Qatar's migrant workers of $440 million—an amount equal to the prize money FIFA will give for World Cup 2022.

So far, FIFA and Qatar have not responded. Amnesty's Romanos hopes the players from the 32 World Cup teams will speak up on behalf of Qatar's migrant workers.

"When FIFA awarded Qatar the right to host this World Cup, it knew or should have known about the labor abuses that would happen as a result of the labor system in place in the country," Romanos told me. "It wasn't a secret. It was well-documented that there is the kafala system, exploitation will happen. Migrant workers will be the ones building this World Cup and preparing Qatar to host it. Yet FIFA chose to give Qatar this right without imposing on the country any labor conditions to protect migrant workers."

"So fast forward 10 years," she went on, "and we've seen lots of abuses. While acknowledging some reforms are being put in place, we shouldn't forget the past abuses. A lot of people suffered: those who died, those who lost their salaries, those who paid recruitment fees. That's why we call on FIFA to work with the Qatari government to set up a remedy program to compensate workers who suffered to make this World Cup."

The migrant workers I spoke to on my visit to Qatar were, to a person, extremely thoughtful. Several had educations that in the U.S. would have targeted them for much higher-paying jobs. Their dignity and honor give them powerful voices.

"Some people might have come through some bad things here by not going through proper channels," one worker told me. "If you go through the proper channels, your government knows you're here, the government of Qatar knows you're here. But if you step out of channels, you won't be treated good. Because they know you're different. The law is not on your side."

Another told me: "We appreciate the improvement made by the [Qatari] government. I don't think they will go back [to previous laws after the World Cup]. But the issues are on ground level. The laws are OK, but implementation at the ground level, there's some improvement needed. The people in management in companies—that's the challenge in implementing the rules."

In almost 25 years at *Sports Illustrated*, **GRANT WAHL** wrote more than three dozen cover stories. His writing included coverage of the World Cup, the Olympics, and the NCAA basketball tournaments; investigative reporting; and features on a variety of topics. Wahl grew up in Mission, Kansas; attended Princeton University; and began his career as an intern with the *Miami Herald* in 1996. He founded his own soccer journalism site, Fútbol with Grant Wahl, and accompanying podcast in 2021. He died from a ruptured aortic aneurysm while covering the World Cup in Doha, Qatar, in 2022. He is survived by his wife, Dr. Céline Gounder, and their two dogs, Zizou (named after French soccer legend Zinedine Zidane) and Coco.

Advisory Board

The Year's Best Sports Writing 2023

J.A. Adande is the director of sports journalism at Northwestern University's Medill School of Journalism, Media, Integrated Marketing Communications. He is also the graduate journalism Sports Media Specialization leader. Adande has worked in sports media for more than three decades, including multiple roles at ESPN and 10 years as a sports columnist at the *Los Angeles Times*, in addition to jobs at *The Washington Post* and *Chicago Sun-Times*. He has covered a broad array of sports and events, including the NBA Finals, Super Bowls, the World Series, the Stanley Cup finals, the Olympics, the World Cup, Wimbledon, the U.S. Open, and the Masters. He continues to appear on ESPN's *Around the Horn*, where he has been a panelist since the show's beginning in 2002.

Paola Boivin is the director of the Cronkite News Phoenix Sports Bureau, a professional newsroom at Arizona State's Walter Cronkite School of Journalism and Mass Communication. She spent most of her career as a sportswriter in Los Angeles and Phoenix and has won numerous awards, including recognition as an APSE Top 10 sports columnist in 2011 and an APSE Top 10 sports feature writer in 2013. She served a four-year term on the College Football Playoff Selection Committee and was only the second woman picked for the group, after Condoleezza Rice. She is a former president of the Association for Women in Sports Media and is a frequent speaker on topics related to the intersection of sports and society. She also listens to way too much '90s hip hop.

Gregory Lee Jr. is senior news editor at Front Office Sports, based in his hometown of New Orleans. During his 30-year career, he has worked in various editing roles at *The Times-Picayune*, *The Washington Post*, the *Boston Globe*, the *Sun-Sentinel*, NBA.com, and The Athletic. He is a director and alum of the Sports Journalism Institute. He is on the Scripps School of Journalism advisory board at Ohio University and is the chair of the School of Communication advisory board at Texas Southern University. He is also a Missouri Honor Medal winner. Gregory is a former president of the National Association of Black Journalists. He is a proud HBCU graduate of Xavier University of Louisiana.

Jane McManus is the executive director of the Center for Sports Media at Seton Hall University and before that taught at Marist College and Columbia University's Graduate School of Journalism, where she received her master's. For nearly a decade, McManus covered the NFL and women's sports at ESPN and espnW as a reporter, columnist, analyst, and radio host and appeared across ESPN programming in those roles. She has written for numerous publications, including the *New York Daily News*, *The New York Times*, the *Journal News* (Westchester, NY), and *Newsday*; she is currently a columnist at Deadspin. More importantly, McManus played for Suburbia Roller Derby for seven years as Lesley E. Visserate, and once scored 99 points as the starting jammer against Jersey Shore.

Iliana Limón Romero is the *Los Angeles Times'* assistant managing editor for sports/sports editor. The El Paso, Texas, native joined the *Times* in March 2021. She previously was sports editor at the *Orlando Sentinel* and co-founder of the award-winning website Pro Soccer USA. Limón Romero is president of the Association for Women in Sports Media and co-chair of the National Association Hispanic Journalists Sports Task Force.

Glenn Stout served as series editor for The Best American Sports Writing for its entire 30-year run. He is the editor, author, or ghostwriter of 100 book titles, among them *Red Sox Century*, *Fenway 1912*, *Nine Months at Ground Zero*, and, most recently, *Tiger Girl and the Candy Kid: America's Original Gangster Couple*. His biography of Trudy Ederle, *Young Woman and the Sea*, is soon to be a film starring Daisy Ridley for Disney+. He also works as an editorial consultant on book manuscripts, long features, and book proposals. A graduate of Bard College, before becoming a full-time freelance writer in 1993 he worked construction, sold minor league baseball tickets, was a security guard, and a librarian. He lives in Vermont and is a citizen of the United States and Canada.

Shalise Manza Young is a columnist at Yahoo Sports, focusing on the intersection of race and gender in sports. She began her career with the *Providence Journal* and also wrote for the *Boston Globe* and was a frequent contributor on New England Sports Network. Her work has been recognized by the APSE, National Coalition of Minority Football Coaches, and Pro Football Writers of America. A Syracuse graduate, she is buoyed by the support of her husband and kids, and fueled by lots of cold brew and Beyoncé.

Notable Sports Writing of 2022

Selected by the Editor and Advisory Board of *The Year's Best Sports Writing 2023*

JENN ABELSON, NATE JONES AND LADKA BAUEROVA
Dying to Compete: When Risking Lives Is Part of the Show. *The Washington Post*, December 7, 2022

HANIF ABDURRAQIB
The Second Coming of Stephen Curry. *GQ*, January 10, 2022
Triple Alley-Oops, LeBron Cameos and Electric Crowds: The Magic of Summer Basketball. ESPN, September 28, 2022

LINDSEY ADLER
Roger Angell Was the Personification of Baseball History. *The Athletic*, May 20, 2022

DAVID ALDRIDGE
Nets, Grasping at Straws, Have Many More Problems than Their Head Coach. *The Athletic*, November 2, 2022

WILSON ALEXANDER
LSU's Other Super Bowl QB: David Woodley, His Mysterious Life and His Search for Acceptance. *The Advocate/The Times-Picayune*, February 11, 2022

MAITREYI ANANTHARAMAN
The Brief, Thrilling Summer of the All-Canadian Quarterback. Defector, November 18, 2022

STEPHANIE APSTEIN
Jeff Luhnow's Next Act: Soccer. *Sports Illustrated*, October 13, 2022

BIJAN C. BAYNE
  Jackie Robinson Wasn't the Only Candidate to Break Baseball's Color Line. *Andscape*, April 15, 2022

HOWARD BECK
  Does the NBA Have a $@&!*% Problem? *Sports Illustrated*, May 11, 2022

ANNA BETTS, ANDREW LITTLE, ELIZABETH SANDER, ALEXANDRA TREMAYNE-PENGELLY AND WALT BOGDANICH
  How Colleges and Sports-Betting Companies 'Caeserized' Campus Life. *The New York Times*, November 20, 2022

JOSEPH BIEN-KAHN
  8.5 Miles per Hour, on a Road with No Limits. *Sports Illustrated*, September 14, 2022

GREG BISHOP
  Scenes and Soul from Saudi Arabia after a World-Famous World Cup Upset. *Sports Illustrated*, November 23, 2022

SAM BLUM
  Twenty Years after His World Series Moment, Scott Spiezio Puts His Life Back Together. *The Athletic*, September 9, 2002

BEN BOLCH
  Thomas Cole Left UCLA Football after a Suicide Attempt. He Hopes His Story Helps Others. *Los Angeles Times*, July 31, 2022

SAM BORDEN
  The Secret Identity of the NFL's Last Barefoot Kicker. *ESPN*, October 21, 2022

JERRY BREWER
  Voices for Change. *The Washington Post*, October 17, 2022
  Football Is America. We Shouldn't Be Satisfied with Either. *The Washington Post*, December 1, 2022

RYAN LENORA BROWN
  The Not-Quite-Redemption of South Africa's Infamous Ultra-Marathon Cheats. *Business Insider*, December 30, 2022

EVA HOLLAND
The Hardest Climb. *Maclean's*, April 25, 2022
BAXTER HOLMES
Allegations of Racism and Misogyny within the Phoenix Suns: Inside Robert Sarver's 17-Year Tenure as Owner. ESPN, September 13, 2022
MIRANDA HORN
Less Pain, Lots of Gain. Chalk, April 20, 2022
WIL S. HYLTON
How Justin Tucker Became the Greatest Kicker in N.F.L. History. *The New York Times Magazine*, August 31, 2022
MARISA INGEMI
How Colorblind NHL Players See the Game. FiveThirtyEight, March 28, 2022
STUART JAMES
Yann Gueho, the Story of France and Chelsea's Lost Star Who Was Rated Better than Mbappe. The Athletic, December 9, 2022
SALLY JENKINS
Another 'Report' on Abuse in Women's Sports. When Is Enough? *The Washington Post*, October 3, 2022
JAYSON JENKS AND MIKE SANDO
'The Most Toxic Environment I've Ever Been a Part Of': Inside Urban Meyer's Disastrous Year with Jaguars. The Athletic, March 21, 2022
CHANTEL JENNINGS AND DANA O'NEIL
'We Went Through Hell': Former Players Accuse Cynthia Cooper-Dyke of Demeaning, Demoralizing and Abusive Behavior. The Athletic, May 5, 2022
TOM JUNOD
How the Dez Bryant No-Catch Call Changed the NFL Forever. ESPN, November 11, 2022
TOM JUNOD AND PAULA LAVIGNE
Untold. ESPN, April 11, 2022

ELIZABETH MERRILL
  Iditarod Rookie Bridgett Watkins Determined to Race Following Moose Attack that Injured Her Dogs. ESPN, March 3, 2022
  How Iditarod Rookie Bridgett Watkins, Attacked by a Moose, Survived Yet Another Near Disaster. ESPN, April 7, 2022

TRAVIS MEWHIRTER
  Travis Mewhirter's 2022 Beach Volleyball Year in Review, and What a Year It Was. *Volleyball Magazine*, December 27, 2022

MICHAEL J. MOONEY
  Seb Audy Is a World Bank Manager Turned Corporate Executive—and One of the World's Most Daring Polar Explorers. *Washingtonian*, March 23, 2022

MITCH MOXLEY
  Two Fathers. *Esquire*, June 2, 2022

STEPHEN J. NESBITT
  Tony Reali on Life, Grief, Empathy and Two Decades of 'Around the Horn.' The Athletic, December 5, 2022

BILL ORAM
  How Slava Medvedenko Found Himself Armed with an AK-47 Fighting a War against Russia. The Athletic, May 23, 2022

IAN PARKER
  A Murder Roils The Cycling World. *The New Yorker*, November 14, 2022

JEFF PASSAN
  Inside the Self-Inflicted Crisis Boiling Over as MLB's Lockout Deadline Arrives. ESPN, February 28, 2022

JEFF PEARLMAN
  'This Whole Thing Has F---ed Me Up.' *Sports Illustrated*, March 29, 2022

BEN PICKMAN
  The Return and Rebirth of AD. *Sports Illustrated*, May 5, 2022

KEN RODRIGUEZ

Secret Philanthropist: Coach Popovich's Gruff Persona Belies His Generosity. San Antonio Report, May 24, 2022

ALYSSA ROENIGK

Loretta Lynn, Motocross Stars and the Unbelievable Comeback of Racing's Most Iconic Track. ESPN, August 11, 2022

CHANDLER ROME

At 39, Proverbial Astros Workhorse Justin Verlander Becomes Tommy John Case Study. *Houston Chronicle*, April 4, 2022

JOHN ROSENGREN

The One-Legged Snowboarder Who Built an Ingenious Prosthetic for Himself—and His Opponents. *GQ*, March 7, 2022

KEN ROSENTHAL

MLB's Owners Had Every Advantage, and Still It Wasn't Enough for Them. The Athletic, March 2, 2022

KATHERINE ROSMAN AND KEN BELSON

Promised a New Culture, Women Say the N.F.L. Instead Pushed Them Aside. *The New York Times*, February 8, 2022

ROBERT SANCHEZ

'I Am Lia': The Trans Swimmer Dividing America Tells Her Story. *Sports Illustrated*, March 3, 2022

LEANDER SCHAERLAECKENS

The Forgotten Men Behind the Ideas That Changed Baseball. Defector, November 14, 2022

LINDSAY SCHNELL

As Women Athletes Compete Later into Their Lives, Family Planning and Fertility Take Center Stage. *USA Today*, August 19, 2022

DAN SCHWARTZ

The Making of a Monster. *Bicycling*, September 27, 2022

TIM SULLIVAN
WinStar Farm Sues Insurers after Expired Libido Med Injection Traced to Stallion's Death. *Courier Journal*, April 14, 2022

MYAH TAYLOR
Black Surfers Find Moments of Reflection, Rejuvenation at 'A Great Day in the Stoke.' *Los Angeles Times*, June 5, 2022

ALANIS THAMES AND JONATHAN ABRAMS
Female College Athletes Say Pressure to Cut Body Fat Is Toxic. *The New York Times*, November 10, 2022

MARCUS THOMPSON II
Warriors' Trio of Stars Leaves No Doubt: They Belong with the Best in NBA History. The Athletic, June 17, 2022

The Enduring Legacy of Bill Russell, a Monument to Black America. The Athletic, August 1, 2022

Stephen Curry, Who Built Himself Up and Returned to Glory: Our NBA Person of the Year. The Athletic, December 20, 2022

WRIGHT THOMPSON
The Final March of Coach K. ESPN, March 2, 2022

JUSTIN TINSLEY
For Allen Iverson, It Was Never Just about 'Practice.' Andscape, May 6, 2022

SPRINGS TOLEDO
Stardust. *Ploughshares*, January 12, 2022

DON VAN NATTA JR., SETH WICKERSHAM AND TISHA THOMPSON
Sources: Commanders Boss Snyder Claims 'Dirt' on NFL Owners, Goodell. ESPN, October 13, 2022

MATT VAUTOUR
Timmy Allen Is Thriving in Act 2. Mass Live, March 2, 2022

TOM VERDUCCI
The Beautiful Life of Vin Scully. *Sports Illustrated*, August 3, 2022

The Year's Best
Sports Writing

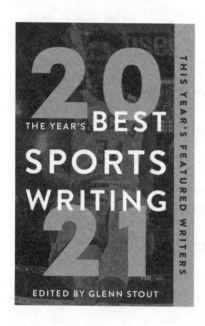
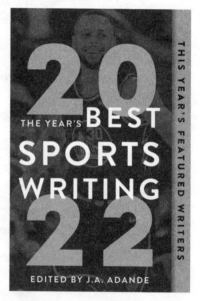

Available wherever books are sold

Submissions for next year's edition: ybsportswriting@gmail.com